MANAGING THE DATA RESOURCE FUNCTION

second edition

MANAGING THE DATA RESOURCE FUNCTION
second edition

RICHARD L. NOLAN

WEST PUBLISHING COMPANY
St. Paul   New York   Los Angeles   San Francisco

LIBRARY OF CONGRESS CATALOGING IN PUBLICATION DATA
Main entry under title:

Managing the data resource function.

Includes bibliographical references and index.
1. Electronic data processing departments—
Management—Addresses, essays, lectures. 2. Management
information systems—Addresses, essays, lectures. I. Nolan,
Richard L.

HF5548.2.M298 1982	658'.054	82-1876
ISBN 0-314-63285-9		AACR2

2nd Reprint—1984

CONTENTS

PART ONE
THE DATA RESOURCE FUNCTION AND STAGES THEORY   1

1
Managing the Computer Resource: A Stage Hypothesis   8
Richard L. Nolan

2
Managing the Crisis in Data Processing   21
Richard L. Nolan

7
What Kind of Corporate Modeling Functions Best?   114

Robert H. Hayes   Richard L. Nolan

8
Orders of Office Automation   130

Richard L. Nolan

18
Data Administration   286
Richard L. Nolan

19
Human Resource Management   297
Barbara J. Lind

20
Personal Privacy versus the Corporate Computer   313
Robert C. Goldstein   Richard L. Nolan

FORWARD

This second edition of **Managing The Data Resource Function** is an important contribution to the body of knowledge that supports the emerging profession of managing computer-related activities. In the first edition Richard L. Nolan alerted management that it is the **data resource** they must manage. Nolan pointed out that the computer itself is only an intermediate resource, though an obviously critical one: computers are important because they add such significant value to an organization's data resources. This fundamental premise provides a sound foundation on which to build a professional body of knowledge.

Over the last ten years, we have seen proof of the value and validity of Nolan's premise. The Stages Theory of data processing (DP) evolution has provided us with a valuable framework for understanding the shift from managing computers to managing data. As a faculty member at the Harvard Business School (HBS), I had an opportunity to work closely with several hundred DP Managers who participated in the HBS Managing the Computer Resource (MCR) course. Those DP Managers have, for the most part, shifted to data resource management approaches. I believe that shift has made them far more effective in meeting their organization's strategic information requirements.

Now in my current position as Director of Nolan, Norton & Company (NNC) MCR programs, I am continuing to work with DP managers in the MCR courses that Nolan, Norton & Company jointly offer with UCLA, the University of Houston, Oxford University, Shell International and IBM. I continue to be impressed with the energy and insight these practicing managers bring to the awesome problems of change and development they face every day. In many respects this second edition would not have been possible without their contributions, or without the efforts of the NNC professional staff who worked to capture and report their ideas in the chapters of this book.

The MCR course is a "living" course. It is based on the concept of data resource management; it is organized around the Stages Theory. But the course changes and evolves every year. The original course was cofounded by Richard L. Nolan and F. Warren McFarlan in 1971 when both were on the faculty at Harvard Business School. Since 1971, the MCR course has been offered each year to DP executives. And each year the course has generated new materials and new perspectives on the profession of DP management. The course "lives" and grows because it brings practicing managers and consultants together with faculty from leading universities; each group learns from the experiences and questions raised by the others.

NNC has played a major role in this development process by working with Information Systems faculties at leading universities such as Harvard, UCLA and Oxford. In addition, NNC has worked closely with large organizations such as IBM and Shell International in tailoring the course to meet the specialized needs of those companies' senior executives. By helping to bridge the gap between academics and managers—between theory and practice—the MCR course has made a major contribution to the emerging body of knowledge about managing data as a resource.

As the current Director of NNC's MCR programs, I continue to search for new case studies and new conceptual frameworks to incorporate into the MCR curriculum. NNC is committed to ensuring that the course remains relevant to today's issues, while continuing to add to that essential core body of knowledge.

The Exhibit on page xvii depicts graphically the 1982 structure for the MCR course; NNC publishes the evolving normative course structure each year in its newsletter, *Stage by Stage.*

This *second edition* of *Managing the Data Resource Function* thus provides a baseline for the professional body of knowledge as of 1982. That baseline continues to evolve and will be built upon over time as new case studies and journal articles are published. I invite you to join in the ongoing effort to strengthen our understanding of the data resource function. Read this book; react to its ideas; debate with your professional colleagues, and share the results of those debates with us. Keep the ideas alive!

James P. Ware, Ph.D.
NNC Director of MCR Programs

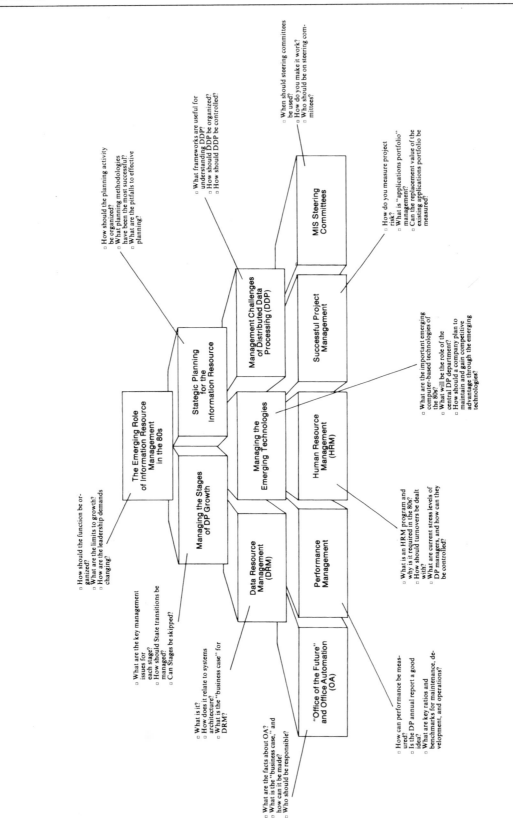

The Emerging Role
of Information Resource
Management
in the 80s

□ How should the function be organized?
□ What are the limits to growth?
□ How are the leadership demands
changing?

Strategic Planning
for the
Information Resource

□ How should the planning activity
be organized?
□ What planning methodologies
have been the most successful?
□ What are the pitfalls to effective
planning?

Managing the Stages
of DP Growth

□ What are the key management
issues for
each stage?
□ How should State transitions be
managed?
□ Can Stages be skipped?

Management Challenges
of Distributed Data
Processing (DDP)

□ What frameworks are useful for
understanding DDP?
□ How should DDP be organized?
□ How should DDP be controlled?

Managing the
Emerging Technologies

□ What are the important emerging
computer-based technologies of
the 80s?
□ What will be the role of the
central DP department?
□ How should a company plan to
maintain and gain competitive
advantage through the emerging
technologies?

Data Resource
Management
(DRM)

□ What is it?
□ How does it relate to systems
architecture?
□ What is the "business case" for
DRM?

Human Resource
Management
(HRM)

□ What is an HRM program and
why is it required in the 80s?
□ How should turnovers be dealt
with?
□ What are current stress levels of
DP managers, and how can they
be controlled?

MIS Steering
Committees

□ When should steering committees
be used?
□ How do you make it work?
□ Who should be on steering committees?

Successful Project
Management

□ How do you measure project
risk?
□ What is "applications portfolio"
management?
□ Can the replacement value of the
existing applications portfolio be
measured?

"Office of the Future"
and Office Automation
(OA)

□ What are the facts about OA?
□ What is the "business case," and
how can it be made?
□ Who should be responsible?

Performance
Management

□ How can performance be measured?
□ Is the DP annual report a good
idea?
□ What are key ratios and
benchmarks for maintenance, development, and operations?

ACKNOWLEDGEMENTS

The first edition of **Managing The Data Resource Function** has been viewed as a landmark work in arguing that data was the resource to build concepts, tools, and techniques to manage. It made good progress in building the conceptual foundation, but reviewers were more critical of deficiencies in providing tools and techniques for data resource management. This second edition has built on the first edition; it makes a major installment to the body of knowledge by tapping the collective consulting experience of the over 200 people at Nolan, Norton & Company, Inc. (NNC)

The task of building the tools and techniques for data resource management is clearly beyond one person, and even one company. But NNC has taken on the leadership task in assembling the second edition. Acknowledgement is due to all the dedicated people at Nolan, Norton & Company. The authors have taken time out of their busy schedules to document and share their experiences on tools and techniques that work in the field. Jill Thomas and Kathy Shea, NNC's professional librarians, directed the unique NNC reference library to the task. Eleanor Rakocy, Millie Rothmel, and their staff in the NNC Consulting Products Group produced the many exhibits. Cheryl Trodella's proficiency with the word processor permitted authors to make multiple revisions to get it "right." Project Manager Taryn Howard was responsible for coordinating the work of all of these people, in addition to providing exceptional editorial and organizational skills to produce this finished product. Even with all these resources, the second edition took three years to develop, which is testimony to the magnitude of the effort.

Acknowledgement is also due to the roots. The roots of *Managing the Data Resource Function* are found in my work as an academic at the University of Washington, the University of Illinois, and Harvard University. As a faculty member of the Harvard Business School from 1969 to 1977, my research was supported by participating companies in the Computer-Based Information Systems Program and the Associates of the Harvard Business School. During my tenure on the faculty, I developed many working papers which provide the foundation for both the first edition and the second edition. I remain deeply grateful for the support and encouragement of my academic and professional colleagues.

Richard L. Nolan, Ph.D.
January 1982

PART ONE

The Data Resource Function And Stages Theory

Data is a resource, and resources must be managed. To manage is to plan, allocate, and conserve resources. The characteristics of the data resource are the same as those of financial and human resources: cost, value, and scarcity. Data resource management involves recognition of these familiar characteristics in a new context.

Although the computer has been the major impetus to recent specialization in the area of data resources, other forces leading to this specialization are not as new. In the early 1800's Babbage described the factors inducing specialization, or division of labor.[1] As organizations since that time have become ever more complex, the forces described by Babbage have led to further specialization for materials (the **production function**), for money (the **financial function**), for the market (the **marketing function**), and for people (the **personnel function**). For each of these resources, the process of specialization has been much the same. Now we are experiencing the rise of the **data function**, more familiarly referred to as **data processing**.

The data function is still evolving, and its evolution is much the same as the evolutionary processes for the other resources. An examination of Babbage's factors leading to specialization is useful for understanding and guiding the evolution of the data function. Babbage outlines six types of factors:

1. Time required to learn about the resources is lengthy

---

[1]From *On the Economy of Machinery and Manufacturers* (London: Charles Knight, 1832), pp. 169-176.

2. The resource is wasted during time spent learning about it

3. Employing the resource requires changes in thinking and manual processes

4. Employing the resources requires new tools

5. Skill can be acquired by frequent repetition of the resource managing process

6. Employing the resource results in contrivance of tools

DATA AS A RESOURCE TO BE MANAGED

There is nothing new about the management of data. Dealing with data, searching out sources, evaluating the quality of data from various sources, and figuring out how to combine different types of data to support decision making have always been important parts of the managerial function. What is emerging, however, is the specialty of data management as part of the general management function. Automatic Data Processing (ADP), Electronic Data Processing (EDP), Management Information Systems (MIS), Information Systems Administration, Information Resources Management, and Data Base Administration are just new names for aspects of the general management function.

To manage is to allocate and control basic resources,[2] to achieve an organizational purpose or goal. The management activities and the degree of specialization associated with these activities change with respect to all resources, so we can assume here that data are a basic resource and should be managed in a manner similar to other basic resources. This assumption is of great help in providing a common sense approach to data management. However, data are often not considered a basic resource, so some justification may be warranted. Samuelson defined three types of resources from the economist's point of view:[3]

1. Natural resources provided by nature in fixed supply

2. Human resources determined by social and biological factors

3. Capital goods produced by the economic system itself to be used as inputs for further production

The first two of these types are considered **primary factors of production** because they are largely determined outside the economic system. Capital goods, however, is considered an **intermediate factor of production**—it is determined within the economic system.

---

[2]Bakke developed a similar discourse in the 1950's for personnel. See E. Wight Bakke, *The Human Resources Function* (New Haven: Yale Labor and Management Center, 1958).
[3]Paul A. Samuelson, *Economics*, *6th ed.* (New York: McGraw-Hill Book Co., 1964), pp. 577-578.

These three resources, defined by Samuelson, are recognized in the field of management but are often broken down further. *Exhibit I* shows six resources recognized in management, and illustrates that, where Samuelson's primary factors of production need no further definition, his intermediate factor, capital goods, is regarded in management as four separate resources. This further breakdown is mainly a matter of convenience, to make it easier to deal with organizational design and management principles.

EXHIBIT I

Basic
Resources

FACTOR OF PRODUCTION TYPE	ECONOMISTS	MANAGEMENT THEORISTS		CARVED-OUT MANAGEMENT FUNCTION
	SAMUELSON	BAKKE*	FORRESTER**	
PRIMARY	NATURAL RESOURCES	MATERIALS	MATERIALS	PRODUCTION
	HUMAN RESOURCES	PEOPLE	PERSONNEL	PERSONNEL
INTERMEDIATE	CAPITAL GOODS	MONEY	MONEY CAPITAL EQUIPMENT	FINANCE
		MARKET	ORDERS	MARKETING
		IDEAS		RESEARCH AND DEVELOPMENT
			INFORMATION	DP DATA PROCESSING

*E. Wight Bakke, *The Human Resources Function*, Yale Labor and Management Center, New Haven, 1958.
**Jay W. Forrester, *Industrial Dynamics* (Cambridge, MA: The M.I.T. Press), 1961.

As organizations become larger and more complex, and as technology advances and is assimilated by these organizations, the degree of specialization and division of labor becomes greater. The difference between the process of data specialization within the management function and specialization processes for the other resources is simply speed. Major advances in computer technology are inducing rapid proliferation of data management specializations: systems analysts, computer programmers, systems and procedures specialists, systems architects, office automation specialists, CAD/CAM (computer-aided design/computer-aided manufacturing) specialists, and data administrators. The speed of this specialization process coupled with computer malfunctionings have led to widely held misconceptions about the field of data management. If we are able to view data as a resource requiring the same type of management attention given the other basic resources, we can proceed toward a greater understanding of this resource and its particular management.

The data resource function is defined as the activities for understanding, developing, employing, and integrating the potential in the resource data. Data are, in turn, defined as observed events. They are manipulated and transformed by an organization to support decision-making activities. The activities required to manage the resources are:

1. Acquisition of knowledge about the nature, potential, and limitations of the resource

2. Procurement, maintenance, and conservation of the quantity and quality of the resource needed

3. Employment and exploitation of the full potential of the resource

4. Integration of the resource with other resources

Before the punch card and before computers, data resource management was highly decentralized. The punch card enabled a datum to be recorded once and stored, to be used as many times and as for as many different purposes as needed. The computer extended this capability by permitting data to be collected, transformed, and retrieved instantaneously. This increased capability and the complex computer technology together created the need for managerial service and advice. This gave rise to the data processing (DP) department, for greater centralization of those activities needed to manage the data resource. It is important to note, however, data as a resource pervades the entire organization, not only the DP department. It is a mistake to identify the DP department as the only group in an organization concerned with the data resource function.

STAGE HYPOTHESIS

When I began my research in 1969 at the Harvard Business School to develop a theory for the assimilation of computer technologies within organizations, it was clear to me that data processing was an area emerging much more rapidly than any other area in business. Growth was (and is) being spurred on by constant advances in computer technology.

I concentrated on formulating an organizational theory which would be effective for structuring knowledge in a new area. *Chapter 1, Managing the Computer Resource: A Stage Hypothesis*, describes my search. The Stage Hypothesis was published in 1973 and satisfied two essential criteria for a meaningful and useful theory. First, it captured the essence of data processing: *growth*. Second, it captured the critical dimension of that growth: the change in data processing activity over *time*. The Stage Hypothesis also included a taxonomy for describing the phenomenon of data processing in terms of tasks, for instance, organizing, planning, and control. However, the tasks taxonomy failed to fully capture the kind of activity introduced by data processing and could not convey the impact of that activity on the organization.

STAGES THEORY

Chapter 2, Managing the Crisis in Data Processing, presents an alternative taxonomy of **Four Growth Processes** which are basic to the evolution of data processing. These growth processes were:

- the applications portfolio
- data processing organization
- data processing planning and control
- user awareness

By 1980, I had further refined the four growth processes into a proven useful taxonomy. The four growth processes now are:

- Growth Process #1:   Applications Portfolio
- Growth Process #2:   Resource—Personnel and Technology
- Growth Process #3:   Organization, Planning, and Control
- Growth Process #4:   User Awareness

I have also refined the dimension of time in data processing growth. The four stage model was expanded into six stages which can be grouped in two general eras of growth and development:

- The Computer Era: Stages I, II, and III
- The Data Resource Era: Stages IV, V, and VI

Exhibit II shows the evolution of the Stage Hypothesis to the Stage Theory between 1972 and 1980. *Exhibit III* shows the current Stage Theory consisting of six stages. Each stage is distinguished by the characteristics of the attributes of the four growth processes identified in the exhibit.

DISTRIBUTED DATA PROCESSING

By the early 1980s, it had become clear that the cost-performance ratio of computers coupled with their technological power provided diverse opportunities to increase productivity. Computers were being coupled with such other technologies as communications technology, graphics technology, and optics technology to increase productivity in virtually every regard. The demands for increased exploitation of the computer

EXHIBIT II

Stage Hypothesis to
Stage Theory

KEY ATTRIBUTES	STAGE HYPOTHESIS (1972)	STAGE THEORY (1980)
TYPE OF HYPOTHESIS/THEORY	DESCRIPTIVE	DESCRIPTIVE
ESSENCE OF PHENOMENON	GROWTH	GROWTH
TAXONOMY	TASK: —ORGANIZING —PLANNING —CONTROL	GROWTH PROCESSES: —APPLICATIONS PORTFOLIO —RESOURCES —ORGANIZATION PLANNING, AND CONTROL —USER AWARENESS
QUANTITATIVE MEASURE	DP EXPENDITURES AND TASKS	DP EXPENDITURES AND GROWTH PROCESSES

TEMPORAL	FOUR STAGES	SIX STAGES
		
		—STAGES I-III
		  (COMPUTER ERA)
		—STAGES IV-VI
		  (DATA RESOURCE ERA)

DETERMINANT OF STAGE MATURITY	ORGANIZATIONAL LEARNING	ORGANIZATIONAL LEARNING

EXHIBIT III

Stage Theory and Attributes of
Four Growth Processes

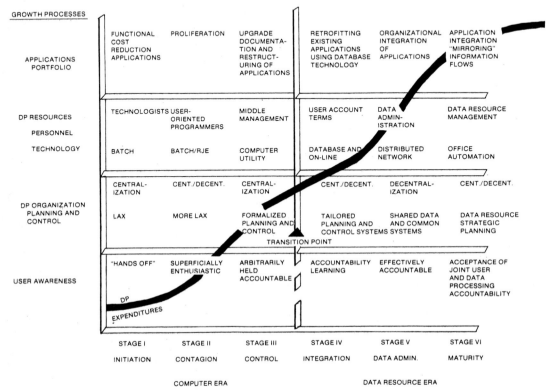

were fast outstripping the capabilities of the traditional DP departments. Decentralization of computer technologies was rapidly emerging as a real requirement.

Distributed data processing (DDP) was fast becoming a "buzz-word." It was an organizational construct for decentralizing responsibility for computers. The issues are complex. Jack Buchanan and Richard Linowes in Chapters 3 and 4 sort out the issues and provide a balance for centralized/decentralized activities in the effective use of computer-based technologies.

The plain fact is that the opportunities of computer technology far exceed the capabilities of any individual or decentralized department. The decentralization described by Buchanan and Linowes is a natural response to reconciling opportunity with user accountability.

Managing the Computer Resource: A Stage Hypothesis*

RICHARD L. NOLAN

Over the past decade, managements have diligently searched for the key to effectively exploit the computer resource. They have been quite successful in using the computer in the operating aspects of their businesses. Most firms have effective computer-based logistics and financial systems—such as inventory control, bill of materials, payroll and accounts receivable. Computer applications for these operational aspects of businesses have been generally successful, even if occasionally marred by costs higher than anticipated. By contrast, managements have had only limited success using the computer for strategic and higher-level decision-making. Computer applications for middle to top management have almost always been plagued with incidences of user dissatisfaction.[1]

Although "how to do it" heuristics abound for use of the computer resource,[2] there is a dearth of generally accepted guidelines for effectively using the computer resource. Indeed, the lack of accepted guidelines for managing the computer resource has resulted in some skepticism as to whether normative theory for the use of computers in organizations is feasible with the current state of knowledge. The complexity of manage-

*Credit Line: "Managing the Computer Resource: A Stage Hypothesis," Communications of the AMC, Vol. 16, No. 7, July 1973. Copyright © 1973, Association for Computing Machinery Inc. reprinted by permission. The research for this paper has been executed under the auspices of the Division of Research and supported by the Associates of the Harvard Business School.

[1]See "Unlocking the Computer's Profit Potential," McKinsey and Company, 1968.
[2]For example, see Arnold E. Ditri, John C. Shaw and William Atkins, Managing the EDP Function (New York: McGraw-Hill Book Company, 1971), Oliver Wight, The Executive's New Computer: Six Keys to Systems Success (Reston, Virginia: Reston Publishing Company, Inc., 1972). In addition, there are several MIS handbooks available.

ment in general, and computer technology specifically, lend support to the skeptics' arguments. **Organization Theory** eclectically draws upon the foundations of the social sciences, such as psychology and sociology, as well as engineering and biology. The study of the use of computers in organizations is a very recent offshoot from Organization Theory. At this point in its development, only a rudimentary foundation exists for developing normative theory for the use of computers in organizations. Even the terminology abounds with imprecision. Nevertheless, the need is great for developing knowledge leading to computer management principles.

In spite of this need, however, researchers must carefully guard against pressures to prematurely attempt normative theory formulation. Research activities must first support a formative period during which the set of variables exerting major influence on the management of the computer resource are identified, the behavior and interrelationship of the variables are determined, and the generality and major determinants of the variables are assessed.

STAGE THEORIES

Stage theories have proven particularly useful for developing knowledge in diverse fields during their formative periods. For example, they have been used in the early development of knowledge in the study of biological growth and of galaxies. The study of economic development of nations in the 19th century was characterized by stage theory formulations. Karl Marx theorized that nations pass through four stages:

- primitive culture

- feudalism

- capitalism

- socialism or communism[3]

Careful formulations of these stages represented an important development in the field of economics. The characteristics of the stages and the study of movement through the stages provided a base for prescriptive theory formulation, such as that of John Maynard Keynes in his work, *The General Theory of Employment, Interest, and Money.*

Stage theories are based on the premise that elements in systems move through a pattern of distinct stages over time and that these stages can be described. Kuznets states two guidelines for a stage theory:

1. The characteristics of each stage should be distinct and empirically testable.

---

[3]Karl Marx, *Das Kapital.*

2. The analytical relationship of any stage to its predecessor or successor should be well defined; it must be possible to identify what processes cause an element to move from one stage to the next.[4]

Two key characteristics of stage theory formulation are the identification of elements and their growth through time. The concept of an element is that it is generic to a particular field, and that it can be specified by a set of attributes. For instance, behavior and physiology are two elements for stages of human development. Maternal dependence and communication are attributes which specify the behavior element, and physical size and appearance specify physiology.

The second key characteristic in stage theory formulation, the concept of growth over time, is that the element changes as its attributes expand or contract in number and nature. For example, behavior changes as an individual progresses from only non-verbal communication to a combination of non-verbal and verbal communication.

A Stage Hypothesis for Use of Computers in Organizations

One of the most interesting phenomena of the use of the computer in business organizations is the behavior of the share of financial resources allocated to using it—roughly quantified by the computer budget. The computer budget typically includes the costs of the physical hardware, software, programmers, systems analysts, and management. It has generally reflected a growth phenomenon. The overall growth of the computer budget itself is not of particular interest given that the use of the computer is an accepted part of doing business and that most established companies have generally exhibited growth in sales and assets over the past twenty years. One would expect the computer budget to grow along with the growth of the company, though the growth might occur as a step function rather than a smooth and steadily increasing function.[5]

What is of interest is the *pattern* of growth for the computer budget and the associated techniques used to manage the computer resource. *Exhibit I* illustrates the computer budget curve for three companies studied in some depth.[6] The curves are estimates, and certainly there are

---

[4]Simon Kuznets, *Economic Growth and Structure: Selected Essays* (New York: W. W. Norton and Co., Inc., 1965), pp. 213-216.

[5]Computer systems usually can accommodate increases in volume of data (e.g., inventory orders) without major changes in the system configuration. For example, a supermarket chain increased its volume of business by 25 percent in one year. The centralized EDP department easily handled the increased volume. The effects on the other parts of the business were great: new warehouses, financing, changes in management structure. Growth or changes in application, however, generally entail changes to the computer system. Of course, overall volume growth will eventually lead to a larger computer system.

[6]It would have been useful to have studied in depth the computer budget behavior of more than three companies. However, it was extremely difficult to find companies with sufficient records and knowledgeable personnel who could interpret the historical records on the computer budget. The study of each of the companies was preceded by the author's three year relationship with the managements through involvement in the Harvard Computer-Based Information Systems research report course. The author's on-site study for the actual research consisted of approximately five days at each company.

EXHIBIT I

Companies A, B, and C
Computer Budget Behavior

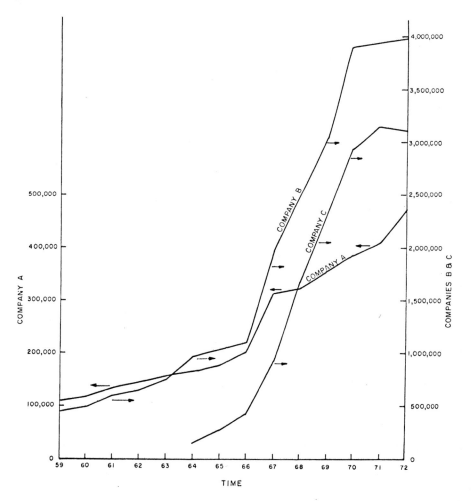

(Annual Computer Budget Dollars)

some consistency problems due to different account classifications between years and poor data for early years. They reflect the effects of
many variables, including situational factors such as changes in the scope
of the business, impact of centralization/decentralization moves, and major
computer acquisitions. Nevertheless, a careful analysis uncovers a crude
S-shaped curve behavior. The points of inflection of a generalized S-
shaped computer budget curve provided the basis for the Stage Hypothesis. As illustrated in *Exhibit II*, four stages, delineated by the points of
inflection on the generalized S-shaped computed budget curve, are
hypothesized: stage I (slow annual increases after computer acquisition);
stage II (highly increasing annual increases—often over 50 percent per

EXHIBIT II

Stages of
Computer Budget Growth

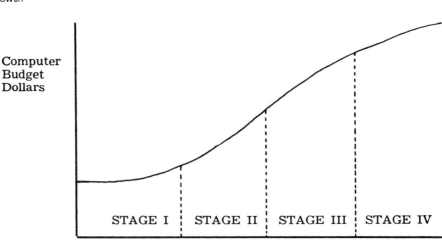

Time

year); stage III (decreasing annual increases, or even a decrease from the previous year); and stage IV (slow, even annual increases). Applying the stages to the companies studied, Company A is experiencing stage II while companies B and C are experiencing stage III.

It is proposed that the computer budget curve serves as a useful surrogate for the growth phenomenon for use of computers in organizations. Further, the *tasks* for managing the computer resource (i.e., planning, organizing, and controlling) are closely aligned with the growth of the computer budget. The tasks are detailed to accommodate the unique characteristics of the set of computer resources to be managed and the objectives to be attained. The stages and the rate of growth of the computer budget affect the way in which the tasks are executed. They also determine where in the organizational structure responsibility and authority are centered for carrying out the tasks. Since the ultimate objective of research on computers in organizations is the development of normative theory, the *tasks* of managing the computer resource is the logical choice for the *elements* of the stage hypothesis. The tasks are generic to the field of Organization Theory.

As shown in *Exhibit III*, the computer budget is a surrogate for the collective effect of multiple situational variables, such as industry, dollar sales, products, business strategy, management, and technology, which determine the set and nature of the planning, organizing, and controlling tasks for managing the computer resource. The situational variables together with a given set of tasks and their attributes result in the profile of computer applications for the organization. Over time, the profile of applications, in turn, influences the tasks.

EXHIBIT III

Process of
Computer Resource Allocation

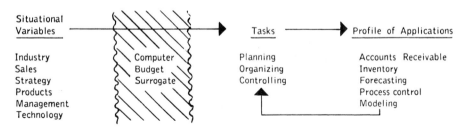

A complete stage theory for the tasks of managing the computer resource must include an explanation for the effects of situational variables and the recursive effects of existing computer-based applications. Ultimately, it is desirable to functionally relate the situational variables to the tasks, and eliminate the need to use the computer budget surrogate. At this point, however, a complete formulation is too ambitious a research undertaking.

A manageable undertaking is to formulate a hypothesis on the relationship of the tasks to the hypothesized stages reflected in the growth of the computer budget. Both situational variables and effects of existing applications are confounded in the budget. However, for the three companies studied, the tasks seemed to be sufficiently associated with the computer budget growth to not be overwhelmed by the effects of situational variables or existing applications. The following description is partially based on the three companies studied and is partially based on generalized experience and discussions with computer managers.

GENERAL DESCRIPTION OF THE STAGES FOR MANAGING THE COMPUTER

The stages for managing the computer[7] are descriptions of central tendencies for the number and nature of planning, organizing, and controlling tasks.[8] By central tendencies, I mean that the nature of the task and its associated attributes seem to be somewhat predictable by stage. Analysis of the computer activity in the three organizations studied indicates that the tasks change character over time and that their attributes evolve in

---

[7]The term "computer" as used here is meant to broadly include the actual computer and all the resources associated with using it in the organization (e.g., programmers, operations personnel, and materials).

[8]For an extended discussion of an analogy between managing the computer and managing the organization see Arnold E. Ditri, John C. Shaw, and William Atkins, *Managing the EDP Function* (New York: McGraw-Hill Book Co., 1971).

patterns roughly correlated with the computer budget growth. The intent, however, is to describe the tasks by stage, and not to assert cause and effect relationships.

Computer Budget Growth	**Stage Description**
Stage I	Initiation (computer acquisition)
Stage II	Contagion (intense system development)
Stage III	Control (Proliferation of controls)
Stage IV	Integration (user/service orientation)

Stage I (Initiation)

Stage I is brought about by the introduction of the computer in the organization. Typically, the computer is introduced into the organization for one of two reasons. The most common reason is that the organization reaches some critical size in which certain administrative processes can be more effectively accomplished through mechanization. Increasing numbers of business transactions justify the capital investment in specialized equipment. Until recently, computer acquisition, either through purchase or lease, dominated the character of the Initiation Stage. Recently, however, low-priced minicomputers, time-sharing, and computer utilities have made the computer resource available to organizations which could not economically justify using computers for processing their data only a few years ago.

A second main reason for acquiring a computer is computation need. Engineering companies, for example, often acquire a computer to aid in the computational work comprising the main business activity. In addition to the two main reasons for acquiring a computer, there are a host of less rational reasons: the competition to acquire a computer, the desire to maintain an image of using the latest technology, and the belief that computing is the wave of the future.

Management generally recognizes the fact that the computer will shock the organization. Thus attempts are made to assimilate it into the organizational structure with the least disruption possible. The original justification for the computer is typically a compelling cost-saving study. It is oriented toward use in one particular system such as payroll, billing, or inventory. The "low-profile" strategy leads to the assignment of responsibility for the computer to the organization that performed the original justification (e.g., controller). If the original justification, however, is partially administrative and partially scientific (computation), an organization conflict for control over the computer often arises. In these cases, scientific and commercial programming groups may spring up and may keep the conflict alive through competition for an extended period of time. This situation is more prevalent among firms in the aerospace and petroleum industries than in less scientific-based industries such as banking. It complicates the implementation of control devices like charge-out systems.

A short time into stage I, it becomes apparent that the computer is a potent change agent in the organization. The computer necessitates a rigor and formalization typically not before experienced in the organization. Its high fixed cost structure focuses management attention on rapidly eliminating underutilization.[9] The forces for rapidly developing production applications create an environment which discourages planning, cost control, and quality assurance. The only control is imposed by programmers themselves. Organization for the computer grows rapidly and haphazardly. The incorporation of highly trained system analysts and programmers also imposes a relatively foreign analytical approach onto the organization ridden with cryptic terminology.

Often even the strongest advocates for computing become alienated by it. The forces of a change not guided by planning techniques and constrained by control devices are too radical to be smoothly assimilated by bureaucratic organization. The result is "those who are committed to computing" despite previous experiences and "those who have become alienated by computing." The experiences engender what has come to be known as the "two culture problem." Those closely associated with computing recognize that their interests and motivations are basically different than operating management. Yet, to make their work purposeful, they are dependent upon effectively communicating with management. Operating management, on the other hand, begins to recognize that the computer resource is different than other resources that they manage. Effective management of the computer is dependent upon an awareness of the nature and potential for computing which is acquired by working with those closely associated with computing.

Senior management by this time has gained enough experience with the new resource to be tempted by the potential power of computing on the one hand, but on the other hand, they are beginning to become sensitized to its dysfunctional effects: changing the way of doing business too rapidly to be smoothly assimilated into the organization; tough internal control problems leading to costly mistakes (e.g., out-of-stock conditions); and human relations problems on the job causd by technological change. Nevertheless, the managerial tendency is commitment to computing. The fallacy and realism of sunk cost seems to play no small part in the commitment. The computer is acquired and old systems have been converted to computer-based systems; the skills required to operate the old manual systems have disappeared. This managerial commitment marks the transition from stage I to stage II. A manifestation of the transition is often an increase in the responsibility and reporting level of the manager of the computer resource. Assignment of responsibility for computing to a specific function such as accounting is usually the cause of many of the planning and control problems. Increasing responsibility and reporting level is also a common technique used by senior management for reacting to problems.

---

[9]Upon acquiring a computer, a company usually does not have enough programs immediately developed to keep the computer busy. It is not unusual during the first six months to operate a new computer less than one shift.

Stage II (Contagion)

Stage II is characterized by a managerial climate of concern. They look for strategies to encourage alienated users to investigate the potential for computing. Generally impressive cost savings in clerical areas as well as a few of the inevitable "spectacular successes" reported in the respective trade journal give a "time is of the essence" element to the movement.

A number of characteristics designed to spark wide computer applications are observable during the Contagion Stage. The need for emphasis on planning tasks is still not recognized. The job of the moment is to use up the capacity of the existing computer. In extreme cases, studies may be initiated on the economics of selling the excess computer capacity on the outside. Inducements include a general lack of project control and budgetary control. Once computer projects are initiated, the management posture is supportive, even if relatively high computer budgets must be absorbed in the process. In fact, most computer projects are noticeably devoid of any project control devices such as PERT (Performance Evaluation Review Technique) or cost/benefit analyses. Centralized systems analysis and operations research groups often render nonchargeable services to user groups.

Inevitably, the capacity of the current computer becomes saturated. The seemingly continued burst of new applications leads to larger and expanded computer systems. More sophisticated computer systems lead to needs for greater specialization in the areas of operations, systems programming, applications programming, and management. Recruiting the highly trained specialized people in a limited market results in a host of high salaries. The budget for the computer organization increases exponentially and quickly soars to a point of crisis for management.

Stage III (Control)[10]

Stage III is entered into as a result of the crisis. Management mobilizes a set of tasks to control expenditures for computing. The inefficiencies in computer applications are the most obvious and usually the first target. Planning tasks are initiated in all aspects of the computing organization. A senior management steering committee is established to evaluate the systems plan and establish prioritie for future systems development. Organization of the steering committee is accompanied by increased responsibility of the EDP manager, often a director or vice president. The tendency is to recentralize the computing activity. By this stage, there has been a general realization of the potential effectiveness of computing in certain areas. The result is a high level of competition for relatively scarce

---

[10]Professor Neil C. Churchill and I explored the Stage Hypothesis together in the spring of 1971. At that time we did not completely agree on the characterization of stages III and IV. Professor Churchill characterized stage III as the turning point where general management learns to manage *with* the computer, and computer management learns to *manage* the computer resource. Stage IV, then, was the maturing of that process. Professor Churchill preferred to characterize stage III as the Restraint Stage, and stage IV as the Control Stage.

systems personnel. Budgetary controls and overall cost justification contain the competition somewhat. Nevertheless, the problem that prevails can be only accommodated by a higher-level managerial committee for establishing priorities.

Formal project management and management reporting systems are instigated during stage III and provide for the beginning of effective management of the computer resource. The existence of these systems leads to the need for and development of standards for programming, documentation, and operations. Often there is also a shift to a user charge-out system for computer services. In the extreme case, the computer organization may be assigned profit center responsibility. Stage III, characterized by a myriad of control devices, is often an overreaction with strong forces toward centralization.

Stage IV (Integration)

Stage IV is marked by the refinement of the control tasks and the elimination of the more arbitrary ones. There is an overall maturation of the tasks for managing the computer resource. Notably, the project control system and the management reporting system become integral components of the management function. Planning tasks become more comprehensive and are effectively linked to the budgeting process and the formal corporate planning activity. The EDP director may spend up to 25-30 percent of his time planning.

The most dominant characteristic of stage IV is a rethinking of the role of the computer resource in respect to organizational goal achievement. The rethinking process is manifested through user empathy and the need to create an organizational design which effectively taps user needs and brings about reconciliation of user needs with the unique comparative advantages of computer processing over other alternatives. The alternatives are evaluated in a manner which brings to bear the economic concepts of out-of-pocket costs, opportunity costs, and cost/benefits.

In support of user orientation, charge-out systems that may have been implemented in earlier stages may be modified to partial charge-out systems, or eliminated entirely. Systems analysts may be moved out into the functional user departments. There is an overall concern for effectively accommodating centralization and decentralization organizational philosophy and business strategy.

Transition into stage IV is more subtle than transitions into the other stages. The computer budget continues to grow as more applications are developed and new technology is integrated, but the growth is slow and even. In addition, the efficiency of using the computer resource increases at a greater rate than the incremental dollars allocated to the computer resource.

GENERAL TASK DESCRIPTIONS FOR THE STAGES

Further analysis of the generic tasks for managing the computer activity and their relative existence and degree of sophistication for the three companies studied leads to the generalization for finer breakdowns of controlling, organizing, and planning tasks, shown in *Exhibits IV, V, and VI* respectively. Rough descriptors are deduced for the attributes of the subtasks associated with the stages. Since none of the companies studied were considered to be in stage IV, stage IV descriptors are fully extrapolated. Although an underlying growth sequence is suggested it is probable that a particular organization will find itself lagging or leading a stage for several attributes of the tasks.

Exhibit IV shows the *control* tasks and subtasks. In general, control tasks are at a rudimentary state or nonexistent (NE) in stages I and II. During stage III, the tasks initiated in the earlier stages become formalized and new ones are initiated. In stage IV, the control tasks are refined and reconciled with organization's goals. Reconciliation with organization goals is indirectly manifested. For example, system objectives are made more explicit and are developed in close conjunction with users. Users express support and respect for the systems organizations.

EXHIBIT IV

Control Tasks and
Stages

TASK	Stage I	Stage II	Stage III	Stage IV
Priority Setting	FIFO	Broad guidelines	Arbitrary	Established Policy
Budget	NE *	Communication	Control	Control
Computer Operations				
a. Scheduling	FIFO	Broad guidelines	Job shop	Job shop
b. Input/output control	User **	User	Policy	Cent. policy ***
c. Security	NE	NE	Policy	Policy/stds.
d. Training	Apprentice	Apprentice	Prereq. †	Internal ††
Programming Control				
a. Documentation	NE	NE	Initiation	Std. Policy
b. Standards	NE	NE	Initiation	Std. Policy
Project Management	NE	NE	Initiation	Std. Policy
Mgt. Reporting System				
a. Project plan	NE	Informal	Formal	Formal
b. Project performance	NE	Informal	Formal	Formal
c. Customer service	Informal	Informal	Formal	Formal
d. Personnel resources	Informal	Formal	Formal	Formal
e. Equipment resources	NE	NE	Formal	Formal
f. Budget performance	NE	Initiated	Formalized	Formal
Data Base Policies	NE	NE	NE	Established
Chg. out/non-chg. out systems	Nonchg. out	Nonchg. out	Chg. out	Best system
Audits	NE	NE	Initiated	Formal
Quality control				
a. Computer system	NE	Initiated	Established	Sophisticated
b. System design	NE	--	Initiated	Established
c. Programming	NE	Initiated	Broad Pol.	Standards
d. Operations	NE	NE	Initiated	Established
Manual Systems and Procedures	NE	NE	NE	Standards

  *NE-nonexistent
  **User-no formal controls; left to user judgment
  ***Cent.-centralized; decen.-decentralized
  †Prereq.-prerequisite minimum standards required
  ††Internal-internal training groups

Exhibit V shows the organizing tasks and subtasks. Three growth characteristics of organizing tasks are important:

1. EDP director's organizational position

2. steering committee

3. specialization

The EDP director's organizational position initially is relatively low and EDP constitutes only a part of his functional responsibility. As EDP grows both in commitment of financial resources and diversity of computer applications, the EDP responsibility rises to higher levels in the organization. Generally the first move is to assign higher level managers in the functional area full-time responsibility. The progression then may continue to the establishment of a director outside a functional area with a title such as Technical Services Director or Administrative Services Director. In some organizations, the responsibility has risen to the vice president level with titles such as Vice President for Information Systems.

The steering committee, consisting of higher level management, indicates an awareness of the potential and importance of the computer resource. Typically, steering committees are initiated at stage III and at stage IV become a refined device for ensuring efficient resource allocation in respect to organizational goals.

Growth processes universally result in increasing specialization and this is true for use of the computer resource. Specialized groups are formed for systems programming, application programming, operations, maintenance, and management.

EXHIBIT V

Organizing Tasks and
Stages

TASK	Stage I	Stage II	Stage III	Stage IV
Steering committee	NE *	NE	Initiation	Established
EDP Director's position	Functional area	Greater respon.	Director	Vice-President
Degree of specialization	Low	Medium	Medium	High
Research	NE	NE	Conducted by S.A.**	Separate function
Program maintenance	Haphazardly done	Loosely organized	Dominant activity	Well defined
Technical services	NE	Initiated	Established	Defined role
Modeling	NE	Initiated	Limited	Well defined
User/analyst teams	NE	NE	Encouraged	Organized for
Centralization/ decentralization	Decent.	Decent.	Cent.	Hard., cent.; S.A. decent.***
Data Base	NE	NE	Initiated	Important Activity
Manual Systems & Procedures	NE	NE	NE	Incorporated †

*NE-nonexistent
**S.A.-systems analyst
***Hardware centralized and systems analysts decentralized
†Incorporated into the EDP organization

Exhibit VI shows the *planning* tasks and subtasks. Virtually no planning takes place during stages I and II, with the exception of conventional budgeting. During stage III relatively wide-spread planning is initiated and becomes refined in stage IV. At stage IV, planning plays a dominant role in shaping the management processes for using the computer resource to reach organizational objectives.

EXHIBIT VI

Planning Tasks and
Stages

TASK	Stage I	Stage II	Stage III	Stage IV
Financial Plan and Budget	Part of other budget	Loose budget	Budget	Budget & Plan
Technological forecasting	NE	NE	Initiation	Developed
Systems plan	NE	NE	Initiation	Developed
Operations and programming plan	NE	NE	Initiation	Developed
Equipment plan	NE	NE	Initiation	Developed
Personnel plan	NE	NE	Initiation	Developed
Conversion plan	NE	NE	Initiation	Developed

CONCLUSION

The study of the use of computers by organizations is in a formative period. The existence of the formative period is reflected by the imprecise terminology in the area and the lack of an accepted body of knowledge for effectively managing the computer resource. In recognition of this, the Stage Hypothesis is presented not as a prescription to computer management, but as a plausible description of the process of using the computer resource in the organization.

The Stage Hypothesis is based on the expenditure patterns of an organization over time. The expenditure patterns are quantified by the computer budget. While the computer budget measurement is crude at best, it does have the virtues of being quantitative and of being reproducible. It is a surrogate for the situational variables that directly determine the nature of the planning, organizing, and control tasks for managing the computer resource. Hopefully, the description of the tasks for managing the computer resource and the logic of their association with computer budget behavior are strong enough to permit others to formulate empirically testable hypotheses on the determinants, development, and attributes of the individual tasks. These will ultimately provide the base for normative theory formulation.

Managing
the Crisis in
Data Processing*

RICHARD L. NOLAN

The member of the corporation's steering committee did not mince words:

> "I'm telling you I want the flow-of-goods computer-based system, and I am willing to pay for it. And you are telling me I can't have it after we have approved your fourth running annual budget increase of over 30%. If you can't provide the service, I'll get it outside. There are now reliable software companies around, and my people tell me that we should take seriously a proposal that we received from a large minicomputer vendor."

The reply of the vice president of information services was not well received:

> "I'm at the edge of control. It isn't any longer a question of financial resources. My budget has grown from $30 million in 1975 to over $70 million in 1978. The technology is getting ultracomplex. I can't get the right people fast enough, let alone provide suitable space and connections to our sprawling computer network."

On returning to his office, the vice president knew that the steering committee member would be going ahead with the minicomputer. There was no way that the corporate technical staff could provide the flow-of-goods functions for the money or within the time frame that the

---

minicomputer vendor had promised. Something was not right, even though he could not put his finger on it.

The vice president mused at the irony of it all. Five years ago he was brought in to set up a corporate computer utility after a similar period of poorly understood growth (that growth had been the undoing of his predecessor). Now key questions were being asked about a similar growth pattern of the data processing (DP) budget, and he did not have the answers. He wished he did!

The plight of the vice president of information services is not singular. The rapid growth in DP services that many companies experienced in the mid- to late 1960s is occurring again in numerous companies. The resurgence is confusing.

The senior managements of some of these companies thought that the DP control structures put in place during the 1970s, such as chargeout, project management, and consolidation of computing activities under tight budgetary control, would contain any future budget growth. Nevertheless, the annual DP budget growth rates are exceeding 30%. Further, just the annual budget *increments* are equal to the total size of the budgets four or five years ago. The confused top executives of these companies are searching for answers to what underlies this growth. Is it good? Will it stop? What are the limits?

The answers are not obvious, but a probing of the status of the DP activities in different companies and of the current technological environment sheds light on the situation and provides insights into the management actions that are needed to prepare for and manage the growth.

SIX STAGES OF GROWTH

Studies I have made during the 1970s of a series of companies—3 large corporations early in this decade, 35 companies several years ago, and then a large number of IBM customer concerns and other corporations since then—indicate the existence of six stages of growth in a company's DP function. These stages are portrayed in *Exhibit I*.

The scheme shown in this exhibit supersedes the four-stage concept I described in HBR in 1974.[1] The four stages described then continue to be valid, but the experience of recent years reveals a larger and more challenging picture.

This exhibit shows six stages of DP growth, from the inception of the computer into the organization to mature management of data resources. Through mid-stage 3, DP management is concerned with management of the computer. At some point in stage 3, there is a transition to management of data resources. This transition involves not only restructuring the DP organization but also installing new management techniques.

---

[1]See my article, written with Cyrus F. Gibson, *"Managing the Four Stages of EDP Growth,"* HBR January-February 1974, p. 76.

EXHIBIT I

Six Stages of
Data Processing Growth

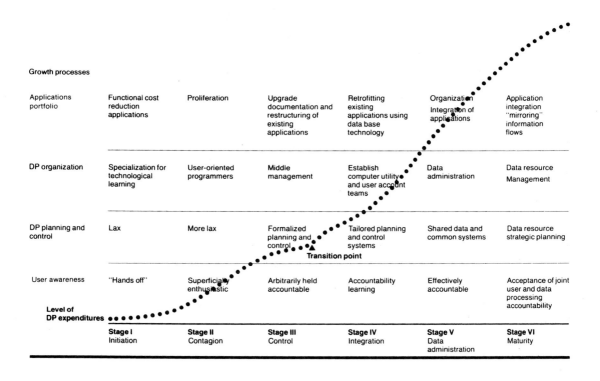

Growth processes	Stage I Initiation	Stage II Contagion	Stage III Control	Stage IV Integration	Stage V Data administration	Stage VI Maturity
Applications portfolio	Functional cost reduction applications	Proliferation	Upgrade documentation and restructuring of existing applications	Retrofitting existing applications using data base technology	Organization Integration of applications	Application integration "mirroring" information flows
DP organization	Specialization for technological learning	User-oriented programmers	Middle management	Establish computer utility and user account teams	Data administration	Data resource Management
DP planning and control	Lax	More lax	Formalized planning and control	Tailored planning and control systems	Shared data and common systems	Data resource strategic planning
			Transition point			
User awareness	"Hands off"	Superficially enthusiastic	Arbitrarily held accountable	Accountability learning	Effectively accountable	Acceptance of joint user and data processing accountability

Level of DP expenditures

Stage I Initiation	**Stage II** Contagion	**Stage III** Control	**Stage IV** Integration	**Stage V** Data administration	**Stage VI** Maturity

To understand the new picture, one must look at the growth in knowledge and technology, at organizational control, and at the shift from computer management to data resource management. I will consider each of these topics in turn.

Burgeoning of Knowledge

Organizational learning and movement through the stages are influenced by the external (or professional) body of knowledge of the management of data processing as well as by a company's internal body of knowledge.

The external body of knowledge is a direct response to developments in information technology. It is concerned with developments in the theory of DP management as well as with the collective documented experiences of companies. The internal body of knowledge, however, benefits from the external body of knowledge, but is primarily *experiential*—what managers, specialists, and operators learn first hand as the system develops.

It is important to realize how greatly DP technology spurs the development and codification of an external, or professional, body of knowledge.

For this reason a company that began to automate business functions in 1960 moved through the stages differently from a company that started to automate in 1970 or 1978. The information technology is different, and the extent of professional knowledge on how to manage the DP technology is much greater in the latter years. Not only is the external body of knowledge more sophisticated, but the information technology itself is more developed.

Control and Slack

Organizational learning is influenced by the environment in which it takes place. One possible environment is what might be called "control"; a second might be called organizational "slack," a term coined by Richard M. Cyert and James G. March.[2]

In the *control* environment, all financial and performance management systems—including planning, budgeting, project management, personnel performance reviews, and chargeout or cost accounting systems— are used to ensure that DP activities are effective and efficient. In the *slack* environment, though, sophisticated controls are notably absent. Instead, incentives to use DP in an experimental manner are present (for example, systems analysts might be assigned to users without any charge to the users' budgets).

When management permits organizational slack in the DP activities, it commits more resources to data processing than are strictly necessary to get the job done. The extra payment achieves another objective— nurturing of innovation. The new technology penetrates the business's multifunctional areas (i.e., production, marketing, accounting, personnel, and engineering). However, the budget will be looser, and costs will be higher. Management needs to feel committed to much more than just strict cost efficiency.

The balance between control and slack is important in developing appropriate management approaches for each stage of organizational learning. For example, an imbalance of high control and low slack in the earlier stages can impede the use of information technology in the organization; conversely, an imbalance of low control and high slack in the latter stages can lead to explosive DP budget increases and inefficient systems.

Exhibit II shows the appropriate balance of control and slack through the six stages. In stage 3 the orientation of management shifts from management of the computer to management of data resources. This shift, associated with introduction of the data base technology, explains the absence of entries in the computer columns after stage 3.

Shift in Management Emphasis

In stage 2 more and more senior and middle managers become frustrated in their attempts to obtain information from the company's computer-

---

[2]Richard M. Cyert and James G. March, "*Organizational Factors in the Theory of Oligopoly,*" Quarterly Journal of Economics, February 1956, p. 44.

EXHIBIT II

Optimum Balance of
Organizational Slack and Control

Stages	Organizational slack		Control		Objective of control systems
	Computer	Data	Computer	Data	
Stage 1	Low		Low		
Stage 2	High		Low		Facilitate growth
Stage 3	Low	Low	High	Low	Contain supply
Stage 4		High		Low	Match supply and demand
Stage 5		Low		High	Contain demand
Stage 6		High		High	Balance supply and demand

based systems to support decision-making needs. *Exhibit III* helps to explain the root of the problem. The exhibit is based on a fictional corporation that represents a kind of composite of the organizations studied. The spectrum of opportunities for DP equipment is called the "applications portfolio."

The triangle illustrates the opportunities for cost-effective use of data processing to support the various information needs in the organization. Senior management predominantly uses planning systems, middle management predominantly uses control systems, and operational management predominantly uses operational systems. At every level there are information systems that are uneconomic or unfeasible to automate, despite managers' desires for faster and better data.

In stage 1 in this organization, several low-level operational systems in a functional area, typically accounting, are automated. During stage 2 the organization encourages innovation and extensive application of the DP technology by maintaining low control and high slack. While widespread penetration of the technology is achieved by expanding into operational systems, problems are created by inexperienced programmers working without the benefit of effective DP management control systems. These problems become alarming when base-level systems cannot support higher-level systems—in particular, order processing, production control, and budgetary control systems. Maintenance of the existing, relatively poorly designed systems begins to occupy from 70% to 80% of the productive time of programmers and systems analysts.

Sometime in stage 3, therefore, one can observe a basic shift in orientation from management of the computer to management of the company's data resources. This shift in orientation is a direct result of analyses about how to put more emphasis, in expanding DP activities, on the needs of management control and planning as opposed to the needs of consolida-

EXHIBIT III

Applications Portfolio
Late in Stage II

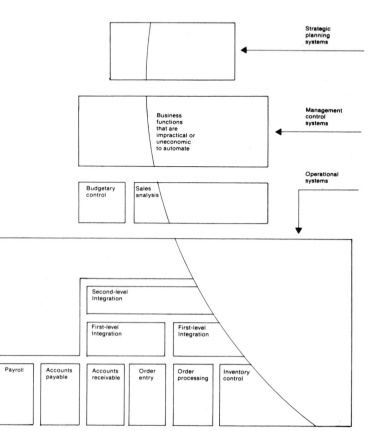

Note: An example of first-level integration is a purchase order application that uses order processing and inventory status information. An example of second-level integration is a vendor payment application that uses accounts payable and purchasing information.

tion and coordination in the DP activities themselves. This shift also serves to keep data processing flexible to respond to management's new questions on control or ideas for planning.

As the shift is made, executives are likely to do a great deal of soul searching about how best to assimilate and manage data base technologies. The term "data administration" becomes common in conferences, and there is much talk about what data administration controls are needed.

But there is little effective action. I believe there is little action because the penetration of the technology is obviously low at its inception, and a combination of low control and high slack is the natural balanced environment to facilitate organizational learning. However, at the same time the seeds are being sown for a subsequent explosion in DP expenditures.

Stage 3 is characterized by rebuilding and professionalizing the DP activity to give it more standing in the organization. This stage is also characterized by initial attempts to develop user accountability for the DP expenditures incurred. Usually these attempts take the form of chargeouts for DP services. Unfortunately, both the conceptual and technical problems of implementing user accountability lead to confusion and alienation; real gains in accountability are not made. Nevertheless, the trends of DP charges in user budgets are rarely reversed.

Consequently, during stage 3 the users see little progress in the development of new control systems while the DP department is rebuilding, although they are arbitrarily held accountable for the cost of DP support and have little ability to influence the costs. Even the most stalwart users become highly frustrated and, in a familiar phrase, "give up on data processing."

Explosive Growth

As stage 3 draws to a close, the DP department accomplishes its rebuilding and moves the data base and data communication technologies into several key application areas, such as order entry, general ledger, and materials requirements planning. In addition, the computer utility and network reach a point where high-quality services are being reliably provided to the users. When these accomplishments are realized, a subtle transition into stage 4 takes place.

Just when users have given up hope that data processing will provide anything new, they get interactive terminals and the various supports and assistance needed for using and profiting from data base technology. Already they have benignly accepted the cost of DP services. Now, with real value perceived, they virtually demand increased support and are willing to pay pretty much whatever it costs. This creates DP expenditure growth rates that may be reminiscent of those in stage 2, rates one may have thought would not be seen again.

It is important to underscore the fact that users perceive real value from data base applications and interactive terminals for data communication. In a recent study of one company with more than 1,500 applications, I found that users ranked their data base and interactive applications as far and away more effective than users of conventional or batch technology ranked their applications. This company has been sustaining DP expenditure growth rates of about 30% for the past four years. More important, the users of the new applications are demanding growth to the limits of the DP department's ability to expand.

The pent-up user demand of stage 3 is part of the reason. But a more important part of the reason is that the planning and control put in place in stage 3 are designed for *internal* management of the computer rather than for control of the growth in use of it and containment of the cost explosion. *Exhibit IV* shows the typical pattern of starting and developing internal and external (that is, user-managed) control systems. Late in stage 4, when exclusive reliance on the computer controls proves to be ineffective, the inefficiencies of rapid growth begin to create another wave

EXHIBIT IV

Growth and Maturation of
Data Processing Planning and Control

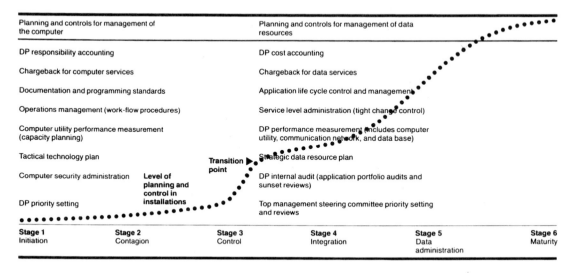

Planning and controls for management of the computer			Planning and controls for management of data resources		
DP responsibility accounting			DP cost accounting		
Chargeback for computer services			Chargeback for data services		
Documentation and programming standards			Application life cycle control and management		
Operations management (work-flow procedures)			Service level administration (tight change control)		
Computer utility performance measurement (capacity planning)			DP performance measurement (includes computer utility, communication network, and data base)		
Tactical technology plan		Transition point	Strategic data resource plan		
Computer security administration	Level of planning and control in installations		DP internal audit (application portfolio audits and sunset reviews)		
DP priority setting			Top management steering committee priority setting and reviews		

Stage 1 Initiation	Stage 2 Contagion	Stage 3 Control	Stage 4 Integration	Stage 5 Data administration	Stage 6 Maturity

of problems. The redundancy of data complicates the use of control and planning systems. Demands grow for better control and more efficiency.

In stage 5, data administration is introduced. During stage 6, the applications portfolio is completed, and its structure "mirrors" the organization and the information flows in the company.

IDENTIFYING THE STAGE

How can executives determine what stage of development their corporate data processing is in? I have been able to develop some workable benchmarks for making such an assessment. Any one of the benchmarks taken alone could be misleading, but taken together these criteria provide a reliable image. I will describe some of the most useful benchmarks so management can gain a perspective on where it stands and on what developments lie down the road. For a visual portrayal of the benchmarks, see *Exhibit V*.

It is important to understand that a large multinational company may have divisions simultaneously representing stages 1, 2, 3, 4, and perhaps 5 or even 6. However, every division that I have studied has its DP concentrated in a particular stage. Knowledge of this stage provides the foundation for developing an appropriate strategy.

First-Level Benchmarks

The first step is to analyze the company's DP expenditure curve by observing its shape and comparing its annual growth rate with the

EXHIBIT V

Benchmarks of
the Six Stages

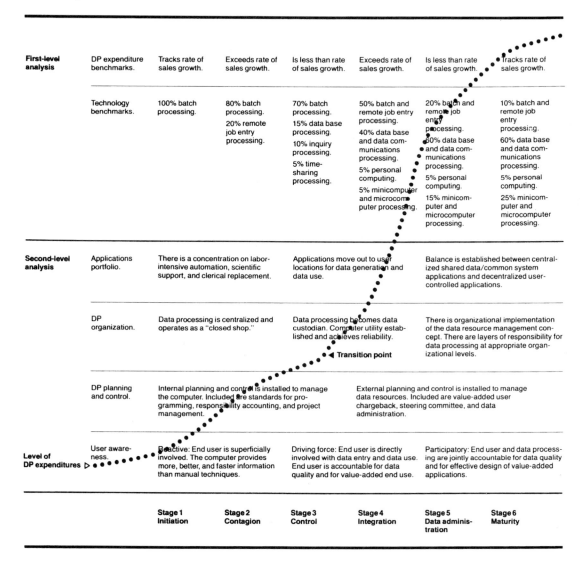

		Stage 1 Initiation	Stage 2 Contagion	Stage 3 Control	Stage 4 Integration	Stage 5 Data administration	Stage 6 Maturity
First-level analysis	DP expenditure benchmarks.	Tracks rate of sales growth.	Exceeds rate of sales growth.	Is less than rate of sales growth.	Exceeds rate of sales growth.	Is less than rate of sales growth.	Tracks rate of sales growth.
	Technology benchmarks.	100% batch processing.	80% batch processing. 20% remote job entry processing.	70% batch processing. 15% data base processing. 10% inquiry processing. 5% time-sharing processing.	50% batch and remote job entry processing. 40% data base and data communications processing. 5% personal computing. 5% minicomputer and microcomputer processing.	20% batch and remote job entry processing. 50% data base and data communications processing. 5% personal computing. 15% minicomputer and microcomputer processing.	10% batch and remote job entry processing. 60% data base and data communications processing. 5% personal computing. 25% minicomputer and microcomputer processing.
Second-level analysis	Applications portfolio.	There is a concentration on labor-intensive automation, scientific support, and clerical replacement.		Applications move out to user locations for data generation and data use.		Balance is established between centralized shared data/common system applications and decentralized user-controlled applications.	
	DP organization.	Data processing is centralized and operates as a "closed shop."		Data processing becomes data custodian. Computer utility established and achieves reliability.		There is organizational implementation of the data resource management concept. There are layers of responsibility for data processing at appropriate organizational levels.	
	DP planning and control.	Internal planning and control is installed to manage the computer. Included are standards for programming, responsibility accounting, and project management.		External planning and control is installed to manage data resources. Included are value-added user chargeback, steering committee, and data administration.			
Level of DP expenditures ▷	User awareness.	Reactive: End user is superficially involved. The computer provides more, better, and faster information than manual techniques.		Driving force: End user is directly involved with data entry and data use. End user is accountable for data quality and for value-added end use.		Participatory: End user and data processing are jointly accountable for data quality and for effective design of value-added applications.	

◀ Transition point

company's sales. A sustained growth rate greater than sales indicates either a stage 2 or 4 environment. Then, analyze the state of technology in data processing. If data base technology has been introduced and from 15% to 40% of the company's computer-based applications are operating using such technology, the company is most likely experiencing stage 4.

In the light of International Data Corporation's research on the number of companies introducing data base management systems technology in 1977 (shown in *Exhibit VI*), I believe that roughly half of the larger companies are experiencing stage 3 or 4. This is further corroborated by evidence that 1978 saw the largest annual percentage growth in the total DP budgets of U.S. companies—from $36 billion to an estimated $42 billion, or a 15½% increase.

As shown in *Exhibit VI*, about 55% of IBM installations in 1979 will have data base technology, compared with only about 20% in 1976. I feel that this means the explosive stage 4 in DP expenditures can be expected in the next two to five years in most companies; the increases may be somewhat moderated by continuance of the impressive technological advances that have improved prices and equipment performance.

Second-Level Benchmarks

The second step is to focus on the four growth processes shown in *Exhibit V*. Each major organizational unit of the company, such as a subsidiary, division, or department, should be listed. Then the growth processes associated with each organizational unit should be identified. For example, a decentralized subsidiary generally has all four growth processes, from expansion in the applications portfolio to an increase in employees' awareness of DP potentials and functions (see the left-hand side of *Exhibit V*). However, a division using the services of a corporate computer utility is likely to have only two of the growth processes—expansion in the applications portfolio and in user awareness.

Next, identify the stage (see the bottom of *Exhibit V*) of each of the growth processes associated with the organizational unit. Use growth as an example in the applications portfolio. The approach used for this process is similar to that for any of the processes. The procedure is as follows:

1. Define the set of business functions for the organizational unit that represents cost-effective opportunities to apply DP technology. I call this the "normative applications portfolio." It represents the business functions that would be receiving DP support if the company had achieved stage 6 maturity. *Exhibit VII* portrays such a scheme.

2. Taking each function in turn, indicate for each set of systems the support that data processing gives to the function in the organization. Ask, "What is it doing for our business?" I suggest doing this by shading the space for the function on the normative applications portfolio; use a ten-point scale to shade the function at 10%, 40%, 80% or whatever amount seems appropriate. Looking at all the shaded functions as a whole, judge the level of support given the system as a whole.

3. Then, match the support given the system as a whole with the benchmarks shown to the right of *Exhibit VII*. For instance, 80% support of operational systems, 20% support of management control systems, and just a faint trace of support for strategic planning systems would show the organization to be at stage 3.

4. Next, look for matches and mismatches between DP investment and the key functions that contribute to the company's return on investment or

EXHIBIT VI

Data Base Management Software Installed and Projected to be Installed on
IBM Medium- to Large-Scale Computers in the United States

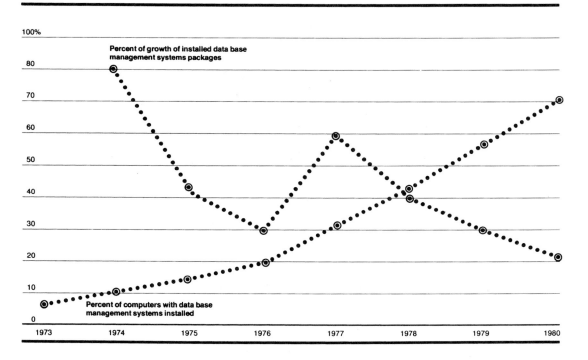

Source: Richard L. Nolan, "*The New EDP Economics*," presentation at the International Data Corporation Conference, San Francisco, April 3, 1978.

profitability. For example, if the company's business is manufacturing, and if half of the DP system investment goes to support accounting, a red flag is raised. The possibility of a mismatch between expenditure and need should be investigated.

After the functional assessment, one should conduct a technical assessment of the applications. The technical assessment gets at the concern of whether the DP activity is using current technology effectively. Benchmarks used include individual system ages, file structures, and maintenance resources required.

Again using a scheme like that described for *Exhibit VII*, compare the support given by data processing to the different corporate functions with the technical assessment. Are the DP systems old, or are the file structures out of date, or are there other shortcomings indicating that up-to-date technology is being neglected? Such neglect may be the result of managerial oversight, of a shortsighted desire to make a better annual profit showing, or of other reasons. In any case, it means that a portion of the company's assets are being sold off.

EXHIBIT VII

Investment Benchmarks for
DP Applications

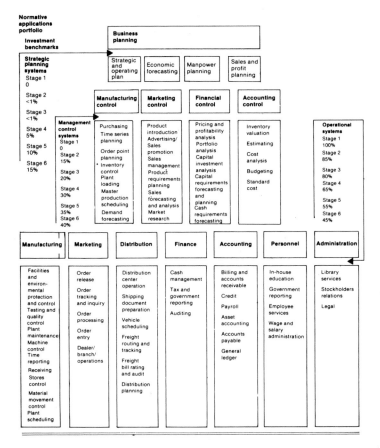

During the definition and assessment of the applications portfolios
for a company, a DP "chart of accounts" is created. The business functions
identified in the applications portfolio are the "objects of expenditures."
Creating the chart of accounts is an important step in achieving the level
of management sophistication required to effectively guide this activity
through stages 4 and 5 and into the stage 6 environment.

So much for the applications portfolio analysis. Using the same sort
of approach, management can turn next to the other growth processes
shown in *Exhibit V* for second-level analysis. When the analysis is
completed, management will have an overall assessment of the stage of
the organization and of potential weaknesses in its ability for future
growth.

If complete analyses of this type are made for all important organizations—divisional and functional—of the company, management will have
a corporate-wide profile. *Exhibit VIII* is an example. Such a profile
provides the foundation for developing an effective DP strategy.

EXHIBIT VIII

One Company's
Stage Analysis

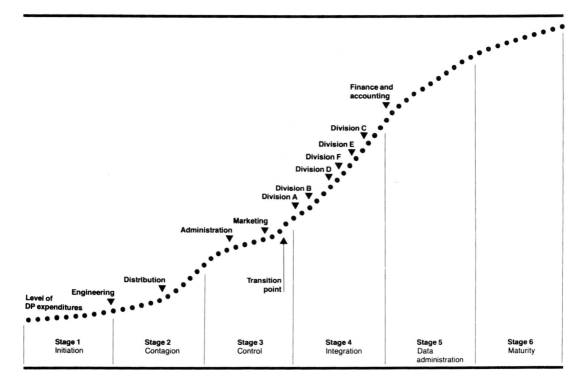

GUIDELINES FOR ACTION

In most sizable U.S. corporations, data processing is headed for an extremely rapid growth in the next five years. This growth is not necessarily bad; in fact, I believe that if the growth can be managed, it will be the most cost-effective growth experienced to date. Here are five guidelines for managing the growth successfully.

1. Recognize the fundamental organizational transition from computer management to data resource management. With the introduction of data base technology in stage 3, an important shift in emphasis occurs—from managing the computer to managing the company's data resources. Obviously, this transition does not occur all at once. It appears first in the analysis of the late stage 2 applications portfolio and is a result of the requirement to restructure it so that applications can be tied together efficiently.

The transition also becomes apparent during the implementation of controls. Difficulties with chargeout systems that are computer-oriented cause management searches for alternative ways to achieve user accountability. This often leads to the conclusion that the user can be accountable for the functional support, but data processing must be accountable for management of shared data.

The key idea is to recognize the importance of the shift in management emphasis from the computer to data and then to develop applications and planning and control systems to facilitate the transition. Applications should be structured to share data; new planning and control systems should be data-oriented.

2. Recognize the importance of the enabling technologies. The emerging information technologies are enabling companies to manage data economically. It is important to emphasize the word *economically*. What companies did only a few years ago in establishing large central DP utilities is no longer justifiable by economic arguments. Data resource management changes the economic picture.

Data base and data communication technologies are important from an organizational standpoint. Sprawling DP networks are enabling new approaches to management control and planning. We can now have multidimensional control structures such as function (e.g., manufacturing, marketing, and finance), product, project, and location. Managers and staff can be assigned to one or more of the dimensions. Through shared data systems, senior management can obtain financial and operating performance reports on any of the dimensions in a matter of hours after the close of the business day, month, quarter, or year.

Last but not least, developments in on-line terminals, minicomputers, and microcomputers are opening up new opportunities for doing business at the operational level. Airline reservation systems, for example, no longer stand alone in this area; we now can include point of sale (POS) for the retail industry, automated teller terminals (ATMs) for the banking industry, and plant automation for the manufacturing industry.

3. Identify the stages of the company's operating units to help keep DP activities on track. A basic management tenet is: "If you can't measure it, you can't manage it." The applications portfolios of a company provide data processing with a chart of accounts. In the past, management lacked a generic and meaningful way to describe and track a DP activity—that is, to locate it in relation to the past and future. However, there is now a generic and empirically supported descriptive theory of the evolution of a DP activity—the stage theory. One can use this theory to understand where the company has come from, which problems were a result of weak management, and which problems arose from natural growth. More important, one can gain some insight into what the future may hold and then can try to develop appropriate management strategies that will accomplish corporate purposes.

4. Develop a multilevel strategy and plan. Most DP departments have matured out of the "cottage industry" era. They have reached the point where they are woven into the operating fabric of their companies. There are many documented cases of the important impact that a computer failure of mere hours can have on a company's profitability.

Nevertheless, many DP departments continue to hold on to the cottage industry strategy of standing ready to serve any demands that come their way. This can have a disastrous effect when stage 4 begins to run its course. The extent and complexity of corporate activity make it impossible for data processing to be "all things to all users." Consequently, decisions will have to be made on what data processing will be—its priorities and purposes; when, where, and whom it will serve; and so on.

If the DP management makes these decisions without the benefit of an agreed-on strategy and plan, the decisions are apt to be wrong; if they are right, the rationale for them will not be adequately understood by users. If users do not understand the strategic direction of data processing, they are unlikely to provide support.

Development of an effective strategy and plan is a three-step process. *First*, management should determine where the company stands in the evolution of a DP function and should analyze the strengths and weaknesses that bear on DP strategies. *Second*, it should choose a DP strategy that fits in with the company's business strategy. And *third*, it should outline a DP growth plan for the next three to five years, detailing this plan for each of the growth processes portrayed in *Exhibit V*.

It is important to recognize that the plan resulting from this three-step process is, for most companies, an entry-level plan. Thus the plan cannot and should not be too detailed. It should provide the appropriate "blueprint" and goal set for each growth process to make the data processing more supportive of the overall business plan. It should also be a spark for all those in DP activities who want to make their work more significant and relevant to corporate purposes.

5. Make the steering committee work. The senior management steering committee is an essential ingredient for effective use of data processing in the advanced stages. It provides direction to the strategy formulation process. It can reset and revise priorities from time to time to keep DP programs moving in the right direction.

From my observation, I think that the steering committee should meet on a quarterly basis to review progress. This would give enough time between meetings for progress to be made in DP activities and would allow the committee to monitor progress closely. Plan progress and variances can make up the agenda of the review sessions.

Understanding Distributed Data Processing*

JACK R. BUCHANAN
RICHARD G. LINOWES

The data processing profession has generated a new set of buzzwords that purportedly describe the next generation of information systems. A new development, referred to as "distributed data processing," or "DDP," will figure in major expansion plans both now and throughout the 1980s. Managers in many organizations are eager to bring some of this state-of-the-art technical capability into their own operations, for distributed data processing, as they see it, is an opportunity to distribute computing facilities and allow access to a machine in a way that was never possible before.

Is distributed data processing just a new technological fad or does it represent a new concept that will enable organizations to make more effective use of their data processing resources? If DDP entails the spread of computing around an organization, what are the hazards of such proliferation? Is there some systematic way for managers to plan and monitor the introduction of DDP into their organizations? In this, the first of two articles, we shall attempt to answer these questions by developing a framework that enables managers to understand DDP and to identify opportunities for its use.

DDP is a concept that has only recently come of age. Technological, economic, and educational developments now allow us to design information systems that may achieve the objectives of matching the

*Reprinted by permission of Harvard Business Review. "Understanding Distributed Data Processing" by Jack R. Buchanan and Richard G. Linowes (July-August 1980). Copyright © 1980 by the President and Fellows of Harvard College; all rights reserved.

organizational structure, supporting the business strategy, and, in general, providing a more natural use of information processing. In essence, DDP involves the exciting prospect of assigning responsibility for DP-related activities so that both business and technical knowledge can be applied more readily to the achievement of an organization's goals.

UNDERLYING DEVELOPMENTS

The move to distributed data processing is possible today in large part because of the drop in cost of computer hardware. Minicomputers and now microcomputers are becoming so inexpensive that it is quite reasonable for a company to buy three or four small computers to do the work previously performed by one central computer or to automate activities previously performed manually. Whereas, in the past, economies of scale may have driven a company to use one large data processing center to perform a wide variety of services, a company now might employ several different computers in different locations to provide more specialized services. Management can now arrange data processing facilities with much less concern for hardware costs.

Technical developments are also responsible for the recent practicality of distributed data processing. Major innovations, primarily from the areas of telecommunications and data base systems, have ushered in many new capabilities. Improvements in both equipment and software have made possible the building of very sophisticated computer networks, and direct links from computer to computer are becoming more common. Tasks that have been handled in large centers may now be partitioned into subtasks, and these in turn may be farmed out to remote sites.

When information systems are designed in this fashion, a whole network of computers often becomes involved in carrying out an operation. Such systems represent prototypes for the distributed data processing of the future; they show how technical developments, perhaps for the first time, permit the decentralization of many data processing activities.

The DP manager has traditionally been responsible for cost center management, capacity planning, systems administration, and adaptation of new technology. Since DDP will increase direct access to the system by the end user, the administrative process of the user must be reflected in system design, and information systems must focus on business tasks.

The DP manager will participate with end users in more joint enterprises and consequently will have to be more concerned with how the user defines productivity. Where computer operations are decentralized, the manager must establish charge-out methods that are understandable to the user and that measure service to the organization. For example, the DP manager should translate from kilocore seconds, computer resource units (CRUs), or other technical terms into measures such as number of transactions processed and reports produced so that both user and top management can make practical use of them. If a user group manager is to have any control over the computer resource, he or she must have this type of information as well as the means to effect change.

Finally, the exposure that most managers have to computerized information systems grows all the time, and their increasing familiarity with data processing leads them to make better use of the systems they have and to demand more from their systems. Thus many of these managers can be expected to set up some kind of data processing activities in their own departments and to become involved in delivering some of their own data processing services.

Declining hardware costs, improving communications and data base capabilities, and the growing data processing experience of users are prime actors behind our projection that distributed data processing, including the extensive use of data bases,[1] will be the hallmarks of the computer era.

COMMON PITFALLS

To take advantage of the power of DDP, managers need a clear conception of the complexities of using and managing the computer resource. Yet managers at all levels too often find themselves in difficulty because of their overly simplistic understanding of data processing, which they see chiefly as a collection of machines and technical issues; and oddly enough, DP managers sometimes are the worst culprits. This narrow view has led to a number of common fallacies.

One manufacturing manager recently pulled us aside to show us a new microcomputer hidden away in his office. He said proudly that it permitted him to do a few small applications unencumbered by the red tape and priority system of the corporate data center, where such applications officially should be done. He was delighted with the department's new toy, and he was eager to expand his operation and bring all his data processing activity in-house. "After all," he argued, "we already have one machine operating successfully. And there is a young engineer upstairs who took some computer courses in school, so we're all set."

In another company, a division general manager was perturbed at the high data processing charges appearing in his monthly income statement, charges that supposedly reflected his actual use of the corporate data center. He felt particularly disgruntled when he stumbled onto an advertisement for a new minicomputer that seemed capable of performing all the processing his division required yet whose monthly fee was significantly less than the figure he was paying. At the next quarterly meeting he complained, "For what we are paying for the data center, we could have our own minicomputer system and control our own priorities."

In a highly diversified conglomerate that has grown by the acquisition of other companies, the corporate controller was concerned about the alarming increase in data processing expenditures by the divisions. He

---

[1] Richard L. Nolan, *"Computer Data Bases: The Future Is Now,"* HBR September-October 1973, p. 98.

appointed a corporate systems planner to investigate the problem. The planner returned with a suggestion: take data processing away from the divisions and place it in regional centers under corporate direction. The plan was rejected out of hand by the controller, who knew that the design would be unacceptable to division managers in the company because they would not give up data processing to a corporate group. The corporate controller exclaimed, "I don't want to *manage* data processing, I just want to *control* it."

Finally, in the federal courts, administrators were planning how computers should be distributed around the country to provide computer support for various administrative functions of the courts. The design of the new system could take any form because there was no existing data processing activity with which to conform. The leadership and development of the project were centered in Washington, and systems analysis and implementation were carried out jointly with district and appellate court administrators. The study team was considering two possible arrangements of data processing facilities: local court minicomputers or regional centers.

Proponents of regional data centers argued that the configuration they favored would permit more responsive systems and more effective control by the courts. Those favoring local minicomputers, on the other hand, felt it was their configuration that offered these benefits, primarily because they saw that physical custody of the machines established effective control of the information processing resource: "How could a court have more control over its information processing at regional centers than it would within its own four walls?"

In all four of these examples, the managers' positions regarding use of computer systems appeared quite reasonable at the time. Only later did the problems or unrealistic features of their stands emerge. As we shall see, their arguments rested on the conventional image of data processing and its role in an organization, a view too limited for data processing planning in the 1980s.

ACQUIRING A BROAD VIEW

How can a manager avoid the pitfalls of the narrow view and systematically plan the placement of DP responsibilities? Primarily, he or she should recognize and work with two fundamental assumptions:

1. Information systems should match a company's structure and strategy.

2. Activities that support information systems are wide ranging and separable.

These basic notions are not only a good general way to understand the data processing resource, but they also allow us to construct a framework for describing and planning distributed data processing systems.

To most technicians, DDP simply means the spread of computer hardware and data to multiple sites around an organization. This definition is deficient, however, because it overlooks a wide range of activities that help make information systems work, furthermore it neglects the linkage of information systems to strategy and structure. In effect, its technical orientation leaves general managers out of discussions about the design of DDP systems.

A broader definition acknowledges that data processing is an organizational resource consisting of many areas of activity, each of which may be executed or controlled by various individuals. These activities, or areas of responsibility, can be spread across an organization in a variety of ways, and a manager should carefully consider the appropriate degree of decentralization for each of them. Assignment of responsibilities by default seldom works.

To facilitate a systematic approach to organizing data processing, one should identify the areas of responsibility that may be operationally assigned in an organization. *Exhibit I* shows suggested areas of activity, grouped rather loosely into the major categories of control and execution, with execution further divided into development and operations. The content of each area may be intuitively clear. Given this division of responsibilities, the major challenges of DDP planning lie, then, in determining the extent to which each should be decentralized, in understanding the interdependencies among them, and in assuring that the appropriate degree of authority and necessary level of competence coexist at the designated locations in the organization.

The areas of execution are the easily identifiable kinds of activities that are commonly associated with data processing. In most companies, technically trained persons, such as programmers, systems analysts, and computer operators, have responsibility for delivering the data processing product or service. The areas of control activity regulate the delivery of data processing in terms of dollars, people, time, quality assurance, and access to data, but they do not require a detailed level of technical knowledge of computers.

To describe the data processing in an organization as "distributed" is to say that authority over one or more of the areas of responsibility shown in *Exhibit I* has been vertically or horizontally decentralized; that is, authority may be delegated downward or assigned laterally. This definition is more inclusive than the definition commonly used. It can imply the spreading out not only of hardware and data but of the whole array of activities associated with managing information processing.

Before describing decentralization of activities within these areas in greater detail, we first consider the forces that shape the design of distributed information systems.

ROOTS OF DECENTRALIZATION

What causes an organization to decentralize? We have identified three general motivations that might lead a company to decentralize or distri-

EXHIBIT I

Areas of
Managed Activity

Execution (Development)	Control
Data base administration	Providing security
Applications programming	Setting priorities
Systems analysis	Standardizing tasks
System documentation	Accessing data
User training	Scheduling tasks
	Personnel planning
Execution (Operations)	Budgeting
Hardware operation	Evaluating products
Telecommunications	
Systems programming	
Application system	
maintenance	

bute its data processing. These are the pressures for differentiation and the resulting needs for selective integration, the desire for direct control, and the wish to reallocate or lend support to authority. Heterogeneity or variability in task, function, or local situation leads to a state of differentiation, which, according to Paul R. Lawrence and Jay W. Lorsch,[2] means that organizational units will differ in goals, time perspectives, interpersonal relationships, and structure. Such differentiation creates the need for various integrative devices. Information systems are common integrative tools which are often used to coordinate operations that span functions, products, divisions, and geographic locations.

Also, uncertainty about such aspects of centralized control as setting of priorities might motivate user group managers to seek control over all system services they see as critical to their operations. When volume permits suitable economies of scale, managers who feel sufficiently competent will have strong motivation to control and even to run their own data processing groups.

Finally, because power to make decisions tends to rest at the level where the necessary information is accumulated[3] and because information support is one of the necessary conditions for effective power,[4] managers can use distributed information systems strategically to bolster the authority of system users in the organization.

Strategy, Structure and Information Systems

Since Alfred D. Chandler's landmark book, *Strategy and Structure*, de-

---

[2]Paul R. Lawrence and Jay W. Lorsch, *Organization and Environment*, Chapter 2 (Homewood, IL: Richard D. Irwin, 1967).
[3]Ibid., Chapter 3.
[4]Rosabeth Moss Kanter, "*Power Failure in Management Circuits*," HBR July-August 1979, p. 65.

EXHIBIT II

Tendency Toward Distributing Data Processing in Relation to
Product Diversification and Corporate Structure

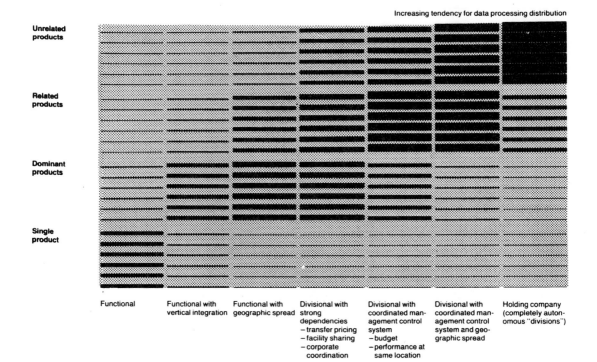

scribing the history of America's first great corporations,[5] writers have
noted how organizations alter their formal structure to facilitate achievement of goals. But the relationship between structure and business plan
has many dimensions. The key to a good design for an organization is not
only the match between strategy and structure but the more complex
match involving strategy, structure, and other administrative systems.
Today many of these administrative systems are embodied in computerized information systems, which assist management in controlling and
coordinating most of the activities of modern, large-scale organizations—
tying together the efforts of diverse departments that pursue different but
complementary ends.

Yet computer applications in general have been so specialized that
many organizations—the data processing profession along with them—
have overlooked potential, and more general, roles for information systems. Information systems are not simply labor-saving devices that
support the activities of people in one or more departments. Rather, they

---

[5]Alfred D. Chandler, Jr., *Strategy and Structure* (Cambridge, MA: MIT Press, 1962).

EXHIBIT III

Responsibility Spectra

Increasing user responsibility ▶

Hardware operation

Prepare source documents	Manage data entry	Operate satellite processor without data base	Operate satellite processor with data base	Manage independent facility

Telecommunications

Specify communications needs	Design network configuration	Specify interface protocols	Implement network	Maintain network

Systems progamming

Use operating system, compilers, and utilities	Interface applications programs to systems software	Maintain updates to systems software	Develop and modify systems software

Applications systems maintenance

Document system errors	Diagnose system errors	Correct system errors

Data base administration

Control source documents	Determine data requirements & conventions	Carry out logical data base design	Carry out physical data base design	Set & enforce conventions for data access	Manage all data bases

Applications programming

Turnkey system	Communicate needs to programmers	Participate on programming team	Supervise development	Select & develop system-building tools

Systems analysis

Conduct preautomation analysis & procedure revisions	Define user data & functional specifications	Evaluate system relative to functional specifications	Participate in high-level system design	Carry out program-level system design

System documentation

Write functional specifications	Write user's manual	Write program design specifications	Write detailed description of all data structures & routine

User training

Conduct preautomation interviews	Prepare user training materials	Conduct user training	Maintain adequate user competence

Providing security

Comply with security procedures	Devise security measures	Authorize security procedures	Manage security facilities

Setting priorities

Accept imposed priorities	Identify needs for system services	Rank alternatives	Authorize commitment of resources

Standardize tasks

Carry out standards	Propose standards	Devise standards	Authorize standards	Enforce standards

Accessing data

Identify available data	Specify data needs	Authorize data collection & distribution privileges	Enforce data collection & distribution privileges

Scheduling tasks

Specify tasks	Determine feasibility of tasks	Sequence tasks	Allocate time to tasks	Approve schedule

Personnel planning

Determine system's impact on user staffing	Designate liaison staff for development & operation	Administer personnel assignments	Evaluate personnel performance

Budgeting

Specify needs in nonfinancial terms	Set upper bounds on system expenditures	Prepare detailed budget	Monitor complete budget

Evaluating products

Collect performance data	Define performance requirements	Monitor performance	Determine appropriate response

are control and coordination devices that should fit an organization's formal structure and facilitate achievement of its business goals.

Most information systems are designed to play such roles, and it is worthwhile to reexamine them in that light. Consider the following typical situation:

- Production managers must maintain control over inventory levels to ensure that operations are not interrupted by sudden depletion of parts. They often establish this control by use of a computerized inventory control system, which, when coupled with formal procedures for requisitioning parts from storage, signals when inventory levels are low and in some cases even orders new parts automatically.

- Managers must coordinate the activities of sales with production, so that when a large influx of orders comes in from the field, production levels will rise to meet the demand. Managers often achieve such coordination by using an automated order entry system that processes sales orders in the field and then, to fill these orders, simultaneously updates the production schedule.

In the first case a computerized information system is used to *control* an important facet of operations, whereas in the second a system is used to *coordinate* different activities. In both cases the information systems fit the structural and strategic features of the organization.

In general, information systems can *support* the organizational structure by providing the information necessary to carry out the assigned responsibility. They can also *make* the structure more elaborate by providing project-based information in a functional organization or function-based information across divisions. Ideally, systems offer managers access to information that can help them fulfill their roles in the formal organizational structure.

What happens if the systems do not fit exactly? What occurs when the design of an information system no longer matches strategy and structure? Of even greater concern, how elastic is the fit of current systems to ever-changing organizations?

The elasticity of an information system may be explored by studying its ability to meet the reporting requirements placed on it. The typical evolution of a system might be:

1. at the outset, the new information system meets the needs of users

2. changes occur in information requirements, and informal channels develop as a result

3. difficulties arise when analysts attempt to modify the system to match current needs—and the system thus becomes distorted, subverted, and inappropriately used, a situation marked by "information overkill"

4. eventually the system is replaced, with varying degrees of disruption

Let us see how this evolution occurs in an example from an actual company that manufactures a variety of products in several plants. The central data processing department developed an information system for plant managers, and most users were happy with the reports they received. Later, top managers formulated a more comprehensive marketing strategy, creating new product lines that grouped products from different plants. Then they appointed new corporate-level product-line managers to monitor both the manufacture and the marketing of each product line.

The information needs of this new group of managers overlapped those of the plant managers to some extent, so they made minor changes in the plant managers' reports, using informal communication channels to meet their remaining needs. As time went on, unrelated additional products were added, so that the old information system became unsatisfactory even for the plant managers. Yet, ironically, nearly all managers clung to the system because they knew it so well and felt they had to have the same data they had always received. These people never stopped to realize that the system had become an encumbrance to rather than an enabler of the business strategy.

Information systems that do not fit the organization they were designed to serve are not uncommon. But with DDP, companies can organize their data processing support groups to better use the competence that exists and to better serve the formal structure. Systems so designed and operated will be less likely to suffer problems such as those just recounted.

Given the ideal that information systems should match an organization's strategy and structure, we can expect that companies with diversified interests and with greater autonomy among their operating units will find DDP particularly useful. DDP will offer them new opportunities for formal control and coordination.

The general influence of corporate structures[6] and product diversification[7] on decentralization of information systems is shown in *Exhibit II*. The exhibit suggests that the motivation to distribute computer resources will be felt more keenly in highly diversified conglomerates but will be less important to single-product companies that are organized according to function. Though other factors, of course, will be important in deciding how and when DDP is appropriate, *Exhibit II* reminds us that efficient information systems are inexorably linked to the strategy and structure of a company.

FRAMEWORK FOR ANALYSIS

To match information systems with the organization they serve, careful

---

[6]Richard P. Rumelt, *Strategy, Structure, and Economic Performance* (Boston: Division of Research, Harvard Business School, 1974), p. 33.

[7]Leonard Wrigley, *"Divisional Autonomy and Diversification,"* (Ph.D. diss., Harvard Business School, 1970).

attention must go into planning the arrangement of the data processing resources that develop and operate information systems. All of the different activities appearing in *Exhibit I* are assigned to different groups in the organization, and it is useful to analyze systematically who has what responsibilities. We shall develop here a multidimensional framework that we can use to evaluate the way a company locates its data processing resources.

The purpose of such a framework, in general, is to divide the overall problem into interrelated subproblems so that each can be solved separately while it contributes to an overall solution. A framework may also be used to provide a system of measures by which to compare organizations or assess the impact of organizational change. The spectra in *Exhibit III* achieve both these ends.

For both of the areas listed in *Exhibit I*, we develop a spectrum of feasible positions, shown in *Exhibit III*, representing the variety of alternative arrangements of activity ranging from complete centralization in a data processing unit to complete decentralization to user groups. Each spectrum shows an increasing and cumulative level of responsibility for the user group manager as the line is traversed from left to right. The ordering of the specific functions is normative, in that if a user participates in some way in a given function as described by a single point along a continuum, he or she will probably participate in all functions shown to the left along that continuum (though some mechanism may be employed to coordinate a shared responsibility). The functions to the right of a given user's position may be carried out by the company's data processing groups or be shared as well.

For example, if the user has technical people who perform data base administration activities up to and including the physical design of the data base, then, according to the fifth spectrum in *Exhibit III*, he or she is most likely responsible for logical data base design, the determination of data requirements and conventions, and the control of source documents. Similarly, the DP manager at some data center performs the remaining tasks, setting and enforcing conventions for data access based in part on the design and, in general, managing all data bases.

The spectra for controlling activities shown in *Exhibit III* are designed to be applicable to either operational or developmental activities under different interpretations. The dual interpretation of the control spectra is a useful feature of the framework. Using the same set of lines, we can analyze control of system development work and control of operations. In most situations, however, control of these two groups of activities is handled in such different manners that it makes sense to discuss them separately.

For example, "accessing data" as a developmental activity represents managements' desires and restrictions on the kinds of data that will be collected within a system. As an operational activity, it is a statement of policy defining authorized access to information within the organization.

The area of "providing security" addresses the engineering (during development) and enforcing (during operation) of mechanisms that prevent unauthorized access. Finally "tasks standardizing" is a control area whose purpose is to coordinate, without direct supervision, a control role that is relevant to all stages of the system's life cycle. It is usually a staff activity designed to magnify the efforts of the line managers and may apply to tasks ranging from defining the phases of system developments, including authorization protocols, to developing programming conventions.

One should recognize that management can control and coordinate activities not only by direct supervision but also by establishing comprehensive guidelines or standard operating procedures. The technical concerns of data base administrators, for example, are commonly controlled in this fashion. Their responsibilities can be either centralized in an individual or a group, decentralized but constrained by centrally designed standards,[8] or decentralized with virtual independence. In the future, the second approach, that is, decentralizing the data base administration activity while using centrally established standards, will probably become increasingly important. In this way, the DP manager can define comprehensive standards that can be enforced by top managers or a highly placed steering committee and that can be used in a decentralized organization to protect the data processing department from excessive control by the user.

Given this introduction to the spectra of data processing responsibilities, consider how the spectra can be applied to a typical application. *Exhibit IV* describes the inventory control system of a medium-sized manufacturing company that currently plays a critical role in production operations. The system is run at the corporate computer center located at headquarters, and the records are kept up to date via terminals located in the plants.

A team of programmers and analysts who came from both the user departments and the centralized systems development group originally developed the system. *Exhibit IV* shows how responsibilities for this system have been and are now distributed across the organization. Note that the control spectra appear twice, once for operations and once for development, because the nature and arrangement of control activities changed significantly when the inventory control system became operational.

In general, user group managers will select the level of responsibility they want for their information processing activities as they traverse the spectra from left to right. This decision is analogous to a company's decision about how far back from the market it wants to be vertically integrated. DP managers, in turn, will determine how much of each user's operation they want to be responsible for. The general manager must then arbitrate between the DP manager and the end user. The general manager

---

[8]Jack R. Buchanan, Rob Gerritsen, and David Root, *"Automated Data Base Programming,"* to appear in Communications of the Associations for Computing Machinery.

EXHIBIT IV

Assigned Responsibilities for a Typical Application:
A Manufacturing Company's Inventory Control System

Execution (Operations)

Hardware operation
The user prepares source documents and manages data entry through terminals to DP center.

Telecommunications
The user specifies his volume and scheduling requirements for communications through his configuration of terminals.

Systems programming
The user only uses the DP center's operating system, compilers, and utilities.

Application system maintenance
The user both documents and assists in diagnosing system errors.

Control (Operations)

Providing security
The user simply complies with security procedures.

Setting priorities
The user identifies his needs for system services.

Standardizing tasks
The user proposes operating procedures and performance standards.

Accessing data
The user authorizes data collection and report distribution.

Scheduling tasks
The user participates in sequencing the tasks.

Personnel planning
The user manages only his own data entry personnel.

Budgeting
The user controls his expenditures by limiting DP use.

Evaluating products
The user defines his performance requirements.

Execution (Development)

Data base administration
The user determines his data requirements and develops a logical data base design.

Applications programming
The user assigns some internal personnel to participate in the programming team.

Systems analysis
The user is quite involved in most analysis work, including some program-level system design.

System documentation
The user develops his own manuals and shares in writing program design specifications.

User training
The user alone is responsible for all internal training activities.

☐ Distributed

■ Centralized

Control (Development)

Providing security
The user devises and authorizes security procedures.

Setting priorities
The user ranks alternative designs for his system.

Standardizing tasks
The user proposes standards and participates in an authorizing steering committee.

Accessing data
The user authorizes data collection and access privileges.

Scheduling tasks
The user participates in approving the schedule.

Personnel planning
The user jointly administers and evaluates all personnel.

Budgeting
The user jointly prepares and monitors the total budget.

Evaluating products
The user decides whether to use the system.

must understand the issues well enough to allocate responsibility so as to best achieve the organization's objectives.

How Much Decentralization?

The framework just described equips us to look inside our own organizations to see to what extent each area of data processing activity is decentralized. By examining the complete set of activities, we see that decentralization of some tasks—be they technical or managerial—is a common occurrence and that even classic types of information systems, such as inventory control applications run on centralized computers, are supported in part by a variety of decentralized, or user, activities. Thus we can say that even these classic information system applications represent a distribution of information processing responsibility.

As we have seen, DDP has implications that go beyond conventional approaches of applying computers to business. Although on the surface it appears to concern itself solely with the arrangement of computer hardware and data around an organization, at a deeper level it involves the management of a wide array of activities that go into the development and operation of computerized information systems.

Managers can organize these activities in many ways, and the choice they make should reflect the strategic and structural decisions they have made before. Thus, even if their information system design leaves hardware at some central site while assigning a few data processing tasks to users, their system is in some sense distributed.

According to this more general definition, nearly all computer applications are distributed. And, indeed, to ensure that information systems fit an organization, data processing should be distributed. Managers should concern themselves now with the question of how they can best distribute data processing for the information systems they require.

The next article in this series will provide tools for managers to help them in this undertaking. For now, however, let us summarize the implications this article has for the role of DDP in organizations:

- Data processing involves distinct types of technical activities and managerial or control activities. Managers can assign responsibility for these activities to different groups in the organization; usually they divide the responsibilities between a data processing manager and a user manager.

- Managers' assignment of data processing responsibilities should create a DP-support organization that can efficiently develop and operate information systems well suited to the organization. Assignment of data processing responsibilities thus may involve considerations more critical than those relating to cost alone.

- Organizations will face competing forces that push for and against decentralization. User groups may argue for more independence to design and operate their systems, to escape what they see as the uncertainties posed by completely centralized operations, or to bolster their own power in the organization. Central data processing groups may counter with arguments for an arrangement that offers economies of scale, ensures a higher level of technical competence, and permits corporate managers closer scrutiny of data processing activities. Both arguments sound compelling.

● Although it is sometimes advantageous to assign control responsibility along with execution responsibility, separation of control activities from execution activities can in fact resolve the dilemma between competing forces. Controls may be distributed throughout an organization to provide checks and balances on activities performed by other groups, to share responsibility between cooperating units, or to assure that the behavior of various units is consistent with organizational objectives and guidelines.

The pitfalls described earlier came about because decision makers were unaware of these crucial considerations. They had only a limited understanding of data processing and so were unprepared to grapple with the problems inherent in the expanded role of computers in their organizations. Managers should seek to understand distributed data processing because, now that it has come of age, they have much to gain by using it to improve the inner workings of their organizations.

Making
Distributed
Data Processing
Work*

JACK R. BUCHANAN
RICHARD G. LINOWES

Recently, a marketing manager defended a key point in his three-year plan thus:

> It's crucial that we put minicomputers in each of the regional sales offices. We're planning to install a sophisticated customer-support information system for tracking orders and storing service records, and we'll need half a dozen minicomputers to make this system work. If we have to depend on the big old machine at the corporate data center, we won't be able to provide our customers the kind of service we claim to offer."

The executive committee listened attentively. Several people looked skeptical, but the controller seemed particularly troubled. He pointed to an unusually large number on the planning document in front of him and retorted:

> "Look at this figure! I'm not convinced we need to spend that much. I think you can get the responsiveness and sense of independence you need at the branch offices without giving each region its own machine."

Then he continued,

> "We can't go around giving minicomputers to any group in the company who wants them. We've authorized too many such plans already, and frankly, I think

*Reprinted by permission of Harvard Business Review. *Making Distributed Data Processing Work* by Jack R. Buchanan and Richard G. Linowes (September-October 1980). Copyright © 1980 by the President and Fellows of Harvard College; all rights reserved.

the whole situation is getting out of control. Right now we're only talking about buying machines, but we don't know what these guys will do with them once they get them. There could be some serious consequences. We need some general policies for handling this kind of proposal."

Variations of this discussion are occurring frequently these days. In many companies, there is a growing call for the large-scale acquisition of minicomputers to serve the needs of a broad cross section of functional areas. This newly surfaced "computer urgeny" puts corporate planners in an awkward position. Many groups are demanding scarce resources for very different hardware and software projects that all look attractive on paper but whose benefits are hard to measure. How can managers plan for the acquisition and use of minicomputers in their companies? What policies should guide them as they enter the era of distributed computing?

This article, our second in a two-part series (see "Understanding Distributed Data Processing" in HBR's July-August 1980 issue), will explore the need to plan for DDP and present a set of planning tools for managers. All levels of management should be involved in planning for distributed computing needs because the decisions have too broad an impact to be left in the hands of functional users or technicians alone.

How can managers get more involved in the planning for the next generation of information systems? The answer is simple: they must understand what DDP is and they must be able to evaluate the implications of various ways of organizing it. Our previous article tackled the first task; it defined the term **distributed data processing**.

In this second article, we introduce some powerful new techniques for evaluating all possible arrangements for data processing resources. These methods will enable nontechnical general managers to contribute to the important data processing (DP) planning meetings of the future.

THE NEED FOR PLANNING

DDP is the systematic decentralization of data processing activities—including a wide range of technical tasks and management responsibilities. It offers an organization the opportunity to develop and operate computerized information systems that both match the organizational structure and promote organizational goals. This definition draws on the fact that data processing, in general, is more than just computer hardware and the work of a handful of programmers; it is a composite of a whole host of activities.

Information systems can support an organizational structure by strengthening communication lines and clarifying measures of performance. To achieve this, managers may choose to decentralize systematically the component activities of data processing within their organizations while paying close attention to overall business plans.

But once managers agree on the advantages of DDP, where do they go from there? How do they plan for distributed computing to ensure that strategy, structure, and information systems all match? Too often either management's planning sessions consist of intense technical advising, not to mention lobbying, or there is no planning at all. In some cases, management involvement and approval are carefully skirted. When managers *are* involved, often their thoughts are overly influenced by considerations. They tend to approve some plans solely on the basis of the potential for reducing operating expenses, and they tend to accept others because they are easy to use and do not require a staff of computer professionals.

Whereas promises of cost reduction or work simplification may be paramount in a go-ahead decision for a new information system, other factors are also critical, such as the availability of technical talent, the degree of coordination between users and programmers on project teams, and the careful construction and enforcement of standards. Unless managers have analytic techniques for assessing these other factors of a DP strategy, they will be severely hampered in their planning; success will depend on luck or on prodigious efforts to rescue a badly planned venture.

In the following sections, we shall introduce some new analytic methods that can simplify the planning process. They use a set of charts and tables that enable managers to describe and plan, with minimal technical terminology, the company's approach to arranging and managing its DP resources. Briefly, these analytic methods embody the following:

1. The DP activity spectra. A set of lines, one for each area of activity of the data processing function, showing the various degrees of involvement that a data processing user may have in managing an information system.

2. The DP participation table. A tabular presentation of the responsibilities assigned to key persons who participate in managing an information system, highlighting the roles they play at each decision point in the system's life cycle.

3. The DP decentralization pattern. A one-dimensional pictorial representation focusing on technical resources and showing the relative degree of decentralization of all technical data processing activities that support an information system.

4. The DP distribution chart. A two-dimensional pictorial representation focusing on both technical and managerial resources. It displays on a summary level the strategic placement of responsibilities for technical and management activities that support an information system.

We shall illustrate these four tools with several examples and then discuss how they are useful in a DDP planning situation. First, we shall describe some dynamics that influence systems planning at a fundamental level.

DYNAMICS OF SYSTEMS MANAGEMENT

In developing systems to support administrative activities, companies tend to go through a process that reflects, among other things, management's growing sophistication in the use and control of computer technology and the organization's ability to use new management methods, a process often referred to as "organizational learning."[1] The finding that the data processing budget of a number of companies follows an S-shaped curve over time prompted the hypothesis that there are four major stages of data processing growth, each with its own characteristics, problems, and opportunities.[2]

The introduction of administrative innovations often produces these growth curves, and of course where we find them depends on what we measure and control and what kind of changes are possible. However, the use of DDP as one form of administrative innovation has the potential of producing complex innovative disturbances, or dynamics, within the organization. These dynamics are difficult to sort out.

To account for extra "ripples" in otherwise mature organizations and to explain the impact of data base systems, Richard L. Nolan proposed a six-stage hypothesis.[3] The "stage hypotheses" will continue to be useful for characterizing a particular application area for a particular user, but in the extensively distributed organizations of the future, on organization as a whole is not likely to show a coherent stage behavior.

Managers will need to understand the causes as well as the results of the forces they experience. Results such as growth in the application portfolio, expansion in size of the data processing organization, and increased use of planning and control methods are important issues for management's attention. However, for planning purposes, there are more basic dynamics that underlie these organizational responses. Some of the more important dynamics may be summarized as follows:

1. Changes in business strategy or organizational structure will create disruptions for DP management. Some may be due to reorganizations of data processing resources as part of a general corporate reorganization. This occurred recently at Citibank, where operations were decentralized to place greater control in the hands of the banking groups.[4] Other changes may come with a reshuffling and redefinition of product lines. Recently at Dun & Bradstreet, computer technology—above and beyond its contribution to management as an administrative tool—became the esence of a brand-new product and the delivery vehicle for an existing product using on-line data base systems.[5] Structure and strategy changes of this sort usually generate a flurry of demands for new information.

2. An organization as a whole displays some stage-line behavior as it

---

[1]James L. McKenney, "*A Field Research Study on Organizational Learning,*" Harvard Business School Working Paper 78-23.

[2]Cyrus F. Gibson and Richard L. Nolan, "*Managing the Four Stages of EDP Growth,*" HBR January-February 1974, p. 76.

[3]Richard L. Nolan, "*Managing the Crises in Data Processing,*" HBR March-April 1979, p. 115.

[4]Richard J. Matteis, "*The New Back Office Focuses on Customer Service,*" HBR March-April 1979, p. 146.

[5]"*Computer Revolution at Dun & Bradstreet,*" Business Week, August 27, 1979, p. 72.

evolves over time.[6] The stages of data processing growth evolve within a larger organizational context. For example, consider a company moving from a functional structure to one organized by product line. Managers working within such transition plans may choose DP departments that are organized by data processing functional structure to one organized by product line. Managers working within such transition plans may choose DP departments that are organized by data processing function—e.g., programming, telecommunications—or operations dedicated to particular users' needs. Some blend these two approaches, using a matrix organizational structure.

3. Changing external and internal technology creates challenges and opportunities to use the appropriate technology. It is often difficult to sort out the differences between the stages of data processing growth in a particular company and the stages of data processing technology in general. First, technical competence must be available to handle the innovation in-house. Second, organizational learning must have progressed to the stage where assimilation of new applications is feasible.

4. Managing multiple projects at various life cycle phases becomes increasingly difficult as the number and sophistication of projects grow and as the need arises to integrate systems with business functions.

Managers can view the growth stages of data processing as a composite of these dynamics. If executives learn to monitor these forces over time and to recognize their implications for DDP planning, crises will be less devastating or may not even arise.

TOOLS FOR ANALYSIS AND PLANNING

Effective information systems depend on the careful assignment of responsibility for areas of data processing activity. The following tools will assist managers in their planning.

Tool no. 1: Activity Spectra

We introduced the first tool—depicting multiple scales of responsibility for data processing activities—in our previous article, and we shall use it here as a measuring stick to assess the way a company organizes its data processing resources. (For the reader's convenience, we reproduce that exhibit here as *Exhibit I.*)

The data processing function involves many kinds of activities. Some are technical and some managerial, and the analytic separation of execution activities from control activities reflects this distinction (see

---

[6]Larry E. Greiner, *"Evolution and Revolution as Organizations Grow,"* HBR July-August 1972, p. 37.

EXHIBIT I

Responsibility
Spectra

Increasing user responsibility ▶

Hardware operation

| Prepare source documents | Manage data entry | Operate satellite processor without data base | Operate satellite processor with data base | Manage independent facility |

Telecommunications

| Specify communications needs | Design network configuration | Specify interface protocols | Implement network | Maintain network |

Systems progamming

| Use operating system, compilers, and utilities | Interface applications programs to systems software | Maintain updates to systems software | Develop and modify systems software |

Applications systems maintenance

| Document system errors | Diagnose system errors | Correct system errors |

Data base administration

| Control source documents | Determine data requirements & conventions | Carry out logical data base design | Carry out physical data base design | Set & enforce conventions for data access | Manage all data bases |

Applications programming

| Turnkey system | Communicate needs to programmers | Participate on programming team | Supervise development | Select & develop system-building tools |

Systems analysis

| Conduct preautomation analysis & procedure revisions | Define user data & functional specifications | Evaluate system relative to functional specifications | Participate in high-level system design | Carry out program-level system design |

System documentation

| Write functional specifications | Write user's manual | Write program design specifications | Write detailed description of all data structures & routine |

User training

| Conduct preautomation interviews | Prepare user training materials | Conduct user training | Maintain adequate user competence |

Providing security

| Comply with security procedures | Devise security measures | Authorize security procedures | Manage security facilities |

Setting priorities

| Accept imposed priorities | Identify needs for system services | Rank alternatives | Authorize commitment of resources |

Standardize tasks

| Carry out standards | Propose standards | Devise standards | Authorize standards | Enforce standards |

Accessing data

| Identify available data | Specify data needs | Authorize data collection & distribution privileges | Enforce data collection & distribution privileges |

Scheduling tasks

| Specify tasks | Determine feasibility of tasks | Sequence tasks | Allocate time to tasks | Approve schedule |

Personnel planning

| Determine system's impact on user staffing | Designate liaison staff for development & operation | Administer personnel assignments | Evaluate personnel performance |

Budgeting

| Specify needs in nonfinancial terms | Set upper bounds on system expenditures | Prepare detailed budget | Monitor complete budget |

Evaluating products

| Collect performance data | Define performance requirements | Monitor performance | Determine appropriate response |

EXHIBIT II

Areas of
Managed Activity

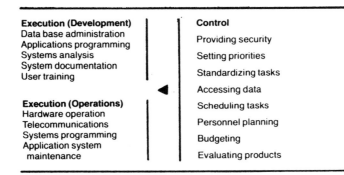

Execution (Development)	**Control**
Data base administration	Providing security
Applications programming	Setting priorities
Systems analysis	Standardizing tasks
System documentation	Accessing data
User training	
	Scheduling tasks
Execution (Operations)	Personnel planning
Hardware operation	Budgeting
Telecommunications	Evaluating products
Systems programming	
Application system	
maintenance	

Exhibit II). For execution activities, we then distinguish the technical tasks associated with systems development from those supporting systems operation. The result is a four-way split of data processing activities into execution of development, control of development, execution of operations, and control of operations.

To visualize where these activities are performed in an organization, we must examine them in further detail. *Exhibit I* will help us here. At the extreme left, a user of an information system is an uninvolved recipient of the services of a completely centralized data center. At the other extreme, the user performs all the tasks himself, and the centralized group—if one exists—is completely uninvolved. At points in between these extremes, activity is divided between the user and the data processing center. In constructing the lines in the exhibit, we followed conventional practices closely, so (usually) if a user performs a task corresponding to one point on a line, he or she probably performs all tasks to the left of that point.

Using all of the lines in the exhibit, we can describe the placement of responsibility for a particular information system. We simply go through the list checking off on each spectrum the right-most point that accurately describes the user's role. For a complete analysis, we must use the eight control activities twice, once for development and once for operations, because control of development is separate and often quite different from control of operations.

Exhibit III shows the results of this analysis for a marketing information system of a medium-sized manufacturer. The system currently has centralized computers at the corporate data center, but it was developed jointly by marketing and corporate DP. During development, marketing had responsibility for many of the control tasks—primarily personnel planning, budgeting, and evaluation. But now, during operations, it controls only the distribution of computer reports.

How are these DP activity spectra useful to management? First, as a descriptive tool; they provide a simple way to describe the placement of DP responsibilities. With minor alterations, they can be used in more

EXHIBIT III

Assigned Responsibility for a Typical Application:
A Manufacturing Company's Marketing Information System

Execution (Operations)

Hardware operation
The user prepares source documents and manages data entry through terminals to DP center.

Telecommunications
The user specifies his volume and scheduling requirements for communications through his configuration of terminals.

Systems programming
The user only uses the DP center's operating system, compilers, and utilities.
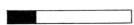

Application system maintenance
The user both documents and assists in diagnosing system errors.

Control (Operations)

Providing security
The user simply complies with security procedures.

Setting priorities
The user identifies his needs for system services.

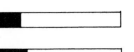

Standardizing tasks
The user proposes operating procedures and performance standards.

Accessing data
The user authorizes data collection and report distribution.

Scheduling tasks
The user participates in sequencing the tasks.

Personnel planning
The user manages only his own data entry personnel.
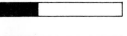

Budgeting
The user controls his expenditures by limiting DP use.

Evaluating products
The user defines his performance requirements.

Execution (Development)

Data base administration
The user determines his data requirements and develops a logical data base design.

Applications programming
The user assigns some internal personnel to participate in the programming team.

Systems analysis
The user is quite involved in most analysis work, including some program-level system design.

System documentation
The user develops his own manuals and shares in writing program design specifications.

User training
The user alone is responsible for all internal training activities.

 Centralized

Distributed

Control (Development)

Providing security
The user devises and authorizes security procedures.

Setting priorities
The user ranks alternative designs for his system.

Standardizing tasks
The user proposes standards and participates in an authorizing steering committee.

Accessing data
The user authorizes data collection and access privileges.

Scheduling tasks
The user participates in approving the schedule.

Personnel planning
The user jointly administers and evaluates all personnel.

Budgeting
The user jointly prepares and monitors the total budget.

Evaluating products
The user decides whether to use the system.

complex situations in which more than two groups provide the services necessary to support an information system. When the functions described are assigned to specific organizational units, they show quite well who does what DP-related activities.

Second, the spectra suggest ways to modify the organization of DP. For a given arrangement of activities, such as that presented in *Exhibit III*, simple shifts in the selected points represent a slightly altered organization and represent transfers of technical tasks or control responsibilities in either a centralized or a decentralized direction.

Suppose now that a manager wants to alter the structure of the DP support organization. He or she should first rank order the spectra of the different activities according to their decreasing degree of rigidity or permanence. Activities that are easily transferable should appear last, while those that are fixed or relatively immobile should appear first.

Next, the manager should step through the newly ordered set of spectra, carefully evaluating the possible shifts that might create the intended effect of redesigning the organization. Clearly, different sets of small shifts may produce similar general effects, so management should explore the consequences of many alternative designs. The spectra organize this exploration process; they structure a manager's search for and evaluation of new options.

Third, the spectra provide the foundation for the other tools we shall describe. By consolidating the spectra in a variety of ways, we shall generate other conceptual devices that involve less technical terminology and hence are more geared toward general management.

Tool no. 2: Participation Table

The second tool is useful in the assignment of specific responsibilities for the DP administrative process. By creating a table that plots both responsibility assignments and the system life cycle, we obtain an outline of how each group participates in the system development process. The resulting DP participation table specifies which tasks and checkpoint responsibilities each group in the organization must bear over each stage.

The table follows nicely from the description of responsibilities provided by the activity spectra. Once a manager has used the spectra to characterize the organizational support for a given information system, he or she can evaluate the roles of key players in the organization over time. The time element appears in the use of the well-established concept of the system life cycle, which captures the important fact that there are distinct phases in the life of an information system: work begins with the planning and design phases, passes through the programming and implementation phases, and enters an operational mode during the production phase.

(Systems also pass *out* of operation, moving through a period that we might call the senescence phase, but those involved in DP are loath to describe this phenomenon as a universal fact of life.)

By examining responsibility assignments over the system life cycle, a manager obtains a table such as the one shown in *Exhibit IV*. This table corresponds to the marketing information system described in the previous section and in *Exhibit III*. We see that at the end of each life cycle phase some milestone document is prepared and passed around to all concerned parties.

EXHIBIT IV

DP Organization
Participation Table

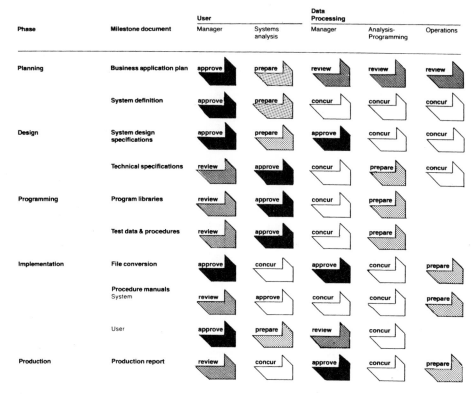

Phase	Milestone document	User		Data Processing		
		Manager	Systems analysis	Manager	Analysis-Programming	Operations
Planning	Business application plan	approve	prepare	review	review	review
	System definition	approve	prepare	concur	concur	concur
Design	System design specifications	approve	prepare	approve	concur	concur
	Technical specifications	review	approve	concur	prepare	concur
Programming	Program libraries	review	approve	concur	prepare	
	Test data & procedures	review	approve	concur	prepare	
Implementation	File conversion	approve	concur	approve	concur	prepare
	Procedure manuals — System	review	approve	concur	concur	prepare
	User	approve	prepare	review	concur	
Production	Production report	review	concur	approve	concur	prepare

The participation table tells us what role each party plays in the overall evaluation of each document. The term approve applies to those who assume responsibility for the communication of resources based on the plans and estimates of those who prepare. Review is provided for information and comments only. Concur requires agreement with the proposed course of action, although the individual assumes no responsibility for the actual commitment of resources.

The organization participation table has value for managers primarily because it clarifies roles to be played over time. Since each company or even each application within a company may have its own distinctive version, the table serves as useful documentation of the administrative processes that have been established to launch and operate a new information system. It also functions as a simple reference sheet to remind all those involved in DP activities about the administrative procedures and protocols that affect their work.

Tool no. 3: Decentralization Pattern

This tool defines a pattern for the organizational arrangement of technical DP activities. It is based on the fact that not all execution activities are decentralized to the same extent. For any given information system, we can enumerate supporting technical activities in a sequence that reflects the degree of their decentralization. As we shall see, such a pattern can function as a shorthand notation in discussions about the organizational features of specific DP plans. For some companies, it may even form the basis of a general design for DP organization.

Exhibit V repeats the spectra for the execution activities associated with the marketing information system example of Exhibit III. Clearly,

EXHIBIT V

Development of the
DP Decentralization Pattern

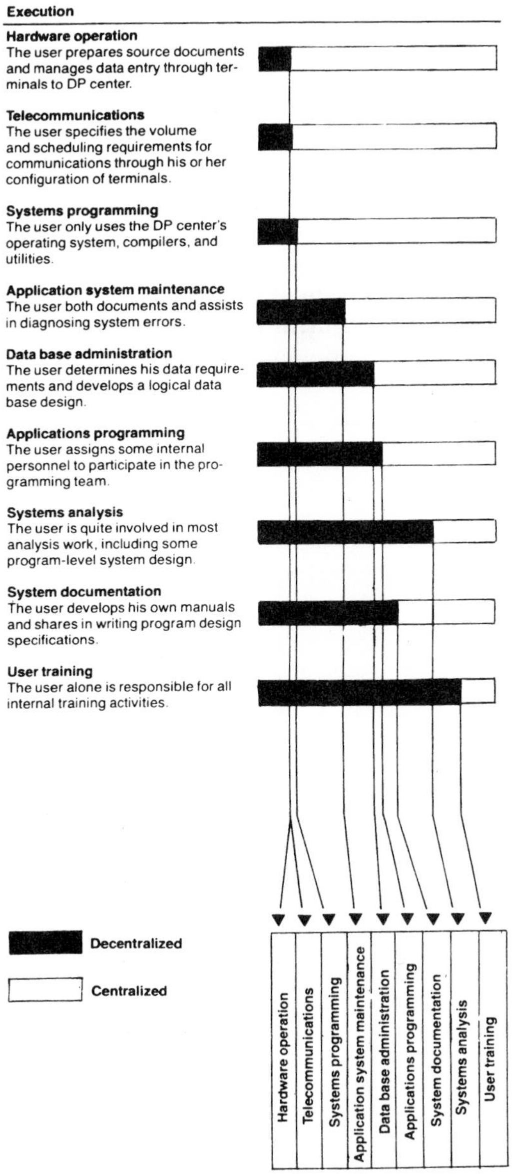

Execution

Hardware operation
The user prepares source documents and manages data entry through terminals to DP center.

Telecommunications
The user specifies the volume and scheduling requirements for communications through his or her configuration of terminals.

Systems programming
The user only uses the DP center's operating system, compilers, and utilities.

Application system maintenance
The user both documents and assists in diagnosing system errors.

Data base administration
The user determines his data requirements and develops a logical data base design.

Applications programming
The user assigns some internal personnel to participate in the programming team.

Systems analysis
The user is quite involved in most analysis work, including some program-level system design.

System documentation
The user develops his own manuals and shares in writing program design specifications.

User training
The user alone is responsible for all internal training activities.

Decentralized

Centralized

Hardware operation
Telecommunications
Systems programming
Application system maintenance
Data base administration
Applications programming
System documentation
Systems analysis
User training

the points on the different lines do not line up perfectly. Some points appear more toward the centralized end of the spectrum ("hardware operations" and "telecommunications"), and others appear more toward the decentralized end ("systems analysis" and " user training").

When these points are projected down to a summary line, the sequence of points reveals neatly the pattern of DP activities arranged according to degree of decentralization. This pattern, henceforth called the **DP decentralization pattern**, characterizes the detailed spread of activities for a single application system. *Exhibit VI* shows a common decentralization pattern found in many companies. "Hardware operations" tend to be most centralized, "user training" and "staff activities" tend to be most decentralized, and "systems analysis" and "data base administration" are usually shared in some manner corresponding to the level of user involvement.

The DP decentralization pattern can aid managers in formulating and clarifying their policies for organizing DP resources. By means of a pattern, or "strip," managers can state succinctly for their organizations the general arrangement of responsibilities that characterizes relationships between DP groups and user groups.

Exhibit VI shows one such pattern for a single application system for a single user group. It is highly likely that the decentralization patterns of other information systems of this user look quite similar. In effect, then, this single decentralization pattern represents a standard decentralization policy for all application systems of this user.

EXHIBIT VI

A Typical DP
Decentralization Pattern

User manager

Staff activities	Systems analysis	Data base admin- istration
User training		
System documentation		
Application programming		
Program maintenance		
Systems programming		
Telecommuni- cations		
Hardware operation		

Data processing management

There are a number of reasons to expect such a standard arrangement. First, resources collected in one place can serve as a pool for a variety of applications. Expertise required on one project can be extended readily to other projects.

Second, any regularities that appear in the relationship between a user and a central group often become a cultural norm, and any new projects are then expected to conform.

Third, the relationship may be so structured and formalized that it is explicitly reflected in the organizational structure. For example, a user who has established a programming group for one project will probably tend to assign this group to other projects. If separate groups perform each activity, these groups may be staffed so that the degree of user participation remains relatively fixed.

Now, assuming some typical pattern for the relationship between a user and a DP center, consider the situation of multiple users sharing a common DP center. In many cases, we can expect the pattern for one user to resemble the pattern for most other users. The differences among the patterns involve not the ordering of activities but the specific point at which responsibilities change hands.

What does this mean? *Exhibit VII* illustrates this situation for a company with separate engineering, marketing, and manufacturing groups. The decentralization patterns are the same for all three, but they are positioned differently. Engineering handles the largest portion of its own technical DP tasks; manufacturing, the next largest portion; and marketing, the least. These organizational variances are most likely due

EXHIBIT VII

DP Decentralization to
Multiple Function Areas—A Typical Distribution

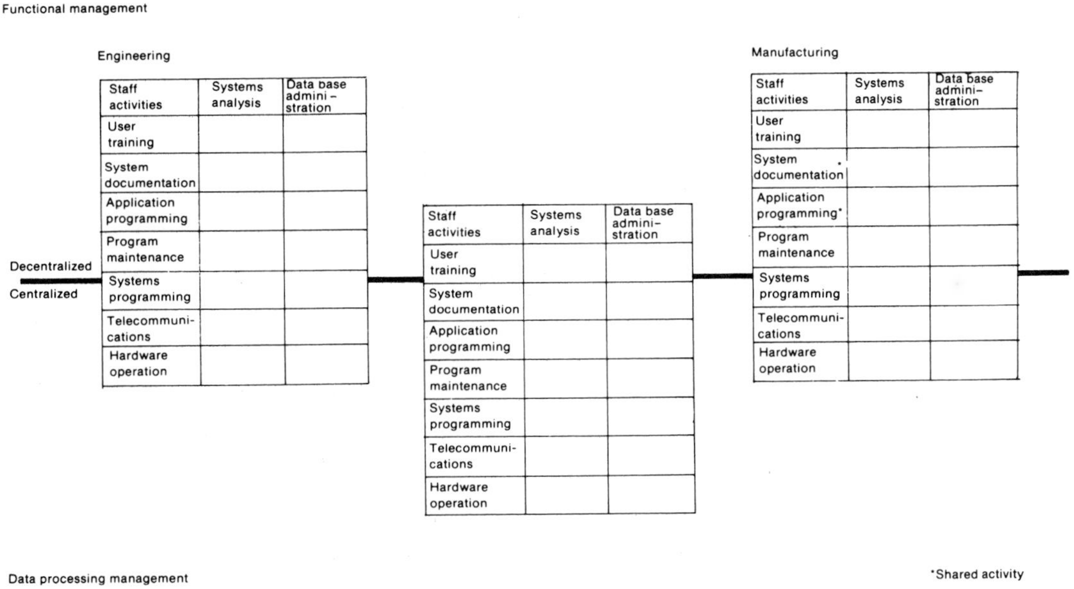

Functional management

Data processing management

*Shared activity

to the differences in the technical competence and data processing experience of the users and to the different requirements of the information systems.

Exhibit VII shows that a company may use a decentralization pattern as a general policy while actual participation in technical work differs considerably from user to user. In general, it is possible to establish uniform policies for decentralization of data processing activities while maintaining the flexibility to vary users' responsibilities.

The example in Exhibit VII shows how the decentralization pattern is useful for expressing policies for DP organization. A company may use it as an expression of its approach to decentralizing DP activities. In the event that a uniform pattern does not hold across all applications of a particular user or across all users, managers should assure themselves that such variations are justified. In this way, the tool can help managers adopt organizational policies that are formulated consciously rather than by default.

Tool No. 4: Distribution Chart

The spectra of activities shown in Exhibit I can be combined in a simple manner to give a concise summary of a company's data processing activities. The separate scales, when consolidated as suggested in Exhibit VIII, generate a two-dimensional picture portraying how a company distributes its data processing resources among organizational subunits.

How are the multiple scales condensed into a simple graph? The multiple "execution" measures of operations and development activities are consolidated into two single summary measures, one for operations and one for development. These new scales may be thought of as projections of the original measures, and they have an appealing graphic simplicity: the selected point or points on each of the original lines in effect "map down" onto corresponding points on the summary lines, defining intervals on the summary lines.

The resulting spread of points in the intervals represents the spread of operations and development activities for a given system within an organization. The summary lines portray what will be called the "execution distribution." These projections and the resulting summary lines appear at the top and the bottom of the exhibit.

The two summary measures obtained so far, however, provide only half the picture. A more complete description of a company's handling of its DP resources must show not only where resources are located but how they are controlled. Consequently, the eight control spectra must appear in the picture. To include them, we must separate control of operations from control of development because the methods, procedures, and philosophy of control for these two areas of activity can differ significantly in any given company. The eight control measures are thus used twice when a company's handling of the DP resource is evaluated—once for operations and once for development.

For each area of activity, now, the multiple control measures are projected on summary lines on the sides of Exhibit VIII as we did at the

EXHIBIT VIII

Development of the
DP Distribution Chart

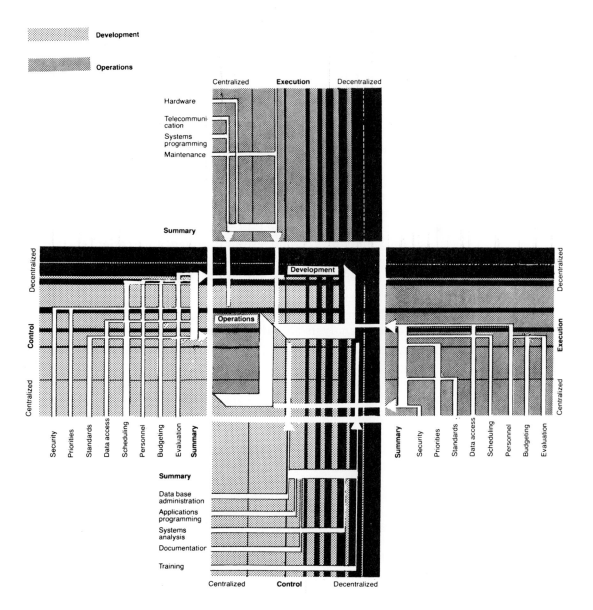

top and bottom. *Exhibit VIII* also diagrams this process for a sample
company. The resulting pattern of points describes the spread of control
responsibility for the DP resource. These summary lines therefore portray
what will be called the "control distribution." They appear on the left and
right sides of the exhibit.

The execution distribution and the control distribution for both operations and development can be visualized simultaneously by using the two-dimensional graph shown at the center of *Exhibit VIII*. Treating operations and development separately, we plot the execution and control distributions against each other, creating regions of distribution for each of the two major areas of activity. The resulting diagram succinctly displays essential features of the decentralization of the information processing resource in an organization. We shall refer to this diagram as the DP distribution chart because the location and shape of its regions reveal in summary form the special features of a company's approach to distributing its DP resource.

Exhibit VIII illustrates how one can consolidate into a simple visual display the multiple dimensions that underlie the data processing resource (according to conventional practice). Managers can use this worksheet to ascertain (and describe) the company's approach to managing its data processing resources.

Here's how:

● Assess the company's practices for a given application system or network by determining the company's position on each of the spectra (while addressing control of operations separately from control of development).

● Determine the summary distributions by projecting the results of the multiple spectra analysis onto the summary lines.

● Plot the execution and control distributions against each other in the DP distribution chart.

The resulting arrangement of shapes presents a summary of conditions in the company that is readily communicable.

One can easily extend this approach to handle the case in which more than two organizational units have responsibility for the DP resource. For example, data center operations can be distinct from systems development work groups even though both are centralized relative to user groups. Such a situation can be handled in the distribution chart by assuming that the tasks on each spectrum completely describe the activities of each area. Intervals within each spectrum represent the activities that separate organizational units might perform.

To apply this notion to the distribution chart, one simply projects the intervals onto summary lines—as was done with points in the earlier situation. The result is a more general strategic view of distributed data processing.

How is this method of summarizing the handling of DP in a company useful? What does it tell managers that will help them plan and better manage the DP resource? In the next section, we shall use the chart to describe the variations in DP practices across a wide array of companies, an exercise that will give more meaning to the patterns appearing in the distribution chart and will help managers characterize their own situations.

DESCRIPTIVE USE

As is the case with any new tool, one should apply it to many situations in order to become familiar with its descriptive powers. Here we shall present the distribution chart of several companies for just this purpose. The companies display widely varying approaches to distributing data processing, and some of these differences are captured in the charts.

Exhibit IX presents the distribution charts for DP applications in six different companies, with key DP tasks labeled. These companies use some of the most common arrangements found in industry and government.

The three examples in the upper half of the exhibit illustrate arrangements that are encountered perhaps most frequently. In the first chart (which describes an airline), both development and operations activity are centralized, and they are controlled centrally also. This company depends on a widely dispersed network of terminals tied in to a very large computer center to maintain its on-line ticket reservation system. The users play some role in operations, but on the whole the show is run centrally.

The second chart, in contrast, depicts a highly decentralized situation in a manufacturing company. Both development and operations are again executed and controlled at the same place, only now the user group does it all. The production department of this manufacturing company develops and runs its own production scheduling system without drawing heavily on corporate resources. The diagram is also typical of divisionalized companies that permit their divisions largely to develop and execute their own applications.

In the third example (a retail store chain), development is executed and controlled centrally while operations are executed and controlled by the user group. The diagram portrays the features of a point-of-sale inventory system that was developed at corporate headquarters and installed in each branch store. The system operates independently in each store under the control of local management.

These first three charts show that operations and developments are often placed primarily along the main diagonal of a chart, extending from the lower left corner to the upper right. This placement is quite natural because it is most often the case that execution responsibility is handled by the group that also handles control responsibility. For example, systems analysts and programmers usually report to technical managers who also budget, schedule, and evaluate their work. It is no surprise to learn that most companies would show distribution charts with placement along the main diagonal.

The fourth chart is the first example of a company that shows a slight deviation from pure alignment along the diagonal. Some of the other examples in the lower row show even greater deviations.

The fourth chart displays the most common arrangement of DP resources. It presents the features of a company that has a centralized computer center whose costs are charged out to the users on the basis of their actual use of the facilities. By this administrative device, the users

EXHIBIT IX

Illustrative Examples of
DP Distribution Charts

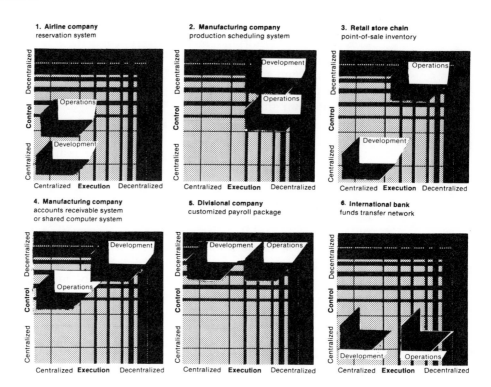

maintain some budgetary control over the central site (if they are free to choose their extent of involvement with the central group). Thus operations are partly controlled by the user and partly controlled centrally.

The development of new applications is undertaken by the users themselves; they have their own computer analysts and programming staffs who can design and implement new information systems as required. The chart depicts a manufacturing company's accounts receivable system, which was developed by the accounting department's DP personnel but is now run by the corporate data center—a joint facility that is paid for by its users.

The fifth example shows a divisionalized company that has adapted a payroll package for use in a division. The division has its own small computer on which to carry out the payroll processing, but it depends on a corporate development group to make the necessary adaptations. In this case, operations are decentralized for execution and control, whereas development is executed centrally under the control of the division. The division controls development by setting priorities, scheduling activities, formulating the budget, and evaluating the work.

In some settings, it makes sense to have centralized development and decentralized operations in DP even though the nature of the application is too critical for its operation to remain under the control of local management. In such cases, the arrangement in the distribution chart of example six might be more appropriate. This chart depicts DP in a large international bank that has developed a sophisticated international computer network to handle the transfer of its funds from bank to bank. The development work is all done at the bank's headquarters, but operations must go on around the world. Control is essential, however, and therefore the company has established procedures that would place both development and operations squarely in the lower portion of the chart.

These six examples illustrate some basic approaches to organizing data processing. Using the distribution chart as a tool, a manager can get a quick overview of his or her organization today and pinpoint similarities with other companies.

USER INVOLVEMENT

How do managers decide how much to decentralize execution and control activities? Or when they do have an idea of the appropriate degree of user involvement in the design and operation of the information system, how do they achieve it? The DP distribution chart can help answer such questions.

Turning to *Exhibit* X, note that the diagonal in the chart moves from centralized to decentralized execution and control. This diagonal shows the possible degrees of user involvement in DP. The range goes from essentially no involvement all the way to complete responsibility for a given system.

We will speak of *user involvement* henceforth to refer to the combination (or "sum") of decentralized execution and decentralized control. The concept is applicable to all regions of the chart, and by definition all points in the lower left offer less user involvement than points in the upper right.

The definition further suggests the idea of lines of "equal user involvement," also identified in the exhibit, which show that a wide variety of organizational arrangements of DP activities can give a user an equivalent of involvement in meeting his or her DP needs.

How are these lines of equal user involvement meaningful to management? They allow managers to consider systematically the alternative combinations of responsibilities that they may assign to user groups to obtain the desired amount of involvement in data processing. For instance, when users experience critical or constantly changing needs for specialized information in their normal business operations, a high degree of user involvement is probably warranted. But what responsibilities should management assign to this user?

An answer to this question begins with the distribution chart. Thinking at a fairly abstract level, we begin by sketching some diagonal equal user-involvement line on the chart that seems to reflect—on the basis of management's judgment of the user's business and information requirements—the general degree of involvement that the user needs to develop

EXHIBIT X

Planning with the Concept
of User Involvement

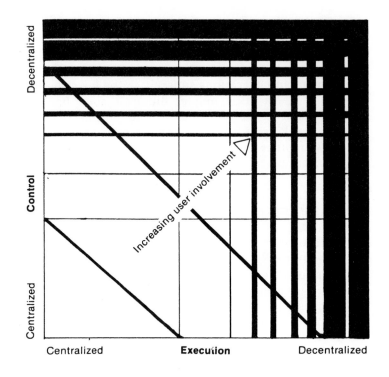

or operate an information system. The more critical the system is to
business operations, the greater the desire for involvement.

Once the desired level of involvement is known, managers must
assign responsibilities that will produce a figure in the distribution chart
that falls on the corresponding line of equal user involvement. They are
free to choose both the kinds of tasks and the variety of subtasks to assign
so long as the corresponding distribution chart reflects their decentralization strategy. Many possible mixes of execution and control activities
satisfy this requirement, so managers have a host of options for achieving
the same effect. Now, with the aid of the chart, they may evaluate their
full range in a very systematic manner. The example that follows will
illustrate this point more clearly.

An Example

Let us return to the planning meeting we described at the outset. There a
marketing manager is expressing the need of his regional sales offices for
greater involvement in data processing. He argues that the company's
sales representatives must have more timely customer information in
order to improve their performance in the marketplace. The solution, as
he sees it, is to put minicomputers in the hands of the regional sales

offices. With these machines, he says, local offices can obtain all types of data on their customers and thus create more responsive sales and service teams. Closing his case in a humble manner, the marketing manager credits a local minicomputer salesman for dreaming up this brillant remedy to his current performance problems.

Although this manager has justifiable reasons for wanting greater sales force involvement in data processing, these concerns by themselves do not imply that regional sales offices should have their own minicomputers. The company can increase user involvement in data processing without giving users their own hardware. The concepts and tools developed in this article make this point clear.

Turning to *Exhibit XI*, we see the DP distribution chart for the customer information system now in operation is the one we have seen before in *Exhibit III* and *VIII*, so we are already familiar with its organization. As noted, operations are predominantly centralized for both execution and control, offering users relatively little involvement in DP. This lower degree of user involvement is reflected by the position of the operations square, falling as it does on line A in the lower left-hand corner of the chart.

If we now want to increase user involvement in the operations of a customer information system, we must rearrange the DP-related activities so that the operations square falls on a line of higher user involvement;

EXHIBIT XI

Increasing User
Involvement: An Example

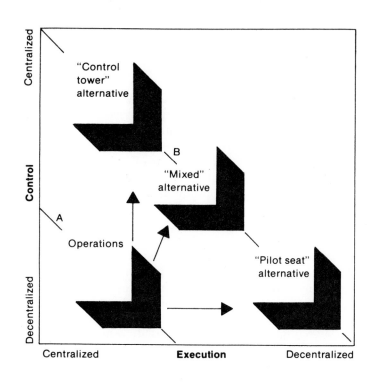

that is, the organization should change so that the distribution chart shows operations along some line B, rather than line A.

As the diagram illustrates, there are several possible shifts that will bring about this state of greater user involvement. These include movement in the directions of pure execution, pure control, or a combination of each. It is a question of putting the user in the "pilot's seat," the "control tower," or in a combination of these roles. Under the shifts that commonly occur, involving a combination of execution and control, the user will probably acquire his own computer.

The pilot seat shift might entail giving the user a computer also, but here the corporate center retains all of the control it had previously, creating a state of affairs that might seem threatening or oppressive to new technical employees at the regional sales offices.

The control tower shift is perhaps the most interesting of the three, for it shows how a state of greater user involvement can be achieved without notable changes in the arrangement of hardware or technical activities. Only managerial processes are changed. Control activities such as budgeting, personnel planning, and task scheduling are put in the hands of the user, while the computer remains in the same place.

If the marketing manager is correct about the need for increased user involvement, the company should consider all possible paths it might take to meet that need. The original proposal—namely, buying minicomputers—probably would have led to a decentralization of both execution and control, some form of "mixed" shift. Though the company may ultimately endorse this particular approach, this shift is clearly not the only one to consider.

Suppose now that management has decided to decentralize some of its DP execution activities to the marketing organization and it rejects the pure control path. If *Exhibit VII* accurately describes the way technical resources are distributed in the company, then decentralization of execution involves simply sliding the decentralization pattern for marketing out toward marketing, as shown in *Exhibit XII*. The pattern probably is pulled out to a position roughly alongside manufacturing's pattern.

This kind of shift still leaves "hardware operation" primarily under the direction of DP management, and so we see that it makes sense to discuss decentralization of execution—that is, technical activities, without requiring the proliferation of computers. As long as an organization's decentralization pattern retains the form presented in *Exhibit VI*, decentralization of execution can go a long way before computers are actually moved out into the field.

The fact that so many departments in this company are requesting minicomputers suggests that the company's implicit decentralization pattern may require conscious modification.

Once the managers of this company have decided to increase marketing's involvement in data processing and have worked out some general path to this end and once they have agreed on a pattern for decentralization technical resources, they then turn the project over to others for more detailed planning. Most likely, representatives from the DP and market-

EXHIBIT XII

Decentralizing Execution:
An Example

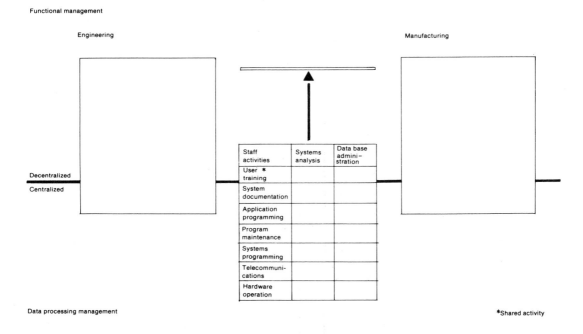

Functional management

Engineering				Manufacturing

Staff activities	Systems analysis	Data base administration
User * training		
System documentation		
Application programming		
Program maintenance		
Systems programming		
Telecommuni- cations		
Hardware operation		

Decentralized

Centralized

Data processing management

*Shared activity

ing departments will get together to hammer out the details and to ensure that the plan is consistent with top management's directives. Tools such as the DP activity spectra and the DP organization participation table can guide them in their deliberations.

IN CONCLUSION

Companies are finding that distributed data processing offers great potential for improving the performance of individual departments and for promoting the success of an organization as a whole. Managers within these companies are turning to DDP to help solve long-standing administrative problems and to help improve the control and coordination of fundamental business tasks. Enthusiasm is indeed strong for the decentralization of computing, and the call to acquire more computers is bound to increase.

Because of the demand, managers will be wise to plan carefully how their organizations will use information systems in the future. Along with these general plans, they should promulgate corporate policies establishing how they will arrange data processing resources to support their information systems. Only with such plans and policies can they assure that information systems will fulfill their potentially powerful roles in the overall success of their businesses.

PART TWO

Frameworks For Computer Opportunity Identification

Most companies are still managing the use of computer technology by focusing on individual applications. This orientation towards pockets of automation is self-defeating. The computer applications base grows to such a size and complexity that the management strategy of focusing on individual applications is analogous to pushing jello down—you push it down at one place, and it pops up in another place. The result in data processing is that maintenance of existing applications usurps all available systems development resources, data processing costs grow exponentially while delivery of new computer-based applications falls preciptously, and valuable data processing personnel become frustrated and leave.

Chapter 5, The Applications Portfolio describes an alternative construct for defining the results of a data processing activity. In designing the Applications Portfolio, a point in time is identified and opportunities for cost-effective use of current computer technology to support a set of business functions are identified. An inquiry is made into how many of those opportunities have been tapped, and key questions are addressed:

- What is the functional quality of the Applications Portfolio?

- What is the technical quality of the Applications Portfolio?

Sometime during the transition from the Computer Era to the Data Resource Era, new technology is required to sustain Applications Portfolio progress. The low-level support applications have been developed. Further progress is dependent upon cross-organizational integration of the operational support applications, as well as support to the control and planning functions. *Chapter 6, Computer Data Bases: The Future is Now*, describes

75

the organizational environment leading up to this fundamental transition and the need for enabling technologies to respond to the transition.

Chapter 7, What Kind of Corporate Modeling Functions Best, lays the groundwork for addressing the top part of the Applications Portfolio triangle, the planning functions. The payoff for support to planning functions can be high, but support to planning functions requires different approaches and different thinking.

Chapter 8, Orders of Office Automation, focuses on information technologies that are reverberating throughout the Applications Portfolio. As the office worker consumes more of the sales dollar, we are seeing natural forces to increase their productivity. Currently, the office worker only receives $2,500 of capital investment compared to over $25,000 of capital investment per factory worker. The economic implications of these facts are clear. In the future we will see an increasing capital investment in information technologies directed at improving the productivity of the office worker.

5

The Applications Portfolio

DAVID P. NORTON

The **Applications Portfolio** is a model which draws a visual analogy between the functions of the organization and the work of data processing. It is based upon calculated values assigned to existing data processing systems support. The creation of an Applications Portfolio for an organization makes it possible to map data processing support to the functions of the organization and the decision-making process. It creates a picture of the specific role of data processing systems in the organization, making more viable both the accomplishments and the potential areas for growth.

CONSTRUCTING THE APPLICATIONS PORTFOLIO

The Applications Portfolio concept draws from several key contributors to the literature on the role and use of information in the organization.

In his work, *Planning and Control Systems: A Framework for Analysis*, Robert Anthony provides a taxonomy for analyzing decision-making structures in an organization.[1] Anthony reviews management planning and control activities at three levels:

1. Strategic Planning. The process of deciding on the objectives of the organization, on changes in these objectives, on the resources used to

---

[1]Robert N. Anthony, *Planning and Control Systems: A Framework for Analysis*, (Boston: Harvard University Graduate School of Business Administration, 1965).

attain these objectives, and on the policies that are to govern the acquisition, use, and disposition thereof.

2. Management Control. The process by which managers assure that resources are obtained and used effectively and efficiently in the accomplishment of the organization's objectives.

3. Operational Control. The process of assuring that specific tasks are carried out effectively and efficiently.

The characteristics of each of these processes tend to be quite different. The strategic planning process tends to focus on highly unstructured problems involving many variables. The management control process tends to encompass all aspects of the company's operations with the objective of initiating action conforming to the policies and precedents established in the strategic planning process. The operational control process focuses on the supervisory level of management where specific tasks are executed. These tasks are performed in accordance with well-defined rules and procedures, requiring a minimum amount of individual judgment. Operational control systems are developed for tasks of limited scope.

The normative Applications Portfolio is a model which describes all of the automatable functions of an organization. It defines the set of an organization. It defines the set of business functions that represent cost/effective opportunities for applying data processing technology. In this sense it is an ideal, the maximum potential for data processing support to the organization.

The normative Applications Portfolio is created by mapping the functions of the organization according to the three levels described by Anthony, and then building vertically from one level to the next in order to show that activity on the lower levels supports activity on the higher levels. *Exhibit I* shows the outline of the normative Applications Portfolio with the division of the three levels indicated.

The next step in constructing a portfolio is to examine the functions of the organization being described and then to indicate in which level of the portfolio they belong. This categorization is based upon Simon's[2] ideas on decision-making and Gorry and Scott Morton's[3] framework for information characteristics required to support decision-making at the three levels.

Exhibit II summarizes the characteristics of information required to support each of the management functions by level. Different sets of decisions require different types of information. An information system that is appropriate for one type of decision will not be appropriate for others. The characteristics of these decisions and the information required to support them have implications concerning the appropriate devices and

---

[2]Herbert A. Simon, *The New Science of Management Decision* (New York: Harper & Row Publishers, Inc., 1960), pp. 5-6.
[3]G. A. Gorry and M. S. Scott Morton, *"A Framework for Management Information Systems,"* Sloan Management Review, 13, no. 1 (Fall 1971):55.

EXHIBIT I

Three-Level
Normative Application

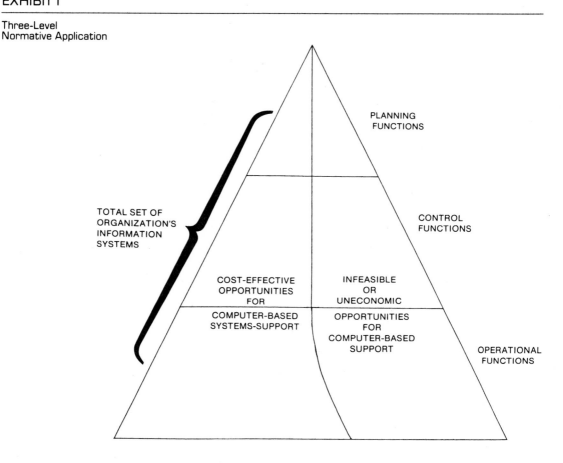

technical aids for data retrieval and processing as well as for the way in which the information resource is structured and stored. These differences in the characteristics of users' requirements, in turn provide the basis for the structuring of organization programs and a data base to support decision-making.

The functions which belong on the operational control level will be repetitive, routine, and highly structured. Functions which appear on the management control level will be less repetitive, less highly structured, and less routine. Functions on the strategic planning level will be non-repetitive and often highly varied and unstructured. For example, a typical set of functions might be marketing on the operational control level, market control on the management control level and business planning on the strategic planning level.

The stratification of business functions into three levels permits analysis of key information characteristics supporting those business functions. However, a more detailed grouping which reflects the unique way in which an organization executes business functions is necessary before the development of an effective systems architecture is possible.

EXHIBIT II

Characteristics of
Information

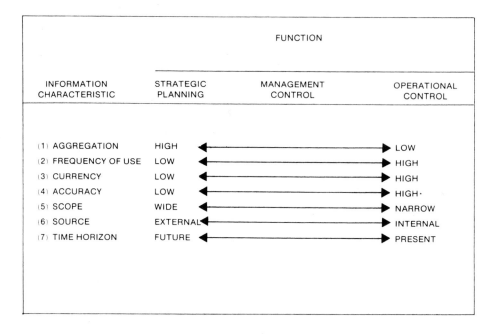

INFORMATION CHARACTERISTIC	FUNCTION		
	STRATEGIC PLANNING	MANAGEMENT CONTROL	OPERATIONAL CONTROL
(1) AGGREGATION	HIGH	←——————→	LOW
(2) FREQUENCY OF USE	LOW	←——————→	HIGH
(3) CURRENCY	LOW	←——————→	HIGH
(4) ACCURACY	LOW	←——————→	HIGH·
(5) SCOPE	WIDE	←——————→	NARROW
(6) SOURCE	EXTERNAL	←——————→	INTERNAL
(7) TIME HORIZON	FUTURE	←——————→	PRESENT

Jay W. Forrester has been a major contributor in providing concepts and methods to understand this complex systems phenomena.[4] He identifies several important attributes of complex systems:

1. They are dominated by counterintuitive behavior.

2. They are insensitive to most parameter changes.

3. They resist most policy changes.

4. They are often affected by policy changes in ways contrary to long-term intent.

Forrester's Industrial Dynamics approach provides a way to look at decision-making modules in business systems, to analyze the flow of information among these modules, and to understand the ways in which such flows affect decision-making. The foundation for Forrester's analytical approach is the construction of six networks describing the flow of resources within the organization:

1. Materials (e.g.; inventory)

---

[4]Jay W. Forrester, *Urban Dynamics* (Cambridge, MA: M.I.T. Press, 1969).

2. Orders (e.g.; requisitions for new employees)

3. Money (e.g.; accounts receivable, accounts payable, cash)

4. Personnel (e.g.; man-hours per week)

5. Capital equipment (e.g.; factory space, tools)

6. Information—rates and levels interconnecting other networks

The key ideas from Forrester which are relevant in constructing an Applications Portfolio are:

1. A decision-making network can be viewed as a series of individual decision-making modules.

2. To understand a decision-making network, one must understand the relationships between the modules as well as the structures of the individual modules.

Sherman Blumenthal builds on the ideas of Anthony and Forrester by providing operational guidelines for developing models of information systems.[5] Blumenthal's approach is of particular value for viewing the design of the programs for operational control and the related data bases. Blumenthal focuses on the development of a model of the information system which, in turn, permits the identification of modules (programs). Modules are the basic unit for systems planning and evaluation.

Blumenthal describes the operational control information system of an organization as a large network consisting of a number of "information processes," all of which are not equally bonded together. The difference in the degree of "coupling" in the information system, that is, how closely linked they are, provides the "basis for initial subdivision of the universe of information processing in a business into conceptually (and developmentally) manageable parts."[6] Blumenthal identifies four major information subsystems which are loosely coupled against one another but more closely coupled within. These subsystems correspond to the four major resources of the organization:

1. materials

2. capital equipment

3. money

4. human

The materials and capital equipment networks are more closely linked to each other than to the remaining networks. Using the degree of coupling

---

[5]Sherman C. Blumenthal, *Management Information Systems: A Framework for Planning and Development.* (Englewood Cliffs, NJ: Prentice-Hall, 1969), p. 45.
[6]*Ibid.*

as his criterion, Blumenthal identifies a hierarchy of information systems which exist in a typical organization. This hierarchy is shown in *Exhibit III.*

Exhibit IV shows the typical relationships among the various modules, as well as the data files required to support them. At this level of detail the model can prove to be of particular value to the systems architect or manager. It identifies each of the modules, or building blocks, of the operational control information system, regardless of whether they are automated or manual. Further, it identifies each of the files required to support these modules, as well as the paths for moving information through the system. Any interfaces with other information systems are also identified.

Identifying, isolating, and specifying a module is, at best, an art that depends upon the characteristics of the specific information system. However, Blumenthal provides several guidelines to aid the artist in this task.

- The size of the module should be sufficient to economically justify its development on a free-standing basis.

- The designer should start with the existing operational system and base the modules on these, rather than vice versa.

EXHIBIT III

Blumenthal Taxonomy of
Operational Control Systems

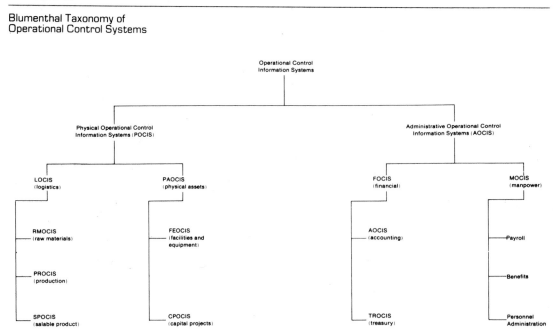

Source: Sherman C. Blumenthal, *Management Information Systems: A Framework for Planning and Development* © 1969, pp. 76, 81. Reprinted by permission of Prentice-Hall, Inc., Englewood Cliffs, N.J.

● The boundaries should be theoretically determined by a cost/benefit analysis whereby the residual value associated with having a particular function in a given module would be the basis for specifying module boundaries. In practice, however, cost and benefit relationships are difficult to determine before actual implementation. Therefore, the segmentation of an information system into modules is generally done on the basis of experienced professional judgment.

Blumenthal cautions that "one should not start out by redesigning the organization merely because that would make its architecture more elegant, or our systems design job easier."[7] The value of Blumenthal's contribution is two-fold:

1. It provides operational guidelines to assist in the development of models of the decision-making process.

EXHIBIT IV

Saleable Product Information System
Submodules and File

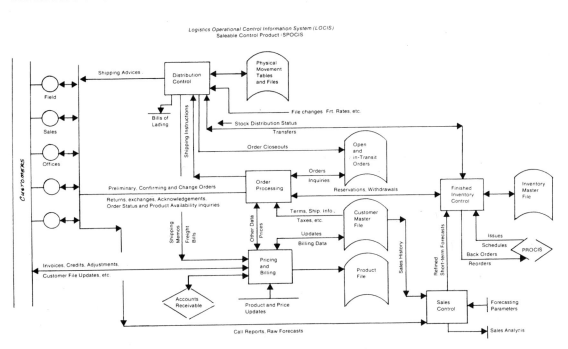

Source: Sherman C. Blumenthal, *Management Information Systems: A Framework for Planning and Development* © 1969, pp. 76, 81. Reprinted by permission of Prentice-Hall, Inc., Englewood Cliffs, N.J.

[7]Sherman C. Blumenthal, *Management Information Systems: A Framework for Planning and Development*, p. 41.

2. It shows that an information system can be divided into major sub-systems which focus on the management of specific resources.

Exhibit V shows a representative division of an organization. It is important to note that certain functions have been excluded from the portfolio in the exhibit. There is actually a "shadow portfolio" or a segment of the portfolio which is composed of functions which cannot now be automated. This segment is excluded from the normative Applications Portfolio, but remains a potential area of expansion as new technologies make it possible to consider automating previously excluded functions. Each of the business functions is supported by a number of activities. These are represented by vertical slices in the triangle under the appropriate function. Activities on the operational control level are the most specific and the most numerous. They comprise the day-to-day tasks of the organization. At the management level there are fewer functions and fewer activities conducted on a less frequent basis. This is explained by the nature of such management level tasks as direction, review, and reporting. At the top of the triangle, strategic planning comprises a few activities which are largely nonrepetitive, infrequent, and broader in scope.

EXHIBIT V

Applications Portfolio of
a Division

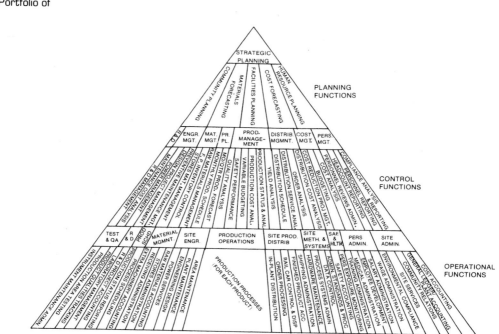

EVALUATING THE APPLICATIONS PORTFOLIO

Once the functions of an organization have been described in the normative Applications Portfolio, that portfolio can be used to show how current systems are supporting those functions. Data processing systems can be mapped against the activities which they support, and can be indicated in the Applications Portfolio by shading the level of automation on the appropriate activity "slices". When all systems have been matched to the functions of the organization and all activity slices have been shaded, the Applications Portfolio will provide a visual balance sheet for data processing support, a snapshot of the extent of data processing coverage in the organization.

It is obviously difficult to estimate the exact degree of data processing coverage in each activity area. it is equally difficult to calculate the maximum coverage equivalent to full automation of that activity. However, it is possible to describe certain measures which provide a close estimation of the quantity of systems support to each activity and to determine to what extent that support is filling the needs of users concerned with that activity. These measures make it possible to shade in the Applications Portfolio and to review the work of the organization in relationship to the work of data processing in a common context.

Quantity of Applications/Systems Support

The number of systems and the size of the systems supporting a given activity can be assigned a relative value and indicated on the Applications Portfolio. This will show, in a general sense, where systems are concentrated (at what level and in support of which activities) and the extent of the data processing coverage in general.

The primary difficulty with quantitative measures of coverage is that they do not show whether or not existing systems are supporting the users successfully. This same problem is reflected in attempts to describe the work of data processing in terms of the size of its budget, the hardware, or the number of systems. This difficulty is responsible for two clearly opposite views of data processing occurring simultaneously: the acknowledgement that it is critical to the organization, and the skepticism about the degree of success attributable to individual systems applications.

To the extent that the Applications Portfolio is built on quantitative measures alone, it cannot explain what is being done by data processing but only how much is being done. For this reason, it is necessary to establish criteria for determining the effectiveness of systems in supporting the functions to which they are assigned. Measures of quantity must be adjusted according to measures of quality.

Quality of Applications/Systems Support

The quality of the systems which appear in the portfolio can be ascertained in two ways:

● In terms of the technical characteristics of those systems

● In terms of the functional characteristic of the systems

In the first case the source of information is primarily the data processing department. In the second, the source of information is the user in the organization who can estimate, according to certain criteria, whether or not the system is actually facilitating the activity it was designed to support.

The technical characteristics used to measure the quality of systems include design, operability, and maintainability. **Design** determines the suitability of the system to the functions it supports. **Operability** refers to both the ease of use of the system and its adaptability. **Maintainability** refers to the suitability of the system for use over time. The first two are indicators of the quality of the support, whatever the quantity, at the present moment, and the third indicates whether or not this quality of support can be expected to continue over time. All of these characteristics are detailed in *Exhibit VI*.

The functional characteristics of systems are related to the information requirements described by Gorry and Scott Morton.[8] They are indicators of whether the system matches the needs for information appropriate to that activity. As Gorry and Scott Morton have shown, each activity in an organization will require different combinations of informa-tion capabilities with differing degrees of priority.[9] For example, data accuracy may be critical to users in one functional area of the organ-

EXHIBIT VI

Technical Characteristics of
an Information System

DESIGN	MAINTAINABILITY	OPERABILITY
1. QUALITY OF DATA INPUT MECHANISMS (SENSOR AND NON-SENSOR BASED)	1. QUALITY OF DOCUMENTATION	1. EASE OF OPERATION
2. QUALITY OF FILE HANDLING— DATA STORAGE AND ACCESS TECHNIQUES	2. ABILITY TO TRACE PROBLEMS THROUGHOUT APPLICATION SYSTEM, TO FULLY TEST CHANGES AND PREDICT IMPACT OF CHANGES	2. OUTAGES
		3. QUALITY OF HARDWARE AND SOFTWARE BACKUP
3. MODULARITY AND LOGICAL FLOW OF APPLICATION SYSTEMS	3. MAINTAINABILITY OF LANGUAGE USED	4. PROBLEM INVESTIGATIONS
4. EFFECTIVENESS OF DATA REPORTING/OUTPUT MECHANISMS	4. MAINTAINABILITY OF HARDWARE	5. CAPABILITY TO RECOGNIZE AND MODIFY VARIABILITY IN PRODUCTION PROCESS
5. ABILITY OF SYSTEM TO BE INTEGRATED WITH BUSINESS SYSTEMS	5. MAINTAINABILITY OF OPERATING SYSTEM AND I/O ROUTINES	
6. ADHERENCE TO DESIGN STANDARDS	6. AVAILABILITY OF TEST DATA (TRANSACTIONS AND FILES)	

[8] *Op. Cit.*
[9] *Ibid.*

ization while users in another area may be interested in detailed reporting and data currency. Effective systems must acknowledge the different functional priorities detailed in *Exhibit VII.*

Each slice in the Applicatons Portfolio represents an ideal or maximum potential for data processing support. If systems met this objective, the organization would have **complete coverage** in all automatable functions of the business. However, even in the most ambitious data processing plans, complete coverage is recognized as an unrealistic goal. Instead, selected tasks or subtasks are identified as potential targets for automation. The totality of these targeted areas is the **attempted coverage**.

The first step in determining system coverage is to measure the attempted coverage for the Applications Portfolio. This measurement is an assessment of the extent to which portions of each function in the portfolio are covered by existing automated systems. It is a measure of *quantity* of support and excludes consideration of the degree to which automated systems fail to fulfill intended functions due to the characteristics of technical or functional quality described below.

The next step in determining coverage for the Application Portfolio is to account for the effects of functional and technical quality on attempted coverage. This is accomlished by rating systems according to certain technical and functional characteristics. The results are applied against the attempted coverage of each function in the portfolio in order to arrive at a rating for **effective coverage** or the actual yield of systems in use.

EXHIBIT VII

Functional Characteristics of
an Information System

DATA ACCURACY:	THE DEGREE OF CORRECTNESS AND INTEGRITY OF THE DATA PROVIDED BY THE APPLICATION SYSTEM IDENTIFIED IN THE PREVIOUS SECTION.
DATA ACCESSIBILITY:	THE PROMPTNESS WITH WHICH INFORMATION AND REPORTS REQUESTED FROM THE SYSTEM ARE RECEIVED.
DATA CURRENCY:	THE DEGREE TO WHICH REPORTED DATA IS CURRENT WITH ACTUAL EVENTS.
DATA SECURITY:	THE DEGREE TO WHICH THE DATA IN THE APPLICATION IS PROTECTED FROM UNAUTHORIZED ACCESS.
SYSTEM RELIABILITY:	THE DEGREE TO WHICH THE APPLICATION SYSTEM IS AVAILABLE WHEN NEEDED, REPORTS ARE RECEIVED ACCORDING TO SCHEDULE, AND OPERATIONAL AND PROGRAMMING PROBLEMS ARE QUICKLY CORRECTED.
EASE OF USE:	THE SIMPLICITY IN USING OR OPERATING THE APPLICATION SYSTEM.
OUTPUT PRESENTATION:	THE QUALITY AND READABILITY OF THE OUTPUT MEDIUM (E.G., VIDEO DISPLAY, PRINTOUT) AND REPORTING FORMAT.
DETAILED REPORTING:	THE ADEQUACY OF THE EXISTING REPORTS IN INFORMATION.
SUMMARY REPORTING:	THE ADEQUACY OF THE EXISTING REPORTS IN INFORMATION.
DEMAND REPORTING:	THE CAPABILITY OF THE APPLICATION SYSTEM OF PROVIDING DEMAND REPORTS, EXCEPTION REPORTS, AND ONE—SHOT REPORTS AS NEEDED.

The process of discounting attempted coverage to determine effective coverage is shown in *Exhibit VIII*. The shading in the single bar in the exhibit can be transferred to the slice in the Applications Portfolio. When all functions have been rated, the shading of the entire portfolio will show how systems coverage is distributed throughout the business. The Applications Portfolio can then be used to determine the penetration of automation in the business and to compare data processing capabilities in the organization to standards for similar organizations. The implications of this analysis for data processing review and planning are discussed in detail in the *Stage Assessment, Chapter 8*.

Based on the portfolio analogies developed by such financial analysts as Tilles, the following parameters can be used to describe the Applications Portfolio:

1. Portfolio coverage. The distribution of coverage of the universe of all possible information systems. This allows analysis of concentration of coverage in areas suporting key missions and functions.

2. Portfolio maturity. Distribution of the age of existing systems. Also includes distribution by point in life cycle, based on the maintenance profiles of the system.

3. Portfolio balance. The distribution of coverage for different levels of systems (e.g., strategic planning, operational control) or for different functions (e.g., order processing, materials management).

EXHIBIT VIII

Measuring Effectiveness ("Coverage") of
an Information System

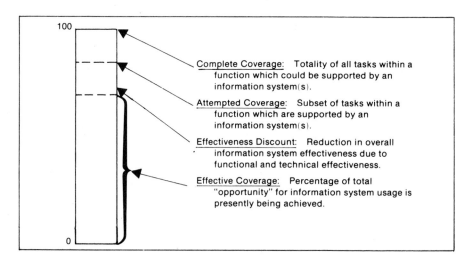

4. Portfolio technology. Distribution of the type of technology used in constructing various components of the portfolio.

5. Portfolio dispersion. Geographic distribution of the portfolio.

APPLICATIONS PORTFOLIO ANALYSIS

The techniques used by financial analysts to perform investment analyses across complex portfolio provide a valuable analogy in analyzing an Applications Portfolio. In discussing the portfolio analysis approach, Tilles states that "the most tangible expression of a company's strategy is its allocation of funds. Few things determine the future of the company as directly as the way it spends money."[10] He describes a set of criteria which should be used in developing a strategy for portfolio management:

1. Mission (function). The relation of resource allocation to individual functions or missions of the company.

2. Risk. The distribution of resources to high risk and low risk activities.

3. Maturity. The balance of age (or maturity) of the elements in the portfolio.

4. Geography. The balance of resources over geographic areas.

5. Excellence. The relationship of excellence in the portfolio to the critical missions of the company.[11]

EVOLUTION OF THE APPLICATIONS PORTFOLIO THROUGH THE SIX STAGES

As data processing matures, the Applications Portfolio will change. Additional applications will be developed, existing coverage will be upgraded and, eventually, business functions will also be altered in response to capabilities and procedures made possible by automation. The growth of the Applications Portfolio is dependent upon growth in the rest of the organization. In some cases applications may take the lead, but in all cases there must be adjustments to match applications to the other growth processes.

The Early Stages

The first activities to be automated will be those in which existing procedures lend themselves to systems design. These include financial

---

[10]Seymour Tilles, "*Strategies for Allocating Funds*," Harvard Business Review Classics, Finance Series, Part III, no. 21092: 14.
[11]*Ibid.*

and accounting procedures where the cost of automation can be justified. Applications will be concentrated in operational level activities where routine procedures and regular reporting are easily adapted to a systems format. Such activities are labor intensive and easily improved by cost-savings systems.

Applications in accounting, payroll, and similar functions are usually successful and generate enthusiasm. In stage II, more and more groups within the organization begin to examine their activities and to look for ways to save time and expense by using data processing services. Successful applications also encourage data processing personnel to go out and sell their services in areas where they feel systems could be used to facilitate nonautomated activities.

This enthusiasm encourages experimentation. It encourages users and data processing personnel to expand their preconceptions about auto-mation and it leads to a much broader idea of "automatable functions." This means that a larger segment of the Application Portfolio is being recognized and can potentially be addressed by systems.

The actual coverage of the Applications Portfolio during this period will increase rapidly and somewhat randomly. Ideally, applications on the operational control level support applications on the management control level, but in fact applications will appear on both levels. In addition, the activities which have been automated on the operations level may not be those which support the applications on the management level. This phenomenon is clear in the late stage II Applications Portfolio. At this point applications have penetrated many functions of the organization, but lack of experience among users and data processing personnel and the absence of controls and planning result in a random pattern of growth.

The crisis which marks the end of stage II and the beginning of stage III is characterized by the effort of data processing and senior management to regain control over this situation. The Applications Portfolio provides an indicator of the specific way in which growth has occurred and shows the areas in which growth has led to inbalance in coverage. It can also be used to determine priorities for future growth. As planning and control capabilities mature, the growth of the portfolio can be managed.

The Intermediate Stages

During stage III the attempt to consolidate and control data processing growth results in an effort to balance the Applications Portfolio. The proliferation of systems has created both an awareness of data processing and a dependence upon it. Finding itself in this situation, the organization begins to ask the question: "What is data processing doing for us?" It is at this point that the Applications Portfolio can become a powerful management tool.

The Applications Portfolio model is derived from an investment portfolio strategy. It is based upon the idea that the field of possible investments is always much broader than the field of actual investments and that, meditating between the two, the investor tries to determine the best or most feasible investment strategy. In the same way, senior management and data processing management can work together to determine the best strategy for managing the Applications Portfolio.

The normative Applications Portfolio can be viewed in this analogy as the field of possible applications. Only a selected number of applications can be considered; this is the attempted coverage. In addition, within the field of investments or applications, not all investments will be equally profitable. The effective coverage shows where applications are successful and where problems exist. This information is supplementd by the indication in the Applications Portfolio of the relationship between effective coverage at the three levels and within each functional area.

During stage III the Applications Portfolio can be consolidated and, as controls are introduced along with planning mechanisms, future growth can be directed according to patterns which will provide for balanced growth. By the end of stage III, the Applications Portfolio should indicate a solid base of applications on the operational control level supporting the development of applications on the management control level. During stage IV this balance will be maintained as applications move up the levels of the portfolio.

During late stage III and early stage IV, there is a transition in the maturity of data processing. As personnel and users become more skilled, as controls are set in place, and as the technology becomes more familiar, the organization can begin to take a more global approach to data processing. Instead of looking at individual systems, individual users, and individual hardware capabilities, management can begin to look for patterns in the flow of information and opportunities for integration.

The Applications Portfolio is a useful tool in this process. The pattern of applications should reflect the pattern of use of applications. This can be compared to patterns of hardware installation, data base administration, and other planning and control efforts. The correlation between data processing and business functions is illustrated in the portfolio so that efforts to integrate the work of the organization can be matched to efforts to integrate the work of data processing in the Applications Portfolio itself.

The Advanced Stages

The initial concept of building applications was directed toward procedures which could be mirrored more or less directly by systems. However, as basic needs are filled, it becomes evident that the power of applications as a means of supporting business functions goes beyond the replication of activities. The accumulation of data, the recognition of the role of data bases, and the growing awareness among users and data processing personnel of the role of information in their work indicate that applications are used for much more than "getting things done faster and more efficiently."

The transition in thinking about data processing which occurs in the later stages is based on the idea that the decision-making process in the organization can be tracked to identifiable information requirements. In the advanced stages, systems growth can be directed along patterns which support the information needs of the decision makers in the organization.

The recognition that systems can support people by providing them with information opens a new frontier for ideas about applications. Segments of the normative Applications Portfolio which had been excluded as infeasible for automation are reviewed and the Applications Portfolio is expanded. Managerial activities, previously exempted from consideration, can now be understood in terms of the information tools and as the source of organizational reports and analyses. This transition is reflected in the activities and functions of the extended portfolio to support not only structured business functions, but also the semi-structured business functions characteristic of both control and planning functions.

At the control and planning managerial levels, only part of the decision-making process can be automated. This may involve interim decision making or it may mean the analysis and presentation of information prerequisite to decision making. In many cases automation is dependent upon the capacity to integrate systems and to use data bases.

Decision making on the strategic planning level is rarely structured, but often final activities are supported by such information-gathering and semi-structured decisions as review of feasibility, collection of possible alternatives, and projections of possible outcome. Systems can be created to support these activities by providing information, simulating outcome, and modeling.

The area of Decision Support Systems, those systems in the Application Portfolio which support decision-making processes as opposed to specific tasks and activities, is still relatively unexplored. Advanced technologies are being introduced at a rapid rate. Each new technical capability introduces the possibility of new applications and ties between applications, and spurs the user to review the ways in which business is conducted and decisions are made.

In the context of such rapid change in technology, the Applications Portfolio is useful for planning. Areas which had been excluded may now be reviewed and added to the existing portfolio. The visual model can be used to show the role of data processing to date and the new areas which are opening up. It can help senior management and data processing management understand how new technologies can support the organization, and can help plan for the introduction of systems where they will be most effective.

6

Computer Data Bases: The Future is Now*

RICHARD L. NOLAN

On July 1, two sets of forecasts from the planning department arrived on the desk of the marketing vice president. The first set forecasted sales for the company's existing line of industrial products for the year beginning the following January. The second set forecasted sales over the same period for a new line of industrial products, similar to the company's established line, to be introduced in January.

The company expected that the two lines would complement each other, permitting an in-depth coverage of its markets which would place the company in an extremely strong competitive position. This was particularly important at this juncture; competition had been making inroads into the company's traditional turf, and the higher level of sales that could be expected would give the company some much-needed profits.

With pleasure, the vice president of marketing noted that the forecasts were more promising than he had dared to hope. The forecasting staff had an excellent track record—there was no reason not to take the high projections seriously. So some thought would have to be given to increasing productions for both lines over the next months.

Production was really not much of a problem. In preliminary talks with manufacturing, the fact had been well established that existing plant and personnel could stretch to produce higher quantities on short notice with relatively little sweat. The forecasts gave adequate indications, too, of just how high a level of production would be needed each month for the succeeding nine months.

Inventory, on the other hand, did present something of a problem. Company sales had distinct regional characteristics; they were made from regional warehouses which the company held on leaseback arrangements. In preparation for the new product line, some provision had already been made to increase the company's regional warehouse facilities, but these high sales forecasts made the marketing vice president wonder whether the expansion had been large enough. It seemed to him that a good many of the regional warehouses might well be severely squeezed—both in sheer physical space and in manpower. With these high projected volumes, he thought, the company could be marketing itself right into a warehousing bottleneck.

Also, the regional variations in sales patterns had not been taken fully into account in making the forecasts, for "technical" reasons—here was the one "soft" area he had agreed to tolerate in the forecasts. Hence he was not clear on which warehouses would be the worst hit and where there might be some excess capacity in closely adjoining regions.

He thought next of the aggressive marketing and promotion strategies he had just approved, for both product lines, to be carried out in various regions over the next few quarters. If they were as effective as he expected them to be, there would be a problem in the warehouses. Perhaps he could cut back on his preferred marketing and sales strategies, but this alternative conflicted with the company's need for increasing sales as quickly as possible.

DEFINITION OF A PROBLEM

He did some simple arithmetic and then headed for the CEO's office. After outlining the situation in light of the final forecasts from planning, he boiled it down to this: "If things work out the way we expect them to, the Chicago warehouses, at least, will have to operate at four times their capacity for at least three months. That's only one group of warehouses. And we really don't have the cash in hand to contract for additional outside space."

They argued about a number of possibilities, making a few calculations and thinking out various consequences aloud. After an hour's discussion, they concluded that they simply had to have a better picture of the impact of the new marketing strategy on sales of both lines, and they also had to have a better picture of the impact of projected sales on inventory turnover and warehousing crowding. They needed, in short, to pull all three of the threads together.

At this point, the CEO pointed out that parts of the puzzle were already on the computer:

● The company had inventory simulation programs which had been developed recently to help adjust inventory policies. Several years' actual data on inventory turnover were also available.

- The sales department had a number of forecasting programs designed to provide sales reports and forecast information by region and product.

- On behalf of marketing, the forecasting staff had developed a model for market penetration of the new product line, based on the sales of the existing product line, which it was intended to supplement.

So the two men went to see the vice president of computing services and laid the problem out for him. Then they asked, "Can you get us a printout that will tell us what impact marketing and sales are going to have on the warehouses?"

His answer was no. He pointed out that the company had no program for running such a simulation. He also pointed out that while the company had most of the data that such a simulation would require, none of the data were in readily available form. The inventory data had been specially prepared for the inventory simulations and would have to be completely recoded before they could be used for such a radically different purpose. The programs for forecasting sales did provide regional projections, but they had not been adjusted to mesh with the new inventory systems as yet—that development was still some months away. Further, the several years' sales data used by the programs, once again, were specially coded for the sales programs and could not be used in different programs without a massive reorganization of the data.

Finally, he pointed out that their computer system could not handle the sheer volume of data required by a simulation that attempted to combine all the necessary inventory data, sales data, and market-strategy data. At a minimum, more main memory for the computer would be required.

The CEO looked glum: "I'm not worried about the size of the computer. If we need a bigger memory, we'll get our hands on a bigger memory. How long will it take you to clean up the data and write a simulation program that will give us some answers?"

"Nine months, maybe a year," said the EDP manager.

"Because all our data are frozen into these other programs?" the CEO asked.

"That's the main reason," the EDP manager replied.

"That's a hell of a reason," the CEO said and stalked toward the door.

"Of course, we could have done it the other way," the EDP man called after him. "But now what we'd have to do is. . . ."

But the two men were gone.

What's the Answer?

The problem in this vignette is not one that has an easy solution. Management asked for a computer simulation that cut across three different departments, and was frustrated primarily because each department's data were locked up into its own applications. Even if time had permitted, the cost of recoding all the data for a cross-departmental simulation would probably have been too high for the company to bear. In other words, the company's own data were a frozen asset—a highly constrained resource, analogous to money which could be used to purchase only one type of asset.

Management requests for such ad hoc processing are increasing. As a consequence, companies are beginning to realize that data are a valuable resource, to be managed like any other basic resource.

What the EDP manager wanted to explain to the CEO, and what the CEO did not wait to hear, is that the company could have been managing its data in such a way that the CEO's request could have been fulfilled.

If the company had maintained all its computer-readable data in a single pool or bank—in a so-called "data base"—and if the company had structured this base of data so that a program for virtually any feasible use could have been run from this data base, then it would have been a matter of sheer expertise and flair for a good, experienced programmer to concoct a program that pulled the desired information together. Further, if the company had been maintaining a data base, its programmers would already have developed the expertise and capability to write such a program, with the aid of a "data-base language," on reasonable notice.

The ability to deal with such ad hoc requests is the special benefit of the data-base approach. It has a more mundane benefit too: in an EDP facility of any size and complexity, it is feasible, and much more efficient over the long haul, to create any program—whether big, small, complex, routine, or ad hoc—and to run it from a data base rather than from a lot of separate files of data locked to specific applications.

The truth of this rather strong statement derives from the fact that the data-base approach frees the programmer from the constraint of working over, under, around, and through the structures of separate data files, an expensive fact of life implicit in the traditional approach to EDP operations and planning. With a data base, he need only work with a single structure, that of the base itself.

This one-main-structure feature also makes it easy to decide how data can be obtained and integrated into the base most efficiently and economically—that is, it eases the data-maintenance problem, once the data base has been set up. Considering the extraordinary percentages of EDP budgets that companies allocate to maintenance today—usually over 50%—this benefit is a highly significant one.

Thus the concept of a companywide data base has emerged. It has two key aspects:

1. The data that computer programs use are considered an independent resource in themselves, separate from the computer programs.

2. There is an art and an approach to managing and structuring a company's computer-readable data as a whole, so that they constitute a resource available to the organization for broad-range applications—especially on an ad hoc basis.

Because of its potential benefits, the data-base concept has received much attention recently in the professional press. What I hope to do in this article is explain it in management terms and present some survey results that indicate how the concept is being received and implemented in a small sample of companies.

A HISTORICAL PATTERN

As the matter now stands, most managements would be hard put to manage—and use—their data to full potential, for reasons that are largely historical. Because of the rapid growth of computer technology, management of data has developed haphazardly and in laggard fashion over the years. A general approach to data management has emerged only very recently, and, consequently, applications have developed discretely from one another in an unintegrated and wasteful fashion. Further, each increase in the complexity and capabilities of computers has brought new generations of applications—but these applications still, for the most part, have been specialized in nature, designed for a specific operational use or for a specialized staff function.

Hence management of data has continued to develop in fragmented fashion and at rather low organizational levels—at a subdepartmental or substaff level.

Today, upper levels of management are seeking information that can be generated only from properly structured, companywide pools that include data from the narrower applications located farther down in the organizational hierarchy. That is, management information today requires that a company have a data base which can be used, in conjunction with broad-range programs, to generate information on a broader and more comprehensive scale than the single, isolated applications of the past could usually do.

Notwithstanding the new demands, tradition is still strong; indeed, it has barely been challenged. *Exhibit I* represents the traditional way of doing things—collecting and coding data for specific programs and thereby gluing them more or less permanently and exclusively to those programs. In retrospect, this approach has had three significant disadvantages.

1. Files and records have tended to become redundant. Suppose Company X originally had only a single, computer-based system—say, for accounts receivable—which is represented in *Exhibit I* as Program I. (At this point, please pay attention to *Exhibit I* only. I shall explain its companion—*Exhibit II*—subsequently.)

Program I has three data files: A, B, and C. File A contains customer records, each consisting of data elements a and b; a might be the customer name and b his outstanding balance. Files B and C contain other data elements needed for the accounts receivable program.

Assume that now the company wishes to implement a second program— Program II, as illustrated in *Exhibit I*—with Files D, E, and F comprehending elements a, b, c, d, f, and g. Note that the company already has all these elements, except g, on file for Program I. In all probability, however, its programmers coded Files A and B (including all the elements a, b, c,

EXHIBIT I

The Traditional Approach to
Programs and Data

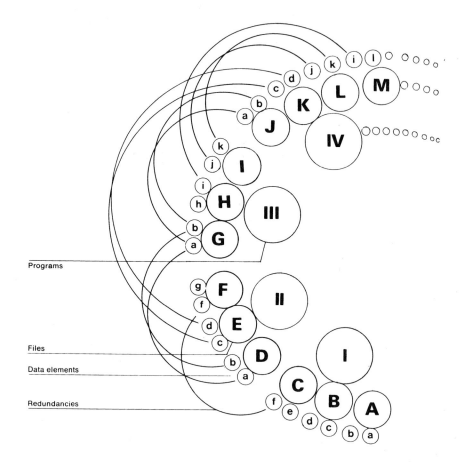

Programs

Files

Data elements

Redundancies

and d) expressly for Program I, and hence cannot now use A and B intact for Program II. Thus the programmers have to make a choice: They can recode A and B so that these files can be used by either Program I or Program II. But this would mean rewriting Program I to take account of the recoding; or they can build two "new" files, consisting of data from A and B but coded for the special convenience of Program II. In the past, when faced with this kind of choice, an EDP department has usually just gone ahead and constructed the two "new" files. Going back over Program I ordinarily seems like too much trouble, so making up the new files seems the easiest way out. It is—in the short run.

But in the long run, as the exhibit shows, Company X might easily find itself creating more and more quasi-duplicate files as it adds new programs. For example: It will need two new versions of File B for Programs II and IV—that is, Files E and K; three new versions of File A

EXHIBIT II

The Data-Base Approach to
Programs and Data

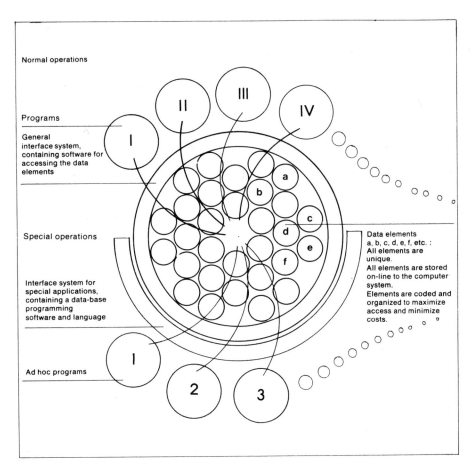

for Programs II, III, and IV—that is, Files D, G, and J; and it will need a new version of File I for Program IV—that is, file L.

And so on. The redundancy of data is obvious. In just this little, highly simplified example, 7 out of 12 (58%) of the data elements in the files are redundant.

Initially, redundancy does not cause a great deal of trouble. As soon as pieces of data must be updated, however, it does cause a great deal of trouble. In an EDP department of any size, it is virtually impossible to update all the redundant files and reports in systematic and synchronized fashion. Consider what must happen if Company X adds a customer: it must update A, B, D, G, and J, and that would only be the beginning.

Once files, records, and reports have begun to overlap and updating becomes a serious chore updating procedures begin to sag of their own weight and different parts of the organization begin to receive inconsistent reports generated from files that are in various states of disrepair. In one large company, the inconsistencies between sales reports at the division level and sales reports at the branch level were so extreme that the salesman began to keep very elaborate manual sales records. These two sets of reports were, in fact, generated in large part from redundant files that were updated at different times.

These particular inconsistencies resulted from a mere difference of organizational level—that is, the divisional versus the branch level. Severe redundancy problems can arise even more easily when reports from one function must be meshed with reports from another function. For example, there is absolutely no reason to expect that a company's inventory-control report will jibe with its accounting report unless the updating disciplines for the files of both functions are synchronized with each other. Even slight variations in the data used for the two functional reports can cause glaring inconsistencies:

In a large retail chain whose applications had developed in the traditional fashion, the needs of the business forced management to request the integration of a number of different functional programs and systems. With great effort, the job was done. However, it was done in such a way that many quasi-duplicate files were created and many separate, but essentially similar, programs were patched together. The company suddenly found itself spending 90% of its programming man-hours just keeping the programs running in concert and the files up to date.

At the very least, redundancy spells confusion and expense for any sizable operation. Perhaps its worst feature is that the longer a company follows the traditional pattern and keeps adding new programs and redundant files of data, coded specifically and exclusively for those programs, the greater the task it must face when it finally assembles all its data in a single pool, so structured and coded that new programs can be run without extensive recollection or recoding of data.

2. The traditional approach undercuts or aborts the advances of computer technology. Computer memory was once a great deal more expensive than it is today. A major computer manufacturer is now predicting that semiconductor technology will reduce the present cost of main memory by many orders of magnitude in the not-too-remote future. Even now the costs of random-access storage have been greatly reduced by the development of extremely large disc devices. Furthermore, new software has introduced new dimensions to computing, dimensions that make possible the more advanced kinds of information systems. For example, virtual-memory techniques allow one to explore, cheaply, relationships between elements in a relatively huge pool of data, not all of which need necessarily be present in literal fact.

Originally, the relatively high cost of on-line storage ("memory," in a rough sense) was a main factor that induced companies to delimit the scope of programming and therewith the amount of data needed during any given run. In effect, this reinforced the practice of creating and maintaining separate files for each application in the company's portfolio—companies tended to store no more data than were needed for the run at hand.

Today, however, many companies that have followed the traditional route, but have acquired up-to-date on-line storage systems, find they have the capacity to keep relatively huge amounts of data alive in the system. But their data are still organized and coded along first-generation computer lines—that is, by specific programs. From a rational viewpoint, this is as awkward, expensive, and absurd as keeping modern accounting records wholly in Roman numerals.

3. The traditional approach obstructs upper management's growing demands for applications that require a data base. The reason for this unfortunate condition is locked into the history of the computer. A brief review of the evolution of computer-based applications runs as follows:

- The computer was first used to replace existing manual functions, primarily within the accounting function.

- Next came the integration of computer-based systems within and between functional areas—this was the cross-functional stage.

- Now cross-functional/interlevel systems are being developed to serve middle and upper-middle management; or, to put it another way, management is now demanding the benefits of computer innovations.

At this third stage, the redundancies and inefficiencies that result from the traditional approach to the management of data become so signal and so extensive that applications can be adequate only if they are developed in such a manner that specific programs are separate from the data. That is, the whole body of a company's data must be structured into a flexible data base.

A MODERN CONCEPT

As *Exhibit II* shows, the data-base concept structures EDP activity in such a way that all of a company's computer-readable data are merged in a single pool, which is used to run both routine programs and programs written in response to ad hoc requests. Note that no files appear in this exhibit—the base of data elements constitutes the general file for the company, and specific files are by and large unnecessary. Note also that two additional software systems are in evidence here which were not in evidence in *Exhibit I*:

- **The data-base interface system**. This enables a specialist data-base programmer to organize and structure the data elements in a manner that minimizes or eliminates redundancy and optimizes the economic costs of data storage and accessibility.

- **The interface system for special programming**. This includes a high-level programming language especially designed for manipulating data elements contained in the data base, solving problems, and producing reports. To write an ad hoc program, the programmer works successively through the interface for special applications and the general interface system to the data base itself.

Comparing *Exhibits I* and *II*, one can see an immense contrast between the traditional concept and the data-base concept, both theoretical and practical. If the company described in the vignette with which I opened this article had had a working data base, the CEO might merely have asked his EDP manager to set a programmer to work on an ad hoc program. No question of data availability would have arisen; the only variable in the case would have been the time required to actually write the program, and this time might only have been a matter of hours.

One can more fully appreciate the contrast if he looks forward to the fourth stage of development in computer applications—applications that senior executives will use in corporate management. This development will most likely emerge from the union of the data-base concept and the corporation-model concept; and while this union is still but a gleam in the specialist's eye, the company that adjusts its EDP policies to the data-base concept now will enjoy a very significant advantage over the company that pursues the traditional patterns until the day of reckoning has actually arrived. (Just how a company should pursue this adjustment is a problem I shall consider later.)

Since much of the computer technology necessary to implement the data-base concept exists and the rest of the technology is being developed rapidly, a strong case for adopting the data-base approach can now be made. Yet, in operational terms, the concept is still novel. To what degree is it being used? What are the issues and problems involved in implementing it? By what strategies can a company work toward a data base? And what benefits can we realistically expect from it?

AN INTERVIEW STUDY

To answer these questions I administered a pattern interview to the data-processing managers of ten companies in six diverse industries. The questions permitted unrestricted responses, and hence the information these managers provided (summarized in *Exhibit III*) is not as clear-cut as one might wish. However, it is informative. It provides some operational perspective from EDP managers on the following topics:

- Current impressions of what a data base should be and do
- Approaches to structuring and organizing a data base
- Strategies for building a data-base system
- The assignment of responsibility for the base's scope and contents— that is, data-base administration
- The role of the data-base administrator

- Access and security

- Organizational and technical problems associated with the data-base concept

The opinions expressed on these topics varied considerably among the EDP managers I interviewed. By and large, a given manager's opinions reflected the particular stage his company had reached in the evolutionary progression toward full use of the data-base concept.

For the reader's convenience I have organized the material in *Exhibit III* in evolutionary sequence. One manufacturing company, Company 1, at the far left, has barely begun to understand and use the concept; in Company 10, at the far right, one finds a fairly sophisticated example of a data base in the operation.

Let me now discuss the topics listed, one by one, with some attention to the way the data base shapes up at various stages of its maturity.

Nature of the Data Base

First of all, I found a certain amount of confusion about what "data base" means. My open-ended question, "What is the data base in your company?" usually brought first a puzzled expression to the manager's face, and then a request for clarification. I answered that I wanted a statement on how he views his company's data base, if, indeed, he views it at all.

Responses ranged all over the lot. Some managers included all the computer-readable data in their company. Othes defined the base more narrowly—for example, as including only the random-access disc files used for routine reporting and analysis.

EXHIBIT III

Evolutionary Stages of
the Data Base

	Company 1— Manufacturing	Company 2— Public Utilities	Company 3— Banking	Company 4— Manufacturing	Company 5— Manufacturing	Company 6— Insurance	Company 7— Manufacturing	Company 8— Manufacturing	Company 9— Wholesale/ Retail Food	Company 10— Manufacturing
Evolutionary stage	Low	Low	Low-medium	Medium	Medium	Medium	Medium-advanced	Medium-advanced	Advanced	Advanced
Data-base concept	All computer-readable data	All computer-readable data	Tape and disc files	Disc files	All computer-readable data	Shared random-access files	Shared random-access files	Shared random-access files	All computer-readable data	Shared random-access files
Data-base structure	Individual applications	Individual applications	Operational, by products	Operational, by functions	Individual applications	Operational, by products	Operational, by functions	Operational, by functions	By key tasks in accounting and distribution	By key tasks in planning and manufacturing
Degree of integration across level	Minimal	Minimal	Low	High	High	Medium	High	Medium	High	High
Degree of integration between levels	Minimal	Minimal	Minimal	Minimal	Minimal	Minimal	Minimal	Low	Medium	Medium
Data-base strategy	Brute force	Brute force	Brute force	Piggyback	Key task	Piggyback	Piggyback	Piggyback	Key task	Key task
Decision maker for data-base contents and designs	Systems analyst	Systems analyst	Steering committee, with an administrative position planned	Systems analyst, with an administrative position planned	Systems analyst	Data-processing manager	Data-processing manager, with an administrative position planned	Steering committee, with an existing administrative position	Steering committee, with an existing administrative position	Data-base administrator
Personnel with direct data-base access	Programmers	Programmers	Programmers	Programmers	Programmers	Programmers	Programmers	Programmers, analysts	Programmers, analysts	Programmers, analysts

The common thread in the responses was "computer-readable." Since all the interviewees were data-processing managers, this common thread is not surprising. But, obviously, the great majority of an organization's data are noncomputer-readable; they are maintained in file cabinets as well as in the minds of management.

Although more and more data are being put into computer-readable form, as the technology improves and makes more sophisticated computer-based applications both feasible and economic, much of the literature on data bases falsely assumes that companies have already translated all the data needed for these applications into machine-readable terms. This simply has not yet happened—indeed, most companies have not even begun to collect the data needed for these applications, in machine-readable form or otherwise.

In general, the more advanced a company's use of the data-base approach, the less naive and more realistic the manager's definition of what the base ought to contain—for example, "shared random-access files used for (periodic) production programs and ad hoc management requests." Such a definition reflects the two key characteristics of the data base:

1. Sharing data between programs

2. Structuring data so that ad hoc management requests can be served

As *Exhibit III* shows, the more advanced companies conceive their data bases in this light.

One data-processing manager articulated the criterion of responsiveness to ad hoc management requests especially well. He said that his company will realize the data-base approach fully when he has incorporated the technology that will permit him to respond to any reasonable request by management for reporting or analysis within one day, and without undue degradation of his continuing data processing. He further described a reasonable request as one that draws on existing computer-readable data.

Structure and Integration

Companies 1, 2, and 5 in *Exhibit III* viewed their data base as structured under the single criterion of individual applications, in the fully traditional manner. Companies 1 and 2 had a minimal degree of cross-functional integration—that is, sharing data between such functional applications as manufacturing and accounting.

Company 5, in the middle of the spectrum, had a high degree of cross-functional integration, as *Exhibit III* shows. In my interview with its EDP manager I had been led to believe that cross-functional integration was minimal. However, further discussion with their lead systems analyst pointed to high integration. With more probing, I found out that this man had taken it on himself to design files to accommodate sharing between programs. He was quite active in the EDP professional societies and expressed strong feelings that this was the "right" approach. Still, all three of these companies had minimal sharing of data between levels of management. In fact, there were very few programs developed for management in any of the three companies.

In addition to Company 5, four other companies (4, 7, 9, and 10) indicated a high degree of cross-functional integration of their data bases, and they had very well-developed computer applications in the operations aspects of their businesses as well. But I should note a significant difference between Companies 4 and 7, and Companies 9 and 10:

Companies 4 and 7 had well-developed applications for general operational activities—accounting, distribution, and inventory control. However, these two companies had not integrated their data bases with middle and upper-middle management applications, such as sales forecasting and production planning. The EDP managers of both companies were rather strong-willed managers, who would stick to their lasts unless induced to do otherwise; and apparently their upper managements had never pressed the issue of interlevel integration.

I found quite a different situation in Companies 9 and 10. The business operations were indeed well supported by computer applications; the operational aspects related to the product flows were supported by highly developed computer applications (for example, the ordering of raw materials, sales distribution, accounting for accounts payable and receivable, and inventory control).

More significantly, however, under strong direction of upper management, the EDP managers in Companies 9 and 10 both used key-task criteria to integrate their data bases. Company 9 viewed distribution and efficient accounting for billing, product movement, and pricing as key tasks, while Company 10 viewed manufacturing and planning as the keys to the overall profitability of the company. In addition, both companies had integrated their data bases for managerial reporting and analysis with their operational data bases.

In both companies one can see the beginnings of interlevel integration—both have been ranked as "medium" on this parameter in *Exhibit III*. Interlevel integration must soon appear, after all, where planning is considered a key focus for company and data-base development, as in Company 10, and where pricing decisions are considered a key focus, as in Company 9.

Without this impetus from upper management to focus integration around key tasks, Companies 9 and 10 could never have reached the advanced stage of computer usage and data-resource management which they have attained. Management's choice of and insistence on this particular strategy was all the more fortunate, considering the popularity of other, far less viable alternatives.

Three Strategies

Thus a main characteristic of the key-task strategy is the capability to respond to management's ad hoc requests for reports and analyses. A company can pursue a couple of other strategies to satisfy such requests without recourse to the data-base concept; but the alternatives are not likely to be very successful.

These are the strategies I can identify:

- brute-force

- piggyback

- data-base/key-task

The strategy of each company interviewed is specified in *Exhibit III*; and in *Exhibit IV* I have attempted to define the three diagrammatically.

Suppose an EDP manager is suddenly given an assignment of the kind I described at the beginning of this article—that is, an ad hoc request for management information that draws across the functions and levels of the company. These are the possible ways he can do the job.

Through Brute Force. He can start from scratch, collecting all the needed data, coding them, writing special programs, and acquiring hardware capability, if it is required. The effort demanded by this approach is likely to be huge, the expense prohibitive, and the time demand wholly impossible. This approach is, as a consequence, very rarely followed.

Now, *Exhibit III* would indicate that Companies 1, 2, and 3 service ad hoc management requests through just this approach. The manager of one of these companies even stated emphatically that this approach is cheaper than any other—and notably cheaper than the data-base approach, which I shall come to presently.

However, he admitted that he has virtually never received such a request for ad hoc reporting. This is no small wonder; such a request would disrupt his department completely, and I suspect that this fact is known to upper management in the company.

The other two companies in this group, equally, have had virtually no experience and no success at all in servicing such requests. Claims for the virtues of brute force should be taken with grains of salt.

Through Piggyback. Using this strategy, the manager attempts to "ride the special project through" on more-or-less existing capabilities. What he does is strip data from existing files, structure them into a special data pool, augment this pool with new data as necessary, expand old programs and write new ones, and increase his hardware capability, if this is required. This approach has two signal disadvantages: it requires the construction of a totally redundant data pool, and, while it consumes less money and time than the brute-force technique, the money and time are still substantial indeed.

The piggyback technique is somewhat more common than the brute-force technique. Companies 4, 6, 7, and 8 have all used it, as *Exhibit III* shows. But since in every case his approach represented a special effort to obtain a special kind of information, its uses were marked by a certain narrowness and shallowness. Possible projects were limited by the quantity and nature of existing data; and the programming skills developed in these companies were not really adequate to create programs tailored to the companies' specific needs. In fact, commercially available data management systems were generally used to structure the new data pools and to generate the programs that produced the reports for management.

Through a Data-Base/Key-Task Strategy. I have already described how an EDP manager would attack the problem of a management request for information; the reader may wish to look back at the organization shown in *Exhibit II*. The diagram for data-base/key-task response in *Exhibit IV* is a close parallel to the general data-base organization, but it contains some new terms and options. To explain what these mean, let me return to a discussion of Companies 9 and 10, which have evolved furthest toward a full data-base mode of operation and have used it most successfully.

Both these companies, 9 and 10, had highly integrated data bases, as I remarked before. These bases were structured according to the companies' key tasks, and were sufficiently developed so that the companies could use commercial data-base software packages. They used one software package for data organization, defining records and files to support multiple applications (the General Interface System of *Exhibit II*), and a different software package to produce ad hoc management reports and analyses (the Interface System for Special Applications in *Exhibit II*).

Both data-processing managers were reasonably satisfied with the commercial software they were using. Nevertheless, they both com-

EXHIBIT IV (continued on pg. 108)

Three Strategies for Responding to
Ad Hoc Requests

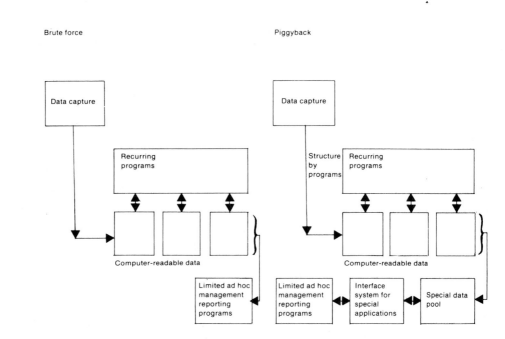

EXHIBIT IV (continued)

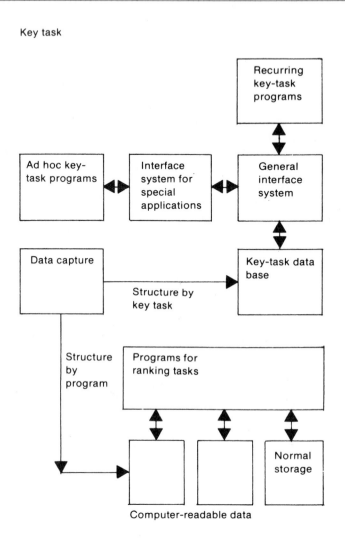

Key task

mented that even the most sophisticated data-base software commercially available did not incorporate the more advanced data-structure methods. Such methods coordinate theoretical data structures (for example, things resembling immense decision trees) with the access constraints of physical storage devices, such as rotating magnetic discs. Suffice it to say that data organization is extremely complex and technical.

It is so complex, in fact, that one is virtually forced into using commercial software. One of the data-processing managers stated that structure technology is so complex today that he could not possibly support an in-house effort to develop the software. The other manager had initially hoped to develop his own data-base software, but, after a preliminary investigation of the costs and problems, he decided to acquire a commercially available package.

However, this complexity ultimately derives from the nature of the key tasks for which top management wants the data base to be used. If upper management focuses on key tasks that embrace all the company's data and require very extensive vertical and horizontal integration of reports and analyses, the job of organizing the data base is tougher than when the key tasks embrace only a part of the data and require less than the complete integration of all functions.

In addition, my interviews led me to a conclusion that may be directly useful to top and senior managers, as they set their sights on the issue of data-base organization: the more closely related the functional uses of the data, the easier it is to design a nonredundant, integrated data base. For example, Company 10, which structured its data base on the key tasks of planning and manufacturing, seemed to be incurring fewer problems in data-base design than Company 9, which structured its data base on the key tasks of accounting/distribution.

The planning/manufacturing structure used by Company 10 focused on vertical integration of the data base. Its manufacturing data were organized at the operations or transaction level; many of the planning data were obtained by summarizing the manufacturing data. The data base was designed to explicitly accommodate the information needs of different levels of management. Also, there was a strong linkage between organizational objectives and use of the data resource through a computer-based planning model. The model provided continuing guidelines for determining important data to be collected at the manufacturing level.

On the other hand, the accounting/distribution structure used by Company 9 required integration of data from two functional areas at the operational level. Although the structure reflected information flow, it did not explicitly recognize middle-management information needs. Thus there was not a continuing source of guidelines and benchmarks for determining which data and which analyses were important, as there were for Company 10.

Generally, then, the data-base/key-task strategy is more effective than brute force and piggyback because it forces cross-functional and interlevel integration in a manner that will suit upper management's needs. For its part, once it has decided that this strategy is the right one, upper management must take a careful look at what it considers its key tasks and make sure that it has settled on the ones that make sense for the company and are clearly understood by the EDP personnel responsible for structuring and maintaining the data base.

Let me return for a moment to the key-task diagram in *Exhibit IV*. This diagram makes provision for the fact that some applications, ad hoc or otherwise, may be remote from the key tasks of the business. If such applications are really required, and if they are really remote from the organizing principles used to structure the data base, a company can always have recourse to special files and special programs, in the traditional fashion. However, it seems clear enough that a company that wants to follow the data-base/key-task concept and at the same time succumbs to the temptation to create a "special" or tangential application every time it needs a new program may find that it is doing neither effectively.

Data-Base Administration

In addition to good decisions on data structure and organization, good decisions on what information will be included in a company's data base are central to the successful use of the concept. The total sum of data must be usefully large—but not ungovernably large, or the system will collapse under its own weight.

In all ten companies I studied, the systems analysts responsible for the various user areas initiated all requests to develop new sets of data or to change old ones. However, the processing of the requests varied considerably:

- Companies 1 and 2, still in the early stages of data-base development, permitted the individual systems analysts to decide what files would be developed and how they should be structured for different applications. These companies had not yet begun to consider data independently from the programs for which they were collected and coded.

- Companies 4 and 5 were just becoming aware of the need to separate data from applications and to recognize a "data resource function," but the systems analyst was still the primary decision maker.

- Companies 3, 6, and 7 assigned decisions on what data should be maintained to a higher and more centralized authority than the systems analysts—namely, to the data-processing manager or to the EDP steering committee.

- Companies 8, 9, and 10 had advanced to the stage at which they had formal data-base administrators who played a central role in monitoring the content and standards of the data base. In these companies, a request for data for a particular application was studied from a number of viewpoints: necessity, redundancy, cost/benefit, procurement methods, EDP planning, and so forth. These analyses had become sufficiently specialized to give rise to another formal administrative position—data-base analyst.

The Role of the Administrator

Exhibit III shows that data-base administrators actually exist in three companies—8, 9, and 10—and that Companies 3, 4, and 7 plan to fill such a position in the foreseeable future (in two to five years).

However, in none of these cases has the company fully delineated the administrator's exact responsibilities or authority. Companies seem to agree that the administrator should concentrate his energies in the areas of planning and designing the data base; and they seem to view the administrator as a useful focal point from which the whole issue of computer data can be viewed as an integrated whole. Too often companies have waked to find a plethora of fractured repositories of data scattered all over the organization.

I might note also that EDP managers with purely technical backgrounds often want to include all possible data—the president's personal files, traffic rates, and so on—in the data base, whereas managers with some executive experience in broader areas tend to take a more realistic view of the elements that ought to be included in a company's working library of data. I have argued elsewhere for the wisdom of injecting the broader managerial viewpoint into EDP department decision making.[1]

The interview discussions on the data-base administrator's responsibilities raised an interesting dichotomy. In the comments on what the responsibilities should be, data were talked about as a corporate resource. In the comments on what the responsibilities actually are, data were viewed merely as computer-readable items.

However, this dichotomy really should not be surprising. The data resource function is being carved out of the general management function. Specialization in data associated with computers is warranted at this time; the conditions for specialization exist.

But the activities for managing data as a corporate resource have not yet developed to the point where specialization is warranted. Senior management within the EDP department can still carry out these activities better than can a specialist.[2] I have already pointed out upper management's responsibility to give guidance on key tasks. Moreover, since the data-base administrator represents a relatively rare, advanced stage of development in the data resource function, it behooves top management to supervise this area closely.

A Note on Access. *Exhibit III* shows that the groups that either directly or indirectly had access to the data base are programmers and analysts. None of the companies provided either managers or their analysts direct access to the data base. Companies 8, 9, and 10 provided an indirect access for analysts through a data management system. Here the analyst communicated a request to a programmer who, in turn, used the data management system to obtain a rapid response.

In all the other companies I studied, the analyst and manager were forced to work through the process of satisfying their needs through a programmer. This process will be changed and greatly simplified as the quality of interface software improves.

Organizational and Technical Issues

The EDP managers expressed concern over these major organizational issues associated with the data base:

● Acquiring personnel that can handle its technical aspects

---

[1]See my article, *"Plight of the EDP Manager,"* HBR May-June 1973, p. 143.
[2]John Dearden, *"MIS Is a Mirage,"* HBR January-February 1972, p. 90.

- Funding and developing suitable chargeout systems to support it
- Setting and enforcing companywide standards
- Using the data resource to best advantage

The major associated technical issues for which they expressed concern were these:

- Converting data to data-base form
- Providing appropriate software for the interfaces
- Designing a data base which will permit ad hoc responsiveness without degrading normal computer processing
- Building in reliability and the ability to reconstruct lost data

Both the organizational issues and the technical issues were greatly felt to be of such magnitude that aggressive action on implementing the data-base concept fully was not warranted at the time. The consensus was that the concept is sound, but that much more needs to be done administratively before it can be effectively realized in practice.

WHAT SHOULD MANAGEMENT DO?

Use of the data-base concept is the next natural milestone in the evolution of EDP applications. It embraces the specialization of EDP functions; it allows management real flexibility in satisfying its need for information; and it permits companies to view and use their data as a real resource. Yet caution and patience are advised in pursuing the concept. What should managers do to deal with this push-and-pull condition?

1. Take the idea seriously. Upper management should provide direction to the EDP manager by identifying key tasks of the business and setting priorities for an improved information capability. Perhaps the single most important factor that permitted Companies 9 and 10 to break out of a parochial treatment of data was upper management's guidance and its insistence on exploiting data for the interests of the business.

2. Set up a data administration function. The issue is when to set up a data administration function, rather than whether to have such a function. Ultimately, an administrator will be needed to implement the data-base concept, anyway. For those companies currently without such a position, an administrative structure is needed for formulating a data-base implementation, and establishing data-base standards, controls, and access procedures. At a minimum, a data-base specialist should be acquired now to provide decision-making guidance for the EDP manager and steering committee. This person can also provide guidance in evaluating and selecting appropriate software.

3. Incorporate data-base technology into the computer system. The hardware technology, as well as the software technology, for data bases has matured to the point that the data-base concept can be both feasible and cost-effective for many orgainzations. While the company will not be noticeably hurt in the short run by ignoring data-base technology, it will in the longer run.

Also, the data-base concept cannot be implemented overnight. If a company begins to plan and act now, it can assimilate even drastic technological improvements into its existing systems in a slow, comfortable, and orderly fashion.

To incorporate the technology that will permit data-base operations, an organization must identify its key computer-based systems and restructure them to remove redundancy and to facilitate their use by higher levels of management. For the present, companies must probably acquire commercial software for structuring data and responding to management requests for ad hoc analyses and reports.

4. Think of data as a resource. For the longer term, management should begin to think of data as a basic resource. It should accept this idea as a natural consequence of functional specialization of the general management function. Since the data-resource concept is closely associated with a fast-moving computer technology, management should expect to see the movement toward specialized data-management activities proceed at a faster rate than, say, specializations in the human resource function. My survey of the ten companies indicates that the emergence of the data-base administrator is a key event in the specialization.

5. Estimate your own company's position in the evolutionary sequence. If you find that your company is still at a rudimentary stage of development, plan for development. If your company is fairly advanced, press forward a little harder. The only thing to lose is redundancy.

What Kind of Corporate Modeling Functions Best?*

ROBERT H. HAYES
RICHARD L. NOLAN

A friend came to us recently with a typical predicament. He would soon give a talk on corporate planning to a group of businessmen and wished to say something about corporate models. However, he did not know of any cases where a corporate model had been successful. All he knew about were "disasters." He wanted a success story or two to balance the picture. Could we help? We were not sure.

WHAT IS A 'SUCCESS'?

To date there is no consensus on what constitutes a successful corporate model. In fact, the history of corporate modeling—that is, of providing formal images of whole companies—reveals many efforts that were unsuccessful by any measure. For this reason, businessmen generally regard corporate modeling with considerable skepticism; hence the defensive attitude of corporate modelers. However, our friend described a "success" as a fairly detailed corporate model that has been used for at least a couple of years to help senior managers make strategic decisions. His success criterion focused directly on the model itself, as complex, integrated, and relatively static. He visualized it as distinct from the corporate decision-making process it was designed to serve.

This criterion, while pragmatic enough, ignores the fact that a model is and can only be part of a broader process for management decision-making and development. It must fit that process; and as the process evolves, so must the model. A simple process requires a simple model; a changing process requires a flexible model. Consequently, trying to identity the inherent characteristics of a corporate model that is "successful" according to our friend's definition is wrongheaded.

Some very inelegant models, which we consider successful because they have evolved and been integrated into a management decision-making process, might be rejected as failures by our aforementioned friend either because of their simplicity or because they evolved over a period of time. In some of these cases the original model was scrapped entirely and a new one developed to fit the particular management process in question. To us, it is the process that is important, not the model.

Granted this criterion, a more optimistic picture of the present and future of corporate modeling emerges. While the past has indeed been grim, it has taught us some extremely valuable lessons about what models, modelers, and corporate modeling can, and cannot, be and do.

Exhibit I shows the three distinct periods through which corporate modeling has progressed. The most salient feature characterizing each period is the particular management approach to modeling that was used:

- bottom-up

- top-down

- inside-out

To appreciate the lessons of the past two decades, one has to analyze the environment in which each corporate modeling period flourished and the changes in this environment that led to the onset of a new period. The current period, characterized by the inside-out approach, appears likely to be the longest period yet, and a successful one at that.

FROM THE BOTTOM UP: 1956-1963

The bottom-up approach to corporate modeling can be characterized by the phrase "corporate modeling as an afterthought." It began with the first commercial use of computers in the mid-1950s. Businessmen were then presented with a powerful new tool that not only promised to increase the speed and reduce the cost of much clerical work, but would also allow them to attempt things that had never been possible previously.

Automating clerical work was a manageable task: the manager could always compare the output of the computer with the output of the previously existent operation, and he needed to defer to the computer specialist only on matters of machine efficiency and speed. Because early computers

EXHIBIT I

The Characteristics of the
Major Periods of Corporate Modeling

Design approach	Period	Prevailing computer technology	Feasible applications	Modelers	Major focus of attention	Major fallacy	Lessons learned
Bottom-up	1956–1963	Second generation: batch processing high-level programming languages	Corporate models designed and implemented by technically oriented personnel	Operations researchers	The model	Models of operating processes can be utilized as planning tools	1 Planning models are different from operating models 2 Operations researchers ("outsiders") do not understand the management decision-making process well enough to build general models
Top-down	1964–1969	Third generation: disk storage time sharing model programming languages	Large models (both in size and in data required) easier to build with special languages	Management scientists and systems analysts	The model	Large, "realistic" models are required for planning, and can be responsive to decision making	1 Large models are relatively inflexible 2 Large models overwhelm the manager's ability to understand the assumptions of the model and to integrate its output into the decision-making process
Inside-out	1970–present	Third-plus generation: mass low-cost storage data bases teleprocessing minicomputers	More efficient use of corporate data Sharing data and programs among geographical areas	Ad hoc project team: managers, systems analysts, management scientists	The process	Undetected, but doubtless there	1 The manager must be intimately involved in the model-building process 2 Simple models are usually the way to start 3 The model should evolve in complexity or size as required by the decision-maker, and at *his* pace

were difficult to use, the priority issue was simple enough: how to master the machine to do traditional chores better.[1]

However, once early success at improving routine tasks—like payroll and accounts receivable—began to whet management's appetite for new horizons in the use of computer technology, the trouble began. Manage-

---

[1] For a lucid discussion of the main concerns of organizations in the use of computers, see Robert I. Benjamin, "*A Generational Perspective of Information Development*," Communications of the ACM, July 1972, p. 640.

ment information systems and corporate planning models were hovering in the midst of the future, it seemed, but who was to lead the manager into the unknown? Who was there to even tell him which unknowns were conquerable?

The only people available were the same computer specialists who had played such supportive roles in automating the familiar tasks. Who were they? Generally, people with mathematical or scientific backgrounds, often with some training in the (then new) field of "operations research," seldom with much business training or experience. They tended to regard the computer with a mixture of awe, affection, and scientific curiosity. In leading the manager by the hand into the unknown, they tended to choose those applications and problems that would cause the computer to shine most brightly and that would stretch its capabilities, and theirs, to the maximum.

One direction they chose was to develop computer "models" of various aspects of the business and to analyze the behavior of those models under various assumptions, through simulation. Usually the parts of the company that were chosen for modeling were operating units: a plant, a distribution center, or even a department within a larger unit.

There were several reasons for this early emphasis on operating models:

- Operations researchers had developed a number of effective frameworks for analyzing operational processes.

- Operating units are very often structured sufficiently well to permit the quantification of their important activities.

- Operating units are relatively easy to observe, and the kind of quantitative data required in the construction of a computer model is generally either already available or easy to obtain.

- The events that occur in operating units are fairly predictable, and many of the decision procedures that were being used at that time for responding to these events could be readily translated into computer programs.

- These events usually occur with such frequency that the operations manager is under continual pressure to respond; hence he is often delighted at the prospect of a computer providing him assistance in the analysis and resolution of these repetitive and pressure-laden problems.

- In manufacturing, where most of these early attempts at modeling were made, the manager usually had an engineering background that made him appreciative of the capabilities of the computer and also allowed him to communicate easily with the computer programmer.

Hence it appeared to be possible for someone without extensive business training, but with some scientific detachment and good powers of observation, to develop an adequate operating model.

Disaster by Addition

Once an operating model had been demonstrated to senior management, someone, in the flush of enthusiasm, was bound to ask how and when such a model could be adapted to provide information for corporate planning purposes. The reasoning seemed impeccable:

1. If a company can develop a model for one function, such as plant operations, then a company can develop a model for all functions of the plant (plant operations, purchasing, accounting, personnel, and so forth).

2. If a company can develop a model for all functions of one plant, it can develop a model for all the plants.

3. If a company puts all these models together and adds a "corporate functions" model to them, then presto—a corporate model will emerge. (Such a model, of course, will require "a slightly larger computer" than the existing one.)

Impeccable through this reasoning appeared, it simply did not work. Attempts to build corporate models in this fashion, from the bottom of the company upward, led to incredible Frankenstein monsters which fortunately died before they could do much harm. For example:

- A large, integrated wood-products company successfully used a computer model to improve the performance of one of its sawmills in the early 1960s. Then it developed similar models for other plants, and attempted to coordinate and optimize the activities of a group of plants. Next, using this coordinated, "optimized" model as a base, the company tried to develop, evaluate, and compare alternative long-range plans. The pyramid of operating models began to crumble as more and more were added, and it collapsed completely when the new burden of long-range planning was added. Today this company has largely abandoned computer planning models.

- A major defense contractor developed a computer model (essentially a job-shop simulator) at one plant to help coordinate and expedite the job flow and improve delivery estimates. The model was quite effective as long as it was used for these purposes, but its extension to long-range planning so discredited it in the eyes of management that it was eventually abandoned as an operating tool.

A note on budget

A 1971 Diebold & Company survey of computer budget expenditures indicates that large companies allocate about 2% of their computer budget to corporate modeling.✳ The companies in the survey had computer budgets that ranged from less than 0.5% to over 2% of sales. Another study of the modeling activities of 36 medium-sized and large companies indicates that they account for up to 10%

of the total computer budget.† Some very well managed companies are spending close to a million dollars a year on modeling.

✶Expenditure Patterns for Corporate Information Systems—1971, The Diebold Group, Inc., 1971.
†Richard L. Nolan, "Strategic Simulation as a Process: Using the Computer in Major Business Decisions," unpublished reaerch study, Harvard Business School, 1974.

In retrospect, the reasons for these disasters are obvious. Operating models—which embrace a variety of inputs, operations, and outputs, and where events occur and decisions are made almost continuously—must contain a wealth of detail. In those days the amount of programming detail and data required for even a simple job-shop simulator was substantial; for a distribution network it was incredible; for a whole complex of plants and distribution centers it was simply infeasible. By the time all the data required to run such a model had been collected, they were out of date, and new data were required.

Faced with such a dismal Sisyphean task, the corporate modeler did exactly what any sane person would do in a similar situation—he made a game out of it. The game was to continuously polish the model, adding "realism" and "precision" to it. Thereby, he was able to pass off his efforts as "research." The fruits of this research were reported to his colleagues through the various professional journals that sprang up during this period.

As the game continued and the model became more complex and sophisticated, more information was required to operate the model, it took longer to produce results, and it was used less frequently. And not only was the output which it generated dissimilar to the actual operating results of the company, but there was often no way to ascertain where and why this divergence existed. The model, in time, became an end in itself.

After a year or so of funding this kind of nonsense, companies quietly dispatched both the model and the modelers; only a stack of boxes filled with punched cards was left to molder quietly in some dark corner. These lessons, however, emerged from the bottom-up period:

1. Operating models are not planning models. The kind of information required is different, procedures are different, and the output required is different.

2. Planning models cannot be built by specialists who are not familiar with the company and its planning process. Knowledge of why and how planning is actually accomplished is necessary.

FROM THE TOP DOWN: 1964-1969

By the mid-1960s, then, the bottom-up approach had fallen into a much deserved disrepute. Meanwhile, a new generation of computers had arrived. They were faster, had larger capacities for storing and retrieving data, and functioned with higher level, user-oriented computer languages. These technological improvements provided a major impetus to corporate modeling activity; one survey indicates that 28 out of 36 companies studied initiated corporate modeling efforts after 1964.[2]

In addition, the increased use of computers in organizations induced specialization among computer personnel and associated groups. Some of these people called themselves management scientists, others, systems analysts, but they all tended to be more aware of practical management problems than their predecessors.

They were also more familiar with the advantages and limitations of the use of computers in organizations. Systems analysts had become conscious that operations models are not usually appropriate for addressing planning problems, and had begun to develop a better understanding of the organizational contexts in which information-gathering and planning take place. They knew by now that the manner in which the enterprise organizes to collect information often determines the kind of planning activity that is possible.

However, the biggest change took place in the echelons of upper management. Somehow—through friends and associates, through books and articles, through speeches and seminars, and through their own inability to deal effectively with a world that was changing faster than ever before—these upper managers "got the faith." A planning model became not just an interesting possibility, one that could be classified as a kind of basic research from which no immediate usefulness was anticipated, but an absolute necessity.

Disaster by Decree

In the pursuit of a competitive advantage (and the "modern image" that publicity about the company's corporate model would engender), upper managements sent forth orders to "create a corporate planning model." This is what we mean by the top-down approach. Earlier corporate modeling experiences were discounted because of lack of commitment, poor technique, or some other equally superficial explanation, and top mnanagement directed that a new start on a global model be made.

The first response to this decree was usually the establishment of a corporate modeling group, generally as a subunit within the corporate planning department, but often reporting directly to a senior officer. The people staffing these departments were a mixed breed; some were old-time operations researchers, some were professional planners who were wise in the ways of the corporate jungle, and some were of the new breed of management scientist, often fresh out of business school. Created by fiat, grafted awkwardly onto the organization chart, and peopled largely

---

[2]Richard L. Nolan, *"Strategic Simulation as a Process: Using the Computer in Major Business Decisions,"* unpublished research study, Harvard Business School, 1974.

by outsiders, such groups were often resented by existing personnel right from the outset.

Suspicions were further aroused by such a group's initial activities. Rather than ask what kind of model was wanted (because nobody really knew), the members attempted to capture in a computer program whatever planning process the corporation was currently using. This required that various people in the organization submit to a rather lengthy interview in which they were asked to describe the decisions they were responsible for, their methods of obtaining the information used to make those decisions, their individual decision-making processes, and the systems by which they transmitted their decisions to those farther down the line.

Nothing, of course, could be more threatening to a middle manager at the staff level, who, on paper, may not appear to do work of very much significance, and who has recurring nightmares about being displaced by a computer. The same is true of a line manager, who is usually already burdened by staff people poking their noses into things they know very little about. Their reactions, almost invariably, were to misinform, either by omission, inaccuracy, or exaggeration. Even those that took the effort seriously found it difficult to respond to such glib questions as: How do you make decisions? (As some have pointed out, this question may be impossible for the manager to answer.[3])

Having collected this information with all the intensity and devotion of priests trying to extract the future from the entrails of animals, the corporate modeling group retreated to its aluminum tower and began to build its model. And what a model it was! This time it was the budgetary process and the flows of funds and resources throughout the company that got the major attention, but the result was the same:

- The model required incredible amounts of data, the useful life of which was often less than the collection period required.

- The model took a long time to run, and it produced piles of output that nobody bothered to look at.

Such models produced another stream of articles, speeches, and comments in trade journals. One such model, for a large petroleum company, was initiated with a team of qualified planners, management scientists, and MBAs. Design efforts began with high level meetings to decide what level of detail would be appropriate for the model, whether optimization or simulation techniques should be used, whether the model should be probabilistic or deterministic, and what data should be collected. Unfortunately, what the model was actually going to be used for was never stated very clearly. As the project continued, support dwindled, and four years later a merger permitted the model to die a merciful death.

---

[3]Russel L. Ackoff, *Management Misinformation Systems,* Management Science, December 1967, p. B-147.

Another such model, for an aerospace company, was championed by the vice president for corporate planning. A team designed a four-module model, comprising a manpower module, a facilities module, an overhead module, and a financial module. The need for and purpose of these modules was clear: to permit analysis of the impact of various contracts and programs on the company's resources. The model was developed, but it proved incredibly difficult to use because of its size and inflexibility. The staff was just unable to keep the model up to date, or utilize it as a planning tool.

History Repeated

History seemed to have repeated itself; the result of the second corporate modeling approach was the same as for the first approach. The corporate model was a myth. It was built by nonmanagers who had no clear concept of how its output was to be used to resolve specific problems, or by whom. By and large, nobody within the corporation had a vested interest in its success, except the modelers themselves. It took so long to build (on the order of two or three years), that by the time it was ready to be demonstrated, its original justification had largely evaporated, as had many of the people who willed its creation. These were the lessons of the period:

1. Top-management commitment to a corporate model is not enough; the managers must actually understand the model.

2. Large, all-inclusive, corporate models pose formidable design and data problems. Moreover, they are almost impossible to understand, except for the people who created them.

The time was then the late 1960s, and the recessionary profit squeeze was on. In many corporations, a new head of corporate planning appeared and was given the mandate to "streamline the operation." Most of the people originally involved in building the model had drifted away, attracted by opportunities to build new and better models for other companies or consulting firms. The corporate model, already infirm, was quietly dispatched, and the new planning director now appeared at corporate planning conferences to give speeches with titles like "The life and death of a corporate model"—addressing the populace over the tyrant's dead body, as it were. Exit the corporate planning model, an unworkable idea condemned by its own naivete to an early demise.

Or so it seemed.

FROM THE INSIDE OUT: 1970-?

During the past five years computers have become much more accessible and easy to use. Teleprocessing, time sharing, and user-oriented languages (such as BASIC and APL) now enable managers and analysts to use the computer directly; it is no longer necessary to work through intermediaries such as computer specialists, data processing department managers, operations research staffs, planning departments, or whatever.

Nor do managers have to rely on others to decide what their problems are and to define the nature of their solutions. They now have direct access to the power of the computer and to canned programs for many of the simple things they need (for example, breakeven analyses, cash flow projections, and market segment analyzers). Without a conscious effort—without even realizing what is happening—many corporations have begun to use the computer to actually develop plans. This is what we call the inside-out approach, and it is in full, if unheralded, swing right now:

- A typical example of the inside-out approach is an interactive budgeting model recently developed for a large commercial bank. The president of the bank had routinely used the budgets of the bank's divisions for control purposes and as a basis for determining bonuses. Consequently, the management of each division had devoted considerable time to these budgets and plans, as well as to analyzing the impact that various business alternatives would have on their budgets.

    Then a young MBA went to work for the bank as assistant vice president; within a year he had automated the budget spread sheet preparation for his division, using a computer time-sharing service. Soon the budgetary and planning process had been automated for all the divisions. The model has continued to evolve through the addition of features such as "trend history" files for revenues and expenses, and statistical tools for analysis and forecasting.

- A second example is provided by the development of the AAIMS interactive planning system at American Airlines. In much the same way as the interactive budgeting system was started at the bank, AAIMS was initiated by some planners who needed computer assistance with their tasks.

    By automating their procedure for assembling forecasts from all parts of the company through a modern programming language (APL), and by designing their key files so that they could be shared among programs, these planners reduced the time required for first-cut planning by 61%. They were then able to shift their major efforts from clerical preparation tasks to "what if?" analyses—of alternative schedules, routings, expense patterns, and the like. (As an added benefit, more and more MS techniques are being assimilated into the company's planning.) Now AAIMS is widely used throughout the company.

These models are not "corporate models," in what has become the conventional connotation of the term—namely, a model that encompasses the strategic planning function of the corporation. Such a model is clearly infeasible; yet this was the illusory objective (although not usually expressly stated) of corporate modeling in the first two periods.

The models resulting from the inside-out approach are designed to exploit the use of the computer within the planning function. Often they simply duplicate activities that had previously been carried on manually. But they respond to genuine, specific needs and are being used intelligently; their output is having an impact on corporate planning decisions. In effect, the inside-out approach has reconciled the requirements of the computer modeling process with those of the corporate planning process.

Why is this Approach Best?

First, decisions are made by people, often while working together in an unstructured fashion. The process by which alternatives are formulated, refined, analyzed, pruned, resolved, and, finally, sold to others is a lengthy and complex one. Seldom does an important corporate decision ever emerge automatically and stand on its own merits; it must be nurtured and defended, often in a hostile environment. And it needs at least one powerful champion—someone who believes in it strongly enough to devote major effort to its acceptance.

No computer can provide this kind and quality of advocacy. Nor will any manager be likely to take on the role of champion unless he believes in both the decision and the analytical process that supports it. Therefore, at best, a computer can take only a secondary role in the decision-making process. Moreover, the computer model must be closely tailored to the person who will use it and assume responsibility for its advocacy. It must make sense to him, and, above all, it must not threaten him.

This sounds obvious, but it lays waste a large part of the conventional wisdom that has surrounded corporate models until recently. For example, it calls into question the validity of "realism" in a model (at least to the extent that "realistic" is equated with "detailed"). What is important is not that the model contain a complete, or even a correct, representation of reality, but that it matches the manager's (or company's) own understanding of the reality that exists. We must replace the concept of "realism" with the concepts of "adequate" and "useful."

Moreover, this viewpoint calls into question the whole concept of a general model—that is, one that can be used by a variety of people for a variety of purposes over a long period of time. Problems, and the environment, change with time. Further, different people look at these problems in different ways and require different kinds of information and different forms of output. A corporate model that attempts to appeal to too many people and address too many problems will often represent an unworkable compromise, too simple to achieve wide credibility, yet too complex to be easily used, updated, and explained. In addition, such models take too long to develop. Models whose expected useful life is only two or three years should certainly require no more than half a year, total, to be created.

Finally, managers are beginning to realize that the real value of a model comes not just from using it, but from creating it. Just as a person advances his understanding of a situation under the tutelage of experience, so does his understanding evolve during the modeling process. Over 50% of the value comes from "getting there"; a model provides an opportunity to gain synthetic experience. As the model is developed and used, it will begin to challenge implicit assumptions of the user and to suggest opportunities for improvement. Hence a good corporate model is not only a decision-making aid, but also a powerful educating and developing tool for management.

Lessons of the Period

Three important facts have emerged from this stage of corporate modeling:

1. The manager must be involved in the process of developing the model. Not only does this ensure that he understands the model and is aware of its shortcomings, so that he is not tempted to make stronger claims than are justified, but it becomes a factor in his own development as a manager.

2. Simple models are best at the outset. One should start with something simple and begin working with it as soon as possible. Often the first model will be based largely on intuition. But as experience is gained, a richer understanding emerges, the level of detail increases as required, and the model becomes more comprehensible and explicable; hence it is more useful for the advocate. Moreover, simplicity tends to ensure that the model's development time will not exceed its expected lifetime.

3. Models (plural), not a single model, are involved in the corporate modeling process. The models should be responsive to the requirements of the problems at hand and should effectively exploit the computer and the modeling resources available.

INHERENT PROBLEMS

Ironically, however, one thing is clear. The facilities and infrastructure that most companies have created to assist the development of more formal corporate models will probably work against the inside-out approach. In our work with companies we have been struck repeatedly by the uneasiness that our work, and even our presence, has created among the resident management scientists. Rather than regarding us as promoters and champions of their efforts, they often regard us as betrayers and usurpers.

In all fairness, in some cases they have proved to be rightly suspicious— it did not require a blazing intellect to determine that some of these people were contributing nothing of value to their companies. Nevertheless, in most cases we were there to encourage and enlarge their activity. Why then do they regard the inside-out approach as a threat? To answer this question, one must look at the typical backgrounds of the people who staff these departments and at the ways these departments are funded.

First, planning departments are ordinarily staffed by professional planners; OR departments, by professional operations researchers; and corporate modeling departments, by professional modelers. These people have special training in the techniques and theories associated with their particular disciplines. They tend to be analyzers, observers, conceptualizers—and outsiders. Their role is usually defined as "in-house consultant." They are rarely intimately familiar with their organizations, nor do they have close working relationships with many of their organizations' line managers. In fact, they tend to work most comfortably and effectively with each other, not with managers.

As a result, they usually prefer to work in teams, relatively isolated from the organizational problems being dealt with. Their only contact with the managers involved generally consists of a rather limited and sterile dialogue. First, there is an initial attempt to understand the problem. Next, some clarifying questions are raised during the course of their analysis. Finally, a formal report is submitted.

As far as funding is concerned, these departments are usually set up as cost centers. The problems associated with assigning costs to projects increases, of course, as do the overhead costs associated with manning and scheduling people's time. Moreover, it is much easier to garner publicity, assign rewards, and negotiate for higher budgets for the following year if the projects are large and highly visible. So, in the natural course of events, a few large projects tend to be preferred to many smaller projects.

Hence most of these departments, because of the inclinations of the people in them and the type of budgetary and control process they are subject to, tend to work on major projects in teams of several people, over long periods of time. Then administration is easy, specialization is possible, training is provided by the team/project orientation, and "career paths" are identifiable. Further, the chances of some sort of perceived success are higher because such projects take so long and are so demanding of resources that the company tends to become psychologically committed to them. In consequence, the initial reaction to their completion is generally favorable.

Under these conditions, it is not surprising that most management scientists feel threatened. Their teamwork-oriented methods, their relative isolation from the rest of the organization, and their quasicynical attitude toward funding and the other organizational pressures that bear on long-term, highly complicated projects are antipathetic to the inside-out approach, which is geared toward simplicity and management involvement.

HOW TO BEGIN

A manager who wants to try this technique needs someone who can offer advice on how to translate a decision process into a computer model; on how such a model might be structured so as to make maximum use of the company's data base; and on how it would relate to others that are being developed. But this adviser needs to be an insider, one who is familiar with the organization and its personnel and who shares the interests of the manager as well as the technician.

To make the inside-out approach work, therefore, the corporate modeling department should be comprised of a few high-caliber people who work informally with a number of managers on an on-going basis. They must have a variety of skills, both managerial and technical, since one of their functions is to recognize the interrelationships between their clients' activities and what is going on in the rest of the organization. Project proposals and funding, except in a very informal sense, are simply not appropriate responsibilities for this kind of group.

Such people might come from a consulting firm—but only if that firm has a long-standing, retainer-like relationship with the company in question, and only if it is understood that the specific consultants will be assigned to this activity over a period of several years. More likely, however, these people will come from within the company itself.

And where would the company get such people? The following scenario seems likely, in our opinion:

A young man—or woman—joins the company and works in two or more line positins over the course of five years or so. At this point he is identified as a "comer," and the process of grooming for higher responsibility begins. He is given a new job in a functional area with which he is not familiar. Once he has a broad grounding in the overall activities of his company, he takes part in a management development program, of which instruction in both planning and the use of computer models is an integral part.

His charge, on returning home from the program, is to develop some simple computer models to aid the decision-making or planning activities he performed in his previous positions. He is also transferred to a special "planning consultant" group, where he is then freed from the day-to-day distractions of line management. This assignment lasts a predetermined time, perhaps a year. While he is with this group, he is also asked to serve as a consultant of the type we described. His ability to inspire confidence and work effectively with those who request his assistance will be one of the bases for his performance evaluation when the time comes for him to be reassigned.

The specific progression is not the most important feature of this scenario. The really valuable points are:

● That assignment to such a group is regarded as a natural and attractive step in a person's career path.

● That highly capable people are appointed to that group.

● That these people are regarded by the organization as having special assignments, rather than as being permanent specialists.

The funding of such a project should be modest, because excessive funding tends to create a dysfunctional pressure: more modeling might be done, but there will be less real commitment to it.

Achieving full utilization of the computer resource in the planning process under this approach will be a rather long process, probably taking a minimum of five years. We regret to say that no shortcuts appear to be available.

Perhaps once a "critical mass" of modeling has been accomplished and models have achieved a certain amount of credibility in an organization, the process will speed up considerably.

THE ISSUE OF URGENCY

Corporate modeling is emerging from adolescence and approaching maturity as a top management tool. As with many other innovations, it was introduced too quickly, sold too enthusiastically to people who had neither the inclination nor the experience to use it effectively, and then debunked and discredited too emphatically. But in the process of compiling a rather dismal ledger of errors, we have learned much. More important, a cadre of experienced, computer-wise managers has been created. Today models are being used pragmatically and effectively in corporate planning and decision-making processes.

However, there still appear to be so many potential pitfalls associated with corporate modeling that many senior managers may question the advisability of getting involved with it at this time. "Wouldn't a wait-and-see strategy be advisable?" We argue no for two reasons:

First, the cost of the inside-out approach is minimal, and the returns can be great. This approach enables the manager to probe tough strategic planning problems—involving markets, products, technologies, and competitive tactics—more deeply and comprehensively than ever before. Moreover, models serve as effective integrative mechanisms; they focus the attention of a number of different people—line managers, planners, and analysts—on a common problem and a common set of data and facilitate communication among them. The value of the model as a communication and educational device is probably as great as its value as a decision aid.

Second, the growth of technology and technological sophistication in management is quickening. There will be more progress in the use of computer models in the next five years than there has been in the past fifteen, for a couple of reasons:

- The cost of computer logic and storage devices has been reduced by more than half every three to five years, and within the next few years it promises to shrink even more rapidly. Consider the hand calculator. Three years ago it cost $250 and few executives used it routinely; two years from now it will cost $25 and almost all executives will use it.

Measuring either by cost or by expertise required, the step from hand calculators to desktop computers and communication terminals is not much greater than the step from the scratch pad to the hand calculator.

- The technology of building computer data bases, through which the basic data about a company's operations can be assessed and used by a computer model, is now available; in five years many organizations will have developed this kind of base. Management will use these bases in precisely the kind of context represented by the inside-out model.

Nothing will ever replace experience and good judgment. But in a competitive arena that is becoming increasingly skill-laden there will be many management teams with experience and good judgment. As has always been the case, success will be a matter of determination and willingness to innovate. Modeling is an idea whose time has come. The technology is here; the cost is down; the people are available. How much longer can one afford to wait?

Orders of
Office Automation

RICHARD L. NOLAN

The Applications Portfolio describes the *automatable* functions of the organization. It is fixed in that a given portfolio may be used to establish a relatively long-term data processing plan and to monitor the progress of that plan. However, in reality, the Applications Portfolio is a balance sheet. It is based upon the conditions within an organization and within the data processing industry at a given point in time. As the technology changes, the potential for automation of organizational functions changes. Similarly, as the organization's understanding of its own activities changes, the possibility of automating is affected.

Recently, this phenomenon has become of critical importance to individuals within the offices of the organization. A flurry of technological innovation has imposed pressure upon the organization to automate the office. Activities which had been treated as individual tasks, built around a complex of relatively inexpensive, personal tools and not included in the Applications Portfolio, are now being discussed as organizational concerns which are related to the general and ever expanding area of computerization.

While no one can deny the need to increase productivity in the office, there is a great deal of confusion as to the relationship of office automation to data processing. This is in part because **office automation** involves an expansion of the Applications Portfolio to include, as automatable, functions of the business which had previously been considered personal or internal department areas. Thus office automation is related to the general Applications Portfolio for the organization and consequently to data processing, but it also includes activities and functions which are distinctly different from traditional data processing service areas. New tools are making it possible to automate clerical, secretarial, and even managerial activities. Many personal daily functions are now considered automatable.

The introduction of office automation brings technology, the use of new technologies, and the problems of planning and control directly into the office. The field of structured and semistructured activities now includes personal and departmental functions which do not fit into the centralized mode of automation. Thus office automation is both related to data processing and separate from it. The growth of office automation applications in the organization reflects this duality.

Exhibit I shows an Applications Portfolio with dots that indicate areas where activities are or could be supported by office automation services. Two things are clear; first, these activities are related to data processing in that they affect a hierarchy of interrelated business functions, and second, they are scattered across this hierarchy of activity. In more concrete terms, technical tools based upon information technologies are being introduced throughout the organization under the auspices of office automation. Currently the overriding factor determining which technologies secretaries and managers use for information tracking, reporting, and communications is their own personal or departmental interest and ability in computerized systems. Thus, office automation seems scattered in a random manner across business activities.

Office automation is data processing related, but the exact nature of this relationship has yet to be defined. The technology and the Applications Portfolio indicate similarity and areas of overlap, but they also

EXHIBIT I

The Network and the Applications Portfolio
Side by Side

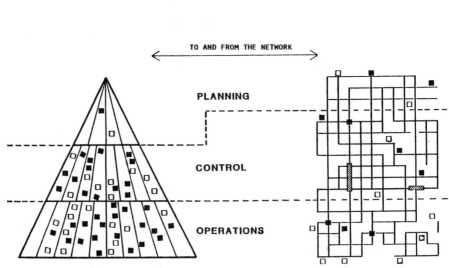

DP APPLICATIONS   COMMUNICATIONS NETWORK

TO AND FROM THE NETWORK

PLANNING

CONTROL

OPERATIONS

BLACK (IN BOTH DIAGRAMS):   OFFICE AUTOMATION APPLICATIONS

suggest differences. In order to fully understand the role of office automation and the nature of its evolution it will be necessary to closely examine its use and the needs of its users. Once these are more clearly understood, it will be possible to describe a pattern of growth and to suggest appropriate control and planning mechanisms.

OFFICE AUTOMATION—A DEFINITION

Office automation is a label which means many things to many people. It is used to refer to equipment, to the automation of procedures with equipment, and to any number of related aspects of change associated with mechanization and advanced technology in the office. For the purposes of clarification and discussion, office automation will be defined here as **the application of information systems technology to increase the productivity of the office and the effectiveness of the managerial, professional, and clerical personnel who work within it.**

This definition is chosen to emphasize several characteristics related to the four growth processes in the evolution of office automation. There is, first of all, a *technology* which is not fixed but expanding. It may begin with a copying machine, a memory typewriter, or a word processing unit. It may eventually include complex integrated electronic systems which are interconnected with data processing and networking facilities.

Second, there are *applications*, functions which have been automated or could potentially be automated. These functions, and their composite activities, can be identified according to the levels and areas described by an Applications Portfolio. Their growth may not follow the same pattern as data processing growth, but its evolution can be followed and planned through analysis and management of the Applications Portfolio.

Third, there are office automation *users* who must move through a learning curve. These users may initially be isolated groups or even individuals, but in the context of long-term planning, they are interrelated and their growth as a whole will affect the evolution of office automation. In particular, the users should be understood to include all groups involved in carrying out the functions described by the Applications Portfolio; i.e., clerical, secretarial, professional, and managerial users.

Finally, the evolution of office automation should be managed through the development of appropriate *controls*. These controls may be initiated centrally or in individual areas by data processing, by senior management, or steering committee groups. The introduction, presence, and adaptation of controls will affect the evolution of the other growth processes.

The definition of office automation is meant to be inclusive. It assumes an openness to activities, technologies, and ways of functioning which are not clear to us now. The factors which will govern the evolution of office automation—the technology, the Applications Portfolio, the users, and the controls—provide the basis for an understanding of office automation and its potential.

ORDERS OF OFFICE AUTOMATION

There is still only incomplete evidence that organizations move through several discrete and identifiable stages of learning about office automation, as some have suggested. However, there are three general **orders** of development in the evolution of office automation to date. These follow a pattern of increasingly complex technological solutions to an increasingly integrated set of organizational functions, utilized by an expanding group of people on all levels of the organization, and governed by a body of controls. While many of the tools of office automation and its functions remain essentially decentralized, there is an overall pattern, identified here in terms of the three orders of office automation which is repeated in most organizations.

The First-Order: Without Combination or Network

Office automation begins with the introduction of tools to assist individuals or small groups of individuals in completing separate, largely clerical functions. The specific technologies will vary as will the applications. Individual offices, or even individuals within those offices, decide which applications and which technologies are the most promising to help them with their work. Similarly, control over the use of office automation facilities begins and remains with the users, and the technology remains in the hands of the users.

Characterized by stand-alone technologies, office automation is recognizable in the office today by appliances used to support tasks of office workers. These appliances, although sometimes quite sophisticated, are generally on the low end of the technological spectrum, serving directed, single tasks. Word processors are typical of these prepackaged appliances, supporting the typing tasks of a secretary and serving as a rudimentary workstation. First-order office automation is present to some degree in almost every large organization today. In some, it is confined to copy machines and memory typewriter. In others, it overlaps individual and organization-wide groups in the form of word processors. In all cases, it is most often used by decentralized groups or by individuals as a largely personal or departmental support.

Second-Order Office Automation: Combination

As office automation evolves, more users are involved. More functions are automated, and both are affected by the combination of technologies, the ability of technology to link activities, and a gradual centralization and interrelation of the work areas involved. In fact, new relationships between individuals and departments become possible. Information support to management as well as clerical and secretarial support are improved, and the office begins to change.

The exact nature of the changes resulting from office automation will vary from organization to organization. General characteristics include the linking of technologies, applications, users, and consequently of controls. But the diversity and adaptability are also important. The following three brief examples will help to illustrate this.

AT&T Conference Facility. AT&T has operationalized the concept of using information technology to conduct business meetings between groups in several large cities. Automated conference facilities have been built in New York, San Francisco, and Chicago. These facilities are equipped with TV cameras that are voice-activated so that conference participants in the different cities have the feeling of face-to-face discussion. Electronic blackboards make it possible to use graphic communication as well. The facilities supplement this by providing instant facsimile transmission of paper documents.

These conference facilities have operated so effectively for AT&T that they have been made commercially available to other corporations. Use of these facilities is becoming more extensive. They answer the problem of geographic dispersion by extending the communication and meeting function to include multiple locations without expensive and time-consuming travel.

Wharton's Experiment. At the Wharton School, members of the faculty of the management science department have taken advantage of office automation to extend their offices into their homes. Electronic terminals allow them to transmit and to receive extensive written material, to check schedules, and even to follow meetings and other department-based administrative activities.

For example, if the chairman of the department needs to stay home for a day to prepare course material, but cannot afford to be "out of the office" for the entire day, office automation makes it possible to do both. At home, before breakfast, it is possible to read mail, check the calendar, and even sketch an article for publication—all electronically—using a terminal connected to the department. The chairman is then free to concentrate on more independent activities at home, undisturbed. Using the terminal, faculty can check as necessary to attend to matters in their offices.

Office automation, in this case, allows the individual to adapt to personal work habits (the need to work on course preparation at home) without neglecting organizational priorities. It maximizes valuable time for higher-level personnel, adding productivity and effectiveness, and avoiding wasteful time in the office itself. In addition, the Wharton system includes clerical, secretarial, and editorial functions, complementing increased productivity on one level with increases on the supporting levels.

Citibank's Letter-of-Credit System. Until a few years ago, the process of issuing and administering a letter of credit at Citibank was lengthy and complex. It involved some thirty-odd processing steps, fourteen people, and many forms, tickets and files. Today, one operator at an automated workstation is responsible for the entire procedure. Through the use of office automation support, a single person can issue, amend, and authorize payment of a letter of credit.

A transaction begins when the operator of the workstation enters information on a new customer request or amendment on a CRT. The CRT responds by displaying a form which indicates the data the operator should provide. The operator then enters this data, according to instructions displayed on the screen, using a keyboard. A central computer system linked to the workstation selects standard paragraphs of text which describe the terms of the credit, and figures the service charges involved. The letter of credit itself is printed out on a printed at the workstation for mailing to the customer. If necessary, the operator dispatches a Telex confirmation simultaneously via a connection with the bank's message switching system.

At the end of the processing day, the workstation reports details of all the day's payments, adjustments, and service charges to the bank's central proof system. This transmission includes information on the kinds of letters issued and the customer groups involved for use in market analysis, business planning, and control. End-of-day processing summaries are also provided to departmental managers, listing items outstanding and exceptions.

The Citibank office automation system makes it possible to increase productivity at the workstation, increase the effectiveness of department management and control, and take advantage of technology to improve internal communications. As a result, the costs for letter-of-credit transaction have been sharply reduced, and customer service has been improved. The combination of automated tasks has resulted in both improved service and improved internal management.

The Third-Order: Integration

Second-order office automation demonstrates several definitive characteristics which provide a basis for extrapolation from existing conditions into the future. First, combined technologies are more powerful than isolated tools and more capable of integration. Second, the integration of technical capabilities allows for the interconnection of such related functions as issuance of letters of credit and internal bank management. Third, the users, while becoming increasingly independent and able to assume more responsibility, are also placed in closer contact with others through expanded communications networks. Reciprocally, controls can be extended in order to improve management of new capabilities.

Third-order office automation is the extension of existing conditions into the future for the purpose of describing the next level of growth. It describes **the furthest point to which one can rationally extrapolate from techniques we now possess**. In many ways, third-order office automation echoes the moods of science fiction. However, it is important to remember the rapid expansion of technology which we have witnessed in data processing over the past twenty years, and the manner in which imaginative scenarios for change have become an accepted part of organizational behavior.

In some ways third-order automation is analogous to the fourth stage of data processing growth. It is characterized by integration of technologies and consolidation of the Applications Portfolio. Controls are established, and users reach a high level of confidence with the technology. The Citibank example of second-order office automation suggests the direction of this progression in much the same manner that stage III data processing organizations suggest the foundations for the transition which marks stage IV. This parallel is, therefore, helpful, but should not be applied literally. Third-order office automation is distinct from second-order office automation in magnitude, but does not exhibit the kind of discrete characteristics which have been used to delineate stages of data processing growth.

The growth of office automation is really a growth in magnitude which is made possible by technical innovation and integration. In the scenario which follows, all of the current office automation techniques are applied freely to a situation which involves comparable functions in a hypothetical organization. Every technical device described now exists in companies or research labs, but few have been integrated and none to an extent which could be called third-order office automation.

Scenario For A Third-Order Organization. At 8:30 on Monday morning, the assistant to the chairman of a major multinational consumer goods manufacturer is handed a note from the company's legal counsel. The handwritten note is something of an anomaly. It is 1995 and most of the senior executives communicate with each other via the high-security lines of the corporation's network. The assistant reads the note and, grasping its significance, sends a signal to the chairman indicating that a top priority item needs his attention.

Moments later, reading the counsel's message on the screen across his desk, the chairman interrupts his activity to call the assistant and asks him to add the item "Bloc announcement" to the agenda for the noontime Asia Bloc Marketing Meeting. The assistant follows up on this order, changing the agenda, confirming the change on a CRT at his desk, and signaling the Legal Department Central in Boston to notify them that the chairman will probably request a full advisory briefing on the Asia Bloc announcement within the next three hours. The necessary staff in Legal can then be held on stand-by for this request.

The Asia marketing meeting begins at 12:00 (noon) Chicago time, and involves representatives from departments located in the United States, Europe, and Asia offices who communicate via electronic consoles and workstations. The intelligence item, received earlier by the chairman via his assistant, is presented to the meeting, displayed electronically on each workstation screen. The significance of the item for marketing strategies is then summarized by the chairman. All communications are translated, on-line, as requested.

The chairman requests projected expenses for Asia for the next three years. Finance responds with displays and hard copy. The representative from the legal department in Boston leaves the meeting to supervise the issuance of a white paper on the Bloc announcement. When he returns, he is asked to transmit the paper on-line as soon as it is ready. Because Legal had been notified earlier by the assistant, this poses no problem. The white paper, like the Finance reports, will be available world-wide within twenty-four hours.

The meeting continues and a run-down of all ads and schedules for Asia are displayed along with patterns of explanation by the marketing representatives in each country. These run-downs have been prepared and programmed into the network earlier. Again, all material, including commercials, is translated on-line automatically. The chairman is able to insert sketches via an electronic blackboard, to be noted by the eastern representatives who will pick up the meeting later and replay the minutes to date.

The group then decides to suspend their discussion on-line until Wednesday so that they can use the intervening time to determine a plan for accelerating marketing plans in response to the Bloc announcement. In the meantime, further analysis from Finance and Legal will be submitted to the electronic meeting record to be reviewed by the participants. In this manner, the meeting can continue, partially on-line, partially via follow-up submissions, until the issue is resolved on Friday. By Friday, the chairman is able to approve new marketing campaigns for Asia.

The assistant places an edited version of the meeting minutes in the organizational archives. It provides a record, a training tool, and a means for analysis and improvement of the meeting process.

In this example, the meeting, a critical function of management and senior level personnel, is made more effective through office automation. In addition, many time-consuming activities including travel, deliberation, and waiting for written communications are eliminated. By allowing the meeting to continue over an extended period of time, input from sub-meetings (e.g. Finance and Legal) can be added as available without necessitating a second meeting. The definition of "meeting" is made more elastic, but the end-result, the work which needed to be done, is the same. The added value is clear.

Although the effects of office automation on organizational behavior in the example are vague, it is clear that this "virtual meeting" provides on accurate portrait of the direction of change. Integration of technologies will allow integration of functions. Interaction between users will be increased without necessitating travel. While specific agendas for automation cannot be described, there are clear trends and corresponding management approaches which can be specified.

THE CHALLENGE TO MANAGEMENT

The general trend in management and control of office automation as an organization moves from one order to the next is a trend of centralization. Initially, applications are in the hands of the users, but as they are integrated, coordination becomes the responsibility of a central technical staff. Similarly, control over the use of office automation facilities begins and remains with the user. But as capabilities, rationales, and budgeting procedures develop, responsibility for setting control guidelines gravitates to a center.

The process of centralization affects many aspects of the office automation process. Data bases will eventually be managed via a centralized function. Even the equipment, located in user areas, must be coordinated centrally to insure consistent quality in the organization's network utility. *Exhibit II* summarizes this evolution. As the circles shrink to ellipses, the control, database, and development all move to the center, indicating that, while processors remain with the users on the periphery of the original circle, the totality is being centralized.

The challenge to management is to determine what is the center depicted in the diagram, and to establish a strategy for planning and control. Whatever organizational rigidities or technical shortfalls may be inhibiting the visualization of second- and third-order office automation, these higher orders are on the horizon and must be addressed. Based on an understanding of technological evolution, it is possible to describe a set of management principles which provide the foundation for an office automation strategy, a center for the converging forms shown in the exhibit.

An Open Definition

The first thing which executives must do is to broaden their thinking about what office automation means. The term traditionally denotes a

EXHIBIT II

Three Orders of
Office Automation

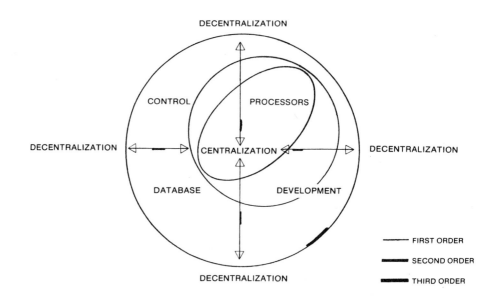

few clerical tasks and an occasional managerial-level task. As the preceding example shows, this is a first-order definition which ignores the potential for office automation support to personnel in all levels of the organization.

In addition, the broadened definition should be used as a basis for design concepts. Adequate tools and software cannot currently be obtained from vendors because, even in the few cases where packages are available, they are company specific and not easily adapted. Management should provide for the evolution of design concepts, development, and implementation of office automation systems. This involves analysis **de novo**, starting with a broadening of the concept of office automation in accordance with the second- and third-order examples cited above.

The office automation systems, elevated by the technology of integration, requires new systems views. Broadening the systems thinking to accentuate communication automation as well as task and processing automation is one of the more important datamation evolutions required in opening up the definition of automation. Traditional systems clearly have not captured this innovation, and need to be reconsidered, building upon current strengths and accepting needed modifications.

Pivot Point: The User

The strategic purpose of office automation is to improve the productivity of the office—a room, a floor, or a decentralized division—as a focus of communications. This involves two things:

1. The network that accepts communications from and delivers communications to the office.

2. The automated applications that support the work that goes on within the office.

Exhibit III shows the communications network for a hypothetical company and the Applications Portfolio of automated applications (which may be centralized or decentralized) side by side. As the Applications Portfolio shows, current office automation installations pepper the portfolio in a random manner which contrast strongly with the apparent order of the network beside it. The strategic problem for management is to find a way to resolve the randomness of the office automation installations so that they will eventually be rationally integrated with the functional hierarchy described by the Applications Portfolio and the network.

Attention here must focus on the user. Insofar as the user represents a business function of the company, all data processing and office automation activities are undertaken on behalf of the user. The network and the automated applications come together conceptually for the purposes of strategic management when they merge to support the users in their work. The user, as the client, is therefore the key to successful management.

In the past, data processing applications were centralized under the control of a data processing department and the user played no significant

EXHIBIT III

An Organization's
Electronic/Processing Network

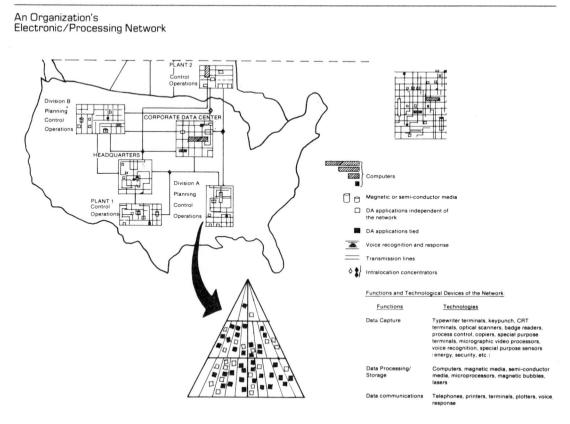

role in the electronic processing network, if indeed there was a network. Ordinarily, the user would ship material to be processed and receive the finished work from data processing. This process is described by the diagram in *Exhibit IV*.

However, once some applications began to be distributed to the users through time-sharing and minicomputers, the user began to play an important role in the network and its operation. By following certain procedures, the user is now able to use directly hitherto centralized data processing services via a communications network. This new relationship is shown in *Exhibit V*.

The experience with data processing decentralization provides indicators of potential problems for office automation as this largely disparate activity becomes integrated in an interrelated but decentralized environment. For example, it is important that users are, first of all, willing to use the capabilities in their areas, and that they are willing to do so according to the correct procedures.

We find the need for two kinds of controls in the case of office automation. These controls must be put into place between the user and the network endings at the user locations. There must be:

EXHIBIT IV

The Centralized DP
Environment

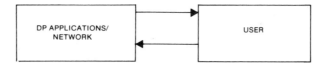

1. Network Integration Controls which ensure that the network and its elements are properly employed.

2. User's Procedural Controls which ensure that the distributed processors are employed correctly.

Inevitably of Merger

Eventually, in third-order office automation, and even to a certain extent in second-order automation, the line will blur which divides office automation applications and applications inside the network. More and more, functions previously performed by data processing will be distributed, and users will take a stronger lead in calling on corporate information processing resources to do their jobs. This is evident in the third-order office automation scenario where technical capability led to a broader notion of what was possible on the part of the users.

The important thing for management is to govern the merger, to insure that the network/user interface is carefully structured so that, when boundaries blur, there will be a firm basis for building an integrated approach. In anticipation of this merger, in addition to monitoring user interface, senior management must treat office automation as a further venture into distributed processing. This means that certain preparation and planning steps should be taken.

In general, all office automation installations in an organization should be audited. There should be an effort to assess the order of automation at each location, noting areas where progress has been made in second- and third-order systems. This assessment should also involve an evaluation of automation of the business functions of the organization, even though they are traditionally viewed as the province of data processing alone. Finally, both office automation and data processing automation should be monitored and encouraged in such a way that they will develop into compatible processes, both internally, and with the communications network.

This strategic implications of the merger of automated office functions and automated business functions must also be examined. For example, data bases used by distributed office automation applications must be fully consistent with the corporate data bases used in data processing

EXHIBIT V

The Distributed
Mode

applications. This is necessary to insure that office work will follow the business strategy effectively. If the organization expects to utilize the two as complementary elements, systems development guidelines for office automation should also be centralized to ensure that systems are congruent with applications organization-wide.

The merger also raises a major organizational issue: should the data processing organizaton subsume office automation strategy and implementation, or vice versa? Data processing departments are not necessarily expert in office automation, but they do have a broad base of learned expertise in information processing. In the long run, they are in a good position to ensure that controls at the ends of the network are structured so that a distributed application fits precisely within the network and the processing resources previously developed. They also have important experience in educating users.

In many ways, the answer to this question will come from careful observance in the future. The juxaposition of different stages of data processing and different orders of office automation make it difficult to be prescriptive.

However, regardless of the specifics, merger is inevitable. In most cases, it is probably aptly described by the name of data resource management.

DATA RESOURCE MANAGEMENT - EVOLVING GUIDELINES

The first step must be for management to communicate the concept of orders of office automation to all potential users in the organization. The exact nature of third-order office automation is a fluid concept which will advance with technology and the mastery of technology. It is important that there be an underlying support for office automation as a **strategic direction**. Overall corporate effectiveness is the chief benefit of high-order office automation. This should be communicated as a concept, regardless of the specific profile of office automation in a given office or department or division.

In anticipation of the merger of both areas of automation—data processing and office automation—compatible controls should be established. Experiments with office automation technologies and combinations of those technologies should be encouraged.

In addition, individuals need to be made aware of the potential for office automation in their areas in a manner which is compatible with, and complementary to, data processing. Managers should be encouraged to try out technologies they believe might make them more productive. Similarly, users should be prepared to experiment not only with the technologies but also with the controls. At the same time, the data processing department must be made sensitive to the issue of developing controls and encouraged in an attitude responsive to office automation.

As a corollary, however, senior management should caution against attempts to combine or integrate prematurely. One way to pace growth is to set up an office automation steering committee which can set strategic direction, reinforce that direction, and encourage rational experimentation by monitoring budgets and providing the necessary slack.

The objective should be to achieve a high-order of office automation in such a manner that, when integration or merger with data processing occurs, little retrofitting, if any, will be necessary. Organizations should learn from the short-term losses which have often accompanied the consolidation of separate files into general data bases. Current distinctions between office automation and data processing should not preclude the eventual integration of the two. Ultimately, both are elements of the general organizational effort to build a strong Applications Portfolio in conjunction with a solid foundation in all of the four Growth Processes.

PART THREE

Direction Setting
And
Planning

Most organizations have budgeting systems which are commonly thought of as one-year plans. When the organization begins to address longer range planning issues, it normally takes seven to ten years to implement a sophisticated planning process. First, the planning horizon is extended and a planning calendar is installed. Then, capital budgeting is integrated. Later the orientation shifts from one-item planning (e.g., hardware, people, and software) to program planning, whereby expenditures are directly related to achieving business objectives.

The planning for computers evolves in a manner very similar to business planning. It must begin with a solid foundation of budgeting, and then it requires the same seven- to ten-year time frame to evolve into a sophisticated process. There are four key ingredients to the computer planning process:

- A substantive planning methodology is required.

- Planning must be executed within an organizational framework which includes input from key personnel.

- The planning process must include people who are willing to internalize the plan and make a commitment to it.

- Planning must begin with a base of organizational knowledge of the opportunities and problems involved in using computers.

Effective planning for computers also must be comprehensive. *Exhibit I* shows a computer planning framework. The top of the triangle represents high level planning detail whereas the bottom represents a low detail level. The first dimension of computer planning involves choosing between a high level of detail ("top-down") and a low level of detail ("bottom-up"). Initially, computer planning usually involves "bottom-up" planning for hardware, and focuses on the second process, Personnel and Technology Resources.

The second dimension of computer planning gradually incorporates all four Growth Processes. The third dimension of planning for computers requires planning for all the Growth Processes at a uniform level of detail. In this dimension, the hierarchy of planning takes the form shown in *Exhibit I.*

Chapter 9, The Direction-Setting Process, describes the linkage between the organization's business strategy and its computer strategy. This linkage is key in providing a focus for the computer activity and establishing guidelines for setting priorities.

Chapter 10, The Stage Assessment, discusses the baselining process. In order to effectively progress through the stages, all Growth Processes must be reasonably aligned. If one process is more advanced than the others, dysfunctional activity impeding progression usually results. Often, this formal planning effort is a first-time attempt to control the Growth Processes and may uncover certain obvious anomalies warranting immediate action. For example, the technical resources available to the organization may be far greater than the organization's ability to use those resources.

EXHIBIT I

Three Dimensions of
Computer Planning

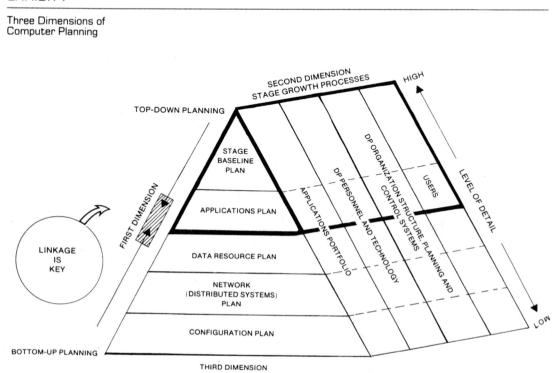

From the foundation of the stages baseline, one moves down the planning hierarchy to application planning. *Chapter 11* focuses on *Application Planning*, a process which begins to formalize the demand for computer systems.

Chapter 12, Data Resource Management, derives the organization's data requirements from the applications plan. At this point, we are able to build a substantive plan for managing the data resource. Although most of this plan is internal to the computer activity, it has broad business implications involving corporate vs. department/divisional data, shared data, and common data. Understanding data resource planning is a major achievement, and is generally a turning point in the effective use of computers to implement business strategy.

Chapter 13, Network Planning, moves into the next level of technical detail where the actual network is planned to implement both the Data Resource and Applications Plans.

Chapter 14, At Last, Major Roles for Minicomputers, places the use of minicomputers into perspective. Mini/microcomputers are an integral part of a company's network and should not be treated any differently than other emerging computer-based technologies.

The Direction-Setting Process: Strategic and Long-Range Planning

DAVID P. NORTON

Direction-setting and planning are, perhaps, the most critical management activities in data processing today. The pace and complexity of technological growth mean that data processing is in a constant state of flux and innovation. Most significant changes require a lead time of several years. Major systems are developed over several years and the hardware capacity required to support them is usually acquired in multi-year increments. Such resources as personnel skills and technical competence also require several years to identify, acquire, and develop. When interdependence between these resources are taken into account, the time horizon for effective managerial action extends well beyond five years.

The paradox for modern data processing organizations is that the same technological complexity and rapid innovation which necessitates foresight and planning also results in an immediate environment which is extraordinarily difficult to manage. The pressures of ongoing operations push planning into the background. There are always important issues which must be addressed without delay lest a multiplicity of problems follow. At the same time that data processing managers see the impending force of change and the need to plan for change, they face equally forceful issues in the here and now. The problem is that without a governing strategy and a long-term perspective, short-term solutions may become long-term weaknesses.

In 1968, McKinsey and Company issued a report on the use of computers at thirty-six major companies and found that those companies which plan data processing activities are more successful than those companies which do not plan.[1] Companies which also audit their actual

---

[1]F. Warren McFarlan, "*Problems in Planning the Information System,*" Harvard Business Review, March-April 1971, p. 78

results against the plan are even more successful. In a similar review of fifteen companies, F. Warren McFarlan found that there was a clear correlation between planning and effectiveness.[2] McFarlan goes on to point out that while some executives consider the volatility of computer technology a deterrent to planning, companies which plan are better prepared to respond to technical innovation. Plans may have to be revised from time to time due to rapid changes in technology, but there is a considerable advantage in the effectiveness of revision from an established base rather than constantly improvising from scratch.[3]

There is no simple solution to the problem of establishing a basis for ongoing operations in a rapidly changing environment. However, management can begin to minimize the impact of day-to-day pressures by coordinating the solution of current problems with a long-term strategy for data processing over the years. If there is a long-term goal, a strategy for the solution of the organization's data processing needs, then immediate problems can be weighed against their long-term impact and management decision-making can be improved. Long-term priorities can be used to derive short-term solutions.

This does not mean that effective ongoing operation is obviated by planning. It does mean, however, that the pressures on management to treat each day-to-day problem with equal concern will be decreased. When there is a long-term plan, a strategy, and a direction, short-term issues can be prioritized. For example, a long-term strategy may involve converting to a data base system. At such a time certain current systems become obsolete. Thus, it is not important to concentrate current efforts on those systems; temporary solutions may be sufficient. On the other hand, some systems may assume critical importance in the long-run, and therefore become important maintenance targets for the present.

The issues of planning in data processing are comparable to planning issues in any management area. It is important that future operations be assured the resources they need in order to be effective. The difference is that in data processing the degree of change is extraordinary and changes are often difficult to implement. The magnitude of ignored questions is constantly increasing in both complexity and cost. A good data processing strategy, a long-term plan, and coordinated plans on the operational level are invaluable resources for every organization today.

THE DIRECTION-SETTING PROCESS

The preoccupation with day-to-day operations affects the effort to introduce long-range thinking in the data processing area. Planning, when it occurs, encompasses a monthly cycle over a one- or-two year period. This results in confusion and unregulated growth which often culminates in crisis situations. Immediate needs are addressed without full understand-

---

[2]Ibid., p. 77
[3]Ibid., p. 76

ing of the scope of the issues involved. The magnitude of plans exceeds the limits of feasibility, overstrains the organization, and in the end weakens data processing capabilities.

It is difficult to make feasible plans in an area fraught with "blue sky" possibilities. There is a sense of infinite possibility associated with data processing counterbalanced by a sense of ongoing frustration. By introducing a multi-level planning process with different planning horizons, management can resolve this conflict. "Blue sky" possibilities can be reconciled with feasibility and need in the organization, choices can be made, and boundaries can be set for translation into ongoing operations.

This is accomplished through a four part process:

- strategic planning

- long-range planning

- operational planning

- and performance monitoring

The **strategic plan** determines overall data processing objectives and establishes a set of directional actions for a time horizon of five to eight years. The **long-range plan** translates strategic planning directions into specific, action-oriented projects, prioritizes these projects, and determines the overall resource requirements for a period of three to five years. The **operational plan** sets the long-range plan in motion, translating it into specific actions by month over a period of one year. The **performance monitoring process** measures actual performance against objectives on all levels at regular time intervals. This sequence is shown in Exhibit I.

EXHIBIT I

Planning
Levels

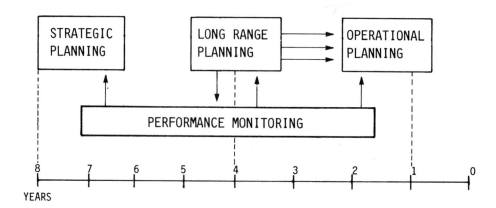

YEARS

EXHIBIT II

Strategic Guidelines Addressed by
Growth Process

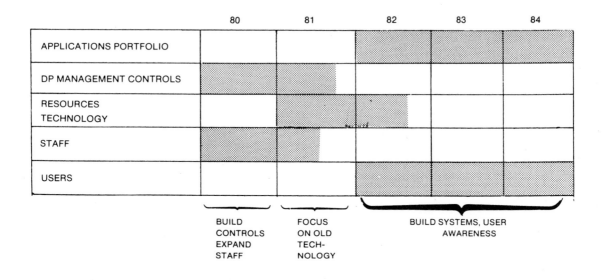

	80	81	82	83	84
APPLICATIONS PORTFOLIO			▓	▓	▓
DP MANAGEMENT CONTROLS	▓	▓			
RESOURCES TECHNOLOGY		▓	▓		
STAFF	▓	▓			
USERS			▓	▓	▓

BUILD
CONTROLS
EXPAND
STAFF

FOCUS
ON OLD
TECH-
NOLOGY

BUILD SYSTEMS, USER
AWARENESS

EXAMPLE: BASE FOR GROWTH DOES NOT EXIST
GUIDELINE 1: STAFF SKILLS AND EXPERTISE REQUIRED IN THE ORGANIZATION
GUIDELINE 2: OPERATIONAL USER SERVICE MUST BE IMPROVED
GUIDELINE 3: DEPENDENCY ON OLD TECHNOLOGY MUST BE BROKEN

The planning process is not driven by technological change alone. It must respond to reciprocal changes among all four of the growth processes. A complete planning program will include plans and performance monitoring of data processing personnel, users, and management control. According to the Stages Model, change in one area will be dependent upon readiness in all of the growth processes. Planning priorities should be designed to maximize coordination of maturity among the growth processes. This is a primary concern of the strategic planning process, and will be reflected in the organization of priorities and activities in the supporting detailed plans. *Exhibit II* shows how one organization has organized priorities among the growth processes over a five-year period. Planning helps the organization grow by extending the planning horizon and placing current issues in perspective. The multiplicity of levels of detail and the scope of concern over time in the various planning elements both function as counterchecks on the intrinsic conflict between changes promising undreamed of capabilities and changes involving unanticipated complications. In order to operationalize this concept it is necessary to understand the degree of detail and the temporal scope of each level of the planning process.

STRATEGIC PLANNING

The first step in the strategic planning process is to identify what data processing can be expected to do to meet the needs of the business (*objectives*) and to decide how it proposes to do this (*strategies*). Although this may be clear in theory, it is actually very difficult to execute. There are two primary reasons for this: confusion regarding the role of information systems, and the complexity of actually determining how to obtain the necessary resources.

In the first case, the strategic link between data processing and the business is often implied rather than explicit. In many organizations the business strategy itself is not explicitly stated. The organization expects support from data processing, but individuals and groups, department personnel and management are all reluctant to go through the process of translating business plans into data processing terms. Where data processing personnel are aware of the potential problems raised by the situation, attempts to get the attention of senior management are frustrated by management's reluctance to get involved. There is a critical lack of understanding at all levels of the organization of the importance of understanding and specifying the role of information systems in the business. In the second case, even if data processing objectives are clearly identified, understanding how they are to be achieved is almost always fraught with complexity. Many organizations developing a first strategic plan discover that they do not possess the resources to achieve their data processing objectives within the time frames specified by the business. Furthermore, when resources are available, the lead time required to put them in place is often in conflict with the time frame for data processing set by business needs and plans.

Given the difficulty of carrying out the strategic planning activity, data processing must accept a certain degree of compromise in its approach to the process. Strategic formulation is often an exercise in understanding available alternatives and choosing which one provides the most (or least) attractive set of expected outcomes. It is a two-part activity in which business needs are matched to unlimited possibilities and then adjusted to available resources.

Step 1 - Determining Data Processing Objectives

In the classical definition of business planning, business strategies and directional action programs develop to achieve business objectives. Data processing objectives can be viewed as elements of the business strategy: that is, as directional actions which the business manager employs to meet business objectives. The initial task in strategy formulation is therefore the development of an understanding of the role data processing plays in helping the organization meet its business needs. In other words, data processing objectives should be aligned with and linked to business strategies.

Many organizations approach this problem by requiring the divisions of the business organization to include information systems requirements in their strategic plans. There are two problems with this approach. First, the business organization may not have a clear idea of its own needs, and second, information requirements may bear little relationship to either information possibilities or limitations. The result of the process is disappointment and further frustration.

A strategy of limited information requirements is certainly better than the situation, prevalent in many organizations, where business strategy is unclear and nonspecific. In either case, however, there must be a large effort on the part of data processing and business groups to communicate both general objectives and the more specific priorities involved. One process for doing this is the Stage Assessment described in Chapter 10. A steering committee can also contribute to this process (Chapter 24).

Step 2 - Determining How to Achieve Data Processing Objectives

Once the information needs of the organization have been articulated, a strategy for meeting those needs can be developed. This is accomplished by surveying the field of possible alternatives and then evaluating those alternatives in terms of the available resources of the organization. This involves, first, maximum openness to and awareness of the available technology and the range of potential approaches to the use of that technology and, second, a realistic perspective on the feasibility of introducing the technology in the organization.

In organizations without a history of strategic planning for data processing, the transition from alternatives to selection of a strategy should be approached with caution. There is a tendency either to be contented with a limited knowledge of the possible strategies or to be overambitious in selecting among them. Most of the previous data processing planning in the organization has probably focused on a shorter time horizon (one to two years). The result is that either overambitious strategies are mapped with foreshortened timetables or current patterns are extended into the future ignoring the need to constantly expand resources and build new technical, personnel, and managerial capabilities.

The second step in the strategic planning process is of critical importance because it **sets the scope of future objectives in tune with the resources of the organization.** If this step is neglected the organization may find that it is unable to carry out plans because one or the other of the growth processes fails to support the increment of growth designated by the strategy. The following example illustrates the problems with such an approach.

Buffalo Nickel Bank. The Buffalo Nickel Bank hired The Consulting Firm (TCF) to assist them in the reformulation of data processing strategy. TCF suggested that the organization conduct a Stage Assessment in order to specify information needs in terms of business needs. On the basis of this survey, business strategies were specified for five to eight years and information needs were overlayed on those plans. Finally, a determination was made of the kinds of data processing systems Buffalo Nickel would need to remain competitive over the next five to eight years.

However, when TCF examined the stage of development of the four growth processes, they found that the organization had not even begun to develop the experience it would need to carry out the strategy it had outlined. This strategy called for the introduction of data resources and the development of interdepartmental integration of information systems. It would take at least two years for Buffalo Nickel to acquire the technology, to hire or train personnel, and to develop the necessary controls.

Accordingly, Buffalo Nickel had to conclude that it could not meet its data processing objectives as they had been articulated. They had to develop an alternative strategy which was a compromise based on their available resources. Buffalo Nickel decided to defer immediate transition to data resources while preparing for that eventuality. In the meantime, they would move ahead with certain critical systems with the understanding that those systems would probably become inflexible sooner than was desired.

THE STAGE ASSESSMENT AND STRATEGIC PLANNING

The Buffalo Nickel Bank case illustrates the advantages of knowing both what is desired and what is feasible given the resources of the organization. This knowledge was gathered in the course of a baseline study or **Stage Assessment**. The key advantage of the Stage Assessment is that it provides a complete and coordinated picture of both business needs and data processing capabilities as described by the stage of maturity of the four growth processes:

1. the applications portfolio

2. data processing personnel and technology

3. management controls

4. user awareness

Exhibit III shows how the Stage Assessment fits into the planning pattern.

As a result of the Stage Assessment effort, Buffalo Nickel was in a position to understand its own limitations and develop effective alternative strategies for ultimately achieving the best possible set of outcomes, even if those outcomes fell short of the full set of data processing objectives. It was able to ascertain all of the "blue sky" possibilities and to select the most realistic alternatives. In addition, awareness of the ultimate objective of introducing data resource meant that short-term decisions about systems were made in light of an eventual goal rather

EXHIBIT III

Strategic
Planning

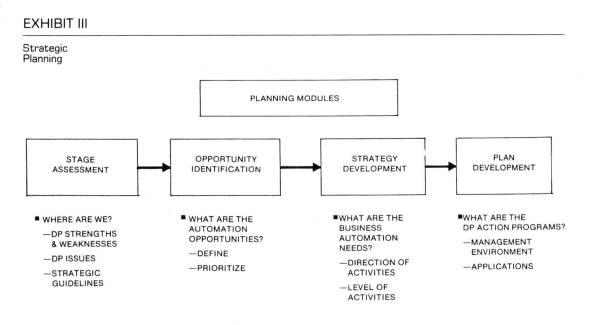

than solely on the basis of their current effect. Immediate relief was not substituted for final objectives except insofar as resources made it a more feasible alternative.

LONG-RANGE OR TACTICAL PLANNING

The **Strategic Plan** lays the groundwork for more specific tactical planning. Once a general strategy has been adopted it can be used as a guide for planning in more detail in a more immediate time frame. The directions set by Strategic Planning for the future, for a five- to eight-year period, are translated into actions plans for the next three to five years. Ideas for data processing growth are converted into projects and plans are laid both for the use of existing resources and for the expansion of resources over the period of the long-range plan.

Exhibit IV shows the planning processes. They are sequenced in a top-down hierarchy whereby the broader decisions made on the strategic level are filtered down and translated into more specific decisions at the lower levels. Over the course of the planning cycle a number of specific planning activities are conducted. These include Data Resource Planning, Network Planning, and Applications Planning. (Each of these planning groups are discussed in detail in Chapters 11, 12, and 13).

The planning sequence is iterative. As decisions are made on one level and plans are determined, the planning process is repeated at the next level of detail. The totality of all of these planning steps is the long-range plan for the organization. It includes consideration at each level of the effect on planning possibilities of all of the growth processes and coordination, guided by the strategic plan and modified by requirements in all of the areas together.

EXHIBIT IV

The Planning
Process

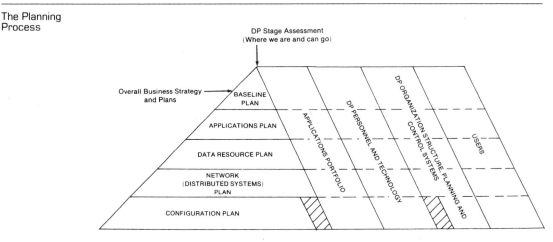

It is of critical importance that organizations recognize the dangers inherent in planning which does not extend to all of the growth processes. When strategy is focused on only one growth process and all of the long-range plans focus on that growth process, expediency in one area of data processing activity becomes the primary criteria for planning. For example, an organization may do a lot of work in business analysis and come up with an applications-only strategy, or develop a Business Systems Plan (BSP) and a data strategy that ignores technical, personnel, and control capabilities. An organization may even become so preoccupied with a limited issue, such as the use of minicomputers, that strategy and long-range plans revolve around that and nothing else.

In the long-range plan, the organization has the opportunity to coordinate a broad number of areas and to insure that strategy is translated into action in a thorough manner. In addition, by setting five- to eight-year goals, long-range priorities can be adjusted so that, when it is time to introduce major innovations (when these innovations are no longer a matter of optimum or ideal solution, but are of critical importance), the organization has the capabilities to implement them.

THE OPERATING PLAN

The final level of planning is the most detailed and also the shortest in temporal perspective. The **Operating Plan** specifies how the long-term plan will be carried out on a month-by-month basis during the upcoming year. It sets up schedules, assigns resources to projects and provides input for the budgeting plan. Projects identified in the long-range plan are broken down into phases so that detailed scheduling can be performed and milestone accomplishments can be tracked. Resources are allocated and the planned projects are summarized in a resource plan which is used to identify personnel and financial requirements.

By the time the organization has arrived at the level of detail of the Operating Plan, the overall objectives and the major priorities have been clearly identified and communicated down the line. It is now a simple matter to address immediate issues by weighing them against eventual goals. The Operating Plan is a means of optimizing resources on a day-to-day level rather than a means of averting complaint on an issue-by-issue basis.

The Operating Plan breaks down the initial strategic priorities into smaller groupings according to the projects described by the long-range plan. At this level of detail activities in each growth process are described in an operating plan for that area. In this manner, general coordination of priorities are carried through in the details of each specific planning area. *Exhibit V* shows how this works for one growth process (i.e., the Applications Portfolio). The same pattern of iteration at a level of greater detail for a more limited time frame is repeated for each growth process or, in some cases, for operational areas within a growth process.

PERFORMANCE MONITORING

The direction-setting cycle is completed by review of performance and adjustment of plans. The foundation for comprehensive review is accurate monitoring of progress against them to interested groups within the organization. If the planning processes have been thorough, there should be natural routes and schedules for periodic response to this information as it is made available.

The first part of the performance monitoring process is the establishment of formal reporting systems which produce recurring, formulated reports addressing the basic elements of the plan. At the strategic level formal reporting might involve periodic assessments of the Applicatons Portfolio coverage. The completion of a specific phase of an applications project, on the other hand, would be reported for review on the Operational Planning level.

EXHIBIT V

Operations Planning:
Applications Planning

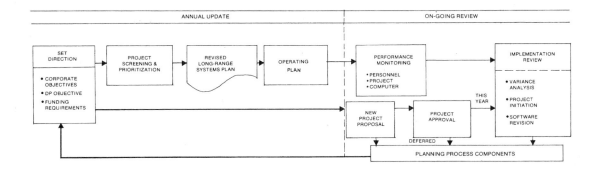

Once the reports are received, they should be reviewed on a formal basis. This is important because without formal review mechanisms, the information from the reports may never really be evaluated. Problems may escalate unnoticed or areas of less interest or familiarity to managers receiving the reports may be ignored. The steering committee provides a formal context for review at the strategic level and the long-range planning level. Project groups and data processing management should review the Operating Plan.

Finally, once variances from the plan have been identified, there should a formal mechanism for updating the plan. On the operational level, this may consist largely of schedule adjustments which are relatively small and independent actions. However, failure to meet the requirements of the long-range plan may necessitate reevaluation of the objectives and the strategies which the organization has chosen to pursue. Changes in strategy should then be reflected in reevaluation and adaptation of the long-range and operational plans.

It is important to understand that the performance monitoring process functions as the final link in the direction-setting cycle. It is not merely a record of events. It provides the basis for a rationale for future action. If reporting and review mechanisms are in place, the organization will remain responsive to the alternation of its growth processes as data processing matures. Organizations will be less likely to become attached to one familiar way of doing things and more likely to keep moving ahead.

RESOLVING THE PARADOX

In the beginning of the chapter, the complex and rapidly changing data processing environment was presented as the source of both hope and frustration for the organization today. The speed of progress demands constant adaptation, but the sophistication of the technology and the skills required places a constraint on the organization's ability to adapt. Direction-setting provides the organization with the self-knowledge and the foresight it needs to overcome this conflict.

In the chapters which follow, the individual elements of the direction-setting process are discussed and explored in more detail. It is important to remember that, although each element should be addressed by an appropriate set of planning activities, the overriding concern must be the cohesion and interrelationship of the elements in the overall plan. This is why the element of time is so critical. Strategies cannot be realized overnight. The plans provide a process whereby constant tuning and adjustment among all of the elements can be continued over the years and within a coordinated framework.

The Stage Assessment

ROBERT J. ABRAMS
JOHN J. FOLEY
LAURENCE G. ROBBINS

Through a **Stage Assessment** the **Stages Theory** is operationalized to tell an organization about its data processing situation. In the execution of the Stage Assessment, the Stages Theory is translated into a practioner's tool which makes it possible to measure the maturity of data processing in terms of the four Growth Processes and to compare those measures to interorganization benchmarks.

The first step in this process is the development of measures for each of the Growth Processes. As Nolan explains in Chapters 1 and 2, the original concept of the **Stages Model** began with observations about the cost of data processing and then broadened to include observations about the underlying reasons for growth represented by the rising curve. In a similar manner, the assessment of the stage of maturity in a given organization can begin with the gathering of information about costs, but must also measure the four Growth Processes which actually drive the development of data processing.

Although the Growth Processes can be mapped according to parallel stages of development, in a given organization there will be deviations from the model. One growth process may lag behind the others, or it may lead them. This can result in problems in a number of areas which are not directly related to the growth process in question. The Stage Assessment measures must be designed to lead management to these discrepancies so that conclusions about the current stage of the organization and plans for future development will be based on a thorough understanding of all of the factors involved.

Many data processing problems are a natural consequence of growth, but others may signal deeper troubles. Temporary growing pains occur during the expansion of data processing because, in setting priorities and working within the constraints of a given situation, growth cannot always be fully coordinated among all four Growth Processes. This situation differs from more critical lags in the growth processes which are not self-correcting. The Stage Assessment supplies the organization with information which helps to distinguish between symptoms of change and symptoms of disease. This makes it possible for management to look beyond the symptoms to the root causes of the problems before taking action.

The role of the Stage Assessment is therefore to provide a comprehensive structure which takes into account all relevant elements. In doing so, it answers questions prerequisite to responsible decision-making:

- Where am I now?

- Where do I want to be?

- How long will it take to get there?

- What is the best route to take?

These questions are answered by measuring the organization against the Stages Model, examining the measures to determine current strengths and weaknesses, and developing a strategy for growth appropriate to existing conditions.

MEASUREMENT OF THE GROWTH PROCESSES

The Stage Assessment begins with examination of data processing costs and the relationship of cost to levels of support indicated by the Applications Portfolio. This provides a general sense of strength and weakness in current operations. It also indicates which areas are of highest priority to the organization and whether data processing dollars are being spent in the right areas.

On the basis of the Applications Portfolio, a general estimate of the status of the organization can be made. This estimate must be qualified and/or amended according to the other Growth Processes. Spending patterns can also be analyzed and compared to areas of need. Finally all of this information can be drawn together in order to arrive at a strategy for future growth and a suitable data processing plan.

The Applications Portfolio

The portfolio provides a basic picture of the relationship between the organization's need for data processing support and the level of support currently being provided by data processing. It does this by mapping the functions of the business by organizational level (operational control, management control, and strategic planning) and analyzing the amount of support provided to the various functions and organization levels by computer-based systems. Many problems, including issues which surface as questions of cost, personnel, or control, can be traced back to imbalances in the Applications Portfolio.

Measurement of the Applications Portfolio is expressed in terms of level and quality of coverage. The **level** or *quantity* of data processing support is the amount of the support being provided to each business function. It is an objective measure based on existing systems and their use. Because it represents the ideal or theoretical support provided by systems as designed, quantity of support is also referred to as **attempted coverage**. *Exhibit I* shows a portfolio with levels of coverage represented by the amount of shading of each functional slice.

The **quality** of data processing is a measure of how well the systems are living up to their potential. It is applied as a corrective measure which is used to adjust or discount attempted coverage to show the actual effect of systems support on the organization, the **effective coverage**. Two measures of quality, technical and functional, are typically used. The technical quality of systems is determined by the data processing personnel who are responsible for the operation and maintenance of the systems. The functional quality of systems is determined by the users who are asked to evaluate the effect of systems support on their activities. The results of this inquiry are factored into the quantity of support in order to

EXHIBIT I

Applications Portfolio with Shading for
Levels of Coverage

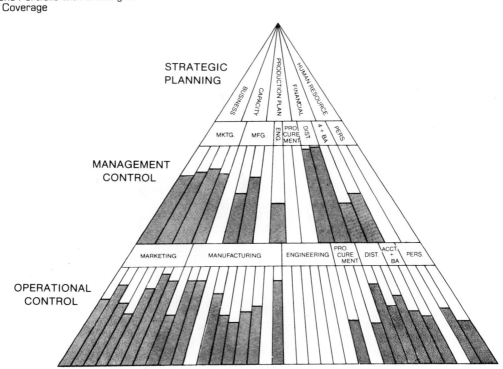

arrive at an effectiveness discount which is used to adjust the level of coverage in the Applications Portfolio.

The Applications Portfolio is then redrawn and adjusted according to the effectiveness of systems support. *Exhibit II* shows the *Exhibit I* portfolio after discounting for effectiveness. When the two portfolios are compared, they show how data processing efforts are related to business needs. They also show where those efforts are having maximum effect and where they are being wasted. On the basis of this comparison the organization can revise and adjust data processing plans to accommodate existing circumstances and channel its efforts into the most profitable areas.

The Applications Portfolio indicates the stage of data processing growth in the organization first by showing the extent of coverage or automation of business functions and second by highlighting the areas of strength and weakness in this effort. Both the portfolio itself and the patterns of strength and weakness are important clues to the stage of growth. By comparing the portfolios of numerous organizations it is possible to identify stages by levels of coverage and by patterns of problems in reaching those levels. The latter is an important indicator of related factors in the other Growth Processes.

EXHIBIT II

Applications Portfolio After
Discounting for Effectiveness

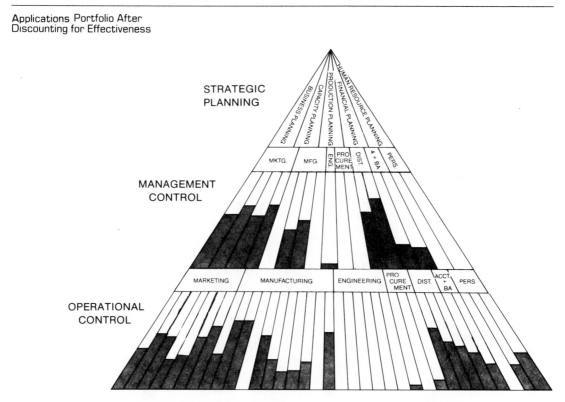

Data Processing Personnel and Technology

The corroboration or qualification of the Stage Assessment made on the basis of the Applications Portfolio begins with a review of the technical capabilities of the data processing area including hardware, software, and personnel. All of these are described and compared to the levels of coverage (attempted and effective) shown in the Applications Portfolio. Data processing personnel are described in terms of their roles and responsibilities in relation to equipment and systems as well as their data processing experience in general. The capability of the technology should be compared to both the skills of the data processing personnel and the requirements of the systems.

The juxtaposition of all of this information will explain many of the discrepancies between the attempted and effective coverage. For example, the organization may not have sufficient data processing personnel or sufficiently skilled personnel to carry out extensive development plans while continuing to keep up with maintenance on existing systems. If plans are carried out, the result will be evident in a growing gap between attempted coverage and effective coverage in the Applications Portfolio. Similarly, if plans for expansion exceed the capacity of hardware, a very costly contingency has been overlooked. Comparison of the Applications Portfolio with data processing personnel and technology can be used to avoid such problems and to set more realistic and profitable goals.

The User

Ultimately, data processing effectiveness is dependent upon the user. It is the user who receives the services and who must apply them to the activities mapped on the portfolio. User experience and user attitudes can be critical factors in systems implementation. Differences between attempted and effective coverage must be examined in light of user needs and user ability. If the systems do not help the user or the user does not understand how to use the systems provided, the systems are effectively nonfunctional. By understanding users, the organization can improve its understanding of the entire data processing effort.

The *experience* of the users is determined by their data processing history, the number of years and the type of experience they have had with data processing in the past. The *ability* of the user to maximize systems can be estimated by looking at this history and by questioning users in order to find out how well they translate their needs into data processing possibilities. The experience and ability of users can then be examined in context of their *motivation*, their attitude toward data processing and its potential role in the organization. If the users are not enthusiastic, they may not use systems regardless of how good the systems are. As a result, effective coverage will be low and growth will be difficult. On the other hand, if motivation is high but data processing is still in an early stage and the Applications Portfolio is very modest, frustration may result in complaints that make data processing coverage sound worse than it actually is. Understanding the user is therefore an important factor for understanding coverage and making a Stage Assessment.

Management Controls

The final growth process which affects the stage of growth of the organization is the presence and quality of data processing controls. There should be a steady evolution of controls paralleling the growing size and complexity of the Applications Portfolio. In many organizations, however, controls may be neglected or may be prematurely elaborate. Controls can support or retard data processing growth, leading a portfolio forward or causing problems which hold the organization back and detract from effective coverage.

The control of systems, procedures, and planning mechanisms can be measured in terms of organizational structure and in terms of existing procedures for monitoring and guiding systems design, development, and implementation. The two are interrelated since organizations are structured around responsibility for decisions and services, and positions are often defined by span of control. The organizational structure can be determined by existing models and through interviews. The first provides a normative picture of roles and responsibilities, the second gives a working picture of the *de facto* allocation of responsibility. Both affect the manner in which data processing controls are installed and applied.

Often misunderstandings about controls, or failures to take advantage of control procedures lead to a sense of disorder. The organization—often senior management in particular—may decide that the entire data processing area is out of control. The Stage Assessment addresses this question directly by providing the organization with broad and accurate information about data processing. It also suggests areas where future information gathering can be directly integrated into monitoring and control procedures.

THREE CASE STUDIES

The motivation for initiating a Stage Assessment is usually the suspicion that data processing is not functioning as it should be. The result of the Stage Assessment should be a better understood data processing situation which can be sustained by continued monitoring of data processing activity and periodic (every two to three years) repetition of the Stage Assessment process.

The Stages Model challenges organizations to ask "Where are we now?" and "How do we compare?" The Stage Assessment provides a methodology for answering these questions and for applying the answers to a planning process. Each of the Growth Process measures can be compared to:

1. the normative model

2. other organizations

3. periodic assessments of the same organization over time

The Stage Assessment supplies corrections for weaknesses, reinforcement for strengths, and proof of progress. It provides a basis for refuting exaggerated fears, for correcting overconfidence and for confirming good progress. It also helps to sort out minor and major issues, to distinguish between symptom and disease.

Each of the cases involves an organization which brought in a consulting group to conduct a Stage Assessment in order to settle the questions "Where are we now?" In this sense they are repetitive, involving the same measurement process described earlier. However, in each case the organization's assumptions about the answer to the question was different. In every case, the Stage Assessment provided an important clarification of circumstances which allowed the organization to make decisions and to move ahead with a more aggressive and self-confident attitude about its data processing future.

The Sarah Stone Health Center

Sarah Stone is a large academic and health care facility. During the late 1970s the management decided to reexamine their data processing function. The organization had made a large investment in data processing, but instead of satisfying users, data processing had become a source of frequent complaints. Rising costs were making it impossible to ignore the growing atmosphere of frustration and disappointment. Two central questions motivated the decision to call in a consultant for the Stage Assessment:

1. Is data processing out of control?

2. Is it costing too much?

Management suspected that the answer to both questions would be yes. The overall credibility of the data processing function had eroded.

The first step in the Stage Assessment was the completion of an Applications Portfolio for the center. According to the concerns expressed by management, the portfolio promised to be spotty with minimal levels of coverage in a few functions. In fact, the Applications Portfolio showed fairly high attempted coverage with more systems installed in support of a wider range of functions than would be expected in an organization like Sarah Stone. Even data processing spending was slightly less than average when reviewed as a percentage of revenue. In sum, spending and coverage looked good.

The next step was a review of the effective coverage and the functional ratings of the systems. If users were complaining about what appeared to be a reasonable level of service, the problem could be rooted in the connection (or lack of connection) between data processing and users. Either data processing had failed to understand what the users needed or the users had not understood how to take advantage of the systems provided them.

Interviews with users and data processing personnel revealed that both of these were true. The users were inexperienced with data processing and unaware of the potential of the service being provided. They did not understand the systems or how to use them. In addition, although management controls were reasonably strong overall, weaknesses in planning and monitoring of systems meant that data processing personnel were not following up efforts once systems were implemented. There was no long-range planning, no means of monitoring departmental performance, and a very weak systems development methodology.

The result of these conditions was that, inspite of a good stage II Applications Portfolio, data processing at Sarah Stone seemed to be in trouble. While systems were potentially effective in supporting the business, adequate communications were not being used. Data processing personnel felt frustrated because users did not respond to their efforts. Users were frustrated because data processing efforts did not correspond to their needs. Development resources were consumed in feasibility studies that ended up as dead-end projects. While systems and costs were not out of control, the inability of data processing and users to communicate meant that data processing investments did not effectively meet the needs of the organization.

On the basis of the Stage Assessment, two key areas were addressed: planning and communications. The Stage Assessment itself was used to establish a baseline understanding of data processing status which was shared by the data processing department and senior management. It was also used to reinforce the recognition that Sarah Stone indeed had the data processing strength it needs if certain weaker areas could be improved. Finally the situation was addressed in the context of the Stages Model to show that many of Sarah Stone's problems are typical of organizations at a similar stage of development. This relieved concerns, restored confidence in data processing, and helped to establish more realistic expectations.

Once there was a common understanding of data processing capabilities, the Stage Assessment information was used to develop a data processing strategy consistent with the strategy of the organization as a whole. For example, a data processing strategy was formulated whereby the separate divisions in competition with each other could, if necessary and if they had the funds, go outside for data processing services. This position was qualified by the statement that this option referred only to services unique to that division for functions which did not involve data considered usable by many users; i.e., corporate data. It was also understood that support in these areas would not eventually be brought in-house, but would continue to be handled as an outside service. Thus the mission of data processing (to provide comparable support to all divisions) was reconciled with the organizational strategy that had put those divisions in competition for resources.

A long-range planning process was then instituted with provisions for input from the users and senior management. This was coordinated with short-range planning procedures which provided information needed to make periodic adjustments to the long-range plan as priorities changed. This insured that future systems would be developed according to user needs and that users would be aware of and able to take advantage of the systems provided.

Finally, in order to guarantee that the planning and monitoring process continued over time, a steering committee was formed. This committee included representatives of senior management, user management, and data processing management. It was chartered to decide on data processing policy, to set goals, and to authorize changes to the long-range plan. In this manner a review process was introduced at a high level in the organization with agreed upon vehicles for management control.

As a result of the Stage Assessment, Sarah Stone avoided overreaction to a difficult situation. Management discovered that problems in data processing were basically problems of communication and control. Users and data processing personnel needed to improve their understanding of one another before systems could be completely effective. Better controls were needed to monitor and guide development and use of systems. Progress in data processing was essentially good, but difficulties in particular areas, identifiable in terms of the growth processes, had to be corrected.

Rothchilde Republic

Rothchilde Republic is a large bank with a "Tiffany" image both within the banking industry and among its international corporate clientele. The emphasis throughout the organization is on quality service. In 1975 the manager of data processing was replaced by a manager who was skilled in banking as well as operations. This change was made in hope that the low quality of data processing could be improved by someone more knowledgeable about the business of the organization.

The new management proved very successful. By 1980 the data processing organization had been rebuilt with a small high quality staff, technology had been upgraded, and communication with users was excellent. A steering committee had been set up to keep senior management abreast and involved in data processing.

The only remaining problem was insuring that this situation remain undisturbed, that data processing growth could continue without affecting the quality of service. The budget had been rising at thirty percent per annum for several years. Priorities had to be set and choices made, but attempts to do this threatened to disrupt a very satisfactory situation. Management was unable to extend the planning horizon without jeopardizing the status quo. The question at Rothchilde was not, "Where are we now?" but "Where should we go?" and "How can we get there unharmed?" The organization felt it was falling behind the industry and might be losing the high quality of service which was the key to its reputation and success.

The bank decided to call in a consultant who suggested a Stage Assessment. The Stage Assessment began with a review of the Application Portfolio which showed that, although applications were widespread, the bank was falling behind similar organizations, particularly at the operational level. This problem was affecting almost all of the functions in the portfolio. The Stage Assessment verified the suspicion that Rothchilde had to move forward, and quantified the extent of the problem. This placed new limitations on data processing plans.

The one-year plan for data processing included objectives suitable to a time span of three to five years. Responding to the need to catch up, Rothchilde developed a plan which involved a high level of inherent risk and required that data processing operate at the limits of feasible growth. The plan might work since the declared level of growth would be achieved in the upcoming year, but in the long run Rothchilde could lose the advantage of quality gained over the past five years.

In order to test the feasibility of these development goals, the consultant decided to examine all four of the Growth Processes more carefully. Only a uniform level of excellence in all areas would allay fears about the feasibility of the current data processing plans. A high-powered effort to move forward at this stage would require maximum support in all Growth Processes if the Applications Portfolio was expanded as planned.

The examination of the other Growth Processes indicated that uniform excellence was lacking. While data processing personnel were good and users were both skilled and well informed, four critical problems emerged.

1. The data center did not have the capacity needed to support the plan.

2. The data center environment was very complex and potentially unstable.

3. System installation procedures were weak.

4. Development schedules were not being met.

In the context of these problems, it was unlikely that the plan could be carried out without exacerbating problems and affecting the quality of data processing.

Three options were identified:

1. The problem areas could be corrected immediately.

2. The plan could be scaled back.

3. Rothchilde could proceed with the plan and prepare for the negative effects that would result.

The first alternative was ruled out because the areas of concern could not be corrected without fundamental changes, and those changes would require two to three years. The second option was more realistic but involved sacrificing the momentum built up over the last five years. It might also result in dissatisfaction among the users and loss of hard-won user rapport. The third alternative, while difficult, promised to maximize the existing strength of data processing in the organization.

In order to proceed with the third alternative, Rothchilde Republic had to institute a long-range planning process. There had to be some way to plan for the eventual repercussions of the short-range plan and to anticipate needs generated by the strain on the organization. The consultant suggested a two-part approach. First, the bank had to establish more realistic expectations about the plan. Missed deadlines and higher risk could not be avoided, but the risk could be minimized by short-term efforts to limit possible loss. The bank could accept small troubles and avoid disaster. Second, they could begin now to understand and to plan for the post-plan environment, to look ahead to the next stage and anticipate problems.

Specific recommendations in the second area, based upon the Stage Assessment, included two key efforts:

1. Preparation for prioritizing development and maintenance needs.

2. Strengthening the steering committee as a means of sustaining good relations and open communications between senior management, data processing, and users.

The steering committee could act as a filter for the balance of supply and demand and serve as a forum for joint decision making. In this way, as user demand rose, prioritizing by the steering committee would eliminate direct rejection of user proposals by channeling them into long-term planning.

The Stage Assessment helped Rothchilde Republic institute long-range planning as a complement to existing plans. It confirmed the feeling that data processing was strong, but also indicated pressures to continue to grow. The idea of evolution through the stages became the basis for a management strategy which answered both present problems (the need to advance rapidly) and future problems (the need to anticipate the consequences of putting pressure on data processing).

Mighty Chemical Bond

Mighty Chemical Bond is a multinational manufacturer of petrochemicals. Data processing management initiated the Stage Assessment in the manufacturing division in an effort to understand why apparently similar levels of service, rendered by a centralized data processing organization, had very mixed degrees of success at the different manufacturing plants. The stage of data processing growth appeared to vary from plant to plant. Central data processing needed to understand the reasons for this variation before deciding upon a course of action.

The Stage Assessment began by addressing the question "Where are we now?" both for the manufacturing organization as a whole and for each plant. An Applications Portfolio was drawn for the organization overall and for each of the plants. Attempted and effective coverage on all Applications Portfolios was compared in order to determine the relative status of data processing among the plants and the status of data processing relative to other organizations in the industry. The same comparison was carried out for each of the other Growth Processes in the organization overall and at each plant.

The result of the Stage Assessment confirmed the mixed environment which Mighty Chemical Bond had suspected. However, the Stage Assessment also indicated that the mix was not so much a result of varied levels of service to the plants as it was a result of varying environments at the plant sites. The uniformity of central systems and data processing personnel was offset by wide variations in the functional quality, that is the effectiveness of the systems, at the plants. The users were having a strong effect on the use of systems because the ability and motivation of users varied according to their familiarity with automation in general. Plants which had served as regional data processing centers before the central facility was created were able to make better use of central systems. In plants with a high level of process control automation, there was also a higher level of effective data processing support.

These varying environments also raised two secondary questions. Mighty Chemical Bond wanted to know if process control computers could be used to provide information in coordination with administrative data processing. The organization was also considering distributed data processing but was not sure whether it would solve problems or create them. The answers to these questions again varied from plant to plant. Some plants were ready to move ahead in both areas; in other plants only the most basic changes would be appropriate.

Future data processing planning at Mighty Chemical Bond would have to consider variations among plants. It would have to involve close coordination among the plants as well as individual initiative and adaptation. Instead of instituting one plan which could be defined and reviewed by a single steering committee, it would be necessary to set up multiple committees which could cooperate to formulate and coordinate plans. For example, distribution of applications and the amount of activity at the plants would have to be introduced gradually, as individual plants were deemed ready. Similarly, the organization could move ahead with plans to coordinate information gathering from process computers and administrative data processing, but implementation would vary from plant to plant.

As technologies are introduced and organizations with multiple environments become more common, the experience of Mighty Chemical Bond will be repeated. It will no longer be possible to summarize the stage of an organization without considering variations in the subdivisions involved. The Stage Assessment and the Stages Theory provide an evolutionary guideline for understanding this phenomenon. They enable an organization to use the Growth Processes to understand the effect of technology in general on the data processing potential within the organization. Without a Stage Assessment, the differences in data processing effectiveness among the plants might have been attributed to problems in central data processing rather than factors in the multiple environments.

CONCLUSION

Application of the stages framework in each of the three cases resulted in very different management actions. At Sarah Stone, the incompatibility of data processing efforts with organizational needs was addressed through strong planning and senior management involvement. At Rothchilde Republic Bank, the competitively driven need to quickly install large new systems was addressed through reducing identified risks and involving senior management for controlling additional demands. At Mighty Chemical Bond, varying levels of service by the data processing department to the various plants was addressed by tailoring plans to achieve a rate of change commensurate with the skills and experience base in each of the sub-organizations.

In each case, the Stage Assessment provided a descriptive model of data processing in the organization. This model was useful in distinguishing normal growing pains from true problems, and helped identify the actions needed to deal with the problems. Because the Stages framework deals with the dynamics of data processing growth, it is possible to provide a context for data processing organization which spans across time rather than one with focus on only a single point in time.

The
Applications Plan

JOHN H. L. BINGHAM
RAYMOND G. FALKNER

In the eyes of the user, applications represent the real value of the data processing resource. They are the most visible connection between what is being done by the business and the use of automated support. For this reason, good applications planning should begin with the business of the organization and should be considered an aspect of business support planning.

This relationship is illustrated by the Applications Portfolio where the functions of the business are represented in terms of opportunities for automation. By reviewing these opportunities and ranking them according to both business opportunities and technical criteria, the organization can develop an **applications strategy** matched to its **business strategy**, and an **applications plan** matched to the **business plan**. This will assure maximum real value for the user while monitoring plans governing technical and economic feasibility.

In the past, applications planning has often been based on a global approach and a generalized planning strategy. Opportunities for development were selected by extending existing systems or introducing applications in new areas on an ad hoc basis. The force of user demand or the technical attractiveness of projects often governed plans regardless of overall business strategies for the organization. As a result of these informal planning methods, the applications plan was often a random and uncoordinated listing of projects which overlooked many important considerations. There was little or no coordination of maintenance and development or the consequent demands upon resources. Lack of specificity, competition among users, multiple demand upon common resources, and similar problems increased as the scope of applications broadened. Eventually this resulted in a general dissatisfaction among users and an erosion of the credibility of data processing.

The disintegration of data processing's reputation under these conditions may or may not be deserved, but it is certainly avoidable. The methodology for applications planning proposed in this chapter eliminates many of these pitfalls of traditional applications development. We introduce an integrative planning process which systematically examines business needs and opportunity for automation before specifying development projects. By following an objective planning process supported by senior management, data processing, and users, the organization can use its Applications Portfolio and its knowledge of the other three growth processes (data processing technology and personnel resources, management controls, and user awareness) to generate a realistic, achievable plan which will result in growth and satisfaction.

This chapter describes the applications planning process and its characteristics throughout the stages of data processing growth and maturation in the organization. First, the applications planning process is traced from the description and analysis of the Applications Portfolio to setting the strategy and developing the plan for implementing projects. Second, the variations and influences are introduced which affect the planning process as an organization matures through the stages. Third, future issues in applications planning are introduced.

THE APPLICATIONS PLANNING PROCESS

There are two key concepts which underly the applications process.

1. Plans should be based upon a sound strategy.

2. That strategy should be the result of an evaluation of a complete range of functional and technical considerations.

The evaluation of planning considerations begins with information gathered from the Stage Assessment about the Applications Portfolio and the other three growth processes. This information is then used to prioritize applications opportunities and resulting projects.

The links to the applications planning process are shown in Exhibit I. As the exhibit indicates, the evolution of the planning process should parallel the management program. For each applications planning issue in Exhibit I there is a parallel management issue. Similarly, for each planning decision there should be a parallel management strategy.

The Stage Assessment

Users often see data processing as a powerful but expensive resource. They are interested in maximizing the value of the support they receive but do not know how to translate their business needs into data processing support requests. The Stage Assessment and the creation of the Applica-

EXHIBIT I

Linkages to
the Applications Planning Process

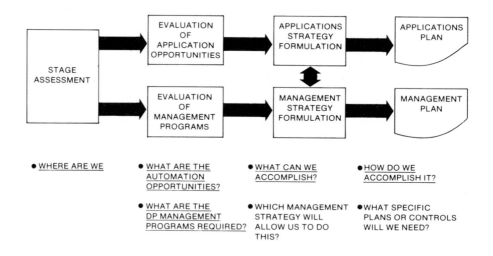

| ● WHERE ARE WE | ● WHAT ARE THE AUTOMATION OPPORTUNITIES? | ● WHAT CAN WE ACCOMPLISH? | ● HOW DO WE ACCOMPLISH IT? |
| | ● WHAT ARE THE DP MANAGEMENT PROGRAMS REQUIRED? | ● WHICH MANAGEMENT STRATEGY WILL ALLOW US TO DO THIS? | ● WHAT SPECIFIC PLANS OR CONTROLS WILL WE NEED? |

tions Portfolio help both users and data processing personnel in this translation effort. They supply a shared answer to the question, "Where are we now?" formulated in terms of business functions and activities.

The Applications Portfolio generated during the Stage Assessment includes *all* of the business functions for which some degree of automated support is feasible and economical. It does not depend upon existing applications for the identification of areas where there is an opportunity for growth. In this way, the Stage Assessment and the construction of the Applications Portfolio avoid the pitfalls of a passive or random approach to application opportunities in which users must initiate systems demands or in which data processing must act as an advocate to sell systems to the users. When there is no overall picture of potential for automation throughout the organization, (i.e., no Applications Portfolio), applications plans are generated on the basis of available and often incomplete information requirements. Critical or potentially profitable areas may be overlooked while applications efforts are concentrated in the most obvious but not necessarily most effective systems areas.

Gap Analysis - The Applications Portfolio

The identification of opportunities for automation makes it possible to decide where applications development efforts should be directed. Once the portfolio has been completed and existing automated support has been described, a **gap analysis** will indicate where there is an opportunity to expand applications, to improve applications, and to initiate new applications. The result of the gap analysis is an applications development perspective which weighs business needs against technical opportunities and constraints.

There are four steps in the gap analysis of the Applications Portfolio. *Exhibit II* illustrates these steps. The first step is the identification of the specific functions (or slices of the Applications Portfolio) where systems support could be improved, expanded, or introduced. In the second step these areas of opportunity are reviewed to find out:

- if existing systems are functioning as effectively as they ought to be according to the needs of the users (functional effectiveness)

- if existing systems are technically sound (technical quality)

- what the business priority of activity in this area is

- how important it will be to automate or increase automation of these functions (functional priority).

When these questions have been answered, the third step is a review of existing systems support and business plans. This information is used to make adjustments to the automation profile of the Applications Portfolio to, in the fourth step, define the opportunities for automation more

EXHIBIT II

Identifying
Application Opportunities

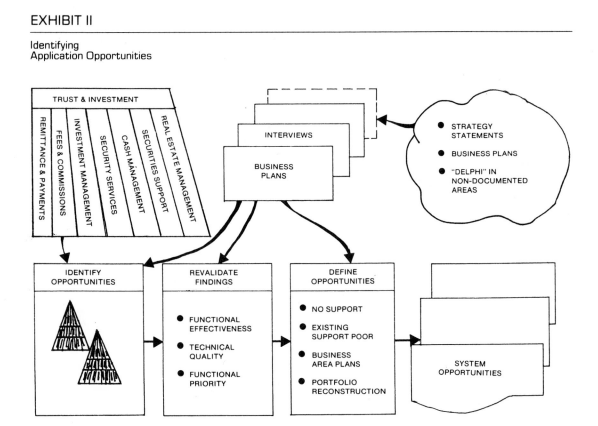

specifically. The result is a list of opportunities for building and improving systems in harmony with organizational priorities and plans.

Evaluating Opportunities. Before the applications plan can be drawn up, there must be some criteria for deciding how to approach the challenge of improving applications and developing applications in new areas. What are the criteria for choosing among all of the possible opportunities? What is going to be the overall direction of applications efforts? How should this reflect and support the goals of the organization? In sum, what does the organization want to accomplish and what support can it realistically expect in the applications area?

These questions break down into more specific considerations which can be sequenced to derive project priorities and project lists. First, the opportunities or gaps must be grouped in systems profiles. Next, these profiles or proposed projects should be reviewed for relative merit and feasibility. Finally, on the basis of a strategy for applications growth, priorities should be set and translated into an applications plan which includes a time-sequenced implementation plan.

There are several key criteria which are helpful in prioritizing applications projects and systems proposals. The weight given to each should reflect the business strategy and the priorities of the organization. These criteria, represented in *Exhibit III*, are:

1. business impact

2. return on investment (ROI)

EXHIBIT III

Key
Evaluation Criteria

(1) BUSINESS IMPACT	THE RELATIONSHIP OF THE PROPOSAL TO BUSINESS OBJECTIVES
(2) RETURN TO INVESTMENT	THE EXPECTED FINANCIAL RETURN RELATIVE TO THE LEVEL OF INVESTMENT REQUIRED, PLUS INTANGIBLE BENEFITS
(3) IMPLEMENTATION RISK	THE LIKELIHOOD THE PROJECT WILL FAIL TO ACHIEVE THE INTENDED OBJECTIVES
(4) CONDITION	THE ABILITY OF EXISTING SYSTEMS TO PERFORM THEIR FUNCTIONS EFFICIENTLY AND EFFECTIVELY

3. implementation risk

4. condition of existing systems

A strategy for applications planning should indicate priority guidelines in these areas so that applications can be selected by balancing their potential contribution to the business against cost and risk involved.

This can be further clarified by examining the question of risk and making a risk assessment of each project. This is accomplished by analysis and evaluation of technical factors (which may reduce the ability of data processing to build the desired system successfully) and operational factors (which may reduce the ability of users to derive expected benefits from the system even if it is built successfully). By analyzing risk, applications opportunities can be seen as business investment issues in which selection and implementation involve a trade-off of risk and potential improvement. Selection of applications in this context is translation of strategy into plans for action.

In a similar manner, funding strategies can be mapped against a prioritized systems list to assist in the selection of an applications strategy. The sequence for applications development and implementation over time will reflect the relative value of systems to the business when compared to their cost and to the technology and resources they will require.

THE APPLICATIONS PLAN

By applying the strategic model for overall applications development to specific situations, planning decisions become fixed and projects are selected. The applications plan is the detailed program for implementing these projects over time. It involves scheduling, budgeting, monitoring, and review of all applications activity. It is a coordinated, organization-wide effort which provides common guidelines, rationale, and review standards. It helps to avoid conflict, oversights, runaway projects, and obsolence.

When this methodology is actualized in a given organization, the assessment process breaks down into two reciprocal implementation sequencing steps. In *Exhibit IV* the prioritized systems list is translated into an implementation sequence. In this case, item 5, "Sales Master File," is placed first in the sequence; item 2, "Order Entry," second; item 4, "Shipment Document Preparation," third; and item 3, "Shipment Data Capture," last. The reason for this adjustment is that although they were sequenced as indicated on the priority list according to **operational criteria**, when **technical factors** are reviewed certain constraints become apparent and the implementation sequence must be adjusted to reflect this modification of feasibility. In *Exhibit V*, the process is extended and a five-year applications plan, sequenced by quarters, is created.

EXHIBIT IV

An Implementation
Sequence

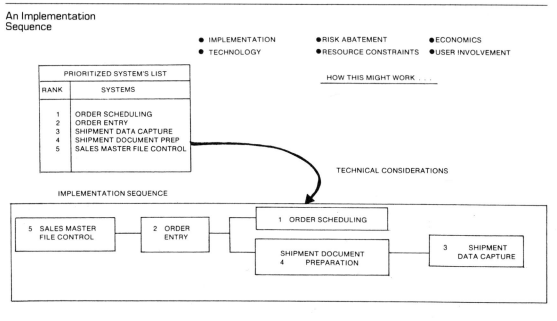

IMPACT OF THE FOUR GROWTH PROCESSES AND THE STAGES

The problem of planning and sequencing illustrates the importance of understanding all four growth processes. The strength of all four will influence the prioritizing and implementation sequence. One application may, for example, introduce a new, critical group of users to data processing. The function supported by the application may be critical to the business; however, since the users are so new to data processing, the risk of failure might outweigh the critical need. In another case, users may be skilled with data processing but, for some reason, no management controls have been put in place and extensive applications plans would be better postponed until sufficient management controls exist.

In other words, for every decision made on the basis of the Applications Portfolio, there must be a reciprocal review of supporting conditions. The adjustments entailed by the recognition of the four growth processes link the applications planning process to the overall evolution of data processing and its maturation through the stages. For this reason, it is important to know not only how to build an applications plan at any moment in time, but to understand how to extend the planning process over time.

APPLICATIONS PLANNING AND DATA PROCESSING GROWTH

The Stages Theory describes an evolutionary process whereby data processing grows from a small, innovative arm of the organization into a

EXHIBIT V

Systems Plan
Sequenced by Quarter

PROJECT	1980		1981				1982				1983				1984				1985			
	3	4	1	2	3	4	1	2	3	4	1	2	3	4	1	2	3	4	1	2	3	4
(1) ORDER SCHEDULING																						
(2) ORDER ENTRY																						
(3) SHIPMENT DATA CAPTURE																						
(4) SHIPMENT DOCUMENT PREPARATION																						
(5) SALES MASTER FILE CONTROL																						
(6) SYSTEM F																						
(7) SYSTEM G																						
(8) SYSTEM H																						
(9) SYSTEM I																						
(10) SYSTEM J																						
(11) SYSTEM K																						
(12) SYSTEM L																						
(13) SYSTEM M																						
(14) SYSTEM N																						
(15) SYSTEM O																						
(16) SYSTEM P																						
(17) SYSTEM Q																						
(18) SYSTEM R																						
(19) SYSTEM S																						
(20) SYSTEM T																						
(21) SYSTEM U																						
(22) SYSTEM V																						
(23) SYSTEM W																						
(24) SYSTEM X																						

HOWEVER: PLANNNING IS AN ON-GOING PROCESS, SCHEDULES AND SYSTEMS WILL BE
REVIEWED AND REVISED PERIODICALLY

sophisticated and integrated part of the organization. This growth is characterized by the transition from data processing plans which are tentative and fairly simple to plans which involve extensive, long-term commitments to both technological strategies and a new management style. In the area of applications planning this transition is characterized by shifts in the planning process.

The most obvious change is the gradually expanding range of planning efforts in data processing throughout the organization. In order to coordinate the four growth processes and to insure that changes in one area are supported by changes in another, new planning groups are formed. These groups illustrate the gradual penetration of the organization by data processing operations and planning. In *Exhibit VI* this change is shown graphically. As the organization moves through the stages, planning becomes more detailed, more extensive, and more complex, and breaks down into disparate elements which themselves require detailed planning efforts. Initial plans concentrate on equipment configuration and personnel; later plans include user development, management control plans, human resource efforts, and data resource planning as well. The

EXHIBIT VI

The Growth of
Data Processing Planning Activities Through the Stages

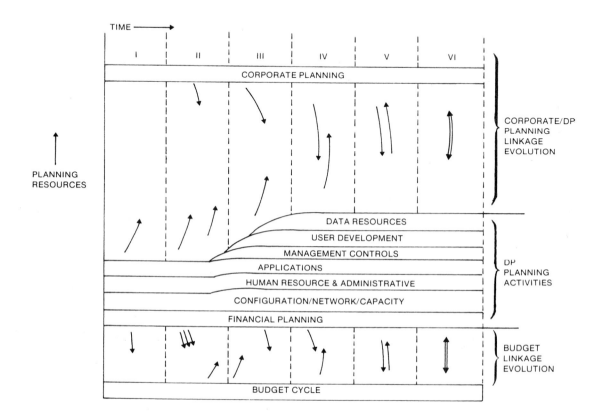

changes in the planning environment as a whole are reflected by changes in the applications planning process.

The three primary factors governing the maturation sequence in applications planning are:

1. Shifts in who determines the applications to be developed.

2. Changes in the way in which these applications are justified.

3. Increasingly sophisticated coordination of planning.

The stages of applications planning are characterized by three major shifts in these factors.

Early Stages - Simple Applications Planning

Initially data processing is treated as an area of technical expertise best managed by the people who know the technology. The data processing manager is viewed as a technical expert who acts as a liaison, bringing automated solutions to the user. He is the one who decides which applications should be developed first, how this can be done, and in what time frame. Users may express preferences in the applications they would like to have, but they trust the data processing manager to tell them what is simple and what is complex, what can be done and what is not feasible.

At this point, the primary criteria for justification of the applications plan is budgeting. In order to prove the value of data processing, the data processing manager will look for return on investment for system justification and use this to prove to senior management that data processing can better the organization through cost savings. The applications plan will be a one- to two-year listing of applications to be developed with an estimate of the required resources.

The applications selected will be simple and probably concentrated in such areas as accounting where automation involves a relatively direct transfer of old methods to a new tool. For the most part, both users and senior management will accept the selection, ranking, and prioritization of systems presented by the data processing manager. Their assumption is that these plans involve the maximum possible planning effort for the time frame given in the existing environment. In addition, the data processing manager will use these applications plans to explain anticipated (and even unanticipated) needs for enlarging staff and increasing equipment capabilities.

Although the applications plan may include both small applications directed at specific user requests and larger development efforts in such labor intensive areas as accounting, the plan on the whole will be simple. Since there is no pressure on the data processing manager to justify or defend his judgment, there is usually no need or effort to construct parallel data resource plans, network plans, or long-range configuration plans.

Intermediate Stage - Applications Planning Matures

As users become more sophisticated in their knowledge of data processing, they begin to question the decisions and the applications priorities set by the data processing manager. Moreover, as the technology becomes more expensive, complex, and pervasive, senior management begins to take a more active interest in what is being done by the data processing department and how it is being managed. The concept of the data processing manager as an expert erodes, and data processing services become a resource which is felt to be understandable by users and providers alike. There is a high demand by users for specific applications, and a parallel demand on the part of senior management for data processing decisions consistent with business objectives. This leads to the feeling that technical expertise should be distinguished from business experience and that data processing decisions should and can be reviewed against nontechnical factors by management.

At this point, two critical changes in attitude are being manifested:

1. The users now see themselves as participants in data processing and want to be included in the selection of applications and the setting of priorities.

2. Senior management sees data processing as a capital investment.

Simple return-on-investment arguments are no longer appropriate justifications for systems. Users and senior management look to data processing for estimates of cost, risk, and timing, but want to govern the overall decision making and applications plan.

In addition to this changing situation, the applications plan itself becomes more complex and sophisticated. Larger development efforts are now clearly distinguished from smaller independent applications in the plan. Multi-year projects which will require large portions of the data processing resource must be coordinated with smaller applications projects. Applications development must be coordinated with maintenance requirements.

The data processing manager's expertise is now considered a factor which determines his responsibility for equipment planning, overseeing of personnel, training of data processing personnel and users, and management of project commitments. In the minds of users and senior management, this shift may also mean that he should not be concerned with selection of applications except in an advisory capacity. While the role of the data processing manager will vary from organization to organization, there will be observable symptoms that applications planning is becoming oriented more toward organization and business-based issues and less toward technical issues.

In this context, all three key factors have shifted. The plan itself is relatively sophisticated and must be coordinated with activity in such other planning areas as users, networking, and data resource management. The data processing manager is no longer the primary decision maker. Users are not interested in determining which applications will be developed. Senior management is asking for business investment justification and has become involved in overseeing the coordination of organizational objectives, budgeting criteria, and applications planning.

The Later Stages - A Sophisticated Planning Process

Senior management direction emerges as a distinctive characteristic of the mature applications plan. It becomes even more pervasive as a coordinating management force as the overall data processing plan expands into a network of plans (see *Exhibit VI*). With the introduction of long-term planning (three to five years), data resource planning, and the effort to use data processing to give the organization a competitive advantage, it becomes necessary to institute a final review of the applications plan by such a central group as a steering committee. This group will coordinate implementation of all planning efforts, and ensure, for example, that the applications plan is reviewed in conjunction with the management plan, network plan, and human resources plan.

At this point, both users and data processing personnel have become supportive adjuncts to and members of the steering committee in formulating applications plans. They participate in the steering committee and assume responsibility for review and selection of systems, budgeting, standards, controls, documentation, and work flow analysis. Through tactical and project-level steering committees, users and data processing personnel take on responsibility for working together to gather and analyze the information necessary for justification of applications efforts and recognition of possible constraints. This includes setting business-oriented priorities as well as reviewing final cost.

In the later stages, a shift takes place to a high-level strategic approach to applications planning based on extensive input from supporting data processing and user groups. This strategic planning activity, represented in body by the decisions of the steering committee, necessitates the development of a feedback loop for review of applications plans. Data processing is expected to initiate controls and mechanisms for monitoring progress in the applications area. Data processing personnel also get information from both technical operators and users so that the steering committee can respond quickly to changing circumstances. The applications plan itself should specify mechanisms for measurement, reporting, review, and adjustment.

The applications planning process is now an ongoing process including both specific projects and overall review procedures. Activity in one sphere or over a given time period becomes input for setting future plans. The Applications Plan, now developed in full, includes both short- and long-term projects and an ongoing system for monitoring, review, and revision at regular intervals.

THE FUTURE OF APPLICATIONS PLANNING-
COMMONALITY AND DIVERSITY

The primary influence on applications planning in the 1980s will be the introduction of less expensive technologies which are easier to acquire and easier to implement. There is already a rapidly expanding trend toward decentralized equipment purchase and utilization. Applications packages are making it possible for users to assume responsibility for applications planning in many areas. Increasingly, new users are being allowed and even encouraged to learn to manage technology at their own place and at their own risk. A 1980s planning issue has arisen from the fact that the degree of risk involved in this kind of decentralization is not yet fully understood.

There is certainly a justification for this trend in the reduction of risk through the development of cheaper systems and applications packages that make trial and error less costly. The possibility of finding inventive new applications tends to offset the cost of implementation failures. In a similar manner, cheaper hardware and software packages mean that redundant applications design, implementation, and processing can often be justified.

On the other hand, opponents of the trend toward decentralization argue that users may be able to start up small systems, but as their data processing activity expands it will outstrip their ability to keep pace with planning and management demands. The result will be an increased long-term management risk which outweighs those temporary limitations on risk inherent in small size or lower initial cost. Even more critical, independent users' efforts in building systems may be inconsistent with a company's overall systems architecture and network.

The future of applications planning must lie somewhere between the extremes of a totally decentralized approach to planning and a single, centrally controlled approach. The same requirements for **coordinated prioritization** and **planning** should apply whether applications planning is carried out by decentralized groups or by a centralized data processing department. Even when striking out independently and attending to their own applications, users and decentralized data processing groups should see themselves as part of an ongoing, coordinated process of growth. Network planning and data resource planning can function as checks in this area, providing common points of orientation for applications planning in a diversified environment.

The arguments for and against decentralized applications planning are both complicated and, as yet, formative. The final decision will be determined by:

- corporate philosophy varying according to the business strategy
- objectives
- policies of the organization

However, whichever way the trend may go, it will certainly be critical for those who are involved with applications planning to be aware that they are acting in a changing environment. The most important factor for successful planning in the long run may not be a decisive choice between any two alternatives, but responsiveness to existing and future opportunities.

12

Data
Resource
Management

STEPHEN J. KING
SUSANNE J. NEHYBA

Voluminous but irrelevant management reports . . . lost sales due to incomplete and inaccurate tracking of product inventory . . . endangered lives of patients who are administered fatal combinations of drugs . . . loss of customers who do not have access to their funds at critical times . . . wasted manpower as the attempt is made to comply with new government regulations—these are just a few symptoms of not managing data as a resource.

Faced with a rapidly changing competitive environment, new government regulations, and scarce resources, companies today realize they cannot succeed without managing data in the same manner as labor, money, equipment, and raw materials are managed. Data allows the company to operate, manage, control, and plan its business activities. In the 1980s data has effectively become the fifth factor of production. It has become a critical company resource which must be managed as such.

Managing data as a resource requires a focus independent of single functional requirements. A broader perspective is necessary to understand how data is used throughout all functional areas and to structure data files to meet multi-functional needs. The objective of data resource management is actually two-fold:

- To satisfy immediate requirements placed on the use of data by business functions and processes.

- To satisfy the long-term data requirements of the business functions and processes.

This chapter provides an overview of **data resource management**, suggests a methodology for instituting and maintaining a comprehensive data resource management program, and concludes with some general guidelines on timing, personnel, and costs and benefits of data resource management.

EVOLUTION OF DATA RESOURCE MANAGEMENT

Historically, the data processing industry focused on the development of individual systems which were designed to produce specific information for their users. As information needs were recognized, they were satisfied through dedicated applications and dedicated data files. The result of this orientation is a rather narrow view of data, where each data structure is designed for a particular, unique business function or task.

Within this framework, the acquisition and storage of data are regarded more as a means to a narrowly defined end of a working functional application rather than as processes with value in themselves. The first step usually focuses on the end-user and identifies which data need to be reported; in other words, what the information requirements of the end-user are. Next, the analyst determines how the necessary data are to be acquired, derived, or aggregated from available sources, as well as how they must be manipulated to produce the desired result. The programmer then designs, implements, and tests the program.

The data files are, therefore, typically designed to be self-sufficient. They provide the data necessary for the execution of the program, but do not share data with other application programs. If data from files of another application are required for a new program, the existing application is usually modified to produce, in effect, a special report in machine-readable format which the new system can treat like raw data gathered specifically for its use.

In this situation, data for the organization as a whole are managed as an afterthought. In many cases, data are recaptured for a new application even though the identical information is already supporting an existing application. In a banking institution, for example, a customer's name and address might appear four times on four different files; one time for each of the four types of accounts he keeps at the institution. This redundancy is clearly a waste of storage space, but the more significant problem is that there is no simple method to insure that the datum remains consistent from one file to another. To illustrate, suppose that the customer moves and remembers to change his address on only three of his four accounts. At the end of the year when accrued interest is reported, the information on one account will be sent to the wrong address. Customer service units typically spend a great deal of time straightening out these problems, most of them caused by inconsistent and unreliable data.

Reports delivered to management are often incomplete and many times irrelevant for supporting the decision-making process. When related data are scattered over many files, the delivery of management information becomes difficult. Query capabilities are nearly impossible to install due to the complicated system interfaces and varied data file structures. The inconsistent handling of data across functional boundaries also contributes to the difficulty. A management summary of financial reports across many departments is completely meaningless if each individual report is based on different criteria and obtained by different calculations.

The system-by-system approach to building data files results in minimal sharing of data between application systems and organizations. **Data sharing** refers to the situation in which two or more application systems have access to the same data file. Having one system produce a file used by another system should not be confused with data sharing. Data sharing, rather, is the opposite of data redundancy. As such, it corrects many of the problems associated with data redundancy, namely increased collection, programming, processing and storage costs, and data inconsistency and unreliability.

Returning to the banking institution example, the four different accounting systems are not sharing data. In some banks, however, new systems have been introduced to maintain a central customer information file. With this system, a new file containing customer's name, address, social security number, demographics, etc., is created. This file can be accessed as necessary by each of the specific accounting systems and its users. In addition, the central information file may contain some summary statistics on the status of each customer's accounts. These summary statistics are updated routinely by the individual accounting systems to provide, for example, an updated day-to-day balance. In this scenario, data redundancy is no longer a problem. Once the central customer information file is updated, each accounting system has access to the most recent and correct information.

When file structures are designed to support individual systems, they are usually designed to make those systems run most efficiently. This design focus means that file organization and access keys are chosen for the convenience of one particular system. These data structures, therefore, cannot be used by another application system unless it happens to require the same structure. An example of this problem occurs when two business areas need the same information, but one needs it by customer name and the other by customer account number. In such a case, the files have to be reorganized, or the application systems have to be modified around a common file structure.

The negative impact of this funtional orientation of data is that communication and integration across departmental boundaries become very difficult. For example, marketing systems do not communicate with the materials requirements planning system, leading to high demand for production and insufficient capacity to produce. Data base management systems can avoid this problem. One of their major functions, in fact, is to provide software which enables any individual application to view data and data relationships and structures within unique functional requirements.

Another significant pitfall of managing data as an afterthought is disparity of coding schemes. As each user area builds its own applications and data files, many naming standards and coding structures start to proliferate throughout the company. There are organizations where product data are used in dozens of different applications, such as inventory, bill of materials, and accounts receivables. The data are defined uniquely for each applications, resulting in different words for the same meaning and different meanings for identical words. A typical example is a company with ten different product codes. Before an accurate inventory level can be obtained these ten different data structures must be consolidated, leading to extensive effort, disruption of present business activities, and loss of valuable time. These problems are addressed by a data dictionary.

BENEFITS OF DATA RESOURCE MANAGEMENT

The benefits of data resource management are realized across the whole corporation, from the user community to data processing management and senior executives. These are tangible benefits which are realized to varying degrees from any data resource management effort. As the scope of a data resource management program broadens, its impact increases to gradually benefit every part of an organization. Knowledge and understanding of data, managed and manageable data structures, and improved productivity are three main categories of these benefits. Let us examine each in more detail.

Knowledge and Understanding of Data

Data resource management provides an insight into how data are used to manage the business. It identifies what data exist, where they are created and used, and how they are created and used. It also defines what these data entities mean, and how they support and are supported by applications systems. By focusing on data in this manner, an organization can further identify how specific data can be used to satisfy the user needs and help achieve overall business objectives. Data resource management becomes a tool which can be very powerful when it is used with good business judgement and understanding.

Managed and Manageable Data Structures

The creation of managed and manageable data structures is another tangible and significant benefit. These data structures logically relate data and minimize the natural tendency within any organization toward data redundancy. An appropriate data structure which is well maintained and publicized can serve many users to their satisfaction. Data can therefore be shared very effectively, and the degree of unplanned and undesirable data redundancy can be reduced.

The data structures also provide a focal point for the establishment of data standards and their enforcement. These efforts assure that the organization has a common understanding of what data exists, what they mean, how they facilitate a common data language spoken throughout the many divisions, departments, and locations of a company. In summary, they are the focal point for the interaction between all information processing activities.

Improved Productivity

Improved productivity in information processing activities is another reason for implementing data resource management. Shared data structures minimize the duplication of efforts inherent in the traditional development of application systems. Instead of several organizations or divisions maintaining identical data elements, a unique data structure is developed and maintained to meet everyone's needs.

In addition to this improvement in productivity, the duplication of efforts caused by a new data reformat and extract file can be decreased significantly. It is no longer necessary to restructure data to fit the requirements of a particular application system or to consolidate like data entities to obtain the complete view of a particular business discipline.

Well managed data structures also optimize the application design process. Applications are planned and implemented as the need arises to manipulate existing data and produce new data. Once these new data become a part of an already built data structure, the design process is never duplicated. Above all, the process is very efficient because the existence, location, accessibility, meaning, and relationships of all necessary data are known. Systems analysts and data administrators do not spend precious time accessing data and making sure they have a correct understanding of data content and meaning.

Data base technology has a significant impact on the management of data by introducing a more powerful and a more flexible means for storing, retrieving, and manipulating data. As such, the data base has become a important tool in many data processing organizations. The data base is typically organized to reflect data relationships and structures existing in the business environment. It can therefore be shared by many applications, and its existence is independent of any one particular application. The data base is stored on direct access storage devices which permit the processing unit to access data quickly and efficiently.

There are major benefits which the data base environment offers over the conventional file environment. The following hypothetical case illustrates how an organization might measure the impact of data base technology on its environment.

At first, the important areas of data processing in the organization are identified. *Exhibit I* classifies these areas into four major categories. A simple chart is developed to reflect the impact of data base on those areas:

+: a favorable effect
0: no effect but potential opportunity
-: a negative effect

EXHIBIT I

Relative Rating:
Data Base Benefits at Organization Y Compared to a Non-Data Base Environment

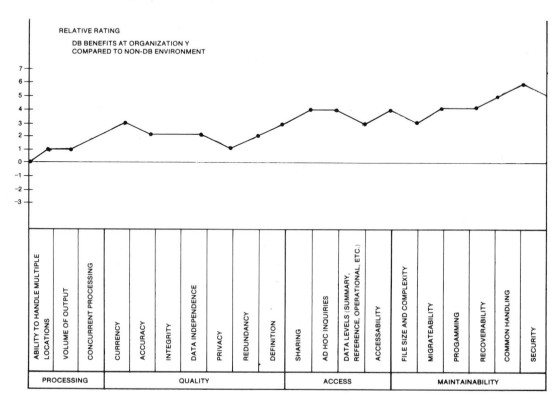

If the relative importance of each area needs to be taken into account, the scale can be elaborated to reflect this factor. Next, all areas are rated for potential benefits, as well as the benefits actually obtained if the data base has already been implemented. In Organization 4, the data base has a favorable *potential* benefit in 19 areas, and a negative effect in one area (a *potential* score of +18). The graph in *Exhibit I* shows that it has obtained a favorable benefit of +5 (10 favorable, 5 negative and 5 no effect). This analysis reveals that the organization is in a good position to take advantage of many more of the potential benefits offered by the data base technology. They have achieved only about five out of eighteen of the recognized benefits.

The sample case developed above is an illustration of how the benefits associated with data resource management can be subjected to measurement and presented quantitatively. Data base technology is by no means the total answer to data resource management. It is also not the only tool offering substantial benefits to an organization. The data base is, however, a powerful tool used extensively in many organizations today, and the challenge remains for many of them to take full advantage of its functional and technical capabilities.

TIMING AND GROWTH OF DATA RESOURCE MANAGEMENT

While many companies will face the transition to the data resource era in the 1980s and many others will ready themselves for this transition, data resource management in its full scope is not appropriate in every specific instance. Data resource management adds a level of complexity to all information processing activities. The learning, both at the organizational and technical level, is significant. It is difficult for an organization to assimilate this level of complexity before they have progressed through the first three stages of growth. The recommended approach therefore concentrates on building the base in stages 1, 2, and early 3, and focuses on data resource management in stages late 3, 4, 5, and 6.

In the early stages, an organization should begin to build the foundation on which future data resource management efforts can be laid. A data dictionary is perhaps the first step. Its implementation should concentrate on data entities which are most frequently used and which are also used across several divisions, departments, or locations. In this way the stage is set for data sharing and data integration, while also building the knowledge and experience level within the organization.

With the proliferation and availability of data base technology that exists today, an organization will acquire and use data bases in these early stages. They will usually be associated with individual applications systems, however, and will not differ very much from traditional data files in their functional capabilities. Although the advantages and capabilities of this technology are not fully capitalized upon at this time, valuable learning is achieved. The role of the data base administrator also emerges during this period, as discussed in the "*Data Administration*" chapter.

As the organization moves into the later stages of data processing growth, data resource management becomes more than an appropriate data processing program and a way to look at data. User demands for data processing services increase steadily, data processing budgets rise dramatically, and the applications backlog increases to unmanageable proportions. User awareness and sophistication is growing as well, and management issues start to dominate over technical data processing issues. The environment is ripe for data resource management; the organization is ready for a new orientation and the benefits it offers.

At the same time that a significant need emerges for data resource management, the capabilities for its implementation have generally also been built. Many diverse technologies such as data base, data communications, and query languages have been assimilated. Organizational learning is well advanced, and the skills and experience base has been built. The organization has moved into the data resource era, and all aspects of a data resource management program become important. Through data resource management, the organization can increase the automated support to the business, integrate its business functions, and increase data availability to meet management reporting and user demands.

Exhibit II presents high-level guidelines for an organization which feels ready for data resource management and intends to commit a significant amount of its resources to the implementation of company-wide data structures. The guidelines are developed around the four growth processes as follows: the first two growth processes focus on how the need for data base technology surfaces and begins to move the organization toward that end. The later two processes focus on how the organization's resources should be channeled and managed to satisfy the identified needs.

The management of risk is a critical success factor in this program. The implementation of company-wide data structures, for example, is a high risk venture for an organization with practically no data base experience. The size of the project is considerable, since its scope is the entire company. The structure is fairly complex because the disciplines of data resource management are not yet absorbed throughout the organization.

And finally, the very limited data base technology experience completes the high risk profile of the program. The suggested course of action is therefore to select a business area and pilot this approach. Such gradual implementation based upon accumulated successes will help to ensure the successful completion of the entire venture.

CONCEPTUAL FRAMEWORK

Our model for the data resource management program consists of the six components shown in *Exhibit III*. The activities modeled by these components are critical to successful data resource management. While each component represents a group of essential, related activities within the overall program, only the execution of the complete process results in an effective and efficient data resource management program.

Although the scope of the activities modeled above is all-encompassing, it is not intended to be the great vision of the future. Data resource management should be instituted gradually, based on a realistic knowledge of the resources and the needs of the organization. It could conceivably begin within a business area such as operations or plant management with just two or three applications and a small base of underlying data. It can then be expanded to product management, technology planning, engineering, and other business areas, until eventually the whole organization has been incorporated into the process. The important point to be made here is that whether the scale is small and only a few business areas are included, or it is large and involves almost the whole company, the model represents a flow of essential activities without which complete success cannot be expected.

An assessment of the current environment is the first set of these activities. It identifies the strengths and weaknesses of the existing resources and supporting infrastructure, and identifies as well those issues and guidelines important to data resource management and the organization. Strategic and tactical plans which focus on the long- and

EXHIBIT II

Characteristics Identifying a Need For
Data Resource Management

APPLICATIONS PORTFOLIO

- Organization recognizes need for standard and consistent data definitions

- Organization recognizes need for improved data accessibility, currency, and security

- Operational need exists to integrate automated support between business functions and between multiple locations

- Organization needs to provide management information from particular operational business functions and their corresponding application systems

- Need is seen for communications linkage between functional areas or with the external environments

- Need is seen to reduce the efforts expended on reformatting, sorting, extracting, and consolidating of data files

USER AWARENESS

- Different aspects of the business have pressing need for multiple views of the same data

- Business needs to efficiently access, update, or create data on-line

- Users build up demand for such processing capabilities as high-level programming or user query languages

- Users desire to become more accountable for the accuracy and security of data

DATA PROCESSING PERSONNEL AND TECHNOLOGY

- Architecture of data base management systems and related software products needs to be established (i.e., product compatibility and upcoming industry announcements)

- Criteria for the use of data bases need to be clearly articulated (i.e., amount of disk space available, benefits acquired per each application system)

- Technical advantages of the data base are recognized, such as standard back-up and recovery procedures, reorganization utilities, and improved access time

- **De facto** responsibilities for data today, right down to the individual programmer, need to be synthesized into a peer group to applications development

- Operationalize the business and data model activities into the data dictionary

DATA PROCESSING ORGANIZATION AND MANAGEMENT CONTROLS

- Data management functions need to be defined and integrated with key data processing management disciplines

- Data organization roles and responsibilities need to be chartered and a plan for the data orientation needs to be developed

- A communications program and a discussion forum for this concentration on data needs to be developed

EXHIBIT III

Data Resource
Management Model

short-term goals of the company are developed next. Finally, an implementation plan is designed. This plan completes the cycle, but also provides for a continuous monitoring and controlling of the entire process. With these mechanisms in place, the data resource management process can be continually improved and gradually expanded to the whole company. The following sections cover each component of the model in greater detail.

Business/Data Model

Business and data modeling represent the first set of activities in a data resource management program. This first component incorporates two kinds of models: a Business Activities Model and a Data Flow Model. Although both are interrelated and based on the specific functional and information flows within the company, these two models are independent and should be considered separately. One represents *what* the business does, while the other determines *where* data originate and are used.

The **Business Activities Model** is a functional representation of the business of an organization. It identifies the business functions, major organizational units and business processes, as well as the interrelationships and interdependencies of these business activities. In other words, it is a model of the flow of the business activities, a process flow diagram.

The Business Activities Model serves as a foundation for understanding the business and the organization. This model is essential for effective data resource management because it provides an overview of the organization and its business processes. Before data resource management can meet its objective of optimizing data use across the whole organization, management needs to focus on this global view.

The **Data Flow Model**, on the other hand, focuses on the data within the company. It first identifies the data, next focuses on where these data originate and are used, and finally focuses in on the interrelationships of those data. The Data Flow Model, as an individual component, is characterized by definitions and cross-references.

The Data Flow Model serves as a baseline for the data resource management program, since it identifies the current use and structure of the organization's data. Management needs to define a common language and to understand the natural attributes of data before it can assess the effectiveness and efficiency of the existing data resource management program, implement changes to this program, or implement a new data resource management program.

An extension of this data modeling process leads us to identifying data flows which currently do not exist due to application systems limitations, but which would make a particular business function or a process much more effective. In the manufacturing area, for example, direct access to manufacturing systems would allow for accurate inventory tracking and materials availability data. In the financial reporting area, direct access to order processing, cost control, and production control data would allow for accurate and relevant tracking of business performance.

In the initial phases of data resource management, the scope of the Business Activities Model and the Data Flow Model is a business area, department or a division. This scope gradually broadens to include the whole organization and to capture the complex interactions and inter-dependencies of all major business processes and data flows. As with any new program or discipline, learning needs to occur before the scope can expand. Yet many times there is a natural tendency to attempt too much, and to do so too soon and too fast. The recommended approach, therefore, is designed to overcome this tendency. It allows an organization to continue to support the ongoing needs of the business, while shifting the primary thrust to data resource management in a focused, controlled manner.

Data Assessment

Data Assessment provides a snapshot of how effectively and efficiently data is managed across the company. In general, strengths and weaknesses in the way the company manages its data are identified, and specific issues critical to effective and efficient data resource management are addressed.

The Data Assessment is structured around the four growth processes and data resource management expenditures. Specifically, the following analyses are included:

- financial analysis

- data portfolio analysis

- user awareness analysis

- personnel and technology analysis

- organization and management controls analysis

Financial analysis examines overall data processing expenditures and then focuses on data resource management related spending. Expenditure patterns are analyzed over time, trends are identified and projected into the future, and ratio analysis is performed. The strengths, weaknesses, and implications of the current and historical data resource management expenditures and financial support can then be evaluated. The analysis finally concludes with recommendations for future spending scenarios, concentrating on efficient allocation of the financial resource.

The **data portfolio analysis** begins by identifying each business function and the data which it creates or uses. Data characteristics such as accuracy, reliability, currency, security, and frequency of use are measured to reflect how well data support the business needs of each function. Reports that are produced during the information dissemination activities of the business functions are also defined and analyzed for their data content. These efforts assess the level and quality of data support to each business function.

The integration of data across business functions, organizational units, and geographic locations is the next step of the data portfolio analysis. Data sharing, data redundancy, data accessibility, and data use are evaluated across application systems and functional departments. This analysis measures how well the company's overall data needs are supported and satisfied.

User awareness analysis examines user involvement, knowledge, and satisfaction with data resource management efforts. Does the user recognize a need for data resource management program and can he/she identify specific benefits of this program? Does he support these efforts and is he willing to dedicate his resources to achieve the identified data resource management goals? Is he knowledgeable and experienced enough to become a valuable resource within the data resource management program? These questions assess the user community and identify existing limitations. They provide guidelines for a feasible data resource management program which will be supported by the users and will expand as their sophistication and experience expand.

The **personnel and technology analysis** evaluates the adequacy of this supply capability. The staff experience level and the staffing profile is assessed. Technical tools which support data resource management are inventoried, and their effectiveness and currency is evaluated. The analysis centers on the organization's ability to support data resource management, identifying weaknesses to be eliminated and strengths to be used as building blocks.

The last analysis examines the current **organizational structure and the management controls** already in place. It measures the effectiveness of data resource management efforts and the appropriateness of the organizational structure. The depth and scope of data resource management activities is evaluated so that plans for future growth can be based on realistic objectives and expectations.

Although it is important to measure the effectiveness and efficiency of current and past efforts, this is not an end in itself. The assessment is only a means to an end. By identifying strengths and weaknesses which currently exist, the appropriate strategy and tactical plans can be developed. As a result, everyone's efforts are well-coordinated and effective, moving the organization steadily toward its objectives.

Data Strategic Plan

Data Strategic Plan is a long-term, direction-setting program which focuses on the data resources of the company. It is a multi-year plan with the objective of effective and efficient use of the data resource. The planning process consists of identifying long-range data resource objectives, developing business policy to support those objectives, identifying areas of opportunity, and selecting those which support the overall business objectives. The coordination of the Data Strategic Plan with the overall business objectives is the key to its success. The plan must be integrated with the business and data processing plans to assure that the company is extending a cohesive effort toward meeting its business objectives and is not counterproductive in its actions.

Data resource management objectives can be classified into three main categories.

1. To increase the effective support which automated systems provide the business through better use of existing data.

2. To separate the data from applications systems to allow integration of business functions.

3. To provide utility programs for more effective and efficient data access and management reporting.

These specific areas of opportunity, then, are based on the overall business and data resource objectives, as well as on the results of the business modeling and data assessment efforts. They are targeted at specific data structures which require consolidation, conversion, integration, distribution, development or functional improvement. Each opportunity, once identified as a particular data entity such as customer or distributor, becomes one of the line items within the Data Strategic Plan.

Then, each item is evaluated and ranked based on return on investment, risk, intangible benefits, business impact, and condition. Funding alternatives are examined and the most appropriate is selected. The result of this process is a three- to five-year plan which concentrates on projects offering the greatest benefit to the business, supporting the overall business objectives, and eligible for financing within the company's funding guidelines. At this point, management should also identify any gaps in the existing supporting infrastructure, to insure that they will not jeopardize the successful execution of the plan.

Data Tactical Plan

The **Data Tactical Plan** defines the way in which the Data Strategic Plan will be implemented. It separates each targeted opportunity of the Data Strategic Plan into specific, finite modules or projects which have a one-to six-month time horizon. It also identifies the short- and long-term resource and management control requirements which are essential for the successful implementation of all projects, addressing business policy issues where appropriate.

The key concept in this planning process is balance. Business and data requirements must be balanced against availability and control mechanisms, and the Data Tactical Plan needs to be synchronized with other tactical plans.

The first step in developing the Data Tactical Plan consists of defining a comprehensive list of tasks for each strategic data opportunity and providing a brief description of each task. Logically organizing these tasks, consolidating them as appropriate, and identifying their dependencies, sequences, and timetables is the next step for tactical plan development. The resulting task matrix is then converted into a PERT (Performance Evaluation Review Technique) diagram. Roles and responsibilities are established for each task, and approval finally is obtained from users and data processing constituencies.

Once the line items of the Data Strategic Plan are transformed into specific projects, the underlying infrastructure needs to be examined. First, the condition of existing resources and management controls is evaluated, and specific opportunities and requirements are identified. Functional descriptions of resources and controls which are required for a well-balanced infrastructure are then developed. The next step involves estimating the time and cost necessary to implement the control mechanisms, and to develop or obtain the resources. And finally, these resources and control projects are sequenced and prioritized to complete the Data Tactical Plan.

The Data Tactical Plan provides three major benefits: large projects are broken down into practical, manageable projects; the efficient management and coordination of company resources and controls becomes feasible across the whole organization; and overall data processing capabilities are enhanced to facilitate management of data as a resource.

Data Structure Development and Implementation

The objective of this module is the actual implementation of the projects defined within the Data Tactical Plan. The process consists of three components:

1. logical data structure design

2. physical data structure design

3. data structure implementation

It is a process resulting in an operational data structure which satisfies user requirements and supports the business needs as well as the overall business ojectives of the corporation.

The logical data structure design represents a functional view of the data from a user perspective. It defines data elements in a standard way, identifies groups of related elements, defines relationships between these data groups, and specifies key field(s) within each group. The logical data structure design is key to user satisfaction, since it determines what data is available, who has access to the data, and how it can be used. To maintain its accuracy and appropriateness, the structure should be periodically updated. It also needs to be carefully documented to assure that the intended benefits and support to the user community are realized.

The physical data structure design first specifies and then analyzes the operational requirements of the data groups. These requirements include frequency of use, volume, response time, and accuracy. It then identifies, evaluates, and selects the storage medium, organization techniques, and access methods, based on the operational requirements and the logical data structure design. Finally, the actual placement and content of the data structures is specified. The physical data structure design therefore identifies where data will be stored, how it will be organized, and how it can be accessed.

Data structure implementation is the last component of this process, and the one which actually puts the data structures into production. First, the structures are loaded according to the physical data structure design specifications. Then utilities required for the support of the structures, such as backup and reload routines, are installed. Next, the data structures are tested for acceptance, and the work flow procedures and user documentation are established. The implementation process is now complete and production can be initiated.

The resource management concept becomes highly critical in this module. A successful data structure implementation requires efficient management of the organization's resources as well as coordination and integration of management control mechanisms. If the infrastructure is lacking, and the necessary level of support is not provided, the timely installation of data resource management projects cannot be guaranteed and should not be expected.

Data Service

The **Data Services** module provides for the successful operation and maintenance of the data structures. The resource and management control projects defined in the Data Tactical Plan build the supporting infrastructure for this ongoing process. Furthermore, both user and technical support staff involvement and commitment are necessary for the preservation of the functional quality and technical integrity of the data structures.

The management control programs are designed to achieve the desired balance between functional requirements and supply capabilities. They represent planned, coordinated, and continuous efforts which grow in scope and complexity as the data resource management program is gradually instituted. The following components, whether comprehensive or limited in their scope, should be included:

- **Standard Enforcement**. Publicize, advertise, and police the data standards of the corporation.

- **Conflict Resolution**. Mediate conflicts over the use, creation, and update of data in data structures.

- **Quality Control**. Assess and improve such data characteristics as accuracy and timeliness by reviewing user procedures and data processing operations.

- **Security Audit**. Inventory and resolve all data security violations.

- **Performance Monitoring**. Monitor technical quality of the data structures, and establish performance criteria and standards.

- **Change Control**. Minimize the potential negative impact of required changes.

- **Tool Support**. Provide technical education and answer issues, questions, and concerns about data resource management technology and its tools.

- **Data Resource Management Activity Support**. Supervise data resource management programs and assure their ongoing execution by providing direction and resources to both management and staff.

RELATIONSHIP OF DATA RESOURCE MANAGEMENT TO EXISTING DATA PROCESSING ACTIVITIES

Data resource management activities have an impact on all aspects of the data processing business. Many of the planning, management, and implementation activities feel this impact to a significant degree. The purpose of this section is to focus on these relationships and shed some light on the complex interdependencies.

Within the traditional information systems planning methodologies, data needs are determined by the applications plan. The data resource plan is therefore only an appendage to this applications plan. With a data resource orientation, however, the data resource plan becomes the integrating force within the overall planning framework. Business functions requirements identify data resource needs. As distributed data processing, decentralization, and telecommunications become widespread, the need to have the required data available in the right place and at the right time must also be met. An applications plan, then, is driven by the need to process data for particular business functions at particular locations. In summary, the data resource plan becomes the driving force behind other planning activities. It becomes, in effect, the common denominator between the business plan, the network plan, and the applications plan by concentrating on the input and output of components of data processing.

As an organization finds itself in stage III, the need becomes evident for managing data in addition to the other management activities. Data storage space increases significantly. Transaction volume experiences large growth. Low terminal availability presents a user service problem.

Data accuracy, security, and accessibility are usually less than satisfactory. Management information reporting is often inadequate.

When the management turns to these factors, an organization soon starts to recognize the importance of managing its data. Since the set of data entities does not change to any appreciable degree over time, the organization begins to understand how the effective management of data can assure its business success. The focus, therefore, will be transferred from application systems to the data resources. The organization establishes a management structure which controls and is accountable for its data resources.

For the many organizations who are currently moving toward decentralization and distributed data processing, effective management of data becomes a critical element in the overall management of data processing. There is a need for central coordination to assure that individual functions and departments are integrated, that the appropriate communication links are established, and that a global corporate plan is developed and followed by the whole organization. It is not an issue of centralized control, but rather of synergy which occurs when the activities and efforts of unique entities are coordinated. Data sharing, appropriate data security, data accuracy, experience and skills transfer, and equipment compatibility are just some of the benefits of this coordination.

Within the systems implementation framework, many data resource management projects will precede system projects, such as the development of a data base with many data structures, or the education of users in the use of a data base management system. The need for these projects is determined through the data and business analysis. The projects are intended to satisfy the multi-functional data needs of the organization and to build the infrastructure for the use of data as a corporate resource.

The implementation of other data resource management projects may be combined with system projects, such as the development of a distributed accounting system for a corporate office. Once the Data Strategic Plan identifies the need for a distributed accounting data structure, the data structure development as well as the data base implementation, and system design and implementation can occur concurrently.

The first step in this project is to decide what locations will perform each business function and what their respective roles and responsibilities will be. The data requirements can then be analyzed. During this process the project staff and management also need to address political issues and sensitivities to assure organizational acceptance of the implemented system.

Systems design, analysis of technical alternatives, selection of any required software and hardware, and systems implementation complete the cycle. The implementation of data structures, documentation in the data dictionary, and other data related activities are an integral part of this cycle. As is apparent in this example, there is sometimes a significant overlap between traditional information systems planning activities and the new disciplines of data resource management.

As personal computers, manager workstations, user-oriented languages and CAD/CAM infiltrate the organization, the central or traditional data processing organization gradually loses control over a large percentage of the company's total expenditures on computers. *Exhibit IV* illustrate how sixty-four percent of the total expenditures will, in fact, be outside the traditional data processing shop by the year 1985.

Managing the many varied disciplines of data processing in this environment is no easy task. Both senior management and user organizations will be looking toward the data processing group for direction and leadership. They will be relying on the experience and expertise which the data processing organization has accumulated over time. And as the management of technology by the data processing organization shifts from exercising complete control to partly establishing guidelines and providing leadership, the management of data becomes a critical element. Data processing management will shift its emphasis to a data orientation. When every division or department of an organization maintains its own files, and does its own data manipulation and data reporting, the management of data becomes as important as the management of technology. Data quality, integration, coordination, and accessibility can become the measures of data processing support to the business.

Data processing management, therefore, needs to assume this responsibility. It needs to bring senior management, data processing staff, and user groups together for the effective management of data across the whole organization. In this role, the data processing manager can become the coordinator, integrator, and quality control officer for the data resources of the organization.

EXHIBIT IV

Changing Computers Technology and
Responsibility Profiles

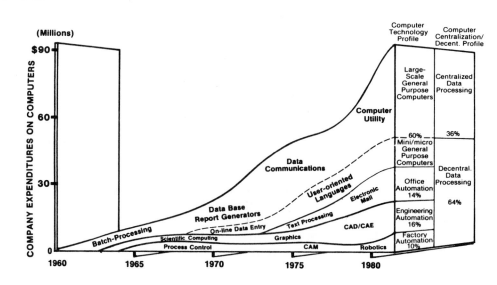

DATA RESOURCE MANAGEMENT ROLES AND RESPONSIBILITIES

Even before a formal data resource management program is implemented within an organization, many of the data resource management activities are already being carried out. They are, however, more often than not very informal in nature and not recognized as data resource management activities. There are three major differences between these informal activities and those within a data resource management program. At the beginning, the application systems focus gives way to a data resource focus. Secondly, some responsibilities which were formerly dispersed among many individuals are now being consolidated as the sole responsibilities of one individual. An example of this is each programmer naming new data versus a single data administrator who is responsible for naming standards of all data. And finally, data-related activities in the traditional data processing shop usually warranted the attention of applications project managers, whereas the data resource management program and its activities become important to data processing management, user coalition groups, and senior management.

There is no single organizational structure that can be recommended for all companies. Some of the factors which are unique for each organization and must be considered include the internal political structure, the existing organizational structure, and the stage of the organization. While no single solution exists, some general guidelines help assure that the organizational environment will have a beneficial impact on the effectiveness of any data resource management program. Each data resource management organization should have two components. The functional organization focuses on data from a business perspective, including data ownership, standardization, and common definitions. The technical organization, on the other hand, is concerned with the physical aspects of data including design, implementation, maintenance, and data security. These two components should be highly integrated into the overall organization by explicit definitions of roles and responsibilities. Their interfaces with users, data processing management and staff, business planners, and executive management are also key to the success of any data resource management program. The size of the data resource management staff is dependent on the size of the whole company, the responsibilities assigned, and the level of demands for service. At the outset, however, it is usually limited to a small staff of ten to twenty highly skilled and motivated individuals. The functional organization has the following mission: to plan for, coordinate, and establish the data architecture necessary to provide the required data and information to all the functional areas of the business.

There are several reporting alternatives for this organization. Reporting can occur within data processing planning and control, directly to the data processing executive, within each business unit, or within the corporate planning and control group. Wherever the organization is placed in the internal structure, however, it should be defined and given support by senior management as the focal point for corporate business data planning as well as the formulator and implementor of data policy cutting across functional lines. Some typical titles of individuals responsible for this group include "data administrator," "data manager," and the new title of "data officer." The skills necessary for these positions are extensive company experience, general management skills, and some data processing experience.

The responsibilities of this functional organization include business/data modeling, determining the quality of data structures, and establishing preliminary priorities for creating or converting data structures. The functional organization is also responsible for developing the Data Strategic Plan and the Data Tactical Plan. This group manages the data structures development process, and evaluates data use across the many functional areas of the business.

To carry out these responsibilities, the functional organization will need to rely on several broad guidelines and procedures. These mechanisms need to be established on a corporate-wide basis, setting one standard for the organization and assuring a cohesive and coordinated data resource management effort. The development of data standards and policies covering such areas as data accuracy requirements, data security requirements, and terminal availability, will allow the organization to monitor the quality of data structures against established standards. The existence of enforcement procedures, including user conflict resolution and data responsibility, assures effective ongoing management of the data structures. The detailed procedures for the interface with the systems development processes allow for the development of appropriate and well-designed data structures. Procedures for the use, control, and access of major data resource management tools, such as data base management systems and report writers, permit the functional organization to supply users with the capabilities to access, organize, and manipulate their data in a controlled and managed environment.

The technical organization is responsible for the management and implementation of the physical data structures as well as the supply of the support capabilities, such as data base management systems, query languages, and the data dictionary. This organization should not be under the direct control of users, systems analysis, computer operations, or systems programming in order to allow it to make physical implementation and design decisions from a company-wide perspective. The logical alternatives, therefore, include placement within the technical support group, placement with the data processing executive, or placement with part of a data resource management organization within the data processing department. The data base administrator is a position typically found in this technical data resource management organization. The individual should have a strong technical background and some management skills to be able to communicate with the technicians as well as users and management.

The responsibilities of this organization consist mainly of data structure implementation, the management of support utilities, and the monitoring of data structures' performance. It is within the scope of these responsibilities to assure complete documentation of data bases, provide proper training in the concepts and techniques of data base to users and data processing staff, and monitor data base use and performance. In short, the technical disciplines of the data resource management activities are the domain of this organization.

The most important guidelines for the technical data resource management organization are the data base design standards and policies. These guidelines must address storage/processing tradeoffs, acceptable access alternatives, general design considerations, and performance criteria. Second are the procedures for restart, recovery, and backup of the data bases. To prevent any conflicts in the transfer of responsibility from one party to another, the responsibilities of users, data processing staff and data resource management staff should be clearly articulated. Also important are the training procedures, guidelines for skills requirements and staff development, and change control procedures.

Once the data resource management organization is installed, its functional relationships and interfaces with other company units must be carefully defined. A new orientation throughout the business, one which focuses on data, cannot be achieved through the establishment of a data resource management organization alone. The five other factions, namely users, business planners, senior executives, data processing management, and data processing staff, also need to assume a supportive role as the organization makes the transition into the data resource era.

The interaction between users and the data resource management organization must be characterized by mutual respect and a close working relationship. User committees or coalitions need to work together with the data resource management organization to resolve ownership and control problems. Jointly they also can sponsor projects to foster data sharing, data standardization, and data definition. User participation during the data resource management development life cycle is important to assure user acceptance and satisfaction with the resulting data structures, their quality, and the future data plans. After all, users are the ones with the business needs. Their involvement in the development life cycle, therefore, assures that these business needs are met.

Within the planning phases of data resource management, the business planners become an important source of information. They inform the data resource managers of company policies, business goals, and objectives. They also provide input to the data resource management funding strategies, instilling in the data resource management organization corporate-wide funding guidelines. Together with the data resource management organization they coordinate data objectives with overall business objectives. Endorsement of the data plans must be obtained semi-annually from the business planners in order to build commitments and relationships within data resource management.

Interface with the senior executives will become increasingly important as the data resource management program gains momentum. Initially, their intervention occurs in an effort to control escalating expenditures on data processing. This probably led to the establishment of a steering committee and an era of control over the use of data processing.

The steering committee becomes the initial forum to review and approve resource plans, to monitor performance, and to resolve data conflicts which cannot be handled routinely. Senior executives support the data resource management organization by providing visible and high-level backing of business policy decisions and organizational impact statements.

The rationale behind the implementation of data resource management should be well understood and communicated by the senior executives to all levels in the company. The senior executives benefit through increased access and availability of data, given the proper training. As one senior executive recently remarked, "Rather than put more into the computer, let's make better use of what we have." Data resource management and senior executives are two major factors in making this happen.

Most data resource management organizations (i.e., both functional and technical) are introduced with the data processing department. All too often though, the bonds with data processing management and data processing staff are not firmly established. Data processing management must view data resource management as one of four or five major programs. The program must be marketed, it must produce results, and it must be well-managed. In order to accomplish this, data processing management influences the assessment, planning, and implementation phases of the data resource management program. Data processing management will detail guidelines and assist in development of data plans to assure overall integration. Data processing management must also make long-term data resource management decisions such as resource limitations, internal conflicts over the creation or use of data, and business extension of the program.

Interface between the data resource management organization and data processing staff is fundamental to establishing a common language and managing common data structures. The involvement of data processing staff will be concentrated in the physical implementation and ongoing use of data. Data processing staff provides consulting or manpower support to assessment and planning activities, participates in data definitions and design processes, and uses data resource management standards, tools, and control procedures. Efforts should be taken not to bring too much formality to this relationship immediately. There is a natural tendency to protect individual territory and not to change what may already be working. This does not alter the fact that the central and visible presence of the data resource management program is absolutely necessary within the data processing department itself.

In summary, the data resource management organization must contain a focus for the business and technical aspects of the program. Balance must be established during the early years. The data resource management organization will always be responsible for performing or executing all data-related activities. The respective roles of other personnel should be:

- users *assist*

- business planners *consult*
- senior executives *review*
- data processing management *approves*
- data processing staff *assist*.

Management of data is as fundamental as execution of business functions. Therefore, every member of the organization must contribute and be an integral part of the data resource management program.

COSTS AND VALUE OF DATA RESOURCE MANAGEMENT

While in the previous sections we alluded to and identified the numerous benefits of data resource management, we have not focused on the demands it places on the organization and the costs associated with implementing it. This concluding section concentrates on these elements and the difficulties, barriers, and costs inherent in data resource management implementation.

Without the commitment, support, and participation of senior and middle management, data cannot be managed as a corporate resource. Business policy issues which have been avoided in the past can no longer be ignored. An overall corporate view of data and efficient management of the data cannot be achieved at the divisional or functional level. Many times, important organizational issues arise and have to be resolved. A case example serves as an illustration.

A retail product company identified an opportunity in the data plan to have the sales office input data directly into the order data base used by the warehouse. It appeared to be a viable alternative and an excellent solution to improving service response and customer satisfaction. The organization, however, rejected this alternative. This change represents an inequitable and unacceptable distribution of work and responsibility in their decentralized environment. The sales manager would be completely responsible for the maintenance of the data structures, the quality of data (i.e., accuracy, validity, and timeliness), and the cost of data entry. The warehouse manager's responsibility would then be simply to follow the instructions in the order data base.

Before accepting and implementing an element within the data plan, senior management needs to consider its implications for the organizational structure. They must ask first if the managers involved are in agreement with this designation of responsibility, and determine how problems would be resolved. Who will be responsible if an order is missed or filled incorrectly? How could the warehouse manager insure that previous precautions inherent in his responsibility for order entry data are continued when sales assumes control over data?

This example clearly focuses on the key issue. Once the data crosses functional responsibilities, data integration and sharing begin to emerge.

Business functions become interdependent through data and the organization's top management must be involved in the data management efforts. Data processing personnel or users alone cannot resolve issues which have deep policy and organizational implications. They also cannot chose the most appropriate alternatives because their view of the organization is very narrow.

As an organization progresses through the early stages toward the data resource era, new technologies, skills, and responsibilities must be gradually assimilated. Although this process is almost self-sustaining due to the availability of technologies, the decreasing cost of hardware, and the "everybody's doing it" syndrome, it is effective only with careful management and planning. Adopting a data resource orientation also requires significant efforts. The leading constituencies, namely data processing, senior executives, and sophisticated user groups, must concentrate and target their actions to successfully bring about this change.

In the initial phases of data resource management, before many of its benefits become a reality, some resistance to the program is only natural. Many users associate the central coordination of data plans and projects with loss of control over their data. The controls introduced to govern the implementation of a data resource management program may be confused with an effort to control the way people do their jobs. These factors represent a difficult mix of tangible and intangible elements which contribute to the resistance. They also teach an important lesson. The organization adapts slowly, and some users are progressive while others prefer little change. Results are necessary before complete acceptance can be achieved. It is therefore important to start slowly, build on prior successes and achievements, and gradually raise the awareness and understanding levels within the organization.

As users place more and more demands on data processing and the Applications Portfolio coverage gradually increases, the data processing budget also grows. By stage III, data processing is faced with a substantial backlog of systems and a significant budget. Focusing on data resource management at this time requires additional resources. While only a few individuals are necessary in the initial phases, the organization's sensitivity to an oversized data processing budget can become a limiting factor.

The expenditures related to data resource management increase with time. As they reach a significant portion of the total data processing budget, an organization will want to justify these additional costs and efforts. *Exhibit V* suggests a framework for such an analysis.

● **Value of Information**

Value of data based on benefits provided, importance to the company, opportunity costs, and replacement costs
Values of data bases
Value of information acquired through applications, ad hoc reporting, or transaction processing

EXHIBIT V

A Financial
Perspective

INFORMATION STATEMENT	1980
VALUE OF INFORMATION	85.0

COST OF PRODUCING INFORMATION
  COLLECTION, PROCESSING,
    STORAGE, DELIVERY
	0.6

ENHANCEMENT, MAINTENANCE DEVELOPMENT	0.8
	83.6
ADMINISTRATION	0.4
DEPRECIATION	3.4
INFORMATION VALUE FOR THE YEAR	79.8

This value assessment should reflect the benefits acquired through data resource management,

Direct manpower savings
Ability to meet business objectives (i.e., service level, market share)
Competitive advantages
Improvements in decision making ability
Improvements in data accuracy, flexibility, currency, security, etc.

- **Cost of Producing Information**

Cost of data projects, including personnel, materials and cost per unit.
Procedural costs (i.e., man-hours equivalent for documentation) in a data dictionary
Tool costs (i.e., data base management system, data dictionary, query languages, etc.)
Data resource management personnel (i.e., on-going personnel support cost)

CONCLUSION

The data resource era is upon us. Organizations must begin to invest today to build stronger, more profitable organizations of the future. Effective use of data is an important vehicle on this path. Data resource management assures that the vehicle runs smoothly and travels great distances.

13

Network Planning

STEPHEN C. HALL

The information systems and the data resource of an organization remain lifeless and useless until there is a provision for the communication of outputs and data to the people and/or machines needing them. Recent technological developments have not only revolutionized the methods of sourcing, processing, and storing data, they have begun to revolutionize the methods of communicating data. By developing a **Network Plan**, an organization can maximize the advantages of these new technologies according to a strategy compatible with its business and management style.

A **Network** is defined as the telecommunications interconnection of computers, mini-computers, and terminals (intelligent and non-intelligent) to provide for the rapid and direct transfer of information from people to people, from people to machines, from machines to people, and from machines to machines. **Network planning** is the process by which the systems and data resource strategies of the organization are developed into specific network architecture, a management implementation plan and systems/network configurations.

The need for careful Network Planning is a result of the enormous technological success of recent years. New technologies are being made available almost more quickly than they can be absorbed by all but the most mature organizations. Hardware costs are decreasing. Systems control and networking software are improving. Off-the-shelf application software is attempting to reduce the impact of development time on the productivity of in-house data processing professionals, a key issue for data processing in the 1980s.

In this atmosphere of rapid innovation it is tempting to embrace solutions in an ad hoc manner. The number of alternatives make improvement seem inevitable. However, unless an organization has made a clear assessment of its particular situation and developed a strategy for addressing its own needs, networking can bring as many problems as solutions. Long-term implementation success in networking depends upon good planning both immediately and for the distant future. Even in the presence of abundant technical progress, management and business planning are irreplaceable assets to successful progress and growth.

However, neither the network technologies alone nor the distribution of processing can solve problems in the area of people and communications. In many cases, the introduction of a technical solution without a management strategy may only highlight existing issues rather than resolve them. Networking technologies should be introduced in response to proposed strategies for addressing policy problems. This Network Plan should anticipate the possible effects of these problems and include choices based upon the needs and the management style of the organization as well as the capabilities of available technologies.

The question for most organizations is not whether they should move into extensive networking, but how to make the move as smoothly and effectively as possible. Successful answers to this question depend upon good understanding of networking and the integration of network planning in both long-range and short-term data processing planning.

This chapter adresses the issues involved in Network Planning by dividing them into three general areas of concern:

1. The availability of networking technology

2. The rationale for Network Planning

3. The process of building a Network Plan

The first section, *Technology: Trends Toward Networking*, demonstrates that the range of technologies currently available makes it possible to discard the notion that technology must drive the Network Plan. The second section, *Network Planning: The Four Growth Processes*, suggests priorities for planning based upon the needs and character of an organization. The final section, *Building a Network Plan*, describes a methodology for generating a Network Plan.

TECHNOLOGY: TRENDS TOWARD NETWORKING

Networking involves the building of an information system for the organization by using a variety of communications systems. While the specific selection of one technology over another should follow the development of a strategy and a Network Plan, it is important to be aware of all of the general categories of systems available, to understand their common characteristics and their differences, before making a decision. Before establishing a rationale for networking, there should be an agreement among the involved members of the organization on general working definitions of the technologies involved. This section provides a blueprint for these definitions.

The computer itself is central to telecommunications and networking activity. Even though there is a lot of talk about the unique advantages of micro, mini, distributed, and central computers and about data resource, office automation, and other new ideas, there is still a great deal of truth to the statement, "A computer is a computer." All computers have input, processing, and output functions. All have systems software to control and manage available resources. All computers have languages which are used to develop applications which automate technical processes, business functions, or personal activities. And all computers have peripherals (e.g., cards, tape, disks, printers, CRT's sensors) which meet the organizational needs of the users to close the people and machine communications loop.

The differences between computers are determined primarily by size, mode of use, and cost benefit. These are the criteria which influence equipment choices. The appropriateness of a computer to the needs of an organization will depend upon the amount of computer power the organization needs, the manner in which that computer power will be used (geographic dispersion and periods of low/high use), the functions to be supported (the volume of data and the way in which it is used), and the economic constraints of the organization.

Computers range in size from microcomputers to large, central computers. They can be used in support of personal activities like problem solving and word processing (smaller computer functions) or for the mechanization of major business functions involving significant volumes of data (batched or on-line production). Microcomputers cost only thousands of dollars and show cost benefit in the enhancement of the productivity of the individual. Central computers cost millions of dollars (for hardware, development, and maintenance) and affect the productivity of the entire business.

Because of the diversity of available technologies, networking planners do not need to depend on any one approach or product for a planning model. To the contrary, in order to insure consideration of a full range of potential solutions, planning for networking should include consideration of as many networking strategies as possible. This also means that there should be a clear sense of what technologies are being offered, what they can do, and in what context they function best.

A good set of working definitions for the kinds of technology available provides a common starting point for examination of networking alternatives. It gives the organization a starting point for matching needs to strategy and strategy to a Networking Plan. The following list of terms illustrates the range of technologies available and offers some basic working definitions. In the future the list will grow and eventually become obsolete but it is useful as an illustration of the scope of networking alternatives available.

Computers

Microcomputer. The microcomputer is a small, independently programmed and operated personal-use computer. A typical configuration might have a thirty-two to sixty-four thousand character memory, a cathode ray tube (i.e., T.V. screen) or keyboard printer, and diskette or cassette disk storage device. These computers cost from $300 to $15,000 and include the Apple II, TRS-80, and the IBM 5100.

Minicomputer. The minicomputer is a medium scale computer capable of supporting multiple computing tasks, business transactions, or processing functions concurrently. It has moderate input/output capacity. A typical configuration includes up to 500k memory, 100mm characters disk and/or tapes, 16 CRT terminals and a line printer. A minicomputer will cost from $10,000 to $100,000. Examples include DEC 11/45, IBM System 34, HP-3000, Data General Nova and Prime/1.

Central Computer. A central computer is a large scale computer capable of supporting multiple, concurrent production processes (e.g., batched jobs, remote batch entry networks, interactive computing (network), database/data communications) with high volume and high quality input/output capacity. Configurations range up to 16 million characters of memory, 100 billion bytes of disk, 6250 bytes-per-inch tapes, 15,000 words-per-minute printers and several thousand CRT terminals. A central computer may cost from $100,000 to $10 million. Some of the more common central computers are the IBM 370 or 303X, Burroughs 6700, CDC 6600, DEC 20, Honeywell 6000, and Univac 1108.

Specialization

Timesharing. Timesharing is a hardware and software specialization that allocates the resources of a central or minicomputer by giving slices of time to users in a way that gives the perception of continuous use and access for multiple on-line users. Timesharing is used for interactive problem-solving, program development, data analysis, or modeling. Examples of time-sharing operating systems include DEC VAX II, IBM CMS or TSO, Dartmouth DTSS, and Honeywell Multics.

Sensor-Based Computers. Sensor-based computers are another hardware and software specialization of micro, mini or central computers. Sensors are used for the direct acquisition and output of digital or analog data which may come from any source and can be fed back to any automated control device. These computers have been used in such applications as the environmental control of a building, laboratory automation or process control in manufacturing.

Word Processing. Word Processing is a hardware and software specialization which uses micro, mini or central computer systems to provide one or many operator work stations with a keyboard, CRT, and printer enabling users to do text entry, editing, printing, storage, and retrieval. This equipment may be used for letters, document preparation, library activities, or, in conjunction with communications equipment, for electronic mail. Examples among microcomputers range from the IBM Memory Typewriter to the Apple II; among minicomputers, Wang, Lanier, and IBM System 6; and among central computers, the IBM ATSS or CMS-Script.

Linkage

Computer Networking. In terms of equipment use, computer networking refers to the hardware and software specialization of computer, telecommunications control, and terminal systems which enables interconnection of computers for the purpose of message or transaction switching, data sharing, workload leveling, or critical functional backup. The network configuration may be primitive (point to point), peer structures (each computer sharing in the network resource), or hierarchical (one computer directing the activities of the entire network). In the context of operational planning, the concept of networking extends beyond equipment to planning with attention to all four growth processes.

Distributed Data Processing. Distributed Data Processing is any form of computer networking providing for the orderly placement of computer power and resources in close proximity to the users. It involves the distribution of some equipment containing computer logic and memory and enables such functions as data entry, transaction processing, and programming using the computer equipment. In the context of this chapter it is considered to be a networking alternative which distributes a greater amount of control over the use and operation of the configuration to the user.

Office Automation. Office automation involves the interconnection of computer, telecommunication, recording, telegraphics, and other equipment to provide centrally and electronically managed office services such as word processing, mail, copying, message communication, transcription, filing, etc. The primary vendors in this area to date are IBM, Xerox, Kodak, Exxon, Wang, and Lanier.

NETWORK PLANNING—THE FOUR GROWTH PROCESSES

There is no question as to the *availability* of the technology necessary in networking. It is clearly a potentially powerful asset which would be a considerable enhancement to the data processing capabilities of all organizations. However, decisions about using the technology should not be made on the basis of the equipment itself. The decision-making process should begin on the direction-setting level in the organization. It should be based on an informed awareness of the available technology as well as a comprehensive understanding of the needs and objectives of the organization.

The Stages Theory provides a framework for building a strong overall understanding of the organization in these terms. It helps the planners describe the capability of the organization to utilize and manage various technologies. By examining the four growth processes, a baseline for network planning can be described. This basic model helps to insure that the Network Plan will be both suitable and feasible.

To summarize briefly, the four growth processes as they relate to the Network Plan can be defined as follows:

- **Application Portfolio**. The business and data communication functions to be automated.

- **User Awareness.** The considerations of managing the impact of change in relation to the ability and motivation of users to absorb new communications technologies and policies.

- **Resources: Technology and Data Processing Personnel.** The use of appropriate computer hardware, software and telecommunication facilities, equipment, and terminals to fit the strategy and architecture, and the corresponding match of skills at the management, design, and operations levels.

- **Management Data Processing Organization, Plans, and Controls.** The building of organization specialties, a management team, and the management processes or infrastructures for enabling the planning, management, and operations of networks.

A complete Network Plan should include the building of a baseline model, an assessment of the current networking environment, a strategy for the functions to be networked (an architecture), and an implementation plan. The balance of activities in the four growth processes will play an integral part in the success of networking and should be considered at each of these junctures in the planning process. It is vital that there exists a clear understanding of the relevant issues in each growth process area before embarking on the Network Plan.

The Applications Portfolio

The Applications Portfolio, as it is prepared for general data processing assessment and planning, provides an overview of information use in terms of the functions and activities of the organization. It can also be used to describe information sources, processing needs, storage, and data resources in terms of potential networking channels. User operational requirements can be used to determine where networking will be most effective. The business model, and the data planning model which is developed from it, are good indicators of shared data requirements. Thus the Applications Portfolio can serve as a good source for the assessments necessary to begin formulating a networking strategy and ultimately defining a network plan.

In addition to the identification of opportunity and the itemization of shared data requirements, analysis of the Applications Portfolio in terms of considerations particular to the network plan can be valuable to developing a thorough and feasible plan. Cost/benefit (or ROI), risk, user goal congruence, and current status of data or information communications can all be assessed through the portfolio. The data model developed for Data Planning in order to specify data requirements can be extended to reflect the operational characteristics of data source, processing, storage, and use which must be considered in building a network plan.

Networking require specific communications in terms of places, people, and machines throughout the organization. The physical location of users and equipment is another factor which can be used to enhance the planning information provided by the Applications Portfolio. All of the information sharing opportunities indicated in terms of the portfolio can also be described in terms of the geographical distribution of personnel, equipment and the performance of functions. This information translates into communications characteristics such as traffic, volume and patterns, latent demand, response time, reliability, accessibility, etc.; all additional factors which will influence the assessment of opportunities and the formulation of a network model.

When all of these factors are analyzed, certain functions will emerge as areas in which networking could be introduced with a maximum of value and effect and at minimum expense and risk. If networking is new to the organization, for example, minimizing risk will be very important. A network supporting only such relatively simple functions as data entry will be the most appropriate. Procedures should also be simple, entailing a lesser degree of change in the existing environment.

In the case of a more mature organization, analysis of the portfolio and related factors may indicate that networking must involve crossing boundaries between functional areas and/or introducing new interfunctional procedures. The situation is more complex and more risk is involved. It will be essential to establish business policies and standards for shared systems and for shared data in order to assure smooth implementation.

In this manner, the Applications Portfolio provides information which allows planners to define the extent and complexity of networking opportunities and to develop a strategy and a plan commensurate with the given conditions. It is the starting point for network planning providing the basis for a model which can be modified to accommodate factors introduced by the status of the other growth processes.

Users

The selection of portions of the Applications Portfolio and data bases which should be targeted for networking must be done knowing the users involved. If networking is the transfer of information from people to people, people to machines, machine to people and machines to machines, then the skill and the interest of the personnel involved will be critical to the success of the Networking Plan. They must be able to use the new technology in carrying out their activities. It should be appropriate to their level of motivation, ability, and responsibility.

Planning should include careful review of which functions in which areas, and which people, information systems, data bases, and eventually which machines to include. The network analysis should include careful enumeration of the information needed by users for the targeted functions and the communications channels which affect their work. These technical choices are based on analysis performed using the Network Model. They should follow applications and user priorities or, where productivity is a problem, prepare and train users so that they will be able to make better use of new modes of activity and make more accurate assessments of potential uses for networking in the future.

Often network planning will involve plans for building user skills and for altering departmental and personal communications policies. It is important to be aware of such changes because they may become explicit in the technical solution but may not be evident in the evaluation of systems capabilities alone. Changes in functional boundaries in the applications portfolio will affect users and their work. A careful analysis of jobs, the tasks involved, and the communications patterns of the users can help to maximize the profitability of networking for the users. Conversely, if an organization already has a serious problem in its communications policies and practices, the introduction of technology may fail if the human resistance and policy issues are not addressed.

The role of the user in successful network implementation should not be underestimated. Patterns of communication and information sharing are often deeply embedded in work habits. Networking should be planned with existing patterns in mind so that implementation will involve minimum levels of disorientation. More extensive and complex networking can be introduced later as people become conditioned to accepting that level of change. For example, the planning of business transaction processing on-line may be well accepted, but electronic mail, calendar scheduling and action follow-up may invade feelings of privacy too much for general acceptance and use.

Management Controls

The introduction of new networks must be accompanied or enabled by the introduction of new management control procedures. These controls should follow existing management style. This is especially important in networking because many of the changes will affect a large number of users and will change their daily activity. It will affect their personnel communication style and, perhaps, their geographical and even organizational position.

Since location of people and management processes are affected by networking, it is especially important to maintain centralized and consistent control of network operations and integrity. Although networking involves dispersal of the networking means (equipment, tasks and responsibilities), the goal is still the integration of information for more effective overall functioning of the organization. Planning and implementing the appropriate management controls is essential to guarantee that as equipment and activities disperse operations and communications integrity are maintained.

There are numerous operational planning mechanisms such as network traffic models which can be used to provide good management control. In addition, controls such as service level assurance, problem management, maintenance and change controls, or traffic monitoring and balancing systems can be established. Organization structures may also be necessary. For example, a network control center or user service desk can be used at the operational level. These management controls will be especially valuable in the 1980s as many organizations develop complex networks (e.g., integrate voice and data communications).

Resources: Network Technology and Personnel

Network technology should not be confused with a network plan or architecture. The strategic plan for networking should provide an overall blueprint or architecture. This architecture is used by detail designers and implementors each year as they develop and install network components. The network architecture in this sense is not the same as the architecture referred to by vendors in describing network implementation schemes in their marketing literature. Network architecture is particular to the organization and is developed by that organization in the course of the planning process.

The network architecture of the organization is a logical extension of the data architecture. It is the high level design of the data flows to be automated in conjunction with the systems and data bases planned for development. The network plan consists of this overall design plus the specification of projects for the implementation of networks according to a stepwise plan. The development of the network architecture is, therefore, an organizational planning activity which is independent of and preparatory to the review of vendor configurations also called "architectures."

This does not mean that an organization should not use off-the-shelf communication configurations in the implementation of the network plan. It does mean that however, that consideration and selection of vendor offerings should *follow* definition of organizational priorities and constraints. This is now possible because of the extensive range of technology available. Once a strategy has been set and a network plan has been built, vendor configurations can be reviewed and evaluated according to the criteria in the network plan. This insures that an organization will be able to select the alternative which is best matched to its functional needs, that which is cost effective and best meets its long-term requirements.

The commercially available product lines provide the network planner with a sense of the range of capabilities and potential configurations which can be used in networking. Each product and its scheme is more or less valuable depending upon the needs and conditions, the Applications Portfolio, the distribution of users and equipment, the motivation and ability of users and data processing personnel, and the management control issues involved. The chart below summarizes the general quality and characteristics of several major network implementations. The task of the organization is to measure the value of each against its own needs.

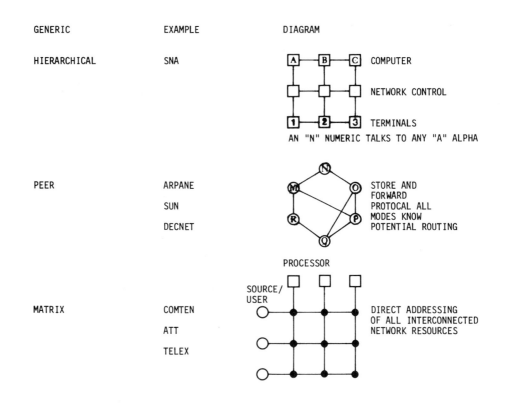

GENERIC	EXAMPLE	DIAGRAM

HIERARCHICAL — SNA

AN "N" NUMERIC TALKS TO ANY "A" ALPHA

PEER — ARPANE, SUN, DECNET

MATRIX — COMTEN, ATT, TELEX

In a **hierarchical network**, several users are linked to one another through a hierarchy of communications equipment while users at the same level communicate through the level or levels above them. In a **peer network**, by contrast, all groups communicate directly. In a **matrix network** each group communicates to a central matrix which processes and communicates with second parties. Each configuration is appropriate to different working habits, data, and information needs.

In summary, the vendor network configurations should be matched to the network architecture of functions and to the required sequencing specified by the organization in its network plan. Technologies are the tools which can be adapted in the course of the networking projects to help bring the networks to life. Different products may be used in different areas and eventually, according to the plan, linked together for greater efficiency.

Good sense in business planning confirms the value of this approach. Good sense makes it possible for the organization to approach networking with the same thoroughness and foresight it would use in any business investment decisions. The Network Model provided earlier in this chapter is the primary tool which the planner uses to determine technology requirements, source, and use. Functional analysis is used to determine what kind of communication functions are required. Volume, traffic, reliability, currency, and other service level analyses help determine the capacity and specifications of the communications systems configurations. Using this model and these analyses, the organization can look for the implementation technology most appropriate to its strategy rather than trying to match planning and implementation to a particular technology.

BUILDING A NETWORK PLAN

The Network Plan is of critical importance to the successful implementation of networking. It can serve as a guide for timing, purchasing decisions, training, and other elements in the installation process. When an organization chooses to use a vendor network configuration, this decision should be based upon suitability of that product to an organization-derived Network Plan. This insures that all learning factors particular to the organization will be accounted for, risks will be assessed, and success will be well managed.

Another advantage of a Network Plan is that it enables the data processing group and the user groups to organize and control changes. These groups are in a good position to assess existing data processing systems, applications, and experience before selecting a specific technology or package. Risk can be minimized by limiting project scope to a level appropriate to the ability and willingness of the people in the organization to accept and adjust to networking. For example, in an organization without much experience in systems engineering and management of technology, the risk of introducing elaborate networking will be high no matter how well the technology has been performing in a test environment or a more sophisticated organization.

Developing a Network Plan

In many organizations the highest priority in the Network Plan is to start simply or in the most labor intensive or least productive communication activities. For example, many organization activities such as data entry, data editing, quality control, and report distribution might be improved by basic network applications. The devices needed to distribute these basic functions to users include keyboard, diskette and cassette equipment, remote batch or on-line printers, and microfiche viewers.

In such projects there is considerable opportunity to speed up data entry and distribution cycles, to improve the quality of the data entered and to reduce the volume of extraneous reports (duplicates, reruns, etc.). The benefit of improvement in these functions is two-fold. First, in the most immediate sense, there will be financial savings, increased productivity, and improved quality of work as the human/machine interface is moved closer to the source and to the user of data. Second, less direct but just as critical, it will allow users to build the necessary skills to move on to the next, more complex networking projects.

Like office automation, networking is a process of extension. No matter how large and sophisticated the existing centralized computer systems may be, moving equipment into user areas means waiting for users to master that equipment. During early projects some user groups will emerge as prime candidates for long-term network plans. Similarly some functions will prove more adaptable than others.

Again, similar to office automation, the first networking projects in any organization will involve a learning period like that of stage I in the overall data processing development. Even in an organization which has reached stage IV in data processing in general, networking technologies may be scant if present at all. Users and data processing personnel will have to pass through another learning process, controls will have to be developed, and the technologies will have to be introduced at a compatible rate of growth. This should be reflected in the Network Plan where anticipation of learning is reflected in terms of a planned, gradual acceleration of activity similar to the modulations described by *The Orders of Office Automation* in *Chapter 8*.

Long Range Network Planning—High Return Projects

Once the basic networking functions are in place and organizational commitment to a more user-oriented environment has been demonstrated, specific plans for the use of networking and distributed processing can be made. On the basis of the initial experience user groups can be designated to participate in long-term expansion of networking and they can be expected to adapt well to the gradual shifts in organization and work methods which may result.

The success and failure of the first projects will also suggest criteria for enhancing the data and networking models for the organization. This can be done by reviewing all major systems and data resources and by identifying opportunities to introduce communication links and ease distribution of the functions. Specific criteria include functional complexity (source, processing, and use of data) and technical complexity (systems prerequisites). In addition, each potential systems user should be reviewed for experience and familiarity with basic networking functions (data entry, systems operations, systems design, and systems management).

When all of the areas of opportunity have been ranked, the plan can be improved. The plan should coordinate advancement of networking in some areas with gradual introduction of networking in others. The plan should include specifications for addressing all four of the growth processes in order to assure that networking promotes rather than hinders the general maturation pattern of the organization.

The final Network Plan should be a year-by-year plan for a period of three to five years. It should build upon a basic network and include specification of the associated changes in central data processing. This entails anticipation of the increasing importance of data resource management as a responsibility of the entire organization and the central data processing group. While specific functions are distributed to the users, the responsibility of data processing for the coordination and maintenance of the corporate data resource increases. Data Resource Management Planning should be coordinated with Network Planning and included as a consideration in the Network Plan. And responsibility for defining and standardizing the structure and format of shared data, at a minimum, should be assigned with plans for defining other such responsibilities and positions as the network grows.

SUMMARY

The network planning process insures that an organization is able to maximize its ability to take advantage of networking without jeopardizing its overall data processing growth. It allows data processing planners to turn to the area of communications and distributed processing without losing sight of the general strategies which drives data processing decisions. A careful start-up period guards against expensive mistakes and provides an updated baseline of information for the data processing long-range planning blueprints.

In organizations where networking is embraced without evaluation and planning, there is no assurance that the prerequisites for long-term success are in place. In an iterative, staged planning process the organization can be sure that it is building its network on a solid foundation. User departments are being educated in their new roles and responsibilities as well as building technical skills. The organizational long-range data processing can be updated to include networking in a cost-effective, functionally-effective and human factors-effective manner. Networking can be managed in a manner consistent with the rest of data processing activity.

Without a Network Plan, there is a danger that unplanned proliferation of computers or networks introduced to meet immediate needs will lead to long-term problems when interface becomes important and incompatibility becomes a costly issue. Planning also insures that data resource and data communications standards are established and maintained so that the new technologies can be coordinated and, eventually, linked in an organization-wide systems network with an effective data resource center.

The ultimate goal of a Network Plan is to build a strategy for introducing technologies which will improve the effectiveness of communications. This includes communication from people to people, from people to machines, from machines to people, and from machines to machines. This goal is impossible to attain without a logically developed plan.

At Last,
Major Roles for
Minicomputers*

GERALD J. BURNETT
RICHARD L. NOLAN

Most companies today are on a path toward centralization of computing. Some have already set up elaborate divisions that provide consolidated computer services for the entire organization, while others have centralized their electronic data processing (EDP) activities into regional facilities, commonly called data centers.

A number of studies a few years ago set in motion the forces for this centralization.[1] Analysts found that a few large computers could do the work of several small or medium ones for less money. A perennial lack of qualified computer specialists reinforced this significant cost benefit, and the emergence of data base technology that enabled a corporation to integrate reports on its operations further fueled the flames of centralization.

But more recent evidence suggests that this path is not necessarily a good one.[2] Regardless of the positive forces mentioned above, service levels seem to be deteriorating: users complain that data centers are lethargic and nonresponsive, and centralization of computer facilities all too often runs against the decentralized operations preferred by many companies.

---

[1]Martin B. Solomon, Jr., "*Economies of Scale of the IBM System/360*," Communications of the ACM, June 1966, p. 435; R. A. Arbuckle, "*Computer Analysis and Thruput Evaluation*," Computers and Automation, January 1966, p. 13; and Kenneth Knight, "*Evolving Computer Performance, 1962-1967*," Datamation, January 1968, p. 31.

[1]The pattern can be analyzed for 16 companies in a Computer Based Information Systems (CBIS) working paper by Richard L. Nolan, "*Internal Pricing of Computer Services*," 1974 (Harvard Business School, Boston, Mass. 02163).

In addition, there have been tough administrative problems in forging formal coordination and control policy for the centralized computer organization. Some of these problems could be viewed as transitional; others are more fundamental. For example, in order for centralized computing to work, corporate management must be willing to endorse and enforce standardized data processing project development.

As a consequence of these administrative and organizational difficulties, a nagging question confronts management: Are the measurable economic benefits of centralized computing worth the side effects? Developments in minicomputer technology have dramatically changed the economic and organizational variables. Today minicomputers are available for a fraction of the cost of large computers and can be operated with less specialized support than the larger ones require. This is not to say that minis are going to replace large computers in the near future. It does indicate, however, that the technology has now matured to the stage where the costs of using a mini for certain data processing jobs compare favorably with using a portion of the capacity of a large machine.

Small companies that formerly used service bureaus are beginning to use general purpose minis for applications such as accounting, order entry, and inventory control. Companies with medium computer requirements still generally use a service bureau or a small- to medium-sized conventional computer. Although large companies are beginning to use minis more aggressively, they use them primarily for specialized communications front-ends to their large computer. We expect that more and more small- and medium-sized companies will discover they can have an in-house minicomputer that will allow them to directly control their data processing needs at a comparable or lower cost than they currently incur with a service bureau or a manual system. In addition, larger companies will provide an increasing number of minis for independent applications or divisions.

In addition, more flexibility in aligning the EDP unit with the organizational philosophy of the company also favors the growth in the use of minis. The economies of scale of large computers led to more centralization in EDP than many companies wanted. By employing minicomputer technology, a company can now economically leave more EDP activities under the control of divisional units.

In order to take advantage of minicomputer technology, management must first understand its status and its potential, since it is management that must provide the initiative, the support, and the guidance for its implementation. Therefore, we shall first examine and assess the capabilities of minicomputers vis-à-vis those of the more familiar medium and large computers. Second, we shall illustrate a range of options for effective use of the new technology by reviewing the way in which four companies have employed minicomputers. Third, we shall examine the process of assimilating minicomputer technology into an organization and outline a set of guidelines for management action.

WHAT IS A MINICOMPUTER?

A minicomputer costs around $50,000 for a typical business application, and it can do a good deal of the work of computers costing $2,000,000. Stated another way, minis cost approximately one fortieth as much as large computers, but they can do a great deal more than one fortieth of the work.

In *Exhibit I*, we have outlined the key architecture and design characteristics of large, medium, and small computers and have assessed the managerial significance of these differences. In this exhibit we represent large computers by the IBM 370/168, medium computers by the IBM 370/135, and minicomputers by the DEC PDP 11/45. Other comparable large computers include the Burroughs B6700, the Honeywell 66/80, and the Univac 1110. Other comparable medium computers include the Burroughs B3700, the Honeywell 2050, the NCR Century 251, andd the Univac 90/60. Finally, other comparable minicomputers include the Data General Nova 840 or Eclipse, and the Varian V73.

Two general observations can be drawn from this exhibit. First, though the minicomputer is not as "powerful" as the large or medium computer, it is surprisingly close, given the substantial price differentials. One reason for this closeness is that it has been possible to utilize new hardware technology considerably earlier in minis than in large machines because there is a smaller investment in hardware and software design for a mini. Consequently, a vendor can produce and integrate a new mini into his line much more rapidly than a large computer.

Since an important characteristic of new technology in the computer area has been rapidly decreasing cost, the price for a given amount of power in minis has been lowered consistently and quite rapidly. For example, in 1965 it cost $25,000 to purchase a machine with 4,096 16-bit words and a 2-microsecond cycle time. Because of advances made in microtechnology, by 1974 it cost only $1,990 to purchase a machine with these capabilities.

The second general observation concerns software. Large machine software is more advanced, and thus applications with substantial multiprogramming or shared multipurpose data bases require a large or medium machine. However, minicomputer manufacturers have recognized that one of their next big markets is the end-user business application, and so over the past two years they have begun to make substantial investments in software developments. As a result, it is now possible to use minicomputers as easily as it is large machines for many business applications.

In fact, it would seem that we are now moving into an evolutionary stage where what is needed is increased investment in people for application programs and software development—not breakthroughs in technology. Our reasons for believing this will become clear as we discuss the services that minis can provide and the steps management must consider in attempting to assimilate them into the organization.

EXHIBIT I

Technical Comparison of
Computers (large, medium, and mini)

Key computer architec-ture characteristics	Large computer IBM 370/168	Medium computer IBM 370/135	Minicomputer Digital Equip-ment PDP 11/45	Effect Minicomputer vs. medium & large computers	Significance Minicomputer vs. medium & large computers
Hardware					
Word length	32 bits (a bit is equivalent to a binary digit)	32 bits	16 bits	Size of readily address-able program or data areas is restricted. Instruction repertoire is smaller.	Efficiently implemented higher level languages are hard to provide, thus only a few exist. Large applications execute less efficiently and are harder to program.
Maximum memory size	8,400,000 bytes (a byte consists of 8 bits which provides enough binary digits to represent one numeric or alpha-betic character)	524,000 bytes	262,000 bytes	Multiprogramming (the ability to execute pro-grams simultaneously) is restricted. Sub-stantial manipulation of large arrays of data is restricted.	The multiprogramming limitation is not signif-icant, since minis are relatively inexpensive and can thus be dedi-cated to one or a few applications.
Data capacity:					
Memory path (width of the link between the main memory and central processor)	64 bits	16 bits	16 bits	Execution is less efficient.	The data capacity architecture of the large computer makes it more effective for large data processing demands in a multi-programming environment.
Interleaving (ability to simultane-ously access more than one part of main memory)	4-way (as many as 3 input/output (I/O) channels & the central processor can be simultaneously transferring data to and from main memory)	None	None	Overlap of program execution and I/O data transfer is restricted (compared with the large computer).	The mini's power com-pares with the medium computer's in a dedi-cated data processing environment, insofar as data capacity is concerned.
Number of channels (channels operate the I/O devices)	Many	A few	One	Configuration and overlap of activity of I/O devices are restricted.	
I/O channel data rate (the rate that data can be transferred over all channels to main memory)	16,000,000 bytes/second	2,400,000 bytes/second	2,360,000 bytes/second	Simultaneous transfer of data from multiple I/O devices is restricted (compared with the large computer).	
Processor architecture:					
Central processor unit cycle time (how fast instructions can be carried out)	80 nanoseconds (1 nanosecond = 1 billionth of a second)	275 nanoseconds	300 nanoseconds	Instruction execution is slower compared with large computer.	The mini is restricted to applications requir-ing substantial proc-essing activity; such activity is not typical of business applications.
Memory cycle (how fast instructions or data can be retrieved from main memory; it should be considered together with the width of the memory path)	480 nanoseconds	800 nanoseconds	850 nanoseconds	Instruction and data transfer to memory is somewhat slower (compared with large computer).	
Number of registers (an indication of more sophisticated programming)	Many	Many	Relatively few	System software devel-opment is limited.	
Number of basic instructions	Approximately 150	Approximately 140	Approximately 80	Execution is less efficient.	

EXHIBIT I continued

Key computer architecture characteristics	Large computer IBM 370/168	Medium computer IBM 370/135	Minicomputer Digital Equipment PDP 11/45	Effect Minicomputer vs. medium & large computers	Significance Minicomputer vs. medium & large computers
Software					
Operating systems:					
Batch (application programs are submitted to computer in self-contained units with no strict timing requirements)	Multiprogramming (batch applications are run simultaneously)	Multi-programming	Multiprogramming (2 programs only)	Computer system resources can be sufficiently utilized in each case.	Systems software for the large and medium computer is complex and designed for multiple tasks in order to share expensive resources; this is not necessary for the mini, since it is relatively inexpensive.
Real time (application programs are called into operation in response to requests from I/O devices)	Separate telecommunications system added to other operating system facilities	Same as for large computers	Telecommunications system is integrated with main operating system	Real time on a mini is usually dedicated to one application.	
Time sharing	Supported simultaneously with other systems by addition of separate facilities	Same as for large computers	Computer must be dedicated to time sharing	Time sharing on a mini is usually dedicated to support of on-line terminals.	
Data base and file management systems	Many sophisticated systems are available	Many systems are available	A few limited systems are available	Data-base systems must be largely developed in-house.	Shared multipurpose data bases are hard to implement on a mini – a significant constraint if these are required.
Programming languages	All 8 major languages	All 8 major languages	Four major languages	COBOL is only gradually becoming available for some minis, which is a significant limitation for companies using COBOL as a standard language.	Language for some applications may not be perfectly appropriate, but this distinction is not critical since there are enough languages available for minis.
Program development aids (e.g., debugging aids, checkout compilers)	Many	Many	Limited	Programming efficiency is inhibited.	More highly skilled applications programmers are required.
Application packages (e.g., payroll, bill of materials, models)	Thousands	Thousands	Hundreds	Users must program more applications in-house.	More cost is involved in programming, if packages available for large or medium machines.
Additional considerations					
Reliability	High	High	Very high; time to fix is brief because of relative simplicity	The mini is likely to be more reliable, but the distinction is unlikely to be important for most applications.	Reliability and vendor support must be considered together.
Vendor support	Outstanding	Outstanding	Good	Caveat emptor applies to mini somewhat.	
Purchase cost	Millions of dollars	Hundreds of thousands of dollars	Tens of thousands of dollars	Minis are substantially cheaper.	Purchase and operational cost are the most significant advantages minis have over large and medium computers.
Operating requirements	Considerable amount of specially prepared space and air conditioning; operators and well-trained systems programmers required	Same as for large computers	One operator per shift, no special site preparation, good systems programmers required	Operational costs are much lower.	

HOW CAN A MINI COMPUTER BE USED

Options for using a mini range from enhancing the service level of the data center to replacing the center entirely. Thus we can first think of the options as being arrayed along the links between the actual user and the central computer. Second, since minis are most often devoted to just one application and are typically located near the user, this same arraying of options can also be thought of as ranging from centralized to decentralized control of the company's EDP resources.

The relationship between these two concepts is shown in *Exhibit II*. For discussion purposes, we have listed four basic options, ranging from using no minis to using only minis. Of course, a company can use minis in more than one way, since these options are not mutually exclusive.

Four Basic Options

Option 1 represents companies that do not use minis at all. Option 2 covers not only companies that use minis as front-ends, that is, minis that handle communications between terminals and central computers, but to those using other combinations of minis and large machines in computing networks as well. Option 3 applies to those organizations in which minis handle independent applications and require no active link to the central computer. In this case, however, the mini and large machines may interchange data on a periodic basis, for instance, nightly. Option 4 represents companies using only minis. It includes those with departmental minicomputers that are tied together in networks with telephone lines to permit sharing of data and programs.

For our case studies we selected four companies whose computer facilities parallel these options. The cases also illustrate how the three with minis incorporated minicomputer technology into their data processing systems.

Central Computer. The first case we studied covers a wholesale manufacturing company that uses only a central computer. This company has a large facility in the Southwest that serves its distribution and sales centers throughout the United States. The primary applications—on-line order entry (using 90 terminals), inventory, distribution, production scheduling, customer billing, and corporate accounting—all share a large data base.

Two years ago the company had a large machine batch system providing those using it with good service. Order entry was a batched keypunch operation. But because of a considerable clerical load and a substantial number of orders that had to be reprocessed because of errors, management decided to place order entry on-line. It expected that this would reduce the clerical load by enabling orders to be verified against the common corporate data base as they were entered.

Though the company considered using a mini, it rejected the idea in favor of full verification of entered orders against a common data base and

EXHIBIT II

Computer Configurations and
Relative Decentralization of Computing

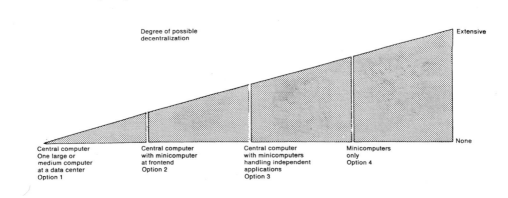

direct data-base updating. A mini could not have handled all the applications and used the common data base, because the company's multiprogramming requirements were simply too large.

When on-line order entry began, no one on the computer staff had had any substantial experience with developing or operating such a system, and thus there were a number of delays. This was particularly true when, at the end of the development stage, the system required substantial tuning in order to achieve proper response time for order entry while maintaining good throughput for normal batch processing.

Six months after installation of the system, the computer center staff still spends the majority of its time on problems associated with the mix of large batch and on-line applications. In addition, the various users are unhappy with their current service; the old, smooth-running batch process that everyone understood has been replaced by a complex mixture of batch and on-line applications. This new environment causes periodic software problems that result in the need to set priorities at the computer center concerning which applications will be delayed or not run. The fact that the center makes these decisions in the best interests of the corporation does not lower the frustration of the operational managers who do not receive their required reports.

These circumstances raise the important issue of the operational effectiveness of using one large computer for all applications. In making the decision, a company should place considerable weight on the value of separate operations for on-line and batch applications—particularly in a system that does not already have on-line applications. In this case, the operational staff could have continued its smoothrunning batch processing while simply introducing an independent minicomputer system for on-line order entry. Admittedly, this approach would have caught fewer entry errors (since there would not have been a current data base available for verification), but increased operational effectiveness would have been gained.

Central Computer With Front-End Minis. Our second case involves the experience of a large bank that runs a large, highly centralized multicomputer activity. The bank investigated running an on-line portfolio management systems on the central computer for its trust department. Management wanted portfolio managers to be able to communicate with a central file containing investment information so that they could quickly analyze various investment trends and alternatives from their own visual display terminals. This was an excellent task for a large computer, but the bank had some additional specific needs. In order to provide fast response, the system had to allow for substantial overlapping of user requests and sharing of common program data. Also, since the portfolio managers were not all centrally located, both local and remote terminals (via telephone lines) were necessary. Finally, for marketing reasons, the bank decided that it was desirable to have a second type of terminal, one that was portable.

The terminal controller, which was the piece of equipment needed to handle the remote and local terminals for the large computer, cost $80,000. But this controller could not support the most cost-effective terminal available for the specific use management had in mind, and thus a more costly (approximately $30,000 more for the 30 terminals required) but less effective terminal would have been required.

The search for a more feasible alternative led management to consider replacing the hardware terminal controller with a minicomputer. The idea was to use the mini as the front-end of the central computer, where it would handle the communications with the terminals and do additional processing that would otherwise be done on the central computer. The minicomputer processing could thus lower the computing load on the main machine, thereby making it available for the more complex processing for which it was better suited.

In total, the minicomputer, its software, and the terminals cost $30,000 less than the proposed hardware controller with its terminals. The bank not only saved $30,000, it also gained exposure to the use of minicomputers and has developed other minicomputer applications as well.

Central Computer With Independent Minis. Our third case involves the corporate division of a service company that compared using a mini for an on-line system with placing the system on a portion of a large batch-processing machine. The division is in the business of compiling and reporting information to its customers. These reports compare the effectiveness of operations at various companies by processing a substantial amount of data received from each service subscriber.

The business had expanded to the point that an on-line data entry system was required for efficiency of input and error correction. To meet these requirements the system would have to serve some 60 analysts at display terminals who would classify, code, and enter data into a computer, then verify, correct, and store it on magnetic tape. During certain peak periods for entering data, additional time beyond the normal eight hours of operation a day would be required; these peaks corresponded to times of relatively heavy loads on the central computing facility for this particular corporation. Finally, adding the on-line application would require additional major software consisting of a real-time operating system, a communicatons controller, and terminal handling hardware.

The company had both a mini and a large machine data entry system designed. The $500,000 estimate covered a five-year life for the large computer's main memory and processing units, the overhead used by the real-time software, and the input/output hardware; this was a fully allocated cost including such items as floor space and operator costs. Corresponding costs for two minicomputers, each handling 30 terminals, totaled $150,000. Software development was about the same in each case.

On a direct cost basis (that is, the application was not charged for operating system overhead, floor space, and operators), implementing the system with the large computer worked out to $170,000. Therefore, even on a direct cost basis a large machine implementation would have been more expensive than a mini implementation. (This would not have been the case if the large machine's hardware and software costs could have been shared among more on-line applications.)

Since peak loading problems for both the large machine and data entry would occur at about the same time, there was an additional value to entering data on another machine under the users' direct control. Thus the company decided to use a mini for the data entry system. Its decision took into account the desirability of user control and the fact that additional new real-time requirements were ill-defined at that time.

Minicomputers Only. The fourth case involves an engineering firm that had been using service bureaus to satisfy the computing needs of its various offices throughout the United States. These requirements include accounting and engineering calculations, data collection and editing for very large computer models, and running computer models. The firm is highly decentralized, and its partners have substantial discretion over all major decisions having an effect on their respective offices.

The firm's managing partners decided to look into acquiring a central computer to handle the majority of its data processing needs. The large computer that was available could handle most of the company's needs at a monthly rental cost of $27,000 (or a purchase cost of $1,200,000). But the cost rose to $55,000 per month when telephone line charges and operating costs were added. Though this cost compared with expenditures at service bureaus, there were other considerations. For one thing, a large internal computer represented a substantial new corporate function that the firm would have to learn to manage centrally. In addition, centralization of computing resources was counter to its decentralized operating philosophy.

Therefore, the firm decided to investigate minicomputer alternatives. It found that four of the larger offices could justify using minis for all of their computing needs (except for the actual running of the large engineering models) and that the smaller offices could continue using service bureaus until minis were warranted for them. The cost of the four minicomputers was $350,000, with operating and telephone line charges being very low—less than $2,000 per month per office. The total for service bureaus and minis was $40,000 per month.

The savings in operating costs of $15,000 per month was attractive, but even more important to the firm was the opportunity to maintain its decentralized operating philosophy. Each office would retain control over new programs to be developed and over daily computer runs. Further, using the local machine for engineering calculations would be easier under direct user control, and local engineers could be encouraged to use the computer and allowed very free use of the machine. These advantages would prove particularly useful whenever a specific job or proposal required a considerable amount of engineering calculations.

Thus for both organizational effectiveness and economic reasons, the firm chose the minicomputer alternative. Since many of the offices have similar requirements, some central coordination of computing is valuable. One individual carries out this coordination, and this has resulted in the standardization of operating systems and a set of programming languages for all offices. In this way, data and programs can be shared among offices at the discretion of the partners in each office.

EVALUATING THE OPTIONS

The use of minis is not necessarily an either/or proposition. Instead, management needs to determine how minis can most effectively be integrated into the overall data processing system of an organization. This determination is best made by first carrying out a high-level design for the application. *Exhibit I* provides such a design framework to use in examining the characteristics of a mini that limit its power with respect to a large or medium machine. In particular, as we discussed in the first case, the primary limitations occur when the application requires either a substantial amount of processing or the establishment of a complex data base common to multiple applications.

After this analysis is completed and has shown a minicomputer to be feasible, the decision to use a mini, medium, or large computer requires a qualitative weighing of three factors:

1. Economics. Cost is perhaps the most compelling justification for using or not using a mini. There are three components of cost: software development, hardware, and operations. Software development costs for large machines and minis will generally be comparable, but the numerous commercial software packages available for large computers will often justify using a large computer for an application.

In analyzing the hardware and operating costs for the large machine, companies must decide whether full costing or direct costing is more appropriate. Full costing would charge the application for all the resources that it uses directly plus a proportionate share of all other resources in the system that are shared, such as people and space. Direct costing charges the new application only for the required incremental resources, such as direct use of the central processing unit and peripheral equipment. If existing computer facilities are idle because of underutilization of a corporation's large machine, arguments can be made for incremental costing of a new application.

Although it may be desirable to use direct costing in some situations, it is important to recognize that there will be pressure from full-cost users to relegate direct-cost users to lower-priority computer time and to suspend them during periods of high load on the large machine. In addition, as the computer needs of a company grow, it may require a larger machine. The direct-cost user will have contributed to making the load heavy enough to justify a new machine and may then have to be charged full instead of direct costs. Thus using direct costing has some pitfalls and must be viewed cautiously.

2. User control. The mini allows the user to be independent of other programs on the main computer. In addition, the user of the mini is free from concern about the computer center's need to keep its machine operational and upgrade its capabilities to meet increasing loads. These issues may arise when some users of a large machine have a heavy, high-priority load that interferes with the needs of other users. This situation is particularly frustrating when one division of a corporation controls the central computer. (This same problem occurs for small or medium-sized companies that utilize a service bureau.) The user with his own mini will not suffer from interruptions of this type. Independence is also particularly useful for a user when there are response time constraints, since response will be fully under the user's control.

3. Operational effectiveness. For substantially decentralized operations, today's economical mini may be more practical and far less disruptive than larger machines for in-house data processing. As the first three cases illustrated, the mini can help relieve the complexity of the operational load on the central computer. With this simpler environment (particularly with on-line systems), the data processing center will require less systems programming talent, which may be shifted to serve users' needs directly.

GUIDELINES FOR MANAGEMENT

Minicomputer technology has now matured to the stage where management can harness its economic and organizational potential. Management's responsibility is to develop an understanding of the appropriate way to integrate minicomputers into the organization. Each company should carefully assess its data processing system in terms of where it is going and how, and it should inspect the opportunities for taking advantage of minicomputers.

We believe that the data processing staff should build a good understanding of the use and programming of minis. Over a three-year horizon this understanding should evolve so that all computer designers and programmers are equally comfortable using large or small machines. Thus for the long run it is inappropriate to separate the computer staff into minicomputer and large machine programmers. However, in order to get this learning started, it will be necessary to build an understanding of minis in the computer staff, and such a separation may initially be necessary.

To provide leadership to engender an appropriate environment and policy superstructure for incorporating minicomputer technology, top management should take the following actions:

1. Direct the EDP manager to acquire and build minicomputer technology capability by integrating technical systems and applications expertise into the current staff.

2. Establish a policy to include minicomputer options among alternatives for all new major applications.

3. Look for an opportunity to use a mini for the computing needs of a small, independent division, for instance, one that refuses to participate in the central computer utility. This could also be an opportunity for the entire company to gain valuable experience.

4. Establish a central function to study an promulgate minicomputer standards for hardware, software, applications development, and data bases. This is a very important function to keep under control when computer systems are being decentralized.

PART FOUR

Management
Controls

I know of no small business of more than $4 million in sales that runs successfully without accounting systems and executive leadership. I can make the same statement about data processing departments with similar operating budgets.

But there is one fundamental difference between the $4 million small business and the $4 million data processing activity. Without accounting systems and executive leadership, the small business fails. Unfortunately the computer activity does not. It only goes into a state of perpetual turmoil which frustrates both senior management and user management. It also leads to high turnover among computer personnel.

My point is a simple one: the computer activity must be run as a business within a business. This is a point I have made often. Understandably many have not heard it, particularly those in the earlier stages of evolution where technical problems tend to overwhelm both computer management energies and senior and user management energies as well. But, as data processing grows and begins to affect the organization as a whole, this fundamental truth can no longer be ignored.

The first thing one must do in order to manage a computer department as a business is measure its activities. If you can't measure an activity, you can't manage it. This means installing basic accounting systems. Installation begins with the design of an appropriate chart of accounts so that expenditures can be tracked throughout the company. Data processing managers often cannot determine exactly how much they spend on computers, software, or key personnel. Next, it means installing responsibility accounting to hold computer managers accountable. Later, the organization must have cost or job accounting for both costs and benefits of computer support provided to business functions.

A data processing controller is needed to pull this together. The target is measurement, accountability, and a basis for bottom-line discipline. The professional data processing controller has accounting expertise to ensure that it is done right.

Executive leadership is the second key ingredient to running the computer activity as one would run a business. This executive leadership must come from the data processing manager. But the data processing manager cannot do it alone; he needs to build a team. He also needs to manage toward an explicit strategy—one that senior management, users, and the data processing managers all can agree is the right one for the organization overall.

This strategy will provide direction for the computer activity. Direction-setting is analogous to the activity of the board of directors of the independent $4 million company. The board is made up of the top management team and elected representatives of the shareholders. The executive steering committee needs to provide the same function for the data processing activity. This committee can establish a computer strategy for employing scarce capability to maximum company benefit. They can also set and pursue computer funding levels, sort out priorities, settle information technology positions, and track performance and leadership.

The long-term performance of the computer activity is measured by the balance sheet. The main asset to be monitored on the balance sheet is the Applications Portfolio. The Applications Portfolio is the result of the stream of investments (that is, the annual computer budgets) a company has made over the past twenty years or so. In large organizations its replacement value frequently runs to the hundreds of millions of dollars. Replacement value, rather than historical cost, is the appropriate measurement on the computer balance sheet because this asset is time-sensitive. Applications, once created, require ongoing maintenance which may triple costs; they also become obsolete, and hence depreciate.

The balance sheet should also show the investments in computer professionals, and here is another place where the conservative historical-cost dictum of the accounting profession breaks down. We need a balance sheet constructed on replacement-value concepts and human resource accounting concepts. The assets which the computer activity represents —the Applications Portfolio, its human and technical resources, and the internal organization it has developed—should be balanced against the equity side, namely the organization's expectations for performance. These expectations rise as the organization's investment in computers grows.

The profit-and-loss statement would aim at the bottom line: service delivered cost-effectively to users. Hits and misses here show whether and where the computer activity is running in the red. Here, much needs to be done to equip the organization with the full analogue of the financial controller's toolkit. All resources, processes, and products need to be defined. Then measures of their use must be designed.

Exhibit I shows the functions of a manufacturing business and the computer "business within the business" equivalents. The listings are meant to suggest the many parallels between an independent manufactur-

EXHIBIT I

The Manufacturing Business and
the Computer Activity: Some Equivalences

BUSINESS	THE BUSINESS WITHIN THE BUSINESS
Board of Directors	Executive Steering Committee
CEO	Computer Manager
Controller	Computer Controller
General Counsel	Computer Service Level Contracting
Product	Application
Product Line	Applications Portfolio
Product Strategy	Applications Development Strategy
Product Development	Project-Phase Cycle
Product Development Management	Applications Management
Product Management	Production Services Management
Product Cost Analysis	Project Estimating
Pricing Policy	Chargeout
Income Statement	Income Expense Sheet
Balance Sheet	Balance Sheet
P & L	P & L Analysis
Financial Ratio	Benchmark
Chart of Accounts	Chart of Accounts
Capital Budgeting	Project Screening
Financial Modeling	Financial Modeling
Consumer Market Research/Analysis	User Demand Analysis
Market Development	User Education
Consumer Surveys	User Satisfaction Surveys
Consumer Service Management	User Liason
Career Planning	Career Management
Staffing	Staffing
Training	Training
Corporate Strategy/Planning	Strategy/Planning
Research	Technology Awareness
Product Planning	Applications Planning
Materials Planning	Data Resource Planning
Facilities Planning	Configuration/Network Planning

ing business and the computer activity housed within an organization. Certain equivalences have greater relevance at one stage of evolution than at another. The parallel between general counsel and level service contracting, for example, is far more important in the later stages than in the earlier ones, when uncertainty of many kinds makes precise contracting difficult or impossible. Eventually, however, virtually every business function has its equivalent in the computer environment.

Chapter 15, Controlling the Costs of Data Services, describes the accounting and management control concepts for the computer activity. The accounting and control systems evolve through the stages. The most common error is for controls to lag behind the requirement for them. Experience has demonstrated dramatically that those computer activities which have maintained parity of controls with the requirements of a stage progress most efficiently.

Chapter 16, Production Services, focuses on the operation of the computer network. Many of the industrial engineering and production control activities apply to running an effective network.

Chapter 17, Strategies for Applications Management, focuses on the systems development process. Usually, this area is referred to as "project management." A lot is known about the project management process. But the real key to the management of the process seems to be striking the balance between structure and the use of disciplined methodology while providing flexibility for professionals to apply their art and experience. Striking this optimum balance is tricky, and it is highly project-dependent.

Chapter 18, Data Administration, describes the administrative aspects of data management as a resource. Once the concept of data resource management is understood, the next step is putting the organization structure in place to make it happen.

Chapter 19, Human Resource Management, describes ways to build a comprehensive personnel program for computer professionals. More than any other factor, human resource programs make the difference between highly effective computer activities and those that suffer from low productivity.

Chapter 20, Personal Privacy Versus the Corporate Computer, discusses an important area. As computers take on more business functions, the access to information about people is greatly increased. Furthermore, networks are interconnecting company's computers. It is important to understand the issues at the outset and incorporate safeguards into long-range plans.

15

Controlling the Costs of Data Services*

RICHARD L. NOLAN

Without exception, the companies that I have studied for the past four years have found it difficult to make their transfer-pricing, or "**charge-out**," systems for data processing services understandable to the managers who use them.

The root of this problem is not the inherent technical complexity of computer technology—it is a historical error made in the management of data processing. To date, we have designed our DP management systems around the computer instead of the data. Consequently, chargeout systems have been designed to hold the manager who uses the data accountable for computer-related resources such as processing time, main memory time and space, and input/output accesses.

However, the user works with output units, such as invoices processed, inventory reports, and production schedules. Thus the user is forced to somehow translate input and processing charges into the information for which he or she receives value. Only then can he take appropriate control and be held accountable. In a sense, what is being asked of the user is analogous to asking a car buyer to make a decision on several automobiles by being given a bill of materials on the different types of cars. The car buyer makes the decision on information such as performance of a V-8 versus the economy of a six-cylinder engine; the convenience of an automatic versus manual transmission; economy,

---

safety, and wear of radial versus belted tires, not on kilos of steel, cast iron, and rubber.

Take, for example, this all too common vignette. On July 1, the vice president of marketing had just received his third monthly bill for his department's use of the order entry system. The bill he received is shown in Exhibit I.

Although he did not understand the detail of the bill (for example, he had no idea what CPU, kilobytes, and EXCP stand for), he felt that it was way too much. In fact, the charge represented a good 25% of his budget. He also knew from the president's recent memorandum that he was now accountable for these expenses. So he picked up the telephone and made an appointment to talk with his newly appointed "data processing coordinator."

Management's experience with data processing had followed the pattern of many other companies. After starting out in the early 1960s by automating payroll, the company had experienced extremely rapid growth in its DP budget as applications were developed for almost all parts of the business. The order entry system was one of the early applications.

It was close to a disaster when the devised estimate of development costs skyrocketed from $100,000 to $275,000 with less than half of the originally promised capability. Nevertheless, the marketing department stuck with it, and the costs were treated as corporate overhead. The bugs were shaken out by 1967, and the system was gradually expanded to the point where the vice president of marketing said that the company couldn't carry on business without it.

A year ago, management had become concerned with ever-rising DP expenses and seemingly declining performance, as maintenance problems with existing applications seemed to have got out of hand. Therefore, the company centralized data processing under a new vice president of information services, and there was a general consensus that users should be held accountable for the services they were using. With the support of the

EXHIBIT I

Data Processing
Services Bill

Resource	Use	Charge per unit	Total
Elapsed time on computer (minutes)	243,000	$0.04	$ 9,720
CPU (seconds)	2,430,000	0.0167	40,500
Kilobytes (1K memory/minute)	14,515,000	0.0016	23,220
EXCP (I/O accesses)	105,000,000	0.0002	21,000
Total due			$94,440

president, the vice president of information services had his staff design a system for charging out all costs on the basis of resources used to support the various applications. He also established data-processing coordinators for each major user group.

It was in this context that the vice president of marketing opened the meeting with his data processing coordinator:

"Although I really don't understand this bill, it has to be too high. Order entry cost us less than $30,000 per month before the computer system was installed. Not only is the $94,400 too high, even taking inflation into account, but the cost has varied from $78,000 to $104,000 in the three short months that the chargeout system has been in effect. How is a manager supposed to plan in such a volatile environment?"

"You are absolutely right about the variance," the coordinator responded. "It is due partly to the volume of orders processed and due partly to the upgrade in the computer operating system software last month. We have also incurred technical difficulty in measuring kilobyte minutes in an MVS operating system environment. You see we have a "meg" of main memory, but with virtual memory software we have a lot more. Our problem in charging equitably is one of. . . ."

The vice president didn't understand this explanation and felt that he was getting the same waffle treatment that he had come to expect from data processing. Somewhat irritated, he said he didn't give a damn about the technical problems but wanted the bill to be reduced by 25%.

The coordinator reminded him that the information services division was only a service department and that it was the vice president's responsibility to provide the guidance for making such cuts. He then asked him what component of the bill he would like to attack: CPU seconds, elapsed time, kilobytes, or EXCPs?

At this point, the vice president of marketing became very angry. Shoving the coordinator out the door with instructions not to come back, he got the president on the telephone: "I'm strapped. Data processing is charging me for services that are essential, and I can't do anything about the cost. When I try to get down to how to control the costs, all I get is technical gibberish. . . ."

DESIGN FOR CHARGEOUTS

Data services have become much too important to companies to be left to technicians. Management must devote the time necessary to understand data processing's current and future impact on the business so that it can provide the guidance that both data processing and users need.

In a sense, the chargeout systems that I have studied (see the ruled insert on page 242) have been attempts to provide this guidance. Unfortunately, many of them were built on shaky DP accounting systems and implemented without a clear understanding of what was expected from the user.

As a result, both DP management and users became frustrated. The extent and intensity of the frustration are reflected in the vignette. The vice president of marketing was confused about what actions he should take to be accountable, and what the control rationale was. Another dysfunctional result is that the user gets too involved in the operational details of data processing.

One manager told me, "I now demand internal reports from data processing to check up on just how well they are running their operation."

How can a company develop an effective chargeout system? Obviously, no one system can work for all companies since the needs of companies vary tremendously. However, I think that one good approach to designing an effective system is to follow these seven steps:

1. Assess the overall status of data processing services within the company.

2. Sort out how data processing is organized.

3. Evaluate capacity of accounting systems to support a DP management control system.

4. Assess current chargeout approach.

5. Develop chargeout system objectives and strategy.

6. Develop implementation goals and milestones.

7. Implement and review.

Description of research

This article is based on a study I conducted in eighteen organizations. All were considered large in their respective industries. Four were major banks with assets ranging from $1 billion to $8 billion. Sales in the remaining companies ranged from $50 million for a division to over $6 billion for a large retailer. Data processing budgets varied from $750,000 for a division to over $120 million for an aerospace company that commercially sold computer services.

In the course of the research, I interviewed 21 executives, 56 managers who used DP services, and 38 DP managers. Following the visits, I sent a questionnaire to a sample of managers to determine their attitudes toward chargeout systems. Thirteen of the companies participated in a follow-up questionnaire that I sent to 222 users; 170 usable responses were returned. The full report on this research is contained in my book, Management Accounting and Control of Data Processing (New York: National Association of Accountants, 1977).

Let's look at each of these seven chargeout system steps in turn.

Assess Status of Data Services

The search for alternatives begins with a careful analysis of the characteristics of a company's industry and management philosophy. For example, managements of companies in high technology industries, such as elec-

EXHIBIT II

Stage Process
Audit Criteria

Criteria	Stage I: Initiation	Stage II: Contagion	Stage III: Control	Stage IV: Integration
DP organization				
Objective	Get first application on the computer	Broaden use of computer technology	Gain control of data processing activities	Integrate data processing into business
Staffing emphasis	Technical computer experts	User-oriented system analysts and programmers	Middle management	Balance of technical and management specializations
Structure	Embedded in low-functional area	Growth and multiple DP units created	Consolidation of DP activities into central organizational unit	Layering and "fitting" DP organization structure
Reporting level	To functional manager	To higher level functional manager	To senior management officer	VP level reporting to corporate top management
User awareness				
Senior management	Clerical staff reduction syndrome	Broader applications in operational areas	Crisis of expenditure growth Panic about penetration in business operations	Acceptance as a major business function Involvement in providing direction
User attitude	"Hands-off" Anxiety over implications	Superficially enthusiastic Insufficient involvement in applications design	Frustration from suddenly being held accountable for DP expenditures	Acceptance of accountability Involvement in application, budgeting, design, and maintenance
Communication with DP	Informal Lack of understanding	Oversell and unrealistic objectives and schedules Schism develops	Formal lines of communication Formal commitments Cumbersome	Acceptance and informed communication Application development partnership
Training	General orientation on "what is a computer"	Little user interest	Increase in user interest due to accountability	User seeks out training on application development and control
Planning and control				
Objective	Hold spending at initial commitment	Facilitate wider functional uses of computer	Formalize control and contain DP expenditures	Tailor planning and control to DP activities
Planning	Oriented toward computer implementation	Oriented toward application development	Oriented toward gaining central control	Established formal planning activity
Management control	Focus on computer operations budget	Lax to facilitate applications development activity growth	Proliferation of formal controls	Balanced formal and informal controls
Project management	DP manager responsibility	Programmer's responsibility	Formalized system DP department responsibility	Formalized system tailored to project DP and user/management joint responsibility
Project approval and priority setting	DP manager responsibility	Multi-functional managers First in, first out	Steering committee	Steering committee Formal plan influence
DP standards	Low awareness of importance	Inattention	Importance recognized Activity aggressively implemented	Established standards activity Published policy manuals
Application portfolio				
Objective	Prove value of computer technology in organization	Apply computer technology to multi-functional areas	Moratorium on new applications Consolidate and gain control of existing applications	Exploit opportunities for integrative systems Cost-effective application of advanced technology
Application justification	Cost-savings	Informal user/manager approval	Hard cost savings Short-term payout	Benefit/cost analysis Senior management approval

tronics and aerospace, are more tolerant and understanding of technical complexities than managements of companies in service industries, such as insurance and banking. Also, managements of companies with sophisticated budgeting and financial controls are more receptive to similar systems for data processing. The general rule is that management control systems for data processing cannot be significantly more advanced than the management control systems used for the company as a whole.

Management's next task is to determine the status of its services. What I call the "stage process audit" is a useful way to structure this analysis.[1] Based upon the status of the Applications Portfolio, data processing organization, control mechanisms, and user awareness, an organization's data services can be thought of as being in one of four stages: initiation, contagion, control, or integration. *Exhibit II* shows the attributes for each of these stages. This detailed audit provides the foundation for tailoring the design of a control system.

A frequent mistake in designing an effective system is to impose sophisticated controls upon organizational units that are not "ready." The organizational unit is not ready if controls hinder its operation or if personnel cannot clearly see the relevance of the controls to their problems.

For example, one user in my study was charged for programming services that he did not fully understand because a new on-line system was being developed. Nevertheless, he was asked to make judgments on the resource commitments being made on the project, as well as to accept an accountability for those judgments even though the development process was largely out of his hands.

Sort Out the Organization Structure

Although many companies for the most part have centralized their data processing, there are usually pockets of activities still embedded within the organization that have not been dislodged.

The question of what constitutes an effective organization is complicated by wide disagreement on which activities should be centralized, even when they are only broadly categorized into systems development and operations. The majority of DP personnel I interviewed agreed that operations should be centralized, at least enough to support the specialists necessary to run and maintain the computer facility. However, proponents of minicomputers believe decentralization is preferable. The main disagreement concerns the location of systems development personnel, even though for the 18 research sites studied, 90% of the central DP departments had programmers and 60% had systems analysts—and over half of the user organizations had programmers and systems analysts.

---

[1]See my article, "*Managing the Computer Resources: A Stage Hypothesis,*" Communications of the ACM, July 1973, p. 300.

Organizing data processing becomes even more complex and difficult when activities are sorted into maintenance, data entry, batch processing, on-line services and processing, and telecommunication facilities.

A study of an organization's structure will expose irrational locations for various data processing activities. The majority of these locations can probably be changed; others may have to be viewed as constraints in the short run.

Even when an irrational structure cannot be altered, the structure must be understood because almost every control action taken for the central DP group will also affect the splinter groups.

For example, in one company I studied, the corporate data processing department decided to charge users the full cost of providing services. The divisional data processing department charged less than full costs because occupancy and employee benefits were excluded from the calculation of costs. The effect of the corporate decision was to shift users to the divisional data processing facility, even though the best interests of the company were not served. If these responses are anticipated, systems may be designed to avoid dysfunctional relationships between the central and splinter groups, as well as between corporate and divisional management.

Evaluate Capacity of Accounting System

Since accounting systems provide the foundation for management control, management control can only reflect the quality of the accounting system. As shown in Exhibit III, a logical progression exists in the development of the accounting systems, from after-the-fact, object-of-expenditure control to budgetary control responsibility center, by program (or job), and by quantitative measure of output units.

Although all 18 companies studied had developed meaningful classifications for expenditures—that is, charts of accounts, 4 companies still had not integrated the DP chart of accounts into the company's general ledger system. In addition, the DP accounting systems were of varying quality, which influenced their reliability.

The development of data processing accounting systems is initially an accounting problem rather than a data processing problem because basic accounting concepts are most important. Unfortunately, this need for accounting skills does not seem to be fully recognized in the beginning. Over half of the companies studied reported that their technical personnel played the dominant role in designing the initial accounting systems. Systems analysts and programmers were usually assigned this task on the assumption that their technical skills were needed to measure computer system resource usage. Rather quickly, however, it became apparent that the real problems were accounting problems concerning responsibility centers, costing, and allocating costs to responsibility centers. Accounting personnel then would be brought into the project.

Cost centers, too, seemed to have evolved from the existing structure of the data processing department rather than from an analysis of basic

EXHIBIT III

Evolution of Accounting and
Control Systems

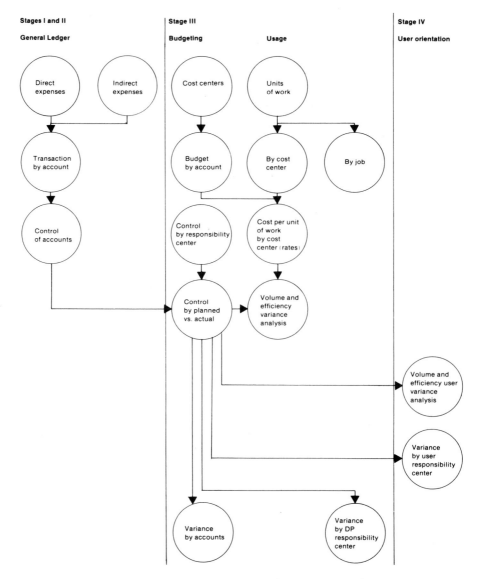

DP functions. Consequently, organizational changes often have a deteri-
mental effect on control. In addition, costs are not consistently categorized
by type—direct, indirect, and overhead.

These fundamental problems seriously hindered the effective design,
implementation, and administration of the chargeout systems. Simply
stated, you cannot build a sophisticated control system on a sandy foundation of weak accounting systems.

Assess Current Chargeout Approach

A useful chargeout system communicates to managers the consequences of their decisions concerning use of services. Cost responsibility will tend to motivate users to employ the resources more effectively and efficiently. Four criteria can be used for determining the usefulness of a chargeout system—understandability, controllability, accountability, and cost/benefit incidence. *Exhibit IV* shows the criteria and questions for determining the maturity of the chargeout system.

As shown in *Exhibit IV*, chargeout systems initially are directed at high-level managers. Summary data processing bills are sent to divisional controllers without much information on the charges being conveyed to end users. With maturity, the chargeout systems become more sophisticated and permit detailed bills to be sent directly to low-level users. It is

EXHIBIT IV

Criteria for
Chargeout Systems

Understandability:
To what extent can the manager associate chargeout costs to the activities necessary to carry out his or her tasks?

Attributes:
High—Manager can associate costs with functions and determine variables accounting for costs.
Medium—Manager can roughly associate costs with functions, but cannot directly determine major variables accounting for costs.
Low—Manager cannot associate costs with functions.

Controllability:
To what extent are charges under the control of the user?

Attributes:
None—No control. The manager has no influence on acceptance or rejection of the charges. These decisions are made at a higher level.
Indirect—Through communication with others, such as divisional or departmental controllers that receive charges, the manager can influence the charges.
Direct/arbitrary—Charges are allocated directly to the manager, but his decision is to either accept or reject the application charges. Little information is provided on controllable versus noncontrollable data processing costs.
Direct/economic—Charges are directly charged in a manner that allows the manager to make decisions that actually reduce controllable data processing costs.

Accountability:
Are costs and utilization of computer-based systems included in performance evaluation of the user?

Attributes:
None—Not included in performance evaluation.
Indirect—Included indirectly in performance evaluation; costs can be related to user, but not done routinely.
Direct—Included directly in periodic user-performance evaluation.

Cost/benefit incidence:
Does the user responsible for task accomplishment also receive the chargeout bill?

Attributes:
Yes.
No.

important that the chargeout system evolve through successive phases so that users and DP managers can learn how to interpret and use the information. It is especially important that the means for accountability be coordinated with the expectations for accountability.

After assessing the status of the existing chargeout system, management's next objective is to develop a strategy that will increase the maturity (and effectiveness) of the chargeout system at an appropriate pace for the major user groups. It is likely that several chargeout strategies may be required for the different user groups.

Develop Objectives and Strategy

In the companies I studied, objectives for the chargeout systems were rarely articulated. Or, if they were articulated, the objectives were often narrowly defined short-term goals. For example, eight of the companies stated that their chargeout system objective was to allocate data processing costs. No mention was made of providing the cost information to users that they needed to make effective decisions about services. In other words, using data accounting systems to allocate costs for financial reporting and budgeting purposes should not be confused with chargeout. Chargeout brings the user into the realm of control and accountability.

In my opinion, the absence of a clear statement of objectives or an excessively narrow statement was the single most troublesome factor inhibiting chargeout system effectiveness. Consequently, systems were not well thought out, but were designed to provide minimal information for accounting, or to support other management tools such as project management systems.

Chargeout objectives should be stated in terms of desirable results for user accountability. Examples of such objectives include:

- Make managers aware of the economic (full absorption) costs of data processing services provided to them.

- Make managers responsible for the economic costs of services they use.

- Motivate managers to make decisions about the use of data processing on the basis of the direct costs of providing the services.

- Charge costs in understandable volume units to facilitate data processing capacity planning.

- Charge costs in a manner to facilitate manager product (service) pricing.

Each of these examples specifies a particular result, and taken together they imply the design of a system much broader than one that simply charges for computer services. Alterations in organization structure, budgeting, and performance review and measurement are often necessary. Once management has articulated an appropriate set of objectives, it should formulate a strategy to achieve them that takes into account the necessary changes in organization and administrative practices.

Develop Implementation Goals

The stage audit I discussed earlier provides an idea of how advanced a company is in respect to data processing. It also specifies a long-term objective.

Keeping in mind that a great deal of difficult organizational changes are required to first synchronize the status of the applications portfolio, organization, control system, and user awareness, and second, to progress through the advanced stages, management can lay out short-run goals and a schedule for longer term goals. A common mistake is to go too fast or to attempt to leap-frog a stage. It is important to remember that learning at all levels within the organization is involved in progressing through the stages.

The more detailed analysis of the organization's chargeout status and specification of management control objectives provide the groundwork for establishing short-run and long-run goals. These goals should also be realistic in terms of schedule and sequence. In addition, they should be initially tailored to the individual user groups with the long-term goal of progressing toward a common chargeout system for the entire organization or, at least, a common chargeout system for each of the major divisions.

Implement and Review

The data processing department should never take it upon itself to implement a management control and chargeout strategy. Implementation of the strategy will have far-reaching effects on the overall management control system of the company, as well as immediate effects on users. It is clear that managers must be able to evaluate information system alternatives since it is the development and operation of their applications that will determine what the costs will be. The chargeout system effectively brings the user into control by matching costs and benefits by responsibility center. Of course, there are complicating factors where applications serve several users in more than one responsibility center.

High-level steering committees play a crucial role in providing a forum for shaking down and ratifying a management control and chargeout strategy. Just as important as ratification is management's agreement on implementation goals and schedules. Organizational changes associated with a realistic strategy will inevitably result in some conflict and disagreement. To constructively negotiate through obstacles that arise, management needs to have a plan or road map on direction and destination.

The steering committee, or some type of quarterly review board, should ensure that the organization maintains progress. In addition to its role of approval and guidance, such a group provides a source of commitment that is necessary for successful management control programs.

THE FUTURE

The 18 companies that I studied are at the forefront of data processing. Their DP organization charts, trends, and plans provide a glimpse of future organization structures and control systems. The extensive incorporation of data-base technology is the most important trend, leading toward a structure that facilitates data-oriented management.[2]

For example, one of the more advanced companies had explained especially well the role of data-base technology in this orientation. The company used a facsimile of *Exhibit V* to compare the traditional computer-oriented accountability scheme with the data-oriented accountability scheme for two applications: an order entry system and an inventory control system. Traditionally, both the definition of data (inventory part numbers, reorder points, customers) and function (the way an order is processed) is contained in the application, using programming languages such as COBOL or PL/1. Chargeout is based on the computer-related resources used, and the user is held accountable for both data and function.

But data-base technology enables management to separate function from data. As a result, users can be held directly accountable for function, and data processing can be held directly accountable for management of the company's data resources.

This company envisions a chargeout system including both simplified user bills and data processing bills from users. In other words, data would be purchased from functional groups that originate them, as well as from outside sources. In responding to requests from users, data processing would provide value-added services by combining, processing, and distributing data. The users would be charged for the cost of the data plus the value-added services of processing them. The value-added concept solves a basic problem of current chargeout systems; it provides a quid pro quo for those who bear the costs of collecting the data but who are not the end-users.

The rapid development of data-base technology will most likely lead to specialized components for data management. *Exhibit VI* shows the three main components: data, processing, and control.

To start with, current processing systems will be relieved of data management functions and will be designed to carry out value-added functions of combining, mutating, and distributing data. Both the data and processing systems will incorporate large-scale and mini/micro-computer technologies.

This division of functions will then lead to a separate control system to facilitate specialized management necessary to account, bill, schedule, monitor, and control the efficiency of the company's data processing

---

[2]See my article *"Computer Data Base: The Future is Now,"* HBR September-October 1973, p. 98.

EXHIBIT V

Comparison of Traditional Computer-Oriented Accountability With
Data-Oriented Accountability

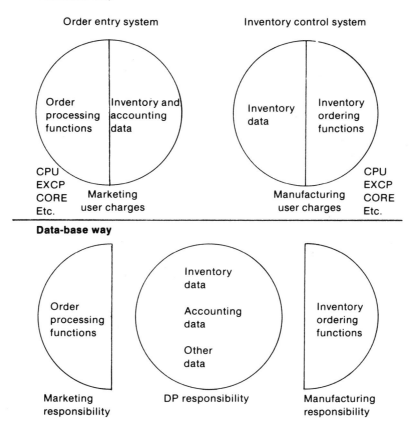

Traditional way

Order entry system   Inventory control system

Order processing functions | Inventory and accounting data

CPU EXCP CORE Etc.   Marketing user charges

Inventory data | Inventory ordering functions

Manufacturing user charges   CPU EXCP CORE Etc.

Data-base way

Order processing functions

Marketing responsibility

Inventory data

Accounting data

Other data

DP responsibility

Inventory ordering functions

Manufacturing responsibility

installation. Although this control component is at present at a rudimentary state, one manufacturer has already entered the market and has delivered such systems to the Social Security Administration and the General Electric Company.

The impact of the evolving data processing installation is distinctly visible on several of the organization charts of the companies I studied. One of the first signs is the incorporation of data administration positions. Data administration separates the management of data from the development of user applications. Another sign is the emergence of the controller position. This position is created to recognize the need for more formal management of data processing, as well as to cope with the need for bringing about effective user accountability. *Exhibit VII* shows my projected organization chart for the future data processing installation.

EXHIBIT VI

Criteria for
Chargeout Systems

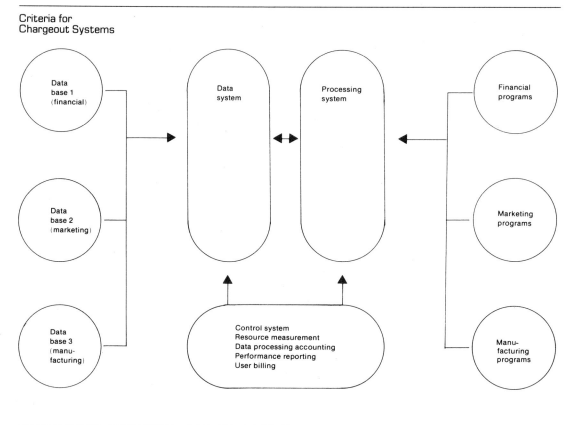

IN SUMMARY

The role and position of data processing has now taken sufficient form to mount effective management programs to fit it into the modern organization. It is clear that organizations progress through stages of maturity for data processing management and the next apparent stage is to establish three separate functions for this management.

In order for it to better control these functions, it is important that top management first understand the natural shift from computer management to data management. This shift cannot and will not take place overnight. It is, and for each organization will be, a gradual shift beginning with the incorporation of data-base technology and an elaboration of control systems.

Next, top management needs to realize that an effective chargeout system is essential if those who use data processing are to be in control and held accountable for the services they receive. It is the users that ultimately justify and obtain the potentially lucrative returns from the company's investment in data processing.

It is this simple fact that should determine top management's orientation and decisions concerning data processing.

Management wants information systems that produce results rather

EXHIBIT VII

Future Data Services
Organization

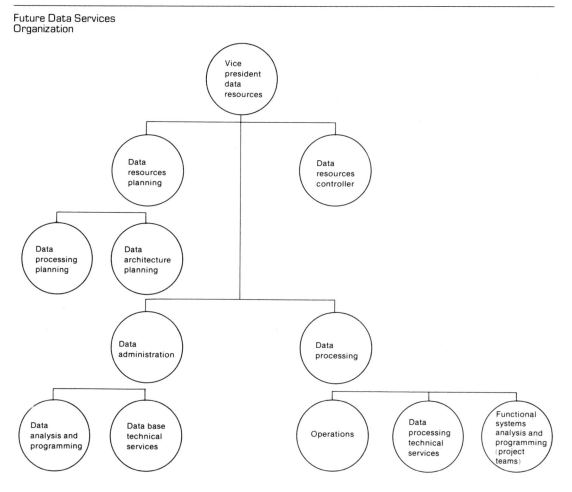

than promises and they want the system to aid them in the real money-making areas of a business—strategic decision making.

Users want the benefit of advanced systems, but the systems must not be so complex and multifaceted that no one can understand, much less use, them.

Finally, cost/performance is still a major criterion for any business investment and particularly for EDP, which has withstood the normal ROI measurements for so many years. It can no longer be rationalized that computer technology and information systems are changing too fast to warrant strict cost justification; therefore cost/performance has become a major criterion. Management wants the networking and the transaction processing and the on-line simulation, but these developments must pay their own way and in a reasonable time frame.*

*From *Management-Oriented Management Information Systems*, by Jerome Kanter, 2d. ed., © 1977, p. 357. Reprinted by permission of Prentice-Hall, Inc., Englewood Cliffs, New Jersey.

16

Production
Services

HERBERT W. PERKINS III

Production services may be defined as the day-to-day functioning of the data center. Production services provide the means by which data processing services are delivered to the user. The quality of service is a critical factor in the overall effectiveness of data processing. Unless there is reliable, effective management within production services, data processing as a whole cannot be effective.

If data processing can be compared to a manufacturing organization, production services may be compared to the production activities in the factory. It involves processing raw materials by people and machines in order to produce a product or service. It is the responsibility of the manager of production services to insure that the factory is run efficiently and effectively.

Since users deal with production services on a daily basis, it is a highly visible area within data processing. Therefore, user's understanding of the efficiency and effectiveness of this department strongly influences the organization's perception of data processing services as a whole. A well-managed data center can sometimes make mediocre development efforts look and function more effectively by compensating for design flaws. However, even the best development group cannot overcome the ongoing difficulties caused by poor management within a production services department.

The relationship between the management of production services and the overall management of data processing is addressed in this chapter. The evolution of this relationship is traced through the stages of data processing growth. Once the relationship has been explored, controls necessary to manage the production services are discussed. Their evolution is discussed in terms of key stage-dependent patterns.

EVOLUTION OF PRODUCTION SERVICES

In stage I the user's only request is, "I want to use the computer." Demand is nonspecific and enthusiasm varies from user to user. At this stage it is easy to become overconfident and to expect that more automation will mean more user enthusiasm. This overlooks the fact that as the user gains experience demand also becomes more sophisticated and more specific and user satisfaction becomes harder to meet. By stage II the user may request use of the computer from nine to five and may expect a steady level of service, equal to the service received when demands were much more limited.

Once user requests become more extensive and more specific there is more pressure for production services to improve and increase services. When problems occur there is a tendency to answer user complaints with technical explanations because the problems appear technical. The management of production services has not yet learned to manage and control the technology. Technical explanations are accepted for a short while, but they are soon dismissed as excuses. The user knows that there is a high level of technical expertise available but does not have the sophistication or the patience to fully understand what is involved in delivering the required service. The management of production services is still grappling with the technology. They do not have the managerial skills necessary to control it.

In stage II it is tempting for production services to become all things to all people. The increased demand for service is encouraging but misleading. There are limitations on the ability to meet demands given the existing capabilities. The tendency of production services management to promise more than it is able to deliver is further complicated by a tendency to depend upon unreliable performance measures.

By late stage II, the user's awareness of technology is improving. It is easier to discuss mutual problems and joint solutions. At the same time, the user is becoming more dependent upon data processing; users are expressing their demands in more specific terms and holding production service accountable for providing increasingly critical services.

In stage III the issue of performance measures surfaces because the system is responding to pressures to contain the cost of data processing, to fix budgets, and to assign more of the cost directly to users. Bartering may replace direct demand and users may begin to offer deals. For example, one user may say that an average eight-second response time and a ninety-seven percent availability is acceptable only if the bill for services is cut by $2000 per month. Another user may agree to an increase in costs in exchange for an improved average response time and increased availability. Since the production services department is still growing, these contracts are mere placebos if the underlying control systems are not present. They may leave problems untouched and do nothing to stabilize growth.

By the end of stage III all of the basic control programs should be installed and working well. Service levels should be defined in user terms.

The tools to measure these service levels should be in place. Production services factory lines evolve. Planning and controlling the network become increasingly important. Decisions regarding the structure of the network must be made. At the same time the network must be kept operational on a daily basis.

MANAGEMENT OF PRODUCTION SERVICES AND ORGANIZATIONAL STRATEGY

The management of production services is different from the management of other data processing areas by the nature of its operational activities. The function of production services is not to set planning strategy or to apply information to the management of the business overall. Instead, the function of production services is to deliver products or services to the users. Products are delivered in the form of predefined reports or transactions. Services are delivered in the form of computing power which the user controls. These products and services are delivered through a series of repetitive production processes. Production services management is the ongoing coordinator and controller of these activities.

Exhibit I graphically represents production services. Input in the form of personnel, machines, and material are presented to the factory. Various production processes act on the input to produce products and services. In *Exhibit I*, five production processes are shown: production staging, data entry, processing, teleprocessing, and distribution. Supporting these production processes is a process support function similar to a plant engineer. Its responsibility is to maintain the factory and keep the lines moving.

EXHIBIT I

Production
Services

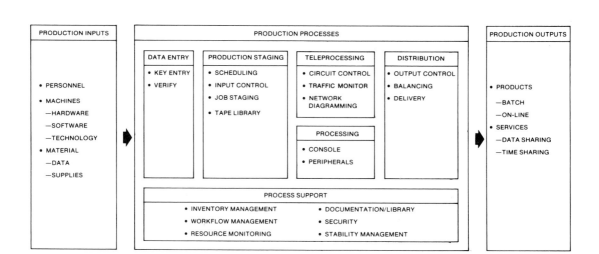

Two things need to be understood about *Exhibit I*. First, the production processes shown are generic processes which evolve through the stages and through the evolution of the industry. For example, distribution may be relatively unimportant in stages I and II. Reports may be sent to users in an unstructured fashion. In later stages, the function will evolve to include a highly formal report compliance/quality control system. In addition, the evolution of the industry has wrought changes on these functions. In passed years, data entry was a very important function of production services. The decline, in recent years, of the cost of technology associated with computing has allowed the data entry function to be distributed to the user organization. As a result, this function has become far less important to production services. Second, the controls shown for process support are those controls which are concerned with keeping the production line working. Other controls not shown in the exhibit are necessary to monitor trends and to expand the capability of the factory. Examples include performance management, resource management, and capacity planning. All controls become increasingly well-defined as the organization evolves.

Because production services are concerned with delivering products and services to users on a regular basis, these services must be linked to the overall strategy and plans of data processing. An awareness of the governing objectives and plans of the organizations must temper the day-to-day decision making process. In the case of production services, long-term goals are tempered and mediated by the very specific, very immediate nature of the work. The production services manager is a coordinator whose ability to sustain a high level of performance in the data center is perceived by users and senior management as the ability to actualize general policy. Thus the quality of day-to-day operations is an indicator of the success of long-term strategy and planning.

The Stages Model of data processing growth provides a key to the successful integration of these two perspectives: day-to-day operations priorities and long-term objectives. The capabilities of production services are affected by the maturity of all four Growth Processes. In particular, growth of the Applications Portfolio and experience of the users defines the way in which the production services department manages the integration of the two perspectives on a daily basis. The development of the other two Growth Processes, organization, planning and control, and personnel and technology resources, define the efficiency and effectiveness of production services.

It is important for the manager of production services to have a clear understanding of the role of production services in the overall data processing organization. The products of production services have broad exposure throughout the organization. By their nature, these products have a far wider audience than the activities of the systems and programming staff. User perceptions of data processing service are heavily influenced by the quality of production services and the attitude of production services staff. In addition, because of the interdependence with other areas, many problems can not be solved by the data center alone. Many of these problems are not technical but instead involve the controls associated with the flow of information between production services and the rest of the organization. It is the responsibility of the production services department to develop, maintain, and install these controls. However, in order for the controls to be effective both management and the applications development group must support the effort. Examples of these controls include the method of distributing reports, the way in which problems are logged, tracked, and monitored, and the manner of coordinating the installation of changes to production systems. The manager must be able to look beyond the daily activities involved in running the factory in order to take a more universal view of data processing and the role of production services within data processing.

EVALUATION OF THE CURRENT STATUS

The first problem in managing production services is to determine where the entire data processing organization stands in relation to the stages of growth. This involves the examination of both internal and external factors. The size of a data center, the skills of the personnel, and the type of technology employed present a rough idea of the stage of the data processing organization, and specifically of its production services. However, these are only indicators. The real test of maturity requires that production services be seen in the context of all four Growth Processes.

Once data processing determines its stage of growth, then the production services management should attempt to identify those areas in which the production services department is most successful and least successful, and to discriminate between internal and external causes. They must determine which areas they can improve internally and in which other areas they are dependent on other functional groups. This helps identify both opportunities and problems. Where problems exist, production services may be expected to compensate for weaknesses in other parts of the data processing organization.

The failure to understand how production services mature in terms of the stages of growth is demonstrated by the attitude of production services managers when discussing the quality of their data centers. Asked to describe their measure for an effective data center, many production services managers respond that a good data center is a data center with "no phone calls", implying that the data center is being measured in terms of user satisfaction. User satisfaction can be a good measure of success, but there is a problem with the manner in which this particular measurement is made. It is subjective and it is communicated informally. The same managers who use this measurement will be among the first to decry the lack of data processing knowledge among the users and to defend their data centers against the criticism of such groups. Yet they persist in striving for success on a day-to-day basis according to an informal standard of user complaints and user satisfaction.

"No phone calls" is an example of a stage-dependent measure of production services effectiveness which is treated as if it were an objective standard. In the case of user satisfaction three separate issues are being subsumed by the "no phone calls" ideal. First, the measure fails to consider the level of knowledge and the reasonableness of user expectations given the stage of growth of data processing. Second, the measure provides of no way of assessing how efficiently production services utilize its resources. Finally, there is no method of evaluating the effectiveness of production services over time.

There are broad misunderstandings and inaccurate assessments made possible by this failure to consider either the stage of growth or level of sophistication of users. Users may have unrealistic expectations. Production services may be less efficient or effective than they should be, given the available resources. Some aspects of production services may be stronger than others. Some users may be more or less aggressive in their demands. "No phone calls" may mean that users have become so disenchanted with data processing that they feel it is a waste of time to report problems or request changes. Clearly, measures must be defined carefully.

The solution is to define specific measures of user service levels. This definition process usually begins in stage II. Measures used include, but are not limited to, such things as:

- **Availability**. The percentage of time during which the routines were scheduled to run when the user was actually able to use those routines.

- **Responsiveness**. The time required for the user to get an answer to his query. In a batch environment this is usually called **turnaround time** and is measured in hours. In an on-line environment it is measured in seconds and called **response time.**

- **Reliability**. This is usually measured in terms of mean time to failure and mean time to repair.

- **Cost**. The cost to process a transaction.

Over time these measures become better defined. By the end of stage III the list of measures should be reasonably complete, targets should be set for all measures, and the data collected for each measure should be relatively accurate. With all of the measures in place, the production services department should develop service level contracts with users. These state:

- The responsibilities of both users and the data processing organization. For example, the payroll department may be expected to pay two payrolls per month with approximately five thousand checks per payroll. Further, the time cards will be entered on the second and fourth Wednesday, production services will produce three edit registers per payroll, and the user will be responsible for balancing the payroll.

- The level of service the user can expect, i.e.; three- to five-second response time 90 percent of the time, 97 percent availability, and mean time to failure of two weeks.

- The cost of that service expressed in user terms.

When defining service level measures, production services management must be careful to define them precisely. Response time is an example of a seemingly specific indicator which can be subjective. First, the required response time may vary from one situation to another. One organization may say that anything less than three seconds is good while another talks about a response time of fifteen seconds or less. Good response time depends on the business needs of the user and the reasonableness of his requests.

Further complications can arise since response time is often measured differently by different groups. The user is concerned with terminal response time while production services managers may measure internal data center response time. Internal response time is the time it takes to process the message at the central site ignoring all delays between it and the user. This can cause a vast difference in perceptions. Unless these measures are compared and coordinated, users and production services personnel may disagree on questions concerning the level of service provided. Unless all parties agree on one set of measurements, there will be disagreements about the effectiveness of the production services. This undermines morale, generates conflict between production services personnel and users, and demeans the data center in the eyes of users and senior management.

In the atmosphere created by these problems, it is difficult to make an objective assessment of the performance of the production services department or to set objectives and stick to a strategy. There is a tendency to function on the basis of ad hoc judgements and to respond to problems on a minute-by-minute basis. This leads to a high pressure situation in which production service management becomes crisis management and confidence erodes within the data center and throughout the organization.

PLANNING

Earlier in this chapter, data processing was compared to a manufacturing organization. In this context, the production services department may be viewed as the factory. The management of production services keeps the lines of the factory moving. Data processing may also be viewed as a business within a business.[1] To function as a business, data processing includes all of the functions normally associated with a business. One of these functions is planning.

Just as data processing must be an integral part of overall business planning,[2] production services must be an important part of data processing planning. Production services personnel must know which skills and types of technology are required to support the needs of the business. In addition, production services staff must know what levels and types of service are required by users. They must understand what capacity and

---

[1]See Part IV Introduction.
[2]See Chapter 25, "Corporate Planning for Information Resources."

capabilities must be available. They must know where these services will be provided. Finally, production services personnel must understand how their department will acquire each of the items necessary to provide the products and services required.

In the early stages of an organization's growth there is often no distinction between the formulation of a strategy and the development of a plan. Briefly, *a strategy is what the organization wants to be, while a plan is the way the organization will get there.*[3] The result of this confusion is two-fold. First, the data processing strategy may not support the business strategy. This assumes that there is a data processing strategy even if it has not been articulated. Second, the applications plan evolves as the long-range strategy for data processing. The result can be an organization which develops flawless applications unsupportive of the business strategy which fail to provide the required levels of service.

In the middle stages, production services are integrated into data processing planning. The business strategy and plan drive the data processing strategy and plan. Once the data processing strategy is defined, the Applications Plan and the Management Plan (involving the other growth processes) are developed.[4] The **Production Services Management Plan** may be thought of as a part of the Management Plan.

In the later stages the management plan evolves to cover all application efforts in data processing. As this happens production services planning expands. Eventually it should be totally integrated into the data processing planning cycle.

While user's awareness of the possibilities of automation becomes more sophisticated, understanding of the production services department may be poor. It is the responsibility of production services management to compensate for this discrepancy through careful planning and the thorough introduction of accurate performance measures and good controls. This insures that information about the production services activities and capabilities is accurate. On the basis of this information weighed against input from users as well as strengths or weaknesses in supporting growth process areas, the growth of the production services department can be both balanced and rapid.

PERFORMANCE MANAGEMENT

On the basis of the probable pattern of growth in the data center and the resulting pressures on managers, it is clear that management of production services must involve the measurement of performance as well as the supervision of the day-to-day activity. To date, in most organizations, the monitoring and control of production services has been informal and subjective. Frequently, measures are applied to the problem of standards

[3]B. B. Tregoe and J. W. Zimmerman, *Top Management Strategy* (New York: Simon & Schuster, 1980), p. 17-18.
[4]See Chapter 9, *"The Direction-Setting Process: Strategic and Long-Range Planning."*

and plans in a random, haphazard manner. As a result there may be a casual attitude toward performance measurement founded on such intangibles as the presence or absence of a high volume of user complaints.

Once this casual attitude passes, a feeling of panic often takes its place. Many managers understand what users require, but find themselves unable to satisfy them. As an example, consider terminal level response time. Quite correctly, the only measure of response time which is relevant to a user is the rapidity with which a message appears on his terminal. Unfortunately, that can be rather complicated and expensive to measure accurately. A stop watch can be used for a short time; however, it is not a long-term solution. Thus the manager may recognize the better measure, but may be unable to provide it for technical or economic reasons.

Instead of depending upon the feel of operations, there should be a formal system for evaluating performance. Specific performance measures should be identified. Associated with each measure should be a standard so that management can determine whether or not their production services are doing well.

Finally, it is necessary for a management group to monitor performance on a regular basis. Regular tracking and evaluation can do a great deal to offset complaints or rumors about activity levels and user services. Moreover, when the results of performance measures are included in planning, future pressures can be anticipated and many problems avoided. Resistance to the implementation of standards and performance measurement should not obscure the ultimate value of the knowledge and the advantages they provide.

There are many specific factors which make up the body of potential performance measures for production services. Some of these involve user input and some are internal; in all cases they are based upon formal communication and standardized measurement. Performance measures are of two types[5]:

- **Measures of effectiveness**. How well the organization's objectives are being accomplished.

- **Measures of efficiency**. How well the organization is utilizing assigned resources.

Each of these measures can be considered in more detail. For example, measures of effectiveness can be grouped into three categories.

- **Timeliness**. The extent to which the objective is accomplished in time to be effective. Typical measures include schedule performance, turnaround, and response time.

---

[5]David P. Norton and Kenneth G. Rau, *A Guide to EDP Performance Management* (Wellesley, MA: Q.E.D. Information Sciences, Inc., 1977).

- **Quality.** The extent to which the objectives are accomplished acceptably. Typical measures include accuracy, usefulness, clarity, acceptability, reliability, and availability.

- **Quantity**. The extent to which the objective is satisfied. Typical measures include volume achieved and amount of backlog. Volume in production services may be expressed in terms of CPU hours, key strokes, lines printed, or, more usefully, business transactions.

Likewise efficiency measures can be considered as follows:

- **Staff**. The amount of human resources utilized per unit of output. These resources can be further classified by skills level, skills mix, and function performed.

- **Machine.** The amount of equipment employed. These can be classified by size, capacity, type, and arrangement.

- **Materials**. Supplies consumed in the accomplishment of the objective.

- **Money.** All resources can be converted to a single common denominator, money. Conversely, the availability of this resource can be converted into required resources.

The identification of points at which performance can be measured provides the basis for initiating a performance management program. In order to obtain accurate measures, there must be a certain level of standardization and systematization. While controls may not be necessary to insure smooth operations in the early stages, they are essential to building the infrastructure for a long-term set of performance measures. Thus, the two are interrelated and are strongest when built into production services management from the beginning.

PERFORMANCE CONTROLS

The introduction of controls in production services follows a pattern similar to the pattern of growth in the Applications Portfolio. The first controls are set up in pockets and are concentrated on basic record-keeping activities. They include very simple documentation and problem logging by production services personnel. They are usually limited in scope. As growth continues, these initial control programs are extended and coordinated. Just as initially disparate applications are eventually grouped in support of higher level functions, initially disparate controls are eventually grouped in support of higher level management concerns.

The manner in which problems are handled provides a good example of this evolution. In stage I, problem management is largely concerned with hardware. The only control systems are machine logs for recording hardware problems. In stage II this expands. There may be a machine problem log, a batch problem log, and a problem log for each major on-line system. These logs may be kept in a consistent manner, but may not be integrated. They are like the coexistent but multiple functions in the stage II Applications Portfolio.

By late stage II the questions which production services management must ask to ascertain capabilities and to carry out planning activities require more coordination of controls. Problem log information is consolidated in order to track trends and to provide feedback to users and data processing management. Integrated logs, representing the integration of controls in general, are designed to support management level decision making and to answer management level questions. In addition, they provide guidelines for monitoring day-to-day activity.

Eventually problem logs, like other control systems, are linked through central networks. In stage III, for example, user input may be channeled through a "user help desk," or problems may be relayed to a war room where interrelationships between problems can be tracked. Thus, like the stage III Applications Portfolio, stage III controls are coordinated and networked in order to facilitate more effective use of available capabilities.

Exhibit II provides an overview of the production services management control systems. On the management control level these controls can be grouped in a few general categories, while on the operational control level they involve six specific control areas: inventory management, work flow management, resource monitoring, documentation library, security, and stability management. Without going into too much detail, it is worth looking briefly at a definition of each area and considering the problems or issues addressed.

EXHIBIT II

Production Services
Management Control System

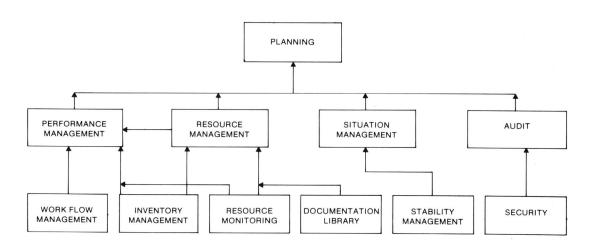

Inventory Management

Keeping up with the individual pieces of hardware and versions or levels of software becomes a complex problem as the organization matures. A formal inventory control system identifies exactly what resources are available in the data center shop and where each is located. It is synonymous with the stores inventory or tools inventory found in the manufacturing environment and provides information related to planning issues. A good inventory control system can be a critical asset in managing change and insuring that stability is not sacrificed as the data center grows.

Workflow Management

The actual control and planning for the shop floor is done through workflow management. Controls are used to monitor and guide the life cycle of individual jobs and to measure and guide scheduling for the entire computer system. In addition to controls which monitor overall activity, workflow controls include specific procedures which define how the work actually flows through the data center. This demands a high degree of discipline but can yield great rewards in an environment where hundreds and often thousands of jobs are processed every day. These controls address the most fundamental process of a production services department: how to move information through the data center.

Resource Monitoring

This is perhaps the most technical control area in the data center. It involves gathering basic statistics which can be applied to chargeout, performance management, tuning, and even portions of capacity planning. In the later stages, the utilization statistics which represent job, resource, and utilization measurement may come from twenty to thirty separate sources. These sources include basic machine accounting (such as SMF), data base accounting (IMS), time-sharing systems, hardware monitoring, recovery management facilities, I/O logs, data entry logs, job set-up sheets, special forms, log, and manpower time reporting. This information is summarized and eventually transformed. It is used to address the increasingly imposing issue of cost. Good resource monitoring is essential to this critical management area of production services. It is especially true that efforts to impose controls in the later stages suffer if controls are not built earlier.

Documentation Library

This area includes specification of all procedures and controls related to the creation, maintenance, and use of documentation and libraries in the production services department. Controls govern creation, modification, access, and use of production services documentation and library in an attempt to insure integrity. Security is the primary issue addressed by such controls. While this may not be a concern in stage I or early stage II by mid-stage III it should become a part of the production services department's control and planning efforts.

Security

Security for the data center involves the protection of corporate assets including the hardware facilities as well as the data. It is often monitored by the corporate auditors who are concerned with the protection of corporate assets. While security in stage I may be limited to physical security, by stage II system security becomes an issue. Typically, in stage III the definition of security is expanded to include a disaster plan as well as a program of graceful degradation.

Stability Management

Stability management includes all of the procedures and controls required to insure that the data center operates in a predictable, trouble-free manner. This area is often known as availability management. The idea that stability management applies only to large organizations is misleading. It can be introduced with as few as ten to fifteen terminals. It is important to install this control early in the stages since attitudes and procedures are harder to change in a larger network. Stability management usually develops in response to a crisis; however, with the help of an awareness of the stages, proper controls can be installed early and drawn upon in critical times. Specific systems include problem management and charge control.

Resource Management

Resource management systems monitor, control, and allocate individual system resources. Resource management systems include capacity planning, network planning, and all of the financial accounting systems. They evolve in order to determine how system resources are being used. They also help determine how the system resources should be used. Subsystems include cost accounting, chargeout, and tuning management.

Performance Management

Performance management is a set of monitoring, tracking, and control systems which manage the data center's delivery of services. The performance of the hardware, systems software, and the applications is monitored. Much of the data used by these systems is generated by other systems. Performance management systems integrate and interpret this data. They provide the feedback necessary for the production services department to manage its performance.

Situation Management

Situation management systems monitor and analyze patterns of problems, changes, and levels of service. It is built directly on the operational control stability management systems with significant support from performance management. Situation management provides the feedback necessary to improve stability and levels of service.

Audit

Various review procedures help the data center determine how well it is operating and managing itself according to its own standards. Audits in this context are internal. They are not punative, but are rather designed to help prepare for an external audit.

SUMMARY

Production services management requires both the macro and micro view of data processing. Specific performance measures and general controls must both be monitored. Effective production services management is dependent upon the foresight of the manager and his willingness to encourage regular record-keeping and general management principles. This is difficult in the context of the numerous small issues which arise on any given day. The control procedures outlined in the chapter may seem unnecessary until a crisis arises; this is why they are difficult to institute. However, like rainfall measures and flood walls, they must be instituted and strengthened before the time of crisis.

The key to management is awareness. If the production services manager knows what the capabilities of the data center are, planning becomes more effective. Ultimately, data processing is better able to match promise to demand. By gradually and consistently extending performance measures and controls. Production service management can insure that management will always be in step with both daily pressures and future challenges. This provides the infrastructure for data processing. Its stability will be echoed throughout the data processing organization. Good coordination between production services and the growth process areas can help an organization side step many problems.

17

Strategies for Applications Management

THOMAS R. MANTZ
ROBERT J. ABRAMS
PAUL CLERMONT

The productioin of computer programs continues to be a most critical aspect of the data processing activity. Both individual user areas and the organization as a whole base a large portion of their judgment as to the effectiveness of the data processing activity on its ability to deliver satisfactory **applications systems** on schedule and within budgets. This phenomenon can be attributed to several different factors which represent basic characteristics of applications systems:

- **Importance**. The applications system is the vehicle through which the power of the computer is harnessed and applied. As the user's primary interface to data processing, the applications system shapes his perception of the extent to which data processing is being effectively applied to meeting his business needs.

- **Concreteness**. Unlike the production services function, whose product is a service which is transient in nature, the systems development function delivers a tangible product. Long before the typical organization comes to view its data resource as a corporate asset, it realizes that its base of installed software is an important, expensive asset. This insight is usually followed by a hard examination of whether the value accumulated therein is commensurate with the resources which have been expended.

- **Variability of Results**. The development of major applications systems is a subtle and difficult process, requiring various business and technical skills to be assembled, coordinated, and managed, often over extended periods of time. Such efforts are occasionally total failures, usually a partial success, and only rarely a complete success—i.e., wholly satisfactory, on schedule and within budget.

● **Mystery of the Process**. Despite the considerable technical complexity of a large computer operations activity, the analogies to familiar production operations make it an activity which most general managers can understand and relate to comfortably. This is rarely the case with the systems development activity. Even though general managers are increasingly being trained in basic programming, they are usually not experienced in the process of medium- to large-scale software development. This lack of real process insight, together with a strong dependence on the process result (and possibly a history of negative experience with previous systems efforts), tends to produce a discomfort which is often expressed as a strong desire to measure and control at short intervals, "before things get too far out of hand."

These characteristics of applications systems led to an early awareness on the part of both data processing and general management of the need to effectively manage applications systems development and maintenance. Over the years, a set of management control programs known generically as **Systems Development Methodologies** have been developed in an effort to address this need.

This has been an active area of research and development. There are at least seven systems development methodologies currently being successfully marketed as commercial products. In addition, dozens of books on the system development process have been published which explicitly or implicitly include systems development methodologies. This has been a fruitful process in that a core of basic principles has emerged from these efforts and become widely accepted in the data processing community as sound and fundamental concepts. However, while many of these results are quite valid, their usefulness is often limited by a failure to view them in a suitable context.

Nolan's Stages Theory provides valuable insights in evaluating the appropriateness of the various **applications management** concepts. Applications management evolves through three primary phases which parallel the stages of data processing growth in the organization:

1. managing the development process

2. managing the systems life cycle

3. managing the applications area

Movement from one phase to another is often prompted by a crisis. In the course of the crisis, there is a recognition that the current methodology is no longer adequate and that it does not include all of the elements now affecting the management field of vision (see *Exhibit I*). This discussion focuses on a description of these crises and their resolution through an expanded management perspective.

EXHIBIT I

Coordinating the
Four Growth Processes

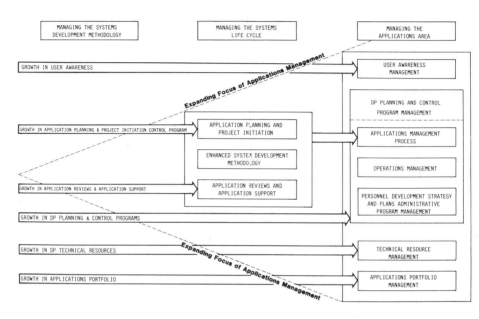

MANAGING THE DEVELOPMENT PROCESS

In the early evolution of data processing, the development of systems is an informal process which focuses on a few well-defined functions by a small group of technicians. Often this involves the automation of such activities in accounting as payroll or accounts receivable. Data processing may even be a part of the accounting department. In this environment, systems developers may have substantial knowledge of existing processes. The first few projects are usually successful, touching off the extension of applications into other functions.

In time, the systems development process moves away from the small and familiar base of its origins. Individual development efforts increase in size, and division of labor is introduced in response to expanding technical complexity. In addition, as data processing matures, systems begin to address management level functions. New processes are introduced and old processes become obsolete. Data processing systems no longer mirror manual systems and the change in business procedures becomes increasingly dramatic. These changes appear gradually, but the resulting crisis occurs suddenly.

The Crisis

The first symptoms of crisis are familiar. In and of themselves they do not necessarily mean that the organization is in trouble. However, each one contributes to a growing sense of anxiety, a burdening sense of suspicion toward data processing and, eventually, a recognition that something must change. The first impulse will be to treat the symptoms, but as they become more numerous the organization will turn on data processing management, demanding both explanations and solutions.

The specific symptoms include schedule slippage, manpower requirements exceeding estimates, segments of coding completed and then abandoned as requirements are more clearly identified, applications systems installed and then pulled out for major rework or even abandoned and written off completely, maintenance difficulties, excessive consumption of computer time, and frequent, error-prone operator intervention. These add up to several larger issues:

1. The notion that systems cannot be developed on schedule or within budget.

2. The sense that, once developed, systems do not meet users' needs.

3. The observation that systems are unreliable anyway.

Altogether there is a growing sense that data processing, daily becoming more important to the functioning of the business, is inept and unaccountable.

The Causes

The growth of data processing is both the cause of these problems and the solution. As the demand for systems increases, specialized personnel and complex technology are required. Even with a steady effort to keep up, the demand for systems taxes the capabilities of data processing. The training of new personnel, for example, may reveal the need for clarification and changes in systems. As more maintenance is required, the lack of coherent documentation becomes apparent. Inefficient use of hardware and software results in systems which consume excessive computer time. Finally the most visable to the users, varied levels of skill and the ad hoc approach to development result in an inconsistency in the quality of systems.

Growth is the underlying factor in all of these problems. Systems development has outgrown the informal, system-by-system approach which characterizes most stage I data processing applications. At this point data processing management must expand the horizons of its awareness and address the systems development process as a whole. It must introduce standards and procedures which are conducive to a reliable level of production and performance and decide upon a systems development methodology.

The Solution - SDM

A systems development methodology (SDM) provides a step-by-step procedure for systems development and the means for regulating and monitoring the systems development process. Although the specific characteristics of an SDM will vary depending on the individual needs of the organization in question, all SDMs have some things in common. These are design activities and implementation activities. All SDMs specify project organization structure, control, and documentation.

The design activities include:

1. a feasibility study

2. a requirements definition/functional specification

3. a general design

The feasibility study helps the user articulate needs in terms of systems and allows data processing to prepare accurate estimates of costs and benefits. The requirements definition/functional specification reinforces the communication initiated in the feasibility study ensuring that user needs are represented in terms of data processing requirements and that the user understands the relationship between what is needed and what will be provided. The general design translates the functional specifications into an overall design which is the input to programming. This careful preparation is carried out in an equally well-defined implementation process. Implementation is broken down into coding, debugging, unit testing, systems testing, acceptance testing, parallel testing, installation and conversion.

The SDM also clearly specifies project organization. The roles of project manager, project director, user, and project steering committee are spelled out along with data processing staff requirements, operations, technical specialists and data processing auditors. Responsibilities are clearly delegated. Project controls are introduced to insure that all decisions are made on the basis of complete information and that there is a periodic reconsideration of decisions at each phase of implementation. Finally, project documentation requirements are established for feasibility studies, financial analyses, functional specifications, and general design along with administrative documentation, including project plans, approval and authorization forms, signoffs, budget, and schedule reports.

IMPLEMENTING THE SYSTEMS DEVELOPMENT METHODOLOGY

The introduction of SDM often occurs in a period of crisis. Data processing is often weakened by poor performance, real or perceived. While SDM may promise data processing managers more control and effectiveness, it also suggests additional burdens and further frustration for both users and data processing personnel. Both groups have become accustomed to informal procedures and may feel things should remain as they were in spite of problems and costs. The challenge of SDM is that it must be sold to the organization. It must be put into effect firmly but cautiously, adapting to both situation and circumstances.

An SDM *addresses* the problems of an expanding data processing development shop, but by itself it does not *solve* them. Managing the development process is far more subtle than purchasing or developing an SDM and promulgating it as the standard "effective immediately." The challenge in installing an SDM that *solves* development problems can be broken into four components:

1. selling

2. focus

3. simplicity

4. customization

The selling of SDM necessitates an important choice of emphasis in its implementation. An SDM can focus on forms, on documentation, or on process. The first two approaches are easier to impose, but the latter offers distinct advantages in the long run. Forms are a necessary element of SDM but as a predominant focus for an SDM they generate an illusion of control because information is often recorded but not utilized. A focus on documentation is some improvement, but it creates the trap of managing the apparent completeness of the documents rather than the quality of their content. To avoid being sidetracked by preoccupation with the *methods* designated by the SDM, management must focus on the *purpose* of the SDM: to put proven processes in place, to train people in those processes, and to guide and monitor their learning.

If SDM is forced upon users without flexibility or customization, the resistance to data processing which emerged in the crisis period will continue, and may increase. Even if SDM is successful in solving many problems, it also could become the scapegoat for continuing problems. Users may object to the paperwork, complaining that systems are supposed to decrease, not increase, their workload. Compliance with SDM may become an excuse for missing schedules and budgets. SDM could be earmarked as an effort by data processing to inflict regimentation on the rest of the organization.

The SDM also must be sold within the data processing organization or the same pattern of complaints will emerge. Data processing personnel, accustomed to the informal atmosphere of the early stages, may object to the structured controls and organizational specifications of the SDM. They may accept the need for improved, more reliable results, but, without careful education and selling, the means to those ends may be interpreted as an attempt to infringe upon their creativity. Paperwork will be blamed for delays and records provided by forms and documentation will be ignored.

Two other important aspects the successful implementation of SDM are simplicity and customization. The need for complexity and detail must be proportional to the risk in current development projects. An SDM provides a risk-reducing structure, but where risks are small to begin with, the benefits of the structure do not justify the overhead. If both the users and the data processing organization have assimilated the SDM process, short-cuts in forms and documentation will reduce overhead and the benefits of the SDM structure will still be realized. As the risks in development projects vary, the SDM must be customized to focus on the specific risks of each development project.

Assimilation will never, of course, be perfect. Some data processing staff members may resist the SDM as an infringement on creativity. Some users will be put off by an apparent increase in paperwork when "all they want is the system". While a little resistance is normal, it should be continually reduced over time in a successful SDM installation.

If an organization has failed to meet the challenge, it has probably lost ground in its development capability from where it was before it started. A better planned attempt to install a more appropriate SDM will have to overcome an initial lack of credibility. But worse, attempting to install an inappropriate SDM by decree will tend to drive away the most competent people—those who understand the SDMs shortcomings and who chafe at unproductive paperwork and regimentation.

To summarize, common development problems in a growing data processing organization have been identified, and we have shown how an SDM addresses these problems, but does not, by itself, solve them. The fourfold challenge of installing an SDM (selling, focus, simplicity, and customization) also has been discussed and the suggestion has been made that failure to meet the challenge can produce negative progress toward improved management of the development process.

SYSTEM LIFE CYCLE MANAGEMENT

The Stages Model explains changes in data processing in terms of growth. As Nolan points out, growth is uneven. For this reason, at any given moment in time the four Growth Processes will generally not all be synchronized. Nonetheless there is an overall pattern of change and a progression which is representative of the stage of the organization. There must be a reciprocal process of change in each Growth Process in response to the overall pace and direction of change in the organization.

The applications area is no exception. Specific procedures and controls must address the issues facing the data processing organization. The SDM addresses a specific set of these issues. As the organization matures, these key issues change, and therefore there must be an accompanying change in the SDM. However, this change is not a permanent solution to the emerging problems of applications management.

In the middle stages, changes in the data processing organization manifests itself along three dimensions. **Automation** is extended from support of operational functions to support of management functions. **Decision support systems** are introduced. The data processing environment becomes increasingly complex. Users develop better data processing skills and become more involved in both the design and use of systems. In addition, older systems require maintenance. In a variety of areas, therefore, applications is becoming a more complex and a more critical part of the business.

The Crisis

Although SDM solves many of the problems of the data processing applications environment in which it is conceived, it is a limited methodology. As the organization grows, new issues emerge. SDM provides mechanisms for handling many of these, but eventually most are outside of the range of activity anticipated by the SDM. There is a discrepancy between the strategies of the SDM and the needs of the organization. The introduction of decision support systems, for example, requires a change in focus and a change in the type of systems being developed. The functions addressed by these systems are less structured and less easily translated into data processing language than those functions automated in the earlier stages. In addition, the new systems must be built on an integrated base of previously developed stand-alone systems. Complicated interfaces between new and existing systems must be developed, resulting in a development process which is a less stable, less predictable activity. For these and other reasons, the standardization of systems development in the SDM is no longer adequate. Variability and unreliability of systems resurface as issues in the organization.

At the same time, data processing is faced with rising demands for maintenance. Development priorities previously determined by the priorities of the users must now be weighed against the need to maintain existing systems. The situation is further complicated by the fact that, in the flush of enthusiasm for growth and development, there is a tendency to neglect maintenance. When attention finally becomes focused on maintenance, problems have already reached crisis proportions.

The size and scope of maintenance problems forces an emergency strategy in data processing. The systems development methodology conceived in the earlier stages of data processing growth did not provide guidelines for balancing development and maintenance. This was not a critical concern at that time and there was no need to exascerbate resistance by including peripheral controls. Now, however, high development demands and the desperate need for immediate efforts in the maintenance of critical systems must be addressed. The result is often a "fire-fighting" maintenance strategy which drains development resources. Data processing is forced to manage systems on a day-to-day basis hoping to hold crises and criticisms at bay.

The Causes

One of the goals of the SDM process is to initiate the user in the systems development process. A direct effect of this is to increase user awareness and involvement in data processing. Users become confident, enthusiastic, and demanding. They value the systems resource highly, they depend upon it and they want to see continued successful performance. This success depends on the maintenance of those systems. Users, however, cannot perform this function for themselves. They are dependent upon data processing for service. The systems are, in this sense, an asset which remains under the custodial care of the data processing department. The users are involved and concerned about systems development but they continue to be dependent upon data processing for the quality of the systems.

The crisis grows out of frustration and dissatisfaction. As maintenance problems escalate, users feel helpless. They turn to data processing for service, but data processing is overtaxed and cannot act on all problems immediately. As a result, the data processing department is seen by users as unreliable and unresponsive. Minicomputers, time-sharing, and service bureaus surface as possible alternatives to dependence upon the data processing organization. This attitude, in turn, generates frustration among data processing management and personnel who are trying to respond but cannot satisfy every demand at once. Data processing finds itself caught in a high-pressure and seemingly endless race to keep up with the accelerating level of demand.

The data processing organization thus finds itself facing a difficult dilemma—on one hand, users begin to expect data processing to be increasingly responsive to their needs; on the other hand, maintenance begins to consume available resources hindering their ability to meet these user needs. Data processing management also recognizes that SDM is an inadequate tool for this crisis. So a new strategy is required, one which focuses beyond the development process. This strategy is systems life cycle management.

The Solution - SLCM

The systems life cycle is not a new concept. In essence, it says that systems have life. They are born during development, maintained throughout their lives, and eventually die. The old system is often the basis for developing a new replacement system, thus beginning the cycle again. At the core of this new strategy is the systems development methodology. Systems Life Cycle Management takes the SDM and expands it. There is a recognition that issues emerge prior to systems development and after systems implementation. Thus, a series of management control programs are developed around the SDM to meet the expanded needs of system life cycle management (SLCM).

The SLCM is a two-part strategy for applications management. As *Exhibit II* illustrates, the SLCM process is composed of procedures for long-range systems planning and annual planning, project initiation, formal applications reviews, and application support. The improvement is brought about through an expanded management strategy. Now the goal of SLCM is not only to regulate development but to optimize resource utilization at every phase of the system life cycle.

The predevelopment or planning phase of SLCM is based on a combination of long-range planning and annual applications planning procedures.

EXHIBIT II

System Life Cycle
Management Process

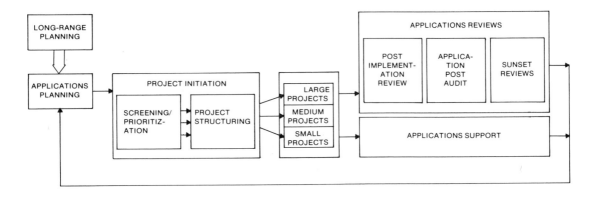

The purpose of the long-range plan is to determine the most appropriate systems for development by balancing the needs of the business organization with the existing capabilities of the data processing organization. The long-range plan then can be translated into a series of annual plans for each applications area containing proposals for development of new and replacement systems and maintenance to existing systems.

The objective of the long-range planning cycle is to develop proposals which are consistent with the overall business strategy. Project initiation is a set of procedures designed to take these proposals and short-term needs and translate them into projects to be executed within the SDM structure. Two fundamental activities occur during project initiation. **Screening/prioritization**, the first of these steps, is designed to balance the long-range proposals with short-term needs to achieve the optimal mix of potential projects for execution. As resources become available, the second step, **project structuring** occurs. Projects are structured by adapting the SDM to consider inherent risk and the capabilities of data processing and user staffs assigned. The resulting projects are released to the SDM for project management.

The SDM continues to be the core of the development phase of SLCM, but it is revised to match the evolution of the data processing environment. The delineation of a single approach to all systems development projects is now revised and made more flexible. Safeguarded by the SDM thinking process which has now become an accepted part of data processing activity, development procedures are formally modified to reflect differences in project size, degree of risk, technology (e.g., data base), and other system-specific considerations. These revisions are incorporated into the planning process as a means of classifying systems and organizing projects.

The postdevelopment phase of SCLM extends the focus of SDM to include two new areas: applications review and applications support. The applications review process consists of a series of reviews designed to capture applications experience. The first of these, the post-implementation review, takes place shortly after application implementation with the objective of reviewing project experience as input to periodic modification of the SDM. After two years, an applications post-audit is conducted which evaluates the quality of the applications finally implemented and establishes a plan for its long-range maintenance. When applications maintenance becomes increasingly difficult, usually after at least five years, a "sunset review" is conducted. This review analyzes the long-term outlook of the system, identifies areas for short-term sustaining maintenance, and captures applications experience as input to the applications replacement process.

In SLCM, applications support is accomplished by means of a maintenance tracking system. This system monitors patterns of maintenance, level of effort required, and other dimensions which describe maintenance activity. An ongoing tracking system is developed and used as an information base for an applications audit. In the applications audit, the ability of the system to meet the needs of the users is reevaluated and recommendations for changes are made. Changes requiring new projects are referred to planning groups. In cases where changes are impossible or too extensive to be considered viable, a "sunset review" is again initiated.

The four phases of the SLCM process extend the scope of the applications management process and allow data processing management to regain control over an increasingly complex environment. They also allow both internal personnel and users to understand systems and the need for systems in terms of long-range planning, maintenance strategy, and a business-based procedure for determining priorities. The success of the SLCM depends upon the ability of management to communicate this new and expanded outlook to data processing personnel, users, and senior management.

Implementing the Solution

As we have seen, system life management is a cyclical process. It begins with system planning and screening and results in a project which is managed under a modified SDM and results in the implementation of a new system. This new system is provided with managed maintenance support. A mid-life review is conducted to develop strategies for continued system support. As its functional value begins to decline, a "sunset review" is conducted to define strategies for maintaining the system as long as possible. As an output of this review new system requirements are fed back to the system planning function and the cycle begins again.

System Life Cycle Management provides the opportunity to integrate data processing into the overall organization. To be successful, the following factors must be present. First, data processing must have mastered the successful development of systems as a routine activity. This means that SDM must be fully understood before SLCM can be attempted. Second, users must become actively involved in the management of this resource. Without this involvement, the chances of misdirecting the data processing function will remain high. Third, data processing personnel must learn to manage multiple integrated management control programs. Without visible management emphasis on all programs, one or more of these programs can atrophy leading to the ultimate failure of all programs. And finally, data processing must shift its emphasis from a focus on development of computer systems to a focus on developing and supporting applications to aid the rest of the organization in the performance of their tasks. If any of these factors are missing, the ability to successfully implement system life cycle management is jeopardized.

Failure to implement system life cycle management leads to the ultimate fragmentation of data processing. Crisis maintenance continues to rise until it consumes one hundred percent of the data processing resources. When this happens, any hope of system development fades and expansion into new applications areas stops. Lack of development experience means that the skills required to mount large new projects implementing new technologies atrophy. At that point, data processing personnel become technological cripples, unable to respond to the most basic needs of users. Data processing becomes a black hole into which requests disappear never to be seen again. At this level of responsiveness, users will do one of two things. If they are not very sophisticated, they will stop using data processing; if they are sophisticated, they will find other ways to meet their needs on minicomputers, time sharing systems, or service bureaus. In either case the result is the same—the total fragmentation of data processing and the loss of any ability to harness data as a resource.

Successful implementation of system life cycle management, on the other hand, provides increased responsiveness and service to the user community. Preventive maintenance is done on a routine basis which leads to a decrease in unpredictable resource sapping crisis maintenance. Resources are provided in a dependable manner for new development. And this development permits the implementation and mastery of the new technologies. These new technologies come to serve as the basis for a transition from clerical stand-alone systems to an environment in which data is available as a resource.

MANAGING THE APPLICATIONS AREA

The shift in management emphasis which occurs at this time is more gradual than previous changes. SDM and SLCM addressed the applications of data processing resources in an efficient and effective manner—SDM on the development life cycle; SLCM on the systems life cycle. The result is a strong central data processing utility. Now, however, issues begin to arise which require management across systems for a functional area and across the four Growth Processes. In essence, there is a shift from an internal data processing management focus to an organization-wide information processing management focus.

The Crisis

During the systems life cycle phase of applications management, concentration on individual systems overlooks the need to coordinate the competing demands of the entire range of applications (existing and planned) in a particular user area. This oversight typically results in a crisis of competing demands for limited development resources. Planned development activities must be suspended as unforeseen, but required, enhancement, maintenance, or replacement activities as other systems consume available staff time. Once again, schedules are missed and dissatisfaction begins to grow.

Failure to manage growth in user awareness manifests itself most frequently in small groups of sophisticated users demanding and successfully constructing conceptually advanced systems which cannot be utilized by the majority of less aware users. Failure to manage growth in technical resources within data processing result in gross inefficiencies, if not outright failures, in the construction and operation of applications. Failure to address the complete set of control programs and instead limiting consideration to only those programs involved with application management leads not only to inefficiencies but also to severe communication failures within the data processing function, with the user community, and with senior management.

Mastery of the systems development methodology and the system life cycle can help avoid many of the pitfalls associated with premature experimentation with alternative approaches to the centralized development approach. Users are not forced to accept inferior external solutions out of a frustration with the quality and responsiveness of internal services. Once controls are fully established, the initial Applications Portfolio fundamentally complete, and user awareness advanced, it becomes appropriate to encourage alternative technological approaches such as:

- distributed systems
- word processing
- time sharing
- minicomputers
- office automation
- service bureaus

As depicted in *Exhibit III*, these technologies, separately and in combination, introduce additional opportunities to the functions represented by the organization's Applications Portfolio and thus constitute additional pages in what might best be described as the organization's "Virtual Portfolio of Applications." The systems development methodology and systems life cycle management approaches to improving the attractiveness of the centralized approach over these alternatives eventually succumbs to the inherent advantages of these alternatives.

The Solution

The crisis manifests itself along two dimensions. The first deals with the need to address issues beyond the scope of centralized data processing controls like SDM and SLCM. Nolan's Stages Theory identifies four Growth Processes which drive organizational learning associated with data processing evolution. They are:

1. the Applications Portfolio

2. data processing technical and personnel resources

3. data processing organization and control programs

4. user awareness

The SDM is a control program associated with the third Growth Process identified above—data processing organization and control programs. The transition to the systems life cycle phase of applications management results from the need to address other control programs of this growth process to ensure that the right systems are developed. The transition to the applications area phase of applications management is prompted by the need to address and manage all four Growth Processes identified above.

Transition to the applications area phase of applications management begins with the recognition that a comprehensive and integrated program is needed which addresses all applications of the functional area, not just individual system's life cycles. This recognition will normally result from a crisis in resource demands in which competing and compelling demands for new systems development (never before automated functions), replacement of existing systems, maintenance, enhancement, and integration of systems cannot all be satisfied. A program of prioritization of demands and resource allocation is required.

Such a program must balance the competing demands of the users Application Portfolio, the first of the four Growth Processes. *Exhibit III* is a representation of a normative Applications Portfolio of a commercial organization. The triangle segment highlighted on the figure contains the existing and potential systems which must be coordinated by the system development life cycle manager in charge of the manufacturing function. Recognizing that his responsibility transcends this entire compendium of applications signals the entry into the application area of applications management.

Acceptance of this responsibility includes acceptance of responsibility for the development of the other Growth Processes. To ensure parallel

EXHIBIT III

Normative Applications Portfolio of a Manufacturing Firm With
An Application Area Highlighted

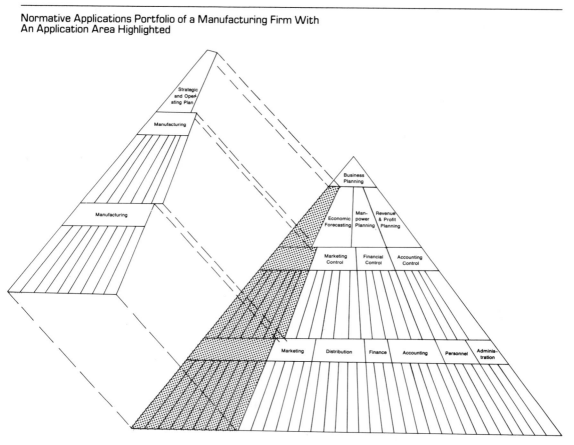

maturation of all Growth Processes, responsibility for their development
is also transferred to the assigned functional area systems and programming manager. This individual is thus tasked with assuring that:

- The Application Portfolio of the user area evolves smoothly under a
  concerted plan.

- User awareness is advanced and is consistent with the evolution and
  sophistication of the applications contained in the portfolio.

- Data processing technical resources including personnel, hardware, and
  software are adequate and do not atrophy faced with the maintenance
  dilemma.

- Planning and control programs used in the area are appropriate, ensure
  effectiveness as well as efficiency, and are understood, used, and useful.

Beyond the need to manage across the four Growth Processes, there is
a need to address the issues which emerge as the second dimension of the

EXHIBIT IV

Evolution of
the Virtual Portfolio Manager

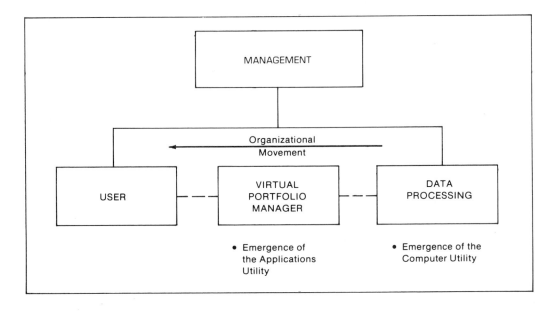

applications management crisis. The organization must accept responsibility for the exploitation of all opportunities contained in the pages of the virtual Applications Portfolio. As depicted in *Exhibit IV*, this requirement will inevitably move the applications manager functionally away from the data processing function in the direction of the user organization, for the virtual portfolio manager must begin to consider the data processing function as one vendor who can satisfy the informational needs of his customer. Having mastered controls in a centralized form, decentralization for heightened effectiveness becomes appropriate and the primary challenge.

Implementing Applications Management

Implementing this final portion of applications management is by far the most difficult. Where SDM and SLCM emphasized the implementation of procedures which for the most part were under the direct control of the data processing manager, this transition requires the direct involvement of areas outside of data processing. To accomplish this, two new constituencies emerge with key roles. First, senior management becomes responsible for setting direction for each of the functional areas. Second, user groups within each of the functional areas assume increasing amount of the responsibility previously held by the central data processing utility. For the data processing manager to be successful in this environment, he must establish an organization-wide orientation and must begin to rely on such management skills as negotiation and conflict resolution.

The shift to applications management may also require the emergence of a new organizational function—the virtual portfolio manager. This individual is responsible for ensuring effective computing support for a particular functional area.

The virtual portfolio manager should be able to enlist alternative technologies as appropriate to the needs and readiness of users, data processing personnel, and control procedures. The virtual portfolio manager, now closer to the user, can view central data processing utility as one among many possible solutions. The objective of virtual portfolio management is to meet the information needs of the organization, not to sustain any particular data processing approach. This manager, shown in *Exhibit IV*, stands between data processing and the user as a channel of communication, a coordinator and an overseer of control procedures. On one side of this manager, in data processing, there is an emergence of the computer utility as a part of the organization which has its own significant role. On the other side, there is the user and the emergence of the applications utility which incorporates data processing concerns but is not strictly a data processing area. The virtual portfolio manager insures the smooth coordination of the two.

The critical need for credibility in this function may require that the virtual portfolio manager report organizationally outside of data processing. Transition to this final step of applications management does not occur quickly, nor does failure to make this transition carry with it quite the severe implications that previous transitions to SDM or SLCM did. Failure will result in accountability for applications, growth processes, and technologies being fragmented, opportunities being missed and progress not being as rapid. While users will inevitably learn to coordinate all applications and technologies, this will not be done without false starts, failures, and inefficiencies. Because of these implied delays, failure to make the transition will prohibit the organization from assuming a leading-edge position in the application of information technology, and will hence result in lost opportunity costs.

The organization which successfully makes the transition to the applications area phase of applications management will find itself capable of meeting the users total information requirements. Responsibility for managing the Applications Portfolio, the Growth Processes and technological alternatives will have been delegated to a degree appropriate to the organization's overall stage of evolution. In effect, a data processing manager will have been created for each functional area—a data processing manager responsible for applications development, service, stage evolution, and total data resource technological management.

SUMMARY AND CONCLUSIONS

Applications management is a component of the data processing function which evolves as the organization matures in its understanding and use of computer technology. Evolution occurs in three predictable and unavoidable phases defined as:

1. managing the development life cycle

2. managing the system life cycle

3. managing the applications area

These phases must occur sequentially and may not be skipped, although an understanding of their characteristics can assist in the mastery of the phase and expediting the transition through any phase.

The first phase, development life cycle management, has a definite operational control program orientation associated with it—emphasis is on doing the systems development job right. The second phase emphasizes management controls and represents a more enlightened attitude toward applications management. It requires an acceptance of the need to manage the entire life cycle of an application including development, operation, maintenance, and replacement. Emphasis in this phase shifts to a broader base of control programs with greater attention being paid to the management of all associated resources and to assuring that the right job is done. The third phase emphasizes strategic planning and represents a still more enlightened attitude toward applications management by including responsibility for coordination of:

- All applications associated with a major functional area of the organization

- The four Growth Processes of the functional area

- Alternative technological approaches and the responsibility for management of the virtual portfolio of applications

Throughout the evolutionary process, in addition to expanded responsibilities, individuals concerned with applications management are inexorably drawn closer to the user organization. Thus eventually assume a status of near independence from data processing as they seek to establish the applications utility function in the organization.

18

Data
Administration

RICHARD L. NOLAN

The question for most organizations is not whether to adopt the data resource approach to information systems but when and how. The transition to data base is ripe with promise but it also involves a shift in many of the basic assumptions guiding computer management today. The reluctance of management to initiate this change threatens to forestall the full benefit of data base technology.

Data administration is the management of data base technology and the plans, procedures, and techniques which support it. The initial responsibility of the data administrator is to provide a data resource perspective and to help the organization to incorporate this perspective in its information planning and processes. As I note in Chapter 2, *Managing the Crisis in Data Processing*, there will be an observable correlation between the effective and smooth transition of an organization to data base and the ability of management to shift from a computer resource perspective to a data resource perspective.

One of the most serious obstacles to implementation of data administration is that recognition of its need usually follows serious problems which result from not having data administration. Most organizations in earlier stages than stage V have been unwilling to accept the shift to a data resource perspective. Data administration has been treated as a technical problem that involves the selection and installation of hardware and software in the early phases of data base use and ongoing technical assistance in the later phases. The full power of data base technology has been masked and aborted by a narrow management perspective which limits the ability of the **data administrator** to plan for the full capacity of the data resource and necessitates a piecemeal approach to data base systems development.

The resistance to accepting the full scale and impact of data resource management is understandable. If data administration is introduced on the scale which the situation demands, the scope of information systems activities in the organization will be expanded and, ultimately, the way in which the business is organized will be affected. However, the advantages of data base technology are so clear and its power to enhance business effectiveness so evident that it is only a matter of time before a more mature, more sophisticated attitude towards data administration evolves.

In order to understand both data administration and the context in which it functions it is necessary to break the discussions of the role of the data administrator into two sections. First, it is important to understand the theoretical functions of data administration in the management of the transition to and the management of the data resource era. Second, it is valuable to review the position and function of the data administrator as it is defined in practice today. Finally, with both perspectives in mind, the stage-affected characteristics of data base technology and the phases of data administration can be outlined.

It is especially important that the contrast between what was predicted by theorists be compared to what has actually happened because it is this comparison which confirms the evolutionary quality of the technical transition we are experiencing today. The Stages Theory helps to anticipate problems before they happen and to understand bottlenecks or apparently retrograde situations. The prediction that data resource management will emerge in the dimensions prescribed by the theoretical model is not undermined by the fact that resistance to change and adjustment to change may take the form of modified or inhibited versions of the final structure. The problems created by the data administrator in practice will only be solved when an organization is ready to assume responsibility for the range and functional quality of change entailed by the data base theory. At such a time, the theoretical prescriptions for data administration will become the guidelines for practice.

Also, before going further, the use of the two forms of the management title in this chapter and in reference to other articles should be clarified. **Data base administrator,** or **DBA,** is the most common way of referring to this function. This appears in several of the sources quoted in this discussion. However, I have chosen to use the title "Data Administrator" to indicate that the function being described is not tied to the technology but extends to organizational data resource management. The data administrator functions as a data strategist as well as a technical manager. He/she is a planner and an operational manager for the organization not merely a data base expert for the data processing group.

DATA ADMINISTRATION—IN THEORY

The use of computer systems in the early stages of data processing revolves around the assumption that the computer and its attendant software are a capital investment which should be managed by a skilled person with appropriate technical experience. This individual is called the data processing manager. The primary function of the data processing manager is to coordinate the operation of the computer with applications development in response to the processing demands of the users. Interaction with users is handled on a one-to-one basis. Data are turned over to the computer systems department for processing and returned in a report format.

The introduction of data base technology changes the terms of this relationship and with it the role of computer-related management in the organization. Data base technology makes it possible to view the data of the organization as an entity to be exploited, and consequently to be managed. It is a resource which can be used to support decision making and to enhance business capabilities by improving the organization and utilization of information. However, in order to exploit this situation, an individual must be able to see both data and data processing in terms of the organization and its business objectives. The data administrator is expected to have this skill, to be both a computer manager and a business manager.

Understood in these terms, the data administrator is new in the organization/data processing configuration. The data administrator is not only a business manager, but must also be technically informed and experienced. On the other hand, the data administrator cannot be a technical specialist but must be able to understand the business and the data or information resources involved. The ideal qualifications for the position include technical knowledge of data base technology, familiarity with the organization and strong administrative skills.

The data administrator is brought into the organization as an internal consultant who helps pave the way for data base technology. Once the scope of the first data base efforts has been defined, the data administrator becomes the organizer and supervisor of installation and start-up. Finally, with the data base in place, he functions as a member of the management-planning group, governing both ongoing data base projects and making plans for future data sharing. By necessity, the data administrator is involved in business decisions because the baseline criteria for data planning will be business support and enhanced profitability.

The basic assumption behind this picture of the data administrator is that the value of a corporate perspective on information is self-evident. The power of data base technology is the power to harbor, on a collective basis, all of the information or data resources of the organization. This involves a broad administrative effort to insure that data processing and data sharing will be coordinated, that procedures will be uniform, that a data dictionary and other supporting technologies will be maximized, and that security and integrity of data are guaranteed. All of these efforts have been foreshadowed by the increasing role of computer technology in the business. Data management is the next logical step.

Out of this picture the data administrator emerges as a new and unique personality in the management group. He is technically oriented but, in addition to using this technical skill to direct and advise computer processing personnel, he must be able to apply his knowledge to planning and policy-making efforts in conjunction with senior management. The selection of data base projects, their timing and scope, are not determined by the technology but rest upon organizational priorities, investment, and commitment. The data administrator must be able to interface with senior management and must help them by providing an expert's perspective on data planning issues.

With this overview of the data administrator in mind, several functions or responsibilities can be listed. First, the data administrator is responsible for strategy and planning. This responsibility includes interaction with senior management planning groups to coordinate data plans with organizational direction setting as well as coordination with user groups and planning activities on a more technical level. Second, the data administrator must define policy and procedures, functioning on more of a middle management level to insure that use of the data base systems will be well-regulated and well-documented. Third, on a more technical or operational level, the data administrator oversees the development of the data dictionary, supervises documentation, and makes sure that issues of protection, security, and integrity of data are handled properly.

This description of the data administrator may seem overwhelming to those who do not fully understand the fundamentals of data base technology. It sounds like a prescription for an information takeover in the business. The concept of privacy at the divisional or departmental level cannot be maintained if data sharing is to become a means of building strength in the business. However, this does not mean that the information group or the data administrator in particular is going to take over subfunctions of the business. The role of the data administrator is to strengthen the whole business by adding the power of a broad data base to the existing power of individual groups. The parts, the contributors of data, will benefit in turn as the value of their own data for them is increased by combination and coordination with data from other sources. Managing the data resource should be seen as an asset and not a threat to the organization as a whole or to its parts.

DATA ADMINISTRATION—IN PRACTICE

The data administrator has been the accepted model for most theoretical discussions of data resource management. Data planning assumes that the data base environment will include a strong, insightful administrator whose presence assures a smooth transition to data base technology. However, studies have demonstrated that, in practice, most data administrators fall far short of this image. They are not policy makers but technicians. They report to the data processing manager and have little or no contact with senior management. They are expected to help users with data base on a one-to-one basis and rarely, if ever, have a chance to function on an organizational level.

The data administrator in theory is not the data administrator in practice. As a result, the promises of the data base of the models are rarely achieved. Data base systems, as they are being implemented today on a user-by-user basis, do not have the additive power promised by theoretical models for data sharing. While this does not mean that things will stay this way forever, it is important to understand the breadth of the current situation and to accept the probable slowness of the management transition in comparison to the rapidity with which the technology has been embraced.

In a study reported at the 1979 National Computer Conference, Jean-Paul DeBlasis and Thomas H. Johnson reported a series of findings which describe the roles and responsibilities of the data administrator today.[1] They found that, although the theoretical model suggests that the data administrator ought to be a skilled corporate manager, in fact most data administrators (referred to in the article as DBA's) have high technical skills and little or no administrative experience. Many have had considerable experience over a long period of time with the company but they have had little or no business training. DeBlasis and Johnson note, "It was felt that administrative skills could be learned on the job."[2]

This is an interesting and contradictory conclusion from the perspective of management science. In most cases, it is assumed that basic administrative skills are of primary importance to someone who must function on a management level. Business training is geared to this assumption and in hiring it is often believed that a good manager can make any business work with a little time.

However, in the case of computer technology the reverse is true. Technical knowledge weighs much more heavily than management skills. This is partly because the role of computers and subsequently of data resource management in business has been misunderstood. If a data administrator can make the technology work, the harboring of the benefits of that work on the part of the organization are expected to be self-evident.

This leads to the second aspect of the practice of data administration, fragmentation. In a study published in 1980 by I. B. McCririck and R. C. Goldstein[3] they found that data administrators spend most of their time on a series of specific technical tasks, primarily those associated with the installation of DBMS, and have little or no planning responsibilities. They observe, "The Data Administrator (sic) is primarily a technician, concerned with implementing a data base system and keeping it working. The planning and coordination of data usage within an organization, an important part of the job in theory, does not in practice seem to be receiving much attention."[4]

The background of the data administrator reflects the data administration function as it has evolved in the organization. Instead of coordination and sharing of data on an organization-wide basis, data base technology is introduced application by application as determined by user

---

[1]Jean-Paul DeBlasis and Thomas H. Johnson, "*Data Base Administration—Classical Patterns, Some Experiences and Trends,*" National Computer Conference Proceedidngs, 1977.
[2]Ibid.,
[3]Ian B. McCririck and Robert C. Goldstein, "*What do Data Administrators Really Do?*" Datamation 26, no. 8, August 1980.
[4]Ibid., p. 132.

willingness and cost. To a certain extent this kind of slow-phased entry into a new technical area is unavoidable. Many of the consequences of this situation, such as redundancy, were anticipated and are part of the learning process. However, the containment of the role of the data administrator to that of a data base technician means that even when these problems are identified, there is no one in the organization with the ability to effect their correction.

The fear of the power of information may be a ghost, a product of incorrect reporting in a science-fiction cast, but its effects are very real. While many organizations have named a data administrator, the administrative function does not exist. Instead of being responsible for organization, planning, and the other management level respponsibilities accorded to the data administrator as a logical result of the demands and potential of data base technology, the data administrator is confined to such technical functions as design and documentation. McCririck and Goldstein summarize, "The Data Administrator of the conceptual literature is responsible for the organization's data resource. . . However, in our survey 77% of the respondents stated that they had no responsibility for any nonmachine readable data and in only one-third of the organizations did the Data Administrator even have control over all machine readable data."[5]

What are the consequences of this for data base technology? What is the data administrator able to do? What are the limitations he faces? And are these characteristics merely manifestations of stages of growth in the data resource function or are they representative of a trend which threatens to alter the objectives and the use of data resource technology?

The data administrator in most organizations today is not a policy maker or a high-level manager. The primary qualifications for the position and the primary responsibilities of the data administrator are technical. They include installation of the DBMS, development of applications, interface with users in response to their requests for assistance, and such support work as data dictionary and security. The data administrator, as the function is described in theory, does not exist.

The result of this situation is that data administration, a function which is critical to the success of data base technology, is not being carried out. Thus, while there is some preliminary use of data base technology to organize data, some data sharing and some attention to procedures and security, the overall management of data as a resource is being neglected. As a result, data base technology is being underutilized and the transition from computer management to data resource management is being inhibited.

Many organizations who suffer from problems in the transition phase associated with the introduction of a data base are looking for technical solutions and technical scapegoats. In many cases the data administrator becomes the object of criticism, deluged by technical problems and forced to scramble for technical solutions. The overemphasis of technical knowledge and responsibilities contributes to this preoccupation with tech-

---

[5]Ibid., p. 132.

nology and obscures the underlying questions. The role of the data administrator is, in practice, the role of the technician but this does not mean that the problems, even where they are attributed to technical sources, are in fact technical problems.

DATA ADMINISTRATION AND DATA RESOURCE MANAGEMENT

In 1977 I participated in a conference, "Database Directions: The Conversion Problem," reported in *EDP Analyser* in 1978.[6] Although the group examined various technical issues, discussions continually returned to the question of data base administration and the role of management in successful conversion. The panel concluded, "While it is appreciated that technological problems exist in data base conversions, it should be recognized that a DBMS conversion is primarily a *management* problem for both executive management and data processing management."[7] In other words, despite the variation in practice, the theoretical role of the data administrator is still considered vital to the success of data technology.

The conclusions of this conference panel demonstrate a fact of learning which the reports on the activities of data administrators overlook. Data base technology as a whole is still new. There is a general learning process which is going on throughout the field and which is reflected in the limited role assigned to the data administrator. Many organizations still think that data base is only a technology and choose to implement it as if it were a piece of equipment. They give the data administrator a technical mandate and assume that management will be driven by the user. As a consequence, certain lessons are being learned.

In the 1977 conference several of these lessons were discussed. First, it was observed that many organizations decide to convert to a data base, initiate installation of a DBMS, and then begin to look for people and processes to support it. Second, as a result of this pattern, the data administrator enters the picture as a technician who must run or fix a given situation. Policy decisions have already been made and suggestions to the contrary would be inappropriate and might be perceived as a challenge to management style. Third, processes of planning and implementation management, like data dictionary, data file organization, application planning, query, and report writing, are treated as technical functions which follow on the heel of the DBMS.

As a result of problems which have developed after DBMS conversions that follow these patterns, the Database Directions conference group concluded that the lesson of data administration in practice is that we must return to data administration as it is described in theory. Support functions must be planned ahead of time, before the DBMS is selected and installed. Data administrators should be brought in early to counsel

---

[6]Richard G. Canning, ed., "*Planning for DBMS Conversions,*" EDP Analyzer 15, no 5.
[7]Ibid., p. 7.

management, to participate in strategy development, and to carry it out. Overseeing technical problem solving should be the assigned role of the data administrator so that technical skills can be assessed and proper resources will be on hand. Finally, the data dictionary, data files, query, and report writing should be organized on a broad basis, not handled instance by instance. In sum, the lesson of previous DBMS conversions has been that the neglect of the data administrator as a management function has led to inappropriate sequencing of the conversion process and neglect of support functions.

THE STAGES OF DATA PROCESSING AND THE PHASES OF DATA BASE ADMINISTRATION

The stages of data processing tell us that data base technology is a critical element in the transition of an organization from stage III to stage IV. The recognition of the value of the data resource and the knowledge of how to exploit that value is a key characteristic of the growth of organizational data processing during this transition. However, within the span of this transition and extending into the increasing skill in data resource management associated with stages V and VI, there are several observable phases in the development of the data administration function. These are already indicated by the differences between data administration in practice and in theory and the observation that the lessons of the theory have been repeated in the lessons learned through experience. The prescriptions of the theorists have become the lessons learned the hard way for the practioners.

In a sense, then, there is an overall stage-learning process for the data base field in which, initially, data base is treated as if it were another technique for processing within the existing organizational environment. Later, after this approach leads to the kinds of problems observed at the Database Directions conference, the need for a stronger management function becomes apparent. The failure to develop a data dictionary or to bring in a data administrator before selecting and installing a DBMS taught many organizations that the scope of data base technology will quickly outstrip any oversimplified treatment of it.

This is where we are now. The lessons of the early stages of data base technology are leading more and more organizations to recognize that there must be better management and administration of the technology. As more organizations try to work with a data base without a full data administration function the lessons of the theoretical models will become lessons of practice.

The phases of data administration are, therefore, both theoretical and practical. For many organizations, the prescriptions in the model may match the things they wish they had done instead of the things they actually did. Nonetheless, the value of these phases is the same. If the lessons of the past are effective, more organizations in the future should choose to follow the prescriptions of these phases. This learning pattern need not alarm us. It has been a part of the learning process throughout the growth of the data processing technology and even now applies equally to various new technical areas. (See Chapter 8, "*Orders of Office Automation.*")

Phase I

Data administration begins before data base is actually introduced into the organization. It begins with the first feasibility and planning efforts. It is especially important that the data administrator become a part of this phase of data base conversion and that the data administrator not only be a technical consultant but someone who is respected for a capacity to respond to the needs of the business organization. Although it may be difficult to promote the data base if the full impact of data management is presented to senior management, the potential power of the data base will always be severely curtailed if it is adopted with the misunderstanding that it is merely another processing tool. It is the responsibility of the data administrator to help senior management and data processing management build the concept of a corporate data resource into their plans.

More specifically, during the planning phase, the data administrator should be involved in selecting applications which will insure the success and promote the visibility of the DBMS. This should include an initial selection of applications which are large enough to have an impact but which are not so critical that they introduce unnecessarily high risks. In addition, initial efforts should be keyed to expansion with an eye to corporate data planning and data sharing.

During phase I, the data administrator should also establish procedures which can be carried to more complex projects in the future. There should be formal project management, standards, and procedures for handling data, data security, and a data dictionary. These measures will all strengthen the data administration function in the future, making it easier to respond to problems and to delegate technical functions.

Ideally the phase I data administrator is someone who has the prestige and skill to participate in high-level policy-making decisions. Although to date this has not often been the case, the advantages of functioning from an organizational perspective cannot be underestimated. Sooner or later the data base will mean organizational data resource management. If the data administrator is aware of this and able to introduce this perspective from the beginning, he or she is at a definite advantage. Practice shows that such situations will be rare. Nonetheless, rarity does not cancel out the value of the model.

Phase II

In phase II the data administrator is responsible for managing the development of the first data base systems and, in time, for setting up the first shared systems. The primary effort in this phase is to see that skilled personnel are brought in, that procedures for filing and documentation are followed to evaluate the implementation effort, and to revise or develop appropriate plans for the future growth on the basis of experience.

In many organizations the data administrator is not even hired until phase II. As I demonstrated earlier, this is a mistake which often leads to an undervaluing of the function of data administration. A similar situation can arise if the data administrator who functioned as a management advisor in phase I is relegated to the role of technical problem-solver in phase II. Once a DBMS has been installed, there may be a tendency to think that data base opportunities will be self-evident. This is a short-sighted view which leads to an application-by-application approach eventually resulting in redundancy and unnecessary expense.

The phase II data administrator should try to maintain a planning and evaluating pattern which follows the management pattern for other parts of the organization. He should be quick to link data base projects to business affects and to see data problems in an organizational context. Data base technology may be serving small and apparently disparate groups during this phase but these efforts are all contributing to the substructure which will be the organizational pattern in the future. It is important that administrative and management habits be put into place so that as the data base grows, the management and control function will be able to handle that growth.

Many organizations today are in this phase and many of these organizations have neglected the management function. The result is that many of the technical characteristics of the phase exist (multiple data bases, new technology, and user training) but these are being treated as situational aids, the data administrator serving as an advisor to the data base user rather than as part of a data base program. As the use of the data base expands this will prove impractical. Users will find themselves competing for the attention of the data administrator who will have no systematic way to prioritize their complaints. Before these organizations can move on to phase III they will have to come to terms with the scope of the data administration function and the data administrator will have to be allowed to assume responsibility for data resource management and data base planning.

Phase III

By the time an organization reaches phase III, data administration has become an organizational function. Juxtaposed on the stages model, phase III will coincide with the later stages of data processing growth both because of technical advancement and because of maturation of users, applications, and management controls. The design, development, and administration of data base systems will be understood to be a part of organizational business strategy. The data administrator along with other high-level information processing managers will be contributors to the organizational decision-making process either directly or through a steering committee format.

DeBlasis and Johnson use the Stages Model to make this same point and agree that maturity—or phase III—cannot be less than this. They conclude, "Some organizations might believe they have matured with only one or two subsystems operating, but until the DBA is involved from the beginning in all database work and also has the final power to make operational decisions, the group has not matured. In fact, during our survey we found very few mature groups."[8]

The absence of phase III groups does not mean that data base technology has reached an impass. The failure to recognize the potential role and the potential contribution of a skilled data administrator is a stage-dependent set-back. As users, management, and data processing personnel become more experienced, the need for data resource management will become the next logical step in the use of technology to build a stronger and more profitable organization. The data administrator will seem less like another presence looking to assume power over user concerns and more like a team member who possesses a new management tool.

---

[8]Ibid., p. 4.

Human Resource Management

BARBARA J. LIND

In the past, data processing planning and development has not paid much attention to **human resource management**. Most planners, managers, vendors, and customers have viewed data processing as an ancillary aspect of a technical field. Progress and plans are determined by such technical factors as the development of hardware, the extension of applications, and the financial resources available to researchers and user groups. The advantage of data processing is often seen in terms of the decrease in clerical manpower made possible by technology. There is an assumption that good management of the technology will be synonymous with good management of personnel, users, and control processes.

In his book, *Managing in Turbulent Times*, Peter Drucker suggests that this assumption is wrong.[1] He points out that the belief that computers would add value to business by reducing personnel costs has been proven wrong. Instead of eliminating clerks, the computer age has replaced them with new clerks called "operators" and "programmers."[2] As a result, management now complains about the cost of personnel in data processing as if it were a hidden expense which, with good management, could be eliminated.

In the context of Nolan's Stages Theory, Drucker's idea sheds an interesting light on the nature of growth in the area of data processing personnel. In the early stages, technology is cost-justified. The emphasis

---

[1]Peter F. Drucker, *Managing in Turbulent Times* (New York: Harper & Row Publishers, Inc. 1980).

[2]Ibid., p. 25.

in management is on using technology to cut expenses. As the technical environment becomes more complex, the personnel aspect of the data processing growth process becomes an increasingly important factor in the effectiveness of the technology. However, because the concentration of effort has been in the area of hardware and software, management feels more confident in these areas and has little or no experience with human resource development.

In many ways human resource management has remained in the early stages of growth even though data processing personnel have developed technical skills and appear to be keeping up with the technology. While applications management, network planning and data administration emerge as long-range planning concerns as an organization matures, human resources continues to be treated in a short-sighted manner. This is happening because data processing managers do not understand the potential value of their personnel investment.

In his new management proposal, Drucker points out that although computers eliminate some jobs and staff, they require new staff who can do new jobs. Consequently, the value added by automation is not the result of eliminating the personnel factor but of altering it. The productivity of people is and continues to be a key to the value of the technology. The ability of the manager to maximize the personnel investment will be as crucial to overall success as the ability to maximize hardware and software.[3] Moreover, following Frederick Taylor's model, Drucker points out that "productivity is not the responsibility of the worker but of the manager."[4]

The implication of this proposal for data processing management is that there must be a change in the attitude of managers toward people. Instead of seeing personnel as an expense to be minimized, managers should see them as an asset to be maximized. As the organization moves through the stages and more personnel with higher levels of skill are introduced, the potential value of this asset increases. Personnel do not become more expensive; they become more valuable.

The problem of turnover provides an interesting illustration of this point. Turnover is considered one of the more expensive problems faced by data processing managers. It also seems to be an unsolvable problem because it arises from the need to keep staff abreast of technology and to fit staff to new technologies as those technologies are introduced. As technology changes, people find that their skills no longer match the tasks they are being asked to do, or in a more stable phase, that they are no longer challenged by the jobs they are doing. In either case the result is that people change jobs.

Personnel migration has become an accepted fact of life in data processing. People see their careers in terms of the industry, not the business or organization. Managers solve their personnel problems through hiring and replacement. The statistics support this pattern and illustrate the

---

[3]Ibid., p. 15.
[4]Ibid., p. 16.

consequences. In a representative organization with a steady rate of growth, turnover can be expected to average twenty percent per year. This means that by the end of two years there will be a cumulative effect of seventy to seventy-five percent turnover in staff. Moreover, instead of increasing the skill level and productivity of a constant staff over that two year period, management will be merely keeping up.

The effects of these patterns are reflected in the presence of problems in the human resources area of data processing which would not be tolerated in a regular business organization. There is little or no continuity of staff. It is difficult to maintain an appropriate distribution of skills and, as the organization matures, the resulting lack of knowledge of the user organization on the part of data processing personnel becomes a constraint on the technology. The more involved data processing becomes in the business, the more the neglect of human resource management affects its success.

There are few organizations who would tolerate these personnel strategies in any other area, yet they continue to make exceptions for data processing. If data processing is going to grow with the organization and become a part of the organization rather than an adjunct to it, human resource management must be introduced as a management priority. Data processing personnel hold the power to draw out the strengths of technological planning and operations. The productivity of people will be echoed by the productivity of the entire organization.

In this chapter a proposal for human resource management of data processing personnel is presented in three parts. First, there is a brief discussion of the key issues which affect people and a review of current practices and problems. Second, in response to these issues, a new perspective for viewing people in data processing jobs and careers is introduced. Finally, drawing on this perspective, several specific management strategies and processes are proposed.

THE ISSUES

Several specific issues appear again and again on the complaint lists of data processing managers who are struggling to maintain a high-level staff in a very competitive environment. These issues can be summarized by four key questions asked by many of these managers:

- How do I get good people?
- How do I keep good people?
- How do I get the right mix of skills?
- How do I maintain that skill balance?

The answer to these questions begins with an understanding of the manner in which they are interconnected. The way in which one question is answered predisposes the organization to a certain set of responses to the other issues.

The ideal of "good people," for example, is largely defined by the demands of an organization *at the moment*. A "good" person is a person who can work optimally in the current technical environment. The statement, "We need more programmers" may justify the hiring of a very strong programming staff but it does not encourage the recruitment of people who may have analytical or management skills as well. As a result, when the needs of the organization change these same people may become "problem" people. Instead of investing in people so that they will be more valuable in the future, there is a tendency to tolerate people until it is better to let them go. In other words, the productivity of a staff is treated as given which can only be changed by changing the staff not by changing the individuals comprising that staff.

The first example leads directly to the second problem. If there is no long-term job security or job improvement opportunity in an individual organization, good people will always be on the look-out for better positions in other organizations. Their loyalty is to their own progress, not to that of the data processing organization. This is made worse by experience which teaches them to move before they find themselves obsolete.

The need to define one's own career apart from any given organization is confirmed by the absence of opportunities for internal growth and training. New skills come with new jobs. Transitional situations are viewed as unstable and risky, which means that in many cases good people are the first to depart an organization in change, abandoning it when it most needs a strong staff. By neglecting training, career planning, and other problematic human resource issues, data processing has opened the door to long-term instability which is much more complex and expensive than the seemingly difficult and costly introduction of human resource efforts. By refusing to manage people as assets today, data processing insures that the asset will be expensive in the future.

"How to get good people" and "How to keep good people" are, therefore, two issues which are intricately woven into the problems of establishing and maintaining good skills distribution. Since the data processing organization is always changing, the mix of skills among its personnel must also be changing. This means that there must be a constant investment in personnel so that staff strength will match technological demand.

To date this issue has been handled primarily by hiring new personnel with new skills at each stage of growth. The emphasis has been on the question, "How do I get good people?" The consequence of this approach is twofold. First, data processing people move from one organization to another because by moving they can be sure of being in a situation where their skills are worth the most. They can even use skill in one area to bargain for training in another, placing themselves in situations where they are confident of success and where they may also learn something new. Second, encouraged to maximize the value of their skills, data processing personnel quickly come to view themselves as specialists (an alternative to upward mobility in the organization) and are reluctant to cultivate skills outside of their initial area of expertise. This increases the inflexibility of the work force and makes it even more difficult for an organization to grow without a turnover in personnel. People become a problem.

In order to cope with this staffing situation, there is a tendency to treat personnel like hardware or software. Replacement becomes the primary solution to changes in the skills requirements of an organization. Hiring and recruitment efforts are driven by pressures to meet the needs of the current data processing environment with little or no attention to long-term issues. Training is treated as a necessary evil which can be minimized by hiring people who have done the same job already for some other organization, hence discouraging flexibility and encouraging specialization.

As a result of these practices, data processing personnel do not expect training or career path planning from any single employer. They plan on moving on when their skills are no longer worth as much to one organization as they are to another. There appears to be no way "to keep good people." In addition, the overall effect on data processing personnel is the generation of a highly individualistic environment in which any effort on the part of an organization to build a staff is in constant conflict with the effort of data processing personnel to protect themselves. This is supported by a management group whose own experience has been similar to that of their staff. They too have had to move from one organization to another in order to train themselves and build their careers.

Unfortunately, these problems are not stage-dependent. They will not go away as the data processing organization matures. Nor are these problems smaller or nonexistent in the early stages. The absence of human resource planning in data processing affects all organizations at all levels. Personnel problems do not appear in the later stages. They are there, in embryonic form, from the beginning and may even be more critical in the expansive environment of stage II, for example, than in the stabilizing environment of stage IV.

Fortunately, the solution to human resource problems in data processing need not be stage-dependent either. An organization can begin to break through these problems at any stage by introducing basic **human resource planning strategies** in its personnel management practices. These strategies can help the organization build staff capabilities and generate an environment which will support continuity and growth of good data processing personnel.

Obviously some problems will continue. No organization can completely eliminate the need for an ongoing search for good people, the need to continually build an environment in which such people will want to work, and the training necessary to keep skills up-to-date. However, through human resource management, data processing can bring these problems under control. The nomadic patterns of data processing specialists can be modified by introducing an emphasis on building skills and staff flexibility. Training and career planning can be used to match personnel goals with the needs of the organization, stabilizing the future of both.

The results of a human resource program will benefit both the organization and the individual. In the long run, productivity will increase if personnel turnover is minimized. Similarly, job security and career potential will diminish the rapid salary inflation which has been the primary motivation for job selection for many data processing personnel. Finally, as a consequence of stabilization and long-range planning, personnel can be better integrated into the overall, long-term data processing plan for the organization, improving the strength and productivity of the entire data resource area.

HUMAN RESOURCE MANAGEMENT

Human resource management answers many of the personnel problems which have surfaced in data processing by providing basic guidelines for developing an integrated management program including personnel planning, recruitment, training, and review. It helps data processing managers apply the lessons of personnel management to the jobs and skills in their area. It suggests basic tools and methodologies for instituting better controlled programs, for monitoring ongoing activities, and for responding to change.

The primary assumption of human resource management is that people are a key resource. They are not adjuncts to technologies but contribute to its efficacy, and consequently to its value. The right combination of people with the right skills and experience can be the critical factor in the effectiveness and profitability of data processing. Nolan has demonstrated (See *Chapter 1, Managing the Computer Resource: A Stage Hypothesis*) that evolution of technology, applications, user awareness, management controls, and data processing personnel are interrelated. If the personnel variable or Growth Process is well managed, its contribution to the success of data processing will be as important as the contribution of any of the other variables.

While this may seem obvious in the context of the stages concept, the data processing personnel problems identified earlier suggest that it has been ignored. Recruitment, hiring, and training are carried out as demand arises on an ad hoc position-by-position, problem-by-problem basis. Career planning within the data processing organization is minimal and performance monitoring is carried out second-hand through informal feedback channels. There are no definite plans, no specific training goals or long-term objectives for personnel. The overriding expectation is simply that data processing personnel will complete the jobs at hand.

The result of the absence of a deliberate human resource management effort is that personnel problems emerge in a nascent, nonspecific manner which carries an air of inevitability. The absence of ongoing training programs, for example, leads to an eventual drop in skill levels. When it becomes necessary to replace an obsolete staff, the resulting pattern of turnover leads to training costs anyway. In addition, as noted earlier, the lost time and the loss of knowledge of the business that results from losing people adds more hidden expense to these changeovers. The hidden costs of not training can be much greater than the costs of training and may never catch up to the potential level of productivity of a well-managed, continuous staff.

When there is no ongoing effort to build strength in the human resources area there is a high probability that demoralization and frustration will not only lower the productivity of the work force but will actually force them to leave. At this point in the cycle, career-minded individuals with the best skills or the best aptitude for learning new skills decide that they must leave the organization, further depleting an already weakened work force. The feeling that this is a "sinking ship" begins to grow. This is made worse by complaints from user groups which focus on data processing in general and on those individuals who work with users in particular.

Data processing management should not be any more willing to accept a status quo or, worse, a degenerating situation in personnel than it is willing to accept such conditions in the other Growth Processes. The attitude of progress, growth, adaptation, and change which motivates the planning of technology, applications, data base, and organizational leadership should apply to personnel planning. Just as technology and applications are enhanced and made powerful through a formal planning process, personnel can be maximized through a strong human resource planning and mangement program.

The transition from the current environment to a more stable and effective environment can be described in terms of a two-part program. First, the organization can begin to build a personnel development program which concentrates on the recruitment, hiring, placement, and training of personnel. Second, the organization can institute a performance management program to monitor and guide personnel, insuring that people are working at the anticipated level, to identify training needs, and to spot problem areas early. Once these two programs have been instituted, they interact to insure that personnel keep pace with development and change in the other Growth Processes.

PERSONNEL DEVELOPMENT

The first step in human resource management in data processing must be a shift from a reactive approach to hiring and training to proactive training and development. Instead of waiting for circumstances (technological factors, for example) to determine the type of people needed, managers should anticipate manpower demand and formulate strategies for hiring and training early.

This means that there must be a shift from concentration on manpower drawn from an external base to building a manpower supply drawn from internal sources. There will always have to be a certain amount of recruitment from outside, but in the transition to a more stable and productive human resource base, there must also be a major effort to build programs to improve the skills of the people already on board. This will insure that the staff as a whole will be able to absorb new demands and take on new responsibilities as they arise. The objective is to develop a long-term asset, an internal resource in the form of a pool of people who can grow with data processing in that organization.

When these concepts are translated into practice some very definite strategies and management actions emerge. First, there must be a human resources plan derived from the strategic plan and the operating plan for the data processing organization. The human resource plan itself must include long-term manpower planning, recruitment, selection, and placement programs or short-term manpower planning, training, and development projects including career path management and, in all cases, a system of performance reviews and controls to monitor and maintain standards. *Exhibit I* suggests the organization of these elements, although the extent of interaction and interdependence of activity among them defies simple illustration.

The personnel development program begins with skills inventory. The objective of this is to establish a data processing skills baseline for the organization in aggregate and for individual positions. The skills inventory consists of a documented appraisal of the skills and knowledge of personnel, an identification of strengths and weaknesses, and a skills training prioritization to suggest patterns for a timetable aimed at eliminating skill gaps. The skill gaps are determined by comparing an inventory of existing skills to an inventory of required skills.

Once the required skills have been specified and the existing skills have been inventoried, a combination of recruitment, internal placement, and training can be instituted to close skill gaps. The objective of this part of the personnel development program is to build a staff base which will grow with the data processing organization. New hiring is matched in emphasis by internal selection and training as long as it is feasible. The product of the program is a more stable data processing personnel group with better skills distribution. It leads to a positive answer to the problem of getting and keeping the right people.

EXHIBIT I

Human Resource
Management

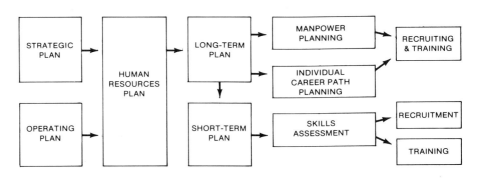

Career path management is an important variable in this stabilization process. It affects the overall data processing environment by bringing the general concept of proactive hiring to bear on individual career plans. The career goals of each staff member are matched to career path structures derived from long-term organizational plans. This is accomplished by means of transfer and promotion programs, dual selection systems, and specified performance criteria.

Exhibit II describes the evolution of a personnel development program. It follows each of the steps described above and indicates points at which they intersect. While a diagram can only begin to touch on the complexity of the program, it demonstrates that personnel development can be broken down into management modules which provide guidelines for the gathering and organization of personnel information. This information gives the data processing manager a knowledge base for the formulation of human resources management strategies and plans.

Performance Management

The diagram in *Exhibit II* indicates a convergence of the assessment and planning elements of the personnel development program in performance measurement. Performance measurement makes it possible for the data processing manager to identify, with some degree of accuracy, the ability and the success of personnel in their jobs. Impressions about the quality of data processing staff can be translated into facts about their ability to get the work done.

Before going into detail about these measurements, it is important to note that performance in general is a function of both motivation and ability. The point of personnel development and performance management, of better recruitment, placement, and training, is to maximize the skills and knowledge of the data processing staff by optimizing the

EXHIBIT II

A Comprehensive
Personnel Program

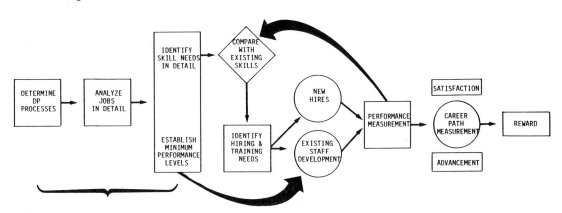

environment in which they work. The transient quality of data processing employment, unspecified performance standards, and lack of opportunity are critical factors because they demoralize people, undermine potential for growth, encourage movement from one employer to another, and make it difficult to trace problems to their source. The objective of performance management is to make sure that skills are maximized by establishing clearly defined job performance levels and requirements and by raising performance levels through a comprehensive appraisal process.

A job performance program begins with the specification of jobs and duties. It asks management to clarify its needs and expectations by setting performance levels for each position. This means that general goals must be converted into specific skill levels and tasks for personnel just as they are translated into systems priorities for applications. Specifically, data processing activity is broken down into processes which translate into positions requirements and, finally, into jobs and staffing. Skill levels and job definitions are developed, with these levels in mind, performance levels are set. Performance management is instituted by means of a series of periodic reviews which lead to position adjustments and/or advancement. *Exhibit III* shows the steps in this sequence.

The final step in the performance management process is the establishment of review mechanisms so that performance can be assessed according to expectations set by job definitions and skill matrixes. Each individual is evaluated according to the skills required for the assigned position or task. In addition, skill gaps or underutilized skill areas can be monitored in order to provide feedback for planning, training, transfer, and advancement. Regular reviews will benefit both staff and management by providing accurate information measuring both the productivity of people and the success of the organization in promoting working conditions in which staff can function productively.

EXHIBIT III

Performance
Management

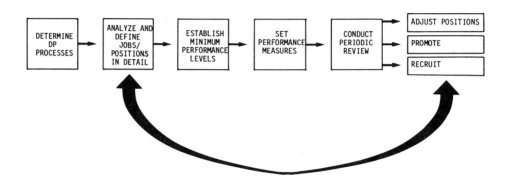

Manpower Planning and Career Planning

Performance management provides important information for long-term planning for the data processing organization and for the individual. The natural follow-up to performance measurement and review is career planning. This provides the foundation for a structured manpower planning approach. This is best understood in terms of the information network resulting from the combination of personnel development and performance measurement programs.

In *Exhibit I*, both short-term personnel development activity and long-term planning provide input for recruitment and training efforts. The short-term aspect of this process involves a match of required and existing skills for the purpose of recruiting and training to close skill gaps. The long-term effort is similar but involves the anticipation of skill gaps and of individual career transitions.

The first part of the long-term process is manpower training. This is an organizational activity which involves the determination of long-range personnel needs based on the overall data processing strategy and data processing plans in all of the Growth Processes. Its objective is to inventory and forecast human resource needs for the data processing organization in accordance with the operating plan and in support of the Applications Portfolio.

The manpower planning process breaks down into several steps which parallel those of the other human resource programs. *Exhibit IV* summarizes these steps. They are:

1. inventory current capabilities

EXHIBIT IV

Manpower
Planning

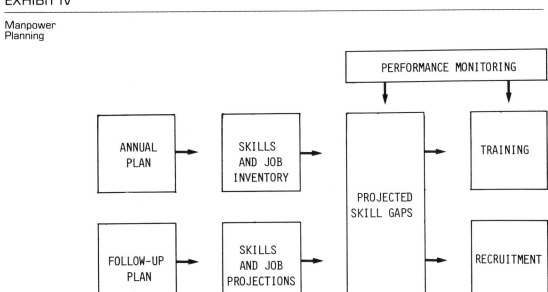

EXHIBIT V

Sample Career Paths for
Junior Programmers

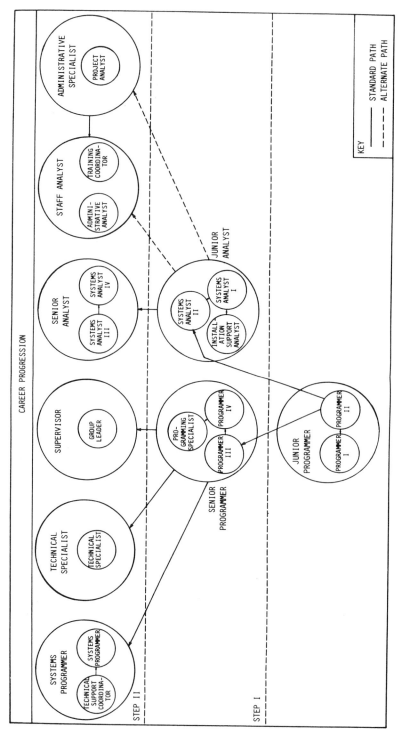

2. forecast future needs

3. monitor and respond to changes which have occurred in the work force because of promotion, transfer, and training

The manpower plan should also include monitoring of turnover, labor costs (current and future), and manpower supply. This information provides the necessary input to keep training and recruitment programs abreast of staffing needs.

Career development programs are constructed parallel to manpower planning programs and function to translate the latter into individual terms. The skills inventories, position definitions, and staffing projections developed in manpower planning can all be translated into career path structures which identify transfer, promotion, and relocation opportunities in the organization. *Exhibit V* shows some representative career path planning patterns.

Career planning makes it possible for the organization to develop internal staff improvement and training programs which complement individual career goals. It eliminates the need for the separation of individual goals from the objectives of the organization and makes it possible for the organization to take advantage of personnel motivation to improve performance. Training and individual growth become assets to productivity for the organization rather than necessary evils. Thus, through human resource management, data processing personnel management is integrated in the overall data processing management effort.

Skills Inventory and Career Paths

The reluctance to introduce human resource management concepts in data processing has been fed by the apparent enormity of the specific tasks involved in the process. There is a tendency to either ignore the need for detailing data processing jobs or for relegating personnel and hiring responsibilities to organizational personnel groups who do not have the expertise necessary to analyze skills and envision career programs. Both of these nonsolutions contribute to the sense of intimidation and frustration which surrounds personnel planning issues in the data processing organization. It feeds the tendency to assume a short-term perspective and the effort to dispense with personnel matters as rapidly and simply as possible.

The processes of job definition, manpower planning, and career planning are tedious but can be made less formidable by introducing several straight-forward mechanisms for organizing the necessary information. These mechanisms are based on a series of matrixes which integrate the various personnel factors discussed in this chapter.

The first step in defining personnel requirements is to describe the work of data processing in terms of tasks and to break these tasks down into their skill components. The list of tasks for a given orgainzation is derived from the business model of that organization and analyzed in terms of data processing skills. This process is shown in *Exhibit VI.* The next step is to create a similar job and skill breakdown for each job

EXHIBIT VI

Business Model Generates
DP Process Task Lists

SKILLS ACQUISITION
- HIRING
- TRAINING

DP PROCESSING
- DEV./MAINTENANCE
- TECHNICAL SUPPORT
- OPERATIONS
- MANAGEMENT

JOB CATEGORY STRUCTURE
- TASKS
- SKILLS
- KNOWLEDGE
- EXPERIENCE
- EDUCATION

CAREER PATHS

PERFORMANCE MANAGEMENT

DEVELOPMENT/MAINTENANCE

PHASE	TASK	Knowledge	Program Logic	Program Coding	Documentation Presentation	Logical Analysis	Design & Planning	Formal writing	Oral Presentation	Negotiations & Decision-Making	Interviewing	Interpreting Documents	Administration	Supervision	Interpersonal Communication	Scheduling & Organizing	Typing
STUDY	Define system components (Files, Input, Output)	1,3 6			● ○ ▲ △ ■	● ○ ▲ △ ■	● ○ ▲ △	● ○ ▲ △			● ○ ▲ △ ■	● ○ ▲ △ ■					
	Perform Cost/Benefit Analysis	1				▲ △ ■						▲ △ ■					
	Identify constraints and assumptions to solve problems	1,5 6				○ △	○					△					
	Identify viable alternatives for probable solutions	1,5				○ △	○					△					
	Understand user organization as it relates to request	1,5				△						△				△	
	Define information usage needed to solve problems	1				△						△					
	Define system objectives	1				△ □	△				△ □	△ □					
	Define overall system information flow	1,5 6				□						□	□				
	Define the scope of the project	1	□	□		□		□			□	□	□		□		

category. This process is shown in *Exhibit VII.* By matching related skill requirements to job categories and tasks, long-term job structures can be delineated. These structures provide guidelines for career path planning. The guidelines can be used by the individual and as a basis for setting training priorities and promotion paths in the organization.

The final step in the introduction of a human resource management program is the establishment of a review process in which performance is assessed according to expectations derived from the job definitions and skill matrixes. Each individual is evaluated according to the skills specific to the assigned task or position. In addition, skill gaps or under-utilized skill areas can be monitored to provide information for planning, training, transfer, and advancement of personnel. Regular reviews benefit both staff and management by facilitating performance management and staff planning. They introduce a control which will enhance the effort to build and maintain internal stability by encouraging growth and advancement.

EXHIBIT VII

A Sample Job
Category Description

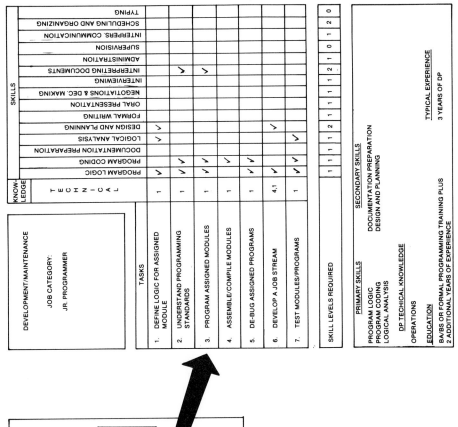

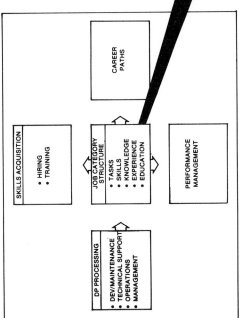

CONCLUSION

For many data processing managers, human resource management represents a new and intimidating area of concern. There is a temptation to postpone the institution of human resources programs by hiding reluctance behind the argument that it is too costly. This sort of thinking detracts from responsible management. Every resource in a business must be maximized if that business is going to succeed, and data processing is no exception. Computers may make it possible to reduce staff in many areas of the organization but they do not eliminate the need for qualified, dedicated data processing personnel. On the contrary, the strength of the technological resources of an organization is dependent upon and enhanced by the strength of its human resources.

The inverse cost curves for data processing technology and data processing personnel are familiar information for the data processing manager. When the cost of computers is compared to the cost of people, it seems that the cost of computers is finally coming under control while the cost of personnel is rising out of control. However, if the entire management picture is reviewed it becomes apparent that it is not the *expense* of people that is rising but their *value*. The data processing facility is only as good as the staff which runs it. The money spent on people, like the money spent on hardware and software, is capital invested in an asset, not funds depleted by an expense.

In order to translate the high cost of personnel into the high value of the human resources asset, data processing managers must begin to learn about their personnel. They must begin to collect information about their staff, their staffing needs, and their potential growth patterns. From this information, management can develop a strategy and institute programs for career planning, training, skills monitoring, and performance review. Management must learn to know and to utilize its human resources. People must be integrated into data processing solutions rather than relegated to the status of data processing problems.

When personnel resources are being fully utilized some very specific benefits can be anticipated. Better human resources management will reduce turnover, not only eliminating the cost of turnover but adding value by building morale and loyalty. The work force will stabilize, while within that work force there will be an increasingly strong sense of opportunity. Increased motivation will lead to improved productivity, and in the long run the investment in people will contribute heavily to the value of the entire organization.

It is certainly difficult to introduce a new management concern in an already complex field, but as Nolan has shown, all of the Growth Process areas are interrelated. Just as the growth of users can inhibit the growth and strength of applications, the growth of data processing personnel can inhibit the power of the technology. Human resources management is not a stumbling block but an opportunity for growth.

Personal Privacy versus the Corporate Computer*

ROBERT C. GOLDSTEIN
RICHARD L. NOLAN

A senior executive of one of the country's largest retail chains recently told us that his company is seriously considering closing down its credit authorization department. Because of what it would cost to comply with proposed laws, not to mention existing regulations, ensuring that computerized information about people will not be handled or used in such a way as to invade their privacy, an organization even as large as his will no longer be able to afford to make its own credit checks, he said. And so he is planning to contract with a national consumer credit company to perform this function for his chain.

When we talked with the general manager of a major consumer credit company, however, he told us that these regulations could drive his company entirely out of business.

While both of these executives are worried about how computer privacy regulations will affect the field of consumer credit, their impact extends far beyond that field to all organizations that use data systems containing personal information. These regulations will affect government organizations at every level, as well as those in the health or insurance fields. In fact, since virtually every organization collects and uses personal information about its own employees, the impact of proposed privacy regulations will be sweeping indeed.

Concern over the privacy invasion potential of computerized data banks is picking up momentum reminiscent of the environmental protec-

*Reprinted by permission of Harvard Business Review. *Personal Privacy Versus The Corporate Computer* by Robert C. Goldstein and Richard L. Nolan, March-April 1975. Copyright © 1975 by the President and Fellows of Harvard College; all rights reserved.

tion activities of a few years ago. A sampling of recent headlines indicates current governmental thinking about this problem:

**"SENATOR ERVIN CHARGES 858 DATA BANKS SHOW REGULA—
TION A MUST"**

**"FORD COUNCIL PUSHES FEDERAL REGULATION, TAKES 14
PRIVACY INITIATIVES"**

"RIGHT-TO-PRIVACY BILL BACKED AT SENATE HEARING"

Several states and foreign countries have already enacted privacy laws, and about 100 privacy bills are currently pending before the U.S. Congress and the various state legislatures. We can now safely predict that within the next year or two privacy will affect every organization that has computerized data about people, for either the federal government will act to impose uniform laws throughout the country or the states will take action on their own. If the federal government does not win this race, another level of complexity will be added to the already difficult process of developing and maintaining useful computer-based systems. With the possibility of having to comply with different requirements in every state, it is no wonder that many forward-looking executives like the two mentioned are worried.

In this article, we shall first look at what the responsibilities of organizations and the rights of data subjects are or no doubt will be under privacy regulations. Then, using a computer model, we shall examine what it will cost various kinds of organizations operating some actual systems to comply with the regulations. Lastly, we offer four steps to take in planning for the new environment.

PRIVACY AND POWER

Privacy proposals recently passed and others currently under consideration go far beyond any strict definition of privacy. For example, giving someone the right to restrict the use of information about himself or herself falls within a limited notion of privacy. But the right to examine information about oneself and add to it if it is felt to be incomplete or inaccurate has little to do with privacy per se. It is a direct effort to increase the power of individuals in their dealings with large organizations, which often seem remote, domineering, and unconcerned about individuals.

The ruled insert, depicted on next page, gives several excerpts from two regulations already on the books in Minnesota and California. Generally, privacy proposals cover three main categories: controls on operating procedures, access rights of data subjects, and usage control by data subjects.

- **Controls on operating procedures**. An organization using a personal data system must take appropriate precautions against natural hazards

Examples of privacy regulations

Minnesota Privacy Act, Chapter 479, Section 4

The California Fair Information Practice Act of 1974

Paragraph E
Upon request to a responsible authority, an individual shall be informed whether he is the subject of stored data and if so, and upon his additional request, shall be informed of the content and meaning of the data recorded about him or shown the data without any charge to him.

Paragraph F
An individual shall have the right to contest the accuracy or completeness of data about him.... The responsible authority shall within 30 days correct the data if the data is found to be inaccurate or incomplete and attempt to notify past recipients of the inaccurate or incomplete data, or notify the individual of disagreement.... Data in dispute shall not be disclosed except under conditions of demonstrated need and then only if the individual's statement of disagreement is included with the disclosed data.

Chapter Three: Rights of Data Subjects

Every governmental body maintaining an automated personal data system in California shall do each of the following:

Item B
Inform in writing an individual, upon his request and proper identification, whether he is the subject of data in the system, and if so, make such data fully available to the individual in a form comprehensible to him.

Item E
Maintain procedures that allow an individual who is the subject of data in the system to contest their accuracy, completeness, pertinence, and timeliness.

Item F
If the accuracy, completeness, pertinence, or timeliness of personal data is disputed, and such dispute is directly conveyed to the governmental body maintaining the personal data, the governmental body shall reinvestigate and record the current status of that personal data.... If the governmental body maintaining the system and the data subject fail to resolve their dispute after reinvestigation of the data, the dispute may be resolved one of three ways to be elected by the governmental body maintaining the system:

1
The data subject may file [a complaint with] the governmental body maintaining the system, [that is,] a brief statement setting forth his views on the dispute.... Whenever a statement of dispute is filed, the governmental body maintaining the system shall, in any subsequent disclosure or dissemination of the disputed data, clearly note that it is disputed by the data subject and provide with the data either a copy of his statement or a clear and accurate summary thereof.
2
The parties to the dispute may agree to binding arbitration of the dispute.
3
The data subject may seek injunctive relief ordering the governmental body maintaining the data to amend, correct, or purge the disputed data.

and other threats to the system and its data, publish descriptions of it periodically in a medium likely to be seen by most of its subjects, establish procedures for responding to inquiries from individuals about their records and for settling complaints about their accuracy, and keep a log of all uses of each person's record.

- **Access rights of data subjects**. A person may examine his own record, request the correction of any information in it that he believes to be erroneous, and append a statement to the record if the error is not corrected to his satisfaction.

- **Usage control by data subjects**. At the time information is collected from someone, he must be told what it will be used for and given the opportunity to refuse to provide it. The subject's permission must again be sought for any new use of the data not covered by his original consent.

One consquence of granting veto power to data subjects is that companies that have sold their mailing lists in the past will no longer be able to do so without the consent of the subjects. Hence these lists may no longer be available to those who have used them as prime sources of sales prospects. Another consequence is that such veto power partially offsets the efficiency gained through data-base technology, which essentially unlocks data from a specific application for wider use.

Although these rights substantially increase the cost of using personal data, everyone will probably benefit from the increased accuracy that should result from giving data subjects access to their records.

MODEL OF SYSTEMS

To determine what it will cost an organization operating a personal data system to comply with privacy regulations, one of us constructed a computer model to analyze their impact on some systems already in use.[1]

The model calculates costs in six categories—programming, computer processing, information storage, data communications, administration, and capital equipment—and analyzes both these costs incurred at the time of conversion to the regulated environment and those associated with the ongoing operation of the system in that environment.

The insert on page 320 gives descriptions of five of the systems analyzed. *Exhibit I* shows some of their characteristics, along with what their conversion and annual operating costs to comply with privacy regulations will be. Although some interesting comparisons can be drawn from this data, it is important to bear in mind the different uses of each system as well as the differences in number of subjects, record size, and transaction volume.

Notification vs. Inquiry Response

The exhibit shows, for each system, the cost of notifications and inquiries for making data subjects aware of their records. Some early legislative proposals required that organizations notify each data subject at least once a year. Because notification seemed prohibitively expensive even without detailed analysis, most later proposals specify that system operators need not notify subjects of their records but must stand ready to respond to subjects' inquiries about them.

Even though it costs more to process a single inquiry than to issue one notification as part of a large batch, the former alternative is generally believed to be cheaper because it is assumed that relatively few individuals will initiate such inquiries. The exhibit shows the fraction of subjects who would have to inquire about their records before it would be cheaper to simply notify all of them.

This break-even point may seem relatively low for all of the systems; however, evidence currently available to the consumer credit company,

---

[1]Robert C. Goldstein, *The Cost of Privacy*, Harvard Business School doctoral dissertation, 1974 (Boston, Honeywell Informations Systems, Inc., 1974.)

for example, suggests that the actual number of inquiries it can expect to receive will be even lower—in the range of 1% to 3%. Thus, if these estimates are reliable, the model's break-even analysis supports the belief that inquiry processing will be cheaper than mass notification.

WEIGHING THE COSTS

Exhibit I clearly shows that the effect of privacy laws on a personal data system will depend on what it is used for. In discussing these effects, we shall divide the systems into three general classes of use:

1. internal

2. financial

3. governmental

In our study, the representative examples for each of these systems were a personal file, a retail credit information clearinghouse, and the automobile registration and license records maintained by a state police department.

Impact on Internal Systems

Systems used only within a company offer excellent opportunities for unilateral action on the privacy front. A company can gain significant experience while working under regulatory conditions without having to contend with external cooperation or actual regulations. At the same time, it can get the necessary mechanisms and procedures in place for the time when they will be required.

Such actions can also serve as a positive demonstration of the organizations's social responsibility in protecting the privacy of its employees. Because all of the data subjects of a personnel system are in one place, or in a relatively small number of places, many of the difficulties of implementing the privacy regulations in a more complex environment do not exist, and consequently costs are lower.

For example, the conversion cost of the one personnel system we studied (System 3) is $142,000, and its annual incremental operating cost is $40,000. These figures are far lower than those for any other systems in the study. In addition, securing the computer installation, a step which should probably be taken regardless of privacy regulations, accounts for slightly more than 80% of the conversion costs. The existence of a free intracompany mail system (free insofar as its marginal cost is concerned) is a major factor in keeping the privacy costs low for an internal system since one of the highest compliance costs is associated with mailing.

Rights of Conflict. Two difficulties arise from the provision specifying that data subjects may examine their own records, because each record usually includes evaluations of the employee by present and past super-

EXHIBIT I

The Cost of
Privacy

	System 1 Medical	System 2 Insurance	System 3 Personnel	System 4 Credit	System 5 Law enforcement
System characteristics					
Number of subjects (in thousands)	1,000	3,300	10	35,000	31
Number of characters in data base (in thousands)	3,500,000	3,600,000	20,000	3,500,000	19,000
Number of users	50	60,000	45	500,000	5,000
Transaction volume per year (in thousands)	2,500	12,000	50	10,000	55
Mode	Batch	On-line	On-line	On-line	On-line
Data-management package	No	Yes	Yes	No	Yes
Development cost (in thousands)	$726	$5,000	$200	$800	$3,000
Annual operating cost before converting to comply with privacy regulations (in thousands)	$4,000	$13,000	$340	$14,000	$2,000
Privacy conversion and annual costs					
Privacy conversion cost (in thousands)	$543	$573	$142	$1,416	$348
Annual privacy cost (in thousands)	$1,797	$1,882	$40	$20,453	$216
Annual privacy cost per subject	$1.80	$0.57	$4.00	$0.58	$6.97
Annual privacy cost per transaction	$0.72	$0.15	$0.80	$2.05	$3.93
Annual privacy cost as percent of annual operating cost	45%	15%	12%	146%	11%
Comparison of record-existence notifications **with record-existence inquiries**					
Cost per record-existence notification	$0.24	$0.09	$0.10	$0.20	$0.48
Cost per record-existence inquiry	$2.76	$1.27	†	$1.40	†
Inquiry/notification break-even point*	9%	7%	†	14%	†

*If more than this percentage of data subjects would be expected to inquire about their records in a given year, it would be cheaper just to notify all subjects.

†The precision of the model and data do not permit the determination of inquiry costs for System 3 because of its small size. Inquiry costs cannot be computed for System 5 because of the nature of this system. Without an inquiry cost, it is impossible to compute break-even points for these two systems.

visors. First, to allow an employee to see information that was assumed would be kept from him violates the privacy of those who provided it. Second, once a new policy has been established, anyone asked to provide an evaluation will know that it will be available to the subject. Thus privacy rights of the evaluator will not be affected, but he is not likely to be as candid as he would be otherwise.

So, on the one hand, this policy could result in bland evaluations that would be virtually useless for personnel planning purposes. On the other hand, of course, it could help eliminate unfavorable reports based strictly on personal dislike. Since such reports could have a significant effect on the subject's career, this protection is rather important. While this is a tough trade-off, the benefit of airing constructive criticism should, in addition to protecting all concerned, more than outweigh the lost benefits of "confidential" information.

Impact on Financial Systems

Privacy regulations will hit financial information systems even harder than personnel systems. Financial information contains some of the most sensitive and most widely circulated data about people. Almost every family has bank accounts of various types, credit cards, charge accounts, mortgages, or other loans. In fact, the statement that you have to give Americans "credit" for their standard of living is more truth than jest. The negotiation of credit requires a person to supply information about his personal financial condition, and in many cases this is supplemented by reports from other creditors or investigative agencies. A complex but nevertheless workable credit information network underlies this essential economic activity.

The data in *Exhibit I* show how severe a strain compliance will place on one consumer credit company. The actual amounts of both the conversion and the annual privacy costs ($1.4 million and $20 million, respectively) are far higher for its system (System 4) than for any of the others. This is primarily because of its greater number of data subjects. Thus, while physical security is the dominant cost for personnel systems, dealing with people (obtaining consent, making notifications, and processing inquiries) is the dominant cost for credit systems.

More specifically, the regulatory variables used in this study indicate that each credit transaction will cost $2.05 more than a current transaction, which costs less than $1.50.

Who Will Pay. In fact, because credit is so central to the American economy, these numbers raise an important question: Who should bear the cost of protecting the privacy of credit records? The credit company executive we interviewed feels that he cannot add $2.00 to his price for a credit check without losing a major share of his business. It is his belief, at least, that retail stores, banks, and loan companies—his major customers— will not pay that additional price for a credit report.

But *Exhibit I* also shows that the increased cost per data subject is $0.48 per year. This does not seem to be an unreasonable amount for people to pay to protect their records, but, of course, collecting it from them would probably be a very complicated and expensive business in its own right.

Unilateral Action Foolish. The provisions included under the general heading of privacy regulations increase the power of individuals in dealing with large organizations. As such, these provisions probably deserve the support of most people as individuals. However, the appropriate response for the affected organizations is not a simple matter for corporate executives. It would be foolish for a bank or credit company to adopt the proposals unilaterally.

In the first place, the costs involved would be substantially greater because of the organization's relatively indirect relationship with data subjects. More important, however, is the fact that unilateral action in this area is simply uncalled for because the major market for credit information is an intercompany one. Unless all involved follow the same set of rules, the protection of privacy will be minimal, and so there is no reason for a single company to handicap itself by incurring the associated costs before its competitors do.

Impact on Government Systems

It is likely that personal information systems within the government will be subject to privacy regulation before those in the private sector. There

Description of personal data systems studied

System 1 processes records of the treatments given one million people at a large network of hospitals. In regular weekly runs, it adds new records to the master file and prepares a large variety of reports. The hospitals use this system almost exclusively for management control and planning purposes. Virtually all its output is in the form of aggregated statistical reports. Only on very rare occasions is information about a single individual retrieved.

System 2 is an on-line system operated by a large casualty insurance company. Its data base covers 3.3 million policyholders and can be queried interactively from any of the company's branch offices around the country. The records may contain financial, legal, medical, or other descriptive information on an individual.

System 3 is an on-line, data-base personnel system for an organization with about 10,000 employees. The company can handle inquiries about any employee's record interactively. Although, like many other companies, it plans to eventually add a skills inventory and other evaluative records to its file, the company is currently using the system only for routine payroll and employee-benefit activities.

Although System 3 is the smallest one in the study, it is one of the most interesting because nearly every organization has one like it. Most of these systems got their start with the payroll function. Over the years, they have been added to, patched up, and modified to meet governmental reporting requirements, provide information for the collective bargaining process, and otherwise facilitate management of the organization's human resources. Expanding personnel systems to serve these additional functions has resulted in the addition of liberal amounts of personal information covering such topics as performance reviews, medical histories, and grievances filed.

System 4 processes information for one of the largest consumer credit companies in the country. This company acts as a clearinghouse for retail credit information, collected from subscribers and stored in an on-line system where any subscriber can obtain a virtually instantaneous credit report on any individual in the data bank. Subscribers can either phone terminal operators, who interrogate the data base and report back verbally, or interrogate the data base directly themselves from small terminals in their own stores.

System 5 is an on-line, real-time system operated by a state police organization with a file of about 30,000 records—some being outstanding warrants on individuals and others stolen car reports. This system is set up in such a way that a state police officer can report a license number to his dispatcher and have it checked in a few seconds against registration and license files as well as against a "wanted and warrants" file. Some police vehicles in the state have even been equipped with mobile keyboard printers so that officers can directly query the files themselves.

are two reasons for this. First, members of both the legislative and the executive branches have expressed the view that governmental systems are a more appropriate target for such regulation. Enforcement is probably easier within the government, as well. Second, the government affects virtually everyone, so moving first in the public sector makes sense.

A great deal of highly personal data is collected by government. The story headlining the existence of 858 data banks was about a survey that covered only the federal government. The systems included contain nearly one billion records on individuals, and these numbers understate the actual situation since several government agencies declined to cooperate fully in the survey.

As a result of the Census and Internal Revenue acts, the personal data banks of the federal government include information on nearly every citizen. In addition, anyone who has ever served in the armed forces is the subject of extensive records relating to his or her service and status as a veteran. All beneficiaries of government-supported health programs have medical information on file, and if a national health insurance for all citizens is established, this particularly sensitive information will be collected about everyone. Information about an individual's brushes with the criminal justice system, another very sensitive type of data, is maintained by government, much of it by the federal government through the National Crime Information Center and the National Criminal History System.

Transaction Costs High. The government system in this study (System 5), an automobile registration and license file used by a state police department, shows some particularly interesting results. The annual privacy cost for this system, while relatively low overall ($216,000), is the highest of all the systems studied when prorated to the individual data subject ($6.97) or to each transaction ($3.93). These results occur because this system requires a relatively large complex of equipment to handle a rather small data base and to process a very small number of transactions. In fact, privacy considerations aside, it costs more than $36 each time a state police officer picks up his microphone and asks for a license check.

While in a commercial enterprise a transaction cost of this magnitude and the concomitant large privacy cost would probably be considered unacceptable, it is characteristic of many governmental systems to consider the benefits so important that cost becomes a relatively minor factor. In fact, of all the data-processing executives interviewed in the five organizations we studied, the executives associated with the two governmental systems were the least concerned about the potential cost of privacy regulations. "If Congress imposes the regulations, then Congress will have to put up the money to implement them"—that seemed to be their general attitude.

CORPORATE POLICY GUIDELINES

In the United States, we are at a crucial point in developing and institutionalizing the concept of personal privacy. The necessary momentum appears to have been achieved, and it seems likely that some sort of federal legislation will be adopted within a year. It is definitely time for those with personal data systems to begin planning for the new environment. What exactly should be done? At least four steps that organizations should take are to:

1. Prepare a "privacy impact statement". A statement analyzing the potential privacy implications should be made a part of all proposals for new or expanded systems. The three categories of privacy proposals we mentioned earlier provide a structure for this analysis: (a) controls on operating practices, (b) access rights of data subjects, and (c) usage control by data subjects. Such a statement should cover not only the system's impact on individuals' privacy but also the effect of privacy regulations on the system.

2. Construct a comprehensive privacy plan. The input for planning is the privacy impact statement, which specifies what has to be accomplished. For new systems, the purpose of the plan is to make sure that the necessary privacy controls are integrated into the design of the system at the very beginning. This procedure will not only be cheaper than grafting controls on later, but it will also ensure that the company will take no steps that are incompatible with privacy objectives. For existing systems, the plan should cover needed changes in programs, equipment, and procedures. Where existing practices will become illegal or excessively expensive, alternatives should be devised.

3. Train employees who handle personal information. The next step in preparing for the privacy regulations is to begin a program of making employees who handle personal data aware of the importance of protecting privacy and the specific policies and procedures to be followed.

4. Make privacy part of social responsibility programs. Finally, data subjects should be kept informed about whatever an organization plans to do on the privacy front without regulatory pressures or in addition to them. Informing subjects will demonstrate a company's awareness and concern for the privacy of its data subjects and may also be of significant help later in obtaining data and the authorization to use it.

Stage I (Initiation)

Taking these steps may reveal that some privacy restrictions will render some systems or portions of them entirely infeasible or unjustifiably expensive, especially those restrictions requiring that all proposed uses of personal data be authorized by the subjects in advance. The need to go back to data subjects to obtain permission for a new use of data already collected may make it almost impossible to expand the usefulness of a system. Organizations should consider this constraint both in deciding whether to go ahead with a new project and in creating initial master plans so that the need for further permission will be minimized.

Capabilities Expanded. The acquisition of new programs and data-processing equipment usually involves fairly long lead times. This may be particularly true in meeting privacy objectives since some capabilities that will be needed to do so are not widely available yet. For example, much of the effectiveness of many of the regulations depends on being able to accurately and reliably identify the source of an inquiry. On-line computer systems, especially, will require additional hardware and perhaps operating software. Suppliers should begin now to develop products to meet these new needs.

Another inadequacy of most systems currently in use is in controlling access to data-bank records. Because the law will require permission from the subject for each use, it will no longer be valid to assume that every record in a system can be used for all purposes. In particular, it will be necessary to keep permission information on each person's record and to have computer systems that can interpret and enforce the restrictions implied by that information.

This problem, like the user identification one, is not technically too difficult to deal with. Current systems handle both problems in ways that will surely be satisfactory. However, for the most part, these are specialized military or research systems. The relevant capabilities have not been included in normal commercial systems up to now because there has been little demand for them.

Data-Management Packages Useful. Our research supports the use of data-base technology in responding to privacy regulations. Of the five systems we have described, the three commercial data-management systems have significantly lower programming costs than the two that do not use them. Much of the specialized-access control programming can be done in a data-management system, and using a standardized version will make it easier to verify implementation of required controls.

Moreover, the law will surely require organizations to provide data to an enforcement agency. Those using data-base technology should find it easier and cheaper to respond, just as did the oil companies who reported with the aid of a data-management package during the recent oil crisis.

For virtually all organizations, the new regulations imply the need to carefully reconsider the technical and economic feasibility of existing and proposed applications. It is not too early to begin planning to reduce the cost and the adverse impact that may result from this legislation.

PART FIVE

Leadership
And
Organization

In the 1960s computers were new to the business scene, and technical leadership was needed to understand how they could be used. Organization was straightforward. Business computing was generally the responsibility of the accounting department, scientific computing was the responsibility of the engineering department, and process control computing was the responsibility of manufacturing. By the 1970s the purview of business computing had dramatically increased with improvements in the technologies of on-line, data base, and software for generation of automated reports. Business applications had widely penetrated the functions of the business—order entry, inventory control, purchasing, and production scheduling. The task of the data processing manager shifted to making business computing a disciplined part of the overall company. In turn, the demand for leadership shifted from technical to management. *Chapter 21, Plight of the EDP Manager* reveals that, in general, the computer manager has been poorly managed during this shift. Senior management is often ill-informed on the processes and risks of using new computer technology.

Exhibit I shows the computer expenditure pattern for a large manufacturing company. Whereas the expenditures for scientific and process control computing remained relatively stable through the 1960s, the expenditure for business computing increased dramatically. Both the growth rate and level of expenditure gave rise to management issues of organization, planning, and control. Through the 1970s, business computing continued to benefit from improvements in technology. Mini/microcomputer technology and communications technology had resulted in the construction of large computer networks which bring a company's geographically dispersed operations into instant contact as well as enabling organizations to structure business functions in such new ways as centralized worldwide order entry and production scheduling of factories located in different countries. Business computing expenditures of the manufacturing company shown in *Exhibit I* increased from $25 million in 1970 to $90 million in 1980. But whereas the data processing manager in 1970 rendered direct control over one hundred percent of the total $25 million expenditure in 1970, he controlled directly only sixty percent of the $90 million expenditure in 1980. This makes the problem of building an integrated efficiently functioning corporate computer network a lot tougher. *Chapter 22, Business Needs a New Breed of EDP Manager*, describes the process in which the data processing manager has taken on general management leadership functions.

An additional complication began appearing in the late 1970s with the widespread use of computers to attack the productivity problem. Scientific computing has expanded into CAD/CAE (Computer-Aided Design and Computer-Aided Engineering) with the combination of computer technology and graphics technology. Process control has expanded into CAM (Computer-aided Manufacturing) and robotics by the combination of computer technology and both graphics and optics technologies. As shown in *Exhibit I*, the manufacturing company's computer expenditure for scientific computing increased from $3 million in 1970 to $24 million in 1980, and process control went from $2 million to $15 million.

In 1970, computers were not used in the office. By 1980, the manufacturing company was spending $21 million to support offices with computers. Combined computer expenditures in 1980 for office, engineer-

EXHIBIT I

Changing Computers Technology and
Responsibility Profiles

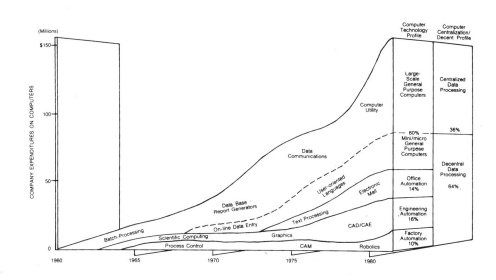

ing, and the factory total $65 million—more than twice the total computer budget in 1970.

COMPUTER ACCOUNTABILITY

In a 1980 meeting with senior management of the manufacturing company shown in *Exhibit I*, the senior vice president for finance insisted that there was no doubt in his mind who was accountable for computers in the company, it was his vice president for data processing. The vice president for data processing had the responsibility for approving all capital expenditures for computers.

This was a living example of "future shock" in the management of computers. The senior vice president of finance was reacting to the 1970 environment. In 1970, the data processing manager directly controlled and was accountable for eighty percent of the computer expenditure, which included one hundred percent of the business computing. The other twenty percent of the expenditures for scientific computing and process control was narrowly focused on engineering and manufacturing. All capital expenditures for computers over $50,000 required approval of the data processing manager. And since it was difficult to purchase a functioning computer for less than $50,000 in 1970, the data processing manager was effectively accountable for the company's use of computers.

Dramatic changes have taken place since 1970. Functioning computers for less than $50,000 are commonplace. Laying out the 1980 facts shown on *Exhibit I* shocked the senior vice president for finance. Currently, the vice president for data processing is directly accountable for only thirty-six percent of the company's annual computer expenditure. And that thirty-six percent now includes only sixty percent of business computing expenses. Furthermore, new computers have been designed to support functional specializations that the vice president for data processing and his staff understood only superficially in 1970. Consequently, the capital expenditure policy for approving all computer expenditures over $50,000 has degenerated into mere ceremony. Clearly a new approach to company computers accountability is needed.

NEW APPROACH FOR COMPUTER ACCOUNTABILITY

The implications of *Exhibit I* provide some clues to an appropriate approach for computer accountability in the 1980s. First, holding one manager directly accountable for company computer expenditures is not workable. The facts are that all types of divisional and functional units in organizations are using computers to carry out their responsibilities. Further, the low capital cost of computers makes capital expenditure controls ineffective.

Secondly, computers are now company pervasive. In 1970 the use of computers could be simply described as business data processing. Business data processing was mostly centralized in a large computer utility. Today the computer technology has been inegrated with such other technologies as communications, graphics, optics, and voice recognition, resulting in highly specialized uses in all functional aspects of the business. The net result has been to shift the balance from the majority of the computers being centralized in the 1970s to the majority of the computers being decentralized in the 1980s. In addition, the highly specialized and diverse use of computers today requires that functional specialists play a key role in the decision-making process.

Thirdly, effective use of computers is one of the most powerful weapons management has to attack the productivity problem being faced by business. Cost performance of computers costing $1,000,000 twenty years ago is equivalent to computers costing one dollar today. This fact has unleashed a powerful economic and entrepreneurial force exploiting the power of computer technology to improve virtually every aspect of business operations from robotics in the factory to electronic mail in the office. There can be no productivity gains, however, without skilled people and management to make them happen. The exponential growth in the use of computers has created a severe shortage of computer professionals. Turnover rates range from twenty-five to thirty-five percent. Accountability for the effective use and management of computer professionals is therefore at least as important and probably even more important than accountability for computer expenditures.

Although no clear-cut solutions can be given, four guidelines have emerged based upon the collective experiences of companies which are successfully making progress with the computer accountability problem.

Guideline #1. Reorient computer accountability from computer expenditure accountability to data resource accountability. Just as accountability in the manufacturing function has shifted from machines to inventories of materials, computer accountability should shift from computers to the data resources.[1] It has shown that effective cost controls are associated with the collection, storage, and processing of data elements.[2] Effective controls consist of differentiating organizational use (corporate, divisional, plant, functional), extent of sharing, and setting standards for quality. The foundation for accountability is built on a scheme for data resource accountability.

Guideline #2. Expand the accountability concept from data processing manager to a joint accountability concept which includes data processing management, senior management, and user management. *Chapter 23, Towards a Theory of Data Processing Leadership* presents a framework for key coalition leadership.

In an analogous manner, the use of computers in most companies has grown from single small projects to multiple projects. When use of

---

[1]See Chapter 15, *"Controlling the Costs of Data Services."*
[2]Ibid.

computer was a small part of the business one person could effectively manage the activity, but this is no longer true. Today, both appropriate organization structure and appropriate definitions of roles and responsibilities are required. Senior management is responsible for linking the business strategy with the computer strategy. Data processing management and user management are responsible for implementing the computer strategy to ensure that the benefits, both cost-saving and productivity improvements, are realized. The executive steering committee is the major organizational mechanism to link business strategy with computer strategy. *Chapter 24, Steering Committees*, describes the use of management steering committees in detail.

Guideline #3. Refocus on the goal of management control from use of computers to save costs to use of computers to increase productivity. In the 1960s and 1970s, computers were used predominately to automate administrative processes. By the late 1970s and now into the 1980s, there are opportunities to apply computers across the company to increase productivity. Formal user plans for each functional area are required to identify the opportunities for productivity improvements and to gain the commitment of users to achieve the productivity improvements. Companies are finding that the identification, commitment, and measurement of these benefits is the key ingredient to effectively using computer technology in the 1980s.

Guideline #4. Make the strategic choices required to link the company's computer strategy to its business strategy. In the environment of the 1980s, it is clear that no company has the financial and personnel resources required to aggressively pursue the myriad of cost-effective opportunities to employ computer-based technologies. Thus strategic choices concerning opportunities must be made. To make these choices in the most beneficial manner, senior management must determine which opportunities are most important to maintaining and gaining a competitive advantage for the company. The management mechanism to make these strategic choices is linkage of the computer strategy to business strategy. More and more is being learned about how best to do this; it is a complex and intricate process whereby the general management perspective is reconciled with the highly complex computer technological perspective. *Chapter 25* describes both leading-edge methodology and a successful practice for effectively making the reconciliation.

21

Plight of the
EDP Manager*

RICHARD L. NOLAN

Over the last year I have talked with a score or more EDP managers about their jobs, and I have noted a curious fact: most of these managers view their jobs and their career prospects in stoic and rather negative terms. In their field, firing seems to have become remarkably common, as have separations and job changes. Of twenty managers I interviewed, seven had been dismissed outright or "voluntarily terminated" within the year, eleven had changed companies within the last three years, and only two had held onto a job for five years.

Admittedly, the sample of managers I have talked with is small, and perhaps this pattern of philosophical depression and firing is not a general one. However, my impression is that it is fairly widespread. It is also my impression that such a condition is quite unusual in U.S. business today—firing, especially, is viewed as a last resort, to be used only after all else has failed. My conclusion is that the EDP manager, as a professional, has come to a sorry pass.

How can one explain his plight? Obviously, any general explanation will fall short of completely explaining all individual situations. Even so, a diagnosis of several specific cases has helped me understand what is happening. The seven cases of dismissal indicate that the firing phenomenon is only symptomatic of a deeper management problem:

● In four of them, the impetus for firing originated with a senior

---

management ill-equipped to deal with a set of problems involving the EDP department which had suddenly become very visible.

- In the other three cases, the impetus was more complex; the EDP managers were held accountable—rightfully enough—for failing to bring about certain kinds of broad organizational change.

I hope the analysis I have to offer in this article will help both the top manager and the EDP manager understand more clearly the pitfalls and obstacles that beset an EDP effort and the man who is primarily responsible for guiding that effort.

THE DEMAND FOR A LEADER

In the last few years, advances in computer applications and technology have forced a unique and complex administrative challenge on the EDP manager:

- His subordinates now range from the most specialized kind of professionals in the corporate structure (computer scientists) to low-skilled clerical workers (key-punch operators).

- His department has developed new layers of management to accommodate the increased complexity and scale of its operations.

- He is responsible for a broad range of activities, from the most routine data-processing assignments to the most experimental information-systems projects.

- His share of the corporate financial resources has increased sharply, often to more than 1% of sales.

The leadership of the EDP department has become an intricate matter, in consequence of these changes, but senior management has not absorbed their full implications because of the sheer momentum of computer technology. The incorporation of the strategic advantages of rapidly improving computer technology has proceeded at a faster pace than most other evolutionary forces acting on the organization (e.g., decentralization, adding a new product line). As a result, the effects of the changes have not been fully assimilated by the organization in general, and most importantly by senior management.

With a Blend of Skills

Once it was possible to assume that a good EDP manager must first and foremost be an expert on computer technology. This assumption was valid enough during the 1960s, when many EDP departments were just getting off the ground. The EDP manager designed and programmed many systems himself, and a relatively low level of leadership skill was acceptable.

In those days, EDP leaders were primarily drafted from the accounting department, and indeed reported to the accounting function. Obtaining leaders from accounting made sense because most of the initial systems automated by companies were clerical financial systems (payroll, accounts receivable, accounts payable, the general ledgers, and so on). Accountants know more than anybody else about these systems, and the computer technology involved is straightforward. In addition, such applications usually replaced manual systems and were justified by cost-savings rationales (although frequently the cost savings were not realized); and accountants are quite comfortable with the cost-analysis discipline used to evaluate proposed computer applications.

> An EDP manager is the person who has prime responsibility for the use of the computer resource in the organization. His title may be Manager of EDP, MIS Manager, Vice President for Technical Services, Vice President for Information Systems, or any of a number of other terms.

In the 1970's, however, most medium- and large-sized companies have long since automated their manual clerical systems. One new thrust in computer applications has been to link together, via cross-functional computer systems, such functional areas as accounting, marketing, and production. A second new thrust has been to build computer capability that can provide middle management with both periodic and ad hoc information—for example, a systems for sales reporting and analysis.

Given these thrusts, it is no longer wise to have a matured EDP function report to the accounting function. That kind of organization may compromise the ideal service orientation of the EDP department, and the tendency to favor the financial applications may linger. For example, in one company that was organized in the old way, design for an order-entry system overemphasized the generation of financial statistics to the detriment of the order-filling logic, and stockouts and automatic backordering became hard to control.

Further, these two thrusts greatly affect the kind of leader needed for a medium- or large-sized EDP function in the 1970's. The EDP manager must now lead three groups of subordinates: key-punch operators and other clerical workers; operators, programmers, and systems analysts, who work in an ever-changing technology; and the highly skilled, highly educated, self-motivated software experts, who supply the department's requirements for applied research in computer technology. He must also mesh them all into an array of functions, projects, and machine configurations.

The more diverse the characteristics of subordinates and tasks, the wider the range of leadership styles required; and the wider the range of leadership styles required, the more managerial skills it takes to do the job. And, as *Exhibit I* shows, the larger the department he heads, the more managerial skills he needs.

Of course, a good understanding of the trends of computer technology is still essential for a successful EDP manager; but it is only one ingredient, and he need not have so high a level of expertise as his computer scientists. The managerial ingredients he needs are more in number, and each is just as important as the technical.

To function effectively, too, the EDP manager must have a good understanding of his company, its capacity for change, and its competitive environment. He must also deftly execute a continuing mission to educate functional managers about how computers can be used in the business. To solve these problems, he will have to revise his own department's organization in some ways, and this is a further challenge.

To some extent, the magnitude of this job is being recognized. A number of companies with sophisticated EDP activities have created a vice presidential position for the EDP manager; others, with a lower level of activity, have the EDP manager report to an executive vice president or a service-oriented vice president (for example, the vice president for administrative services). These are good signs—they indicate that some companies, at least, appreciate the new and broadened dimensions of the EDP manager's job. However, in most cases, the way in which the man himself is treated does not reflect much real enlightenment.

MANAGE AN EDP CHIEF FAIRLY

The chances are the EDP manager in a given company does not have all the skills he could use, but let us assume that he has the potential to acquire them. Top management is responsible for providing him with the guidance and opportunities for developing them. Short executive training

EXHIBIT I

The Skills of
the EDP Manager

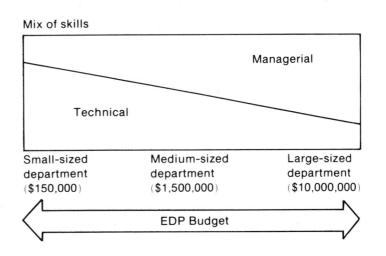

programs are one way of doing this, and there are other formal devices that can be used.

It is equally or more important, however, to recognize the true complexity of the task that has been assigned to him and to treat him with understanding and forbearance. In practice this may be difficult to do, since the very novelty fo the field guarantees mistakes and errors in judgment, and his contingency planning cannot be perfect. Still, top management has a responsibility to treat the EDP manager as a permanent, bona fide member of the management group, to evaluate his performance properly, and to provide him with a career path should his performance be good.

Don't Use Him as a Scapegoat

Senior management has a tendency to treat the EDP manager as an expendable scapegoat, to be sacrificed when computer operations go wrong. Part of the difficulty here is that computers have been consistently oversold to senior management. The more advanced computer applications that have been huckstered to business require a good deal of dense systems analysis and programming before they can be used, and these tasks must be done by people. Deficiencies in either the analysis or programming are almost inevitable; they appear in strange ways, and they often appear at very inconvenient times. Classic examples have been rapidly publicized:

- NASA was forced to abort a multimillion dollar rocket because a hyphen was left out of a program.

- A large aircraft manufacturer mailed a computer-printed check to a supplier for $3,000,000 instead of $3,000—and the supplier proceeded to embarass the company by coming to its sales office to purchase a commercial aircraft for cash.

Senior management naturally has a difficult time reconciling such glaring mistakes with the technical claims made for computers. Too often the conclusion is drawn that the EDP manager is incompetent; too often the search for a scapegoat for an embarrassing mistake stops with the EDP manager.

Unfortunately, this scapegoat syndrome has penetrated the more mundane areas of operations. For example, the EDP manager of a large wholesale company described the pressure of day-to-day processing operations as almost unbearable. Daily orders were completely processed on the computer, including warehouse purchasing, supplier payment, warehouse picking, and customer billing. Thousands of products (many perishable) and over 200 suppliers and customers were involved. These complex operations had evolved gradually, over a period of five years, with the result that the company had become almost exclusively dependent on the computer for processing its mainstream transactions.

However, the company had rapidly increased its sales within this period, and its senior management simply was not aware of the extent of the company's dependence on computer processing. Consequently, senior management was not sympathetic to requests for seemingly expensive backup systems. As luck would have it, the computer finally broke down for a 24-hour period, disrupting large segments of company activity. Senior management's reaction was to fire the EDP manager and hire another, whom it directed to make the thing work.

The new EDP manager has been no more successful than his predecessor in communicating to senior management the need for adequate backup. He is now waiting for the inevitable major disruption in computer processing that will lead to the loss of his own job. I have no evidence to prove the point, but I suspect that the expectation of being made a scapegoat by an ill-informed senior management does nothing to improve this man's morale or effectiveness.

I do not mean to imply by this example that an EDP manager cannot make a mistake for which he should be fired. He can, obviously. But when firing is in question, senior management should search the facts to see where the responsibility for the snafu really lies. It may lie with senior management itself.

Evaluate Him Properly

As in other service functions, the performance of the EDP function is extremely difficult to evaluate. In evaluating the EDP manager, senior management must ask itself this question: Has he developed the "right" set of computer-based applications—the applications that will best help the company reach its objectives?

Unfortunately, there is no straightforward way to answer this question; and all too often the EDP manager's performance is routinely judged on quantitative measures (budget variances) and general efficiency measures. These measures poorly reflect the important performance characteristics of the EDP manager. Budget targets measure only cost inputs, and the departmental unit in this case is not very meaningful.

Instead, senior management should make itself aware of the potential uses of its computer resource in the company. The uses should correspond to the important aspects of the business and be somewhat aligned with competitors' uses of the computer. Given this framework, senior management will be better able to judge whether the right applications have been developed and the most lucrative opportunities for computer processing have been pursued.

The evaluation question, of course, is a highly subjective one. Further, it is ordinarily more than one senior manager can do to reconcile the needs of the business with the feasibility and cost effectiveness of computer processing. Hence the preferred evaluation strategy is to work through a standing, involved, senior-management steering committee that closely interacts with the EDP manager.

Unfortunately, this strategy is too seldom used. In many cases senior managers continually spin their wheels trying to make sense out of quantitative performance measures. The company's only hope in such cases is that the EDP manager will take the initiatives necessary to ensure that his department is responsive to the needs of the business.

The Consultant Syndrome: A more and more popular approach is to call in a consultant to assess the effectiveness of the EDP department. Typically, the consultant analyzes the business and its competitive environment, interviews the EDP users, and makes a report on the effectiveness of the EDP manager. His report usually enumerates the areas of the business effectively being served by EDP and those not being effectively served. Naturally, this list represents his own highly subjective judgments; there is no reliable objective way to determine "effectiveness" or assess trade-offs between items in the list. Hence appropriate senior-management action on the report depends on cautious interpretation, and a real danger exists that unwise decisions may be taken on the basis of it.

A case in point is a large company where the EDP manager has built up what is considered in the industry a well-developed department. A consultant was asked to audit his activity. Both the EDP manager and the consultant have been fervently trying to obtain agreement on what measures of effectiveness should be used.

In part, this is a useful exercise, but quite unsettling for the EDP manager. He knows that this particular consulting firm offers a well-developed executive search service. Given the subjective nature of the problem of evaluation, the objectives of the consultant, and senior management's rather narrow understanding of computing and its rather narrow ability to discern the information in the consultant's report, he feels far from secure.

Ironically enough, the EDP manager views the consultant's activities as his only chance to get senior management to recognize his activities and become involved with them. He feels that a third party of recognized competence may succeed where he has not. EDP performance evaluation in this country has clearly come to a sorry pass.

Provide Him With a Career Path

By failing to provide the EDP chief with a managerial career path, top management is freely squandering its very scarce resource of managerial talent. One EDP manager remarked, with a great deal of truth: "My subordinates think of me as a manager, but my boss thinks of me as just a technician."

EDP management in most companies is a dead end largely because of its fallacious association with technical aspects of computing. Nevertheless, the demands for effective leadership in the EDP department provide an extremely valuable training ground for managers. In addition, the fact that the EDP manager must coordinate his area with virtually all the other areas of a company provides him with a near-unique opportunity to build a perspective on the operation of the business as a whole.

Another force makes it imperative that senior management reassess the EDP function as a source of material for more responsible management positions. The EDP group offers a real opportunity for rapid advancement through the lower stages, and, in this sense, the EDP group is attractive to the young, aggressive manager or MBA who wants to short-circuit the training patterns traditional in the other functional areas of a company. It all too often happens, however, that the young manager reaches the position of EDP director and discovers it to be a dead end. Frustration and a job change generally follow.

Top management cannot afford to ignore EDP management as a valuable source for senior managers. Equally, to obtain properly qualified people for the EDP management job, companies must offer a pathway for advancement beyond the department.

HIS ROLE AS CHANGE AGENT

Just as there is confusion as to what senior management's role in EDP should be, there is also confusion as to what the EDP manager's responsibilities should be.

The EDP manager has a greater responsibility than is generally realized by either senior management or the EDP manager himself. He is responsible for *effecting organizational change*, through providing computer services to assist the operations and decision-making activities of the company. Much more is involved here than just an efficient computer operation; the manager must communicate with and coordinate the users and potential users of computer services in marketing, manufacturing, and other functional areas.

In essence, his job is to invest computer resources (systems analysts, programmers, and computer time) in various applications. As the ouput from these applications is used in the operations and decision-making activities of the organization, the company receives a return on the manager's investment of computer resources. His investment in developing computer applications can be thought of as a portfolio of computer applications. The EDP manager's prime responsibility is, of course, to build a portfolio that maximizes this return.

His Portfolio of Applications

In managing his portfolio, the chief of the EDP must continually eliminate marginal applications. However, his major contribution is made through his decisions to allocate resources to the development of certain new applications and to the redesign and integration of old applications.

As in financial portfolio management, the time dimension of the returns of the various applications is important. Some applications pay back rapidly, others more slowly. Also, each bears a certain level of risk; some will not pay back as expected, and others will incur unexpected losses. Identifying needs for services in the company, judging feasibility, and trading off applications until a decent portfolio takes shape is not a simple procedure.

It is important that senior management understand the process of identifying new investment alternatives. First, each company can be thought of as having a unique set of opportunities for effectively using the computer. The nature of the opportunities depends on such factors as the size of the company, its industry, its products, the nature of the value-added processes, and the various managers' attitudes toward use of the computer.

In general, the opportunities themselves are of two kinds:

1. To process data for operations (for example, order entry and billing) and provide computer-based reports for decision making (for example, sales reports).

2. To automate decision making (for example, using an economic order quantity decision rule when replenishing inventory).

A map like the one in *Exhibit II*, which shows where these two kinds of opportunities are likely to be found, is a good structure with which to begin the search for desirable applications.

The triangle in this exhibit reflects a hierarchical organization with three levels—senior management, middle management, and operations. Within each level there are three different areas management ought to analyze: an area where computer applications are infeasible or uneconomical; an area where it is advantageous to use the computer for operations processing and generating reports for decision making; and an area where it is advantageous to use the computer for automation. Of course, the map of any given company's opportunities is likely to be more complex than this simplified diagram indicates, but the basic layout is

EXHIBIT II

Basic Map of Opportunities for
EDP Applications

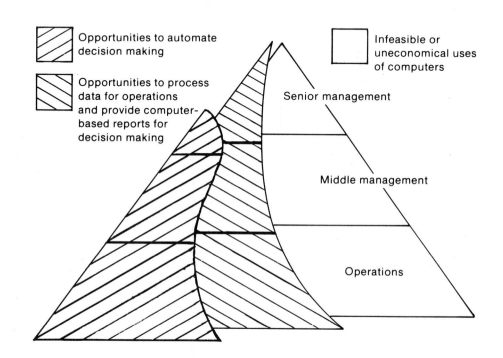

generally valid. Once a company's opportunities have been mapped, the next step is to compare the current uses of the computer with the set of possible applications.

The gap between uses and opportunities for use provide the foci for further investigation. At the lower levels, applications will characteristically be automation of highly structured clerical operation systems; these are low risk and relatively low return. At the higher levels, the applications will usually be more sophisticated, with higher risk and potentially higher return.

A balanced portfolio will include both. The usual pattern is to implement lower-level systems first, since the risks are low and the returns are more certain. From this base one can tackle the more difficult systems—for example, information systems for middle managers—and the portfolio will take form.

Although these analyses can be described fairly easily, they are not easy to carry out; nor are the trade-offs between possible applications easy to make. Most senior managers are quite unaware of the difficulty of the decisions the EDP manager must make when he designs a portfolio, and if they are aware of the portfolio at all, they tend to judge it only by its "success." Unfortunately, "success" here is not a clear-cut criterion, by any means.

THE CRITERION OF HIS SUCCESS

High returns from any computer application in the portfolio only result if an organizational change has been successfully consummated. Four major interacting variables are involved: task, structural, human, and technological.[1] The EDP manager initiates an organizational change by directly influencing the technological variable—the application of computer services. He influences the others only indirectly. He must work with users to ensure that the other variables are managed properly:

- Where tasks are concerned, new ones may be required and old ones may have to be eliminated.

- Where structure is concerned, communication networks may have to be altered and decision-making centers may need to be changed.

- Where human variables are concerned, the skills, attitudes, and activities of personnel may have to be altered. This process is complex.

Organizational change of this kind is successfully consummated by initiating the technological change and then orchestrating the structural, task, and human variables so that the change is lasting and really becomes a

---

[1] See Harold J. Leavitt, "*Applied Organizational Change in Industry: Structural, Technological, and Humanistic Approaches,*" in Handbook of Organizations, edited by James G. March (Chicago, Rand McNally & Company, 1965), p. 1144.

more effective and efficient way of realizing organizational goals than the process that has been replaced.

Here are three cases that illustrate the role and responsibility of the EDP manager in consummating organizational change. Unfortunately, as the reader will see, each resulted in a termination. Each has a lesson to teach, however, about the strategic constraints on the amount of change an EDP manager can inaugurate in a given time. Each also offers a lesson on the management of the EDP manager.

A Turnaround Manager

Many companies allow their computer systems to evolve with little managerial direction. Eventually, a crisis, such as an unacceptably increasing computer budget, an unfavorable management audit, or an economic downturn, spurs top management to action. One common response is to bring in a new manager and centralize EDP. The case of a large electronics company is representative of the situation in which an EDP manager is brought in to straighten out such an operation and subsequently loses his job.

In 1968 this electronics company was spending abut $6 million for computing. About $4 million of the total was being spent outside for computer time and programming. Each of the plant managers acquired his own computing; some acquired and ran their own computers, while others contracted with outside firms. Since the plants were involved in similar activities, there was a great deal of redundancy in applications.

At the same time, applications development was slow and uncertain. One of the larger plants had tried unsuccessfully for several years to develop a computer-based materials management system. The lack of such a system was jeopardizing the award of future government contracts, on which the plant was heavily dependent.

The general manager brought in a consultant to evaluate the company's EDP activity and to recommend a course of action. The general manager reacted favorably to the consultant's recommendations—in fact, he hired him to implement them. In the space of four years, the new manager centralized budgetary and administrative control for EDP, eliminated in-plant computers (except for terminal mode operations) in lieu of a large central computer, brought all systems analysts and programmers into a central facility, initiated centralized system design, set up a charge-out system for allocating EDP costs to users, and developed a five-year EDP plan.

At the end of this period, although sales had doubled, EDP expenditures dropped from $6,000,000 to $4,500,000, with only $500,000 being spent for outside computer services. In addition, the materials management system was developed for the one plant, and implementation was planned for the other plants in the near future. In 1972, the EDP manager lost his job.

Diagnosis. The amount of organizational change this EDP manager initiated by shifting from a decentralized to a centralized strategy is simply staggering. In making the change, however, he put into place only the bare essentials needed for administration—his chargeout system, for example, was cumbrous and rather ill-conceived.

He also failed to follow through on the structural, task, and human variables his moves were affecting. In several instances, severe confusion arose on how new systems were to function, and user anxiety ran high. He did not see to it that plant personnel were intimately involved in the planning process for the technological changes; he preferred to view them as natural resisters or enemies of his "new way," and they, accordingly, rose to the occasion. In addition, he made invalid assumptions about the skills of the users in operating the new systems. Intense training systems were installed, but somewhat late.

In short, this manager had initiated a lot of computer applications, but he had not properly engineered the other variables involved. As a result, only a few of the applications were actually used. For example, the materials management system met with great user resistance, and the returns were not forthcoming as planned. In addition, this resistance seems irreversible, and no end to the problem is in sight.

On the surface, however, the statistics appear to show that the manager has been effective: the EDP budget has been reduced and needed systems developed. A deeper analysis indicates that he has only affected the input or cost side and has not been able to consummate the organizational changes which would result in full returns. Had senior management been tracking the situation properly, however, the firing might have been avoided.

An Overinvested Manager

In 1965, the EDP manager of a trucking company with sales of $40,000,000 was given the go-ahead to develop a real-time, computer-based system for improved freight control and operations planning. Development cost was estimated at $289,000, and the continuing computer costs were estimated at $420,000 annually. The system was to be operational by March 1968.

By late 1967, the design was complete and programming had begun. In April 1968, the design was deemed inadequate and a larger computer was acquired. On July 1, 1969, an even more expanded computer design was used for initial operational testing. A substantial number of problems were uncovered, and the manager requested additional funds for systems development. He also submitted a revised cost figure: the system would now run about $826,000 plus additional annual personnel costs of about $318,000.

In November 1969, the company decided to discard the project completely. The concept was still considered sound, and, despite problems, the preliminary results looked promising—the system would probably have met its original objectives. However, the costs simply got out of hand.

Diagnosis. A couple of problems are involved here. First, the manager took on the development of a system that had too long a time horizon before returns would be realized. The project had a potentially high payoff, but it also had too high a risk for the company to bear for an extended period.

Second, the EDP manager did a very poor job in estimating the magnitude of the system changes and the organizational changes involved. Although he was reasonably proficient in managing the organizational change in terms of constructively influencing the task, structural, and human variables, he simply underestimated the complexities of the technological unknowns of the project. As these were successively uncovered, their solutions had multiple impacts on the rest of the project.

As matters turned out, then, this manager did not have the capacity to consummate the organizational change he had inaugurated by this system, and the system was too ambitious and impacted on too many areas of the business at once to be successful. If senior management had audited the project more effectively, it might have been able to redirect the manager and extricate him from his all-the-eggs-in-one-basket position.

A Manager in Balance

What happens when the EDP manager has completed the major systems needed by the company and desired by top management? When this stage is reached, a major change in the skill mix of the computer organizations is required, from systems development to efficient systems operation.

The case of a medium-sized wholesale/retail company illustrates this situation. The company operated in a highly competitive environment with many low-margin products. Its strategy for using computers was to wait until the technology looked promising and had been proved out by a major competitor. The company's EDP manager proficiently executed this strategy, and in 1972 effective computer applications were in place in all the major functional areas of the business. In 1972 he was initiating feasibility studies in advanced areas. Then he left the company, abandoning what looked, to an outsider, like a golden opportunity for development of higher-level systems.

Diagnosis. While the EDP manager was planning to forge ahead with the same level of effort as in the past, top management was reluctant to do so and expressed a desire to cut back the computer organization. Top management's position was that the EDP manager had effectively exploited the use of the computer in the business, and further investment opportunities for computer applications were simply too risky. This meant a reduction in the computer organization. The reduction was not acceptable to the manager; further investment of the magnitude of previous years was not acceptable to senior management. A stalemate resulted. Since no career path was open, the manager left.

Senior management is privileged to set limits to its EDP activities; no one would argue with that. However, this company allowed a capable manager to leave without so much as a thought whether he might still be valuable in some more advanced capacity.

When a company evaluates its EDP manager, then, it should be attentive to the circumstances of "success" and "failure." Did he succeed or fail because of constraints within his control? Or were they outside his control? How could senior management have improved his chances of success? Should it have monitored his portfolio more astutely? And what will success mean—organizationally, and to the manager himself?

POINTS TO REMEMBER

Undoubtedly, many EDP managers will continue to be fired or separated from organizations by mutual consent in situations similar to the ones I have described. Yet such firings and separations are not solutions; they are symptoms of serious mismanagement. To resolve the problem of mismanagement, it is incumbent on senior management to better understand the EDP management challenge and create an organizational climate in which the changes the EDP manager must initiate can be made properly. It is incumbent on the manager, for his part, to take a larger and more "managerial" view of his job.

For the EDP Manager

The EDP manager is a focal point for change in the organization. For all practical purposes, computer technology progresses unconstrained by considerations of how it will be used by organizations. The EDP manager's role is thus one of linking the efficiency of new computer technology with the needs of the organization. His effectiveness is determined by how well he can bring about organizational changes suggsted by advancing technology—the knowledge of advancing technology being only one small part of his job.

Hence the most important point for the EDP manager to recognize is that his prime responsibility is to consummate the organizational changes that are necessary if computer applications are to be used. The computer activity is a service function. If the service is not used, nothing is gained.

He must also work toward a balanced portfolio of computer applications. This means maintaining dialogues with functional management and performing analyses to ensure that the right systems for the company are being pursued, as well as assessing the company's general needs. The important points here are that the processing needs of the organization be viewed as a whole, and that individual applications in his portfolio make good investment sense, given the company's current operating environment and computer experience.

For Top Management

Generally, the movement from a development stage to an operation stage is simply not fully recognized either by top management or by the EDP manager. The evolution is natural, however, and should be acommodated by a career pattern for the EDP manager that involves increased responsibilities. It is entirely to senior management's advantage to create such a path.

In some companies the first step has already been taken; namely, increasing the responsibilities of the managers and recognizing them by titles such as vice president of administrative services or technical services. The second step is to seriously consider the EDP manager as a candidate for other senior executive positions. It is important to recognize that the EDP manager is a manager, not a technician, and that his particular job challenges and attracts a growing number of bright, young, aggressive managers.

Senior management should also relate to the EDP manager as a manager, not as a computer technician. The competence of the manager largely focuses on his leadership skills. Internally, he must manage subordinates and tasks with a wide range of characteristics. Externally, he must effectively coordinate his activities with other managers' to integrate his technology with their activities. The demand for leadership skills is high. Thus he should be selected on the basis of his managerial skills, and thereafter treated as a manager.

There are two additional points for top management to bear in mind. First, it is unfair to hold the EDP manager accountable for reasonable technological risks involved in using computers. Some disruptions and mistakes are legitimately the result of poor controls at the top-management level or the lack of adequate backup facilities. Other incidents are the result of poor controls at the top-management level or the lack of adequate backup facilities. Other incidents are the result of reasonable technical risks that either cost too much to insure against or are inherent in advanced technology. When a disruption or mistake occurs, it should be traced to its origin. If the EDP manager ought to have devised controls to prevent the error, he obviously should be held accountable; otherwise, the need is for senior management to understand the nature of the technical risks and the practical limits of controls.

Second, senior management cannot legitimately delegate the performance evaluation of the EDP manager. The fact that no straightforward performance measures exist for determining the effectiveness of the EDP department may be unsettling, but a consultant's subjectivity is a poor substitute for senior management's subjectivity. This is not to say that an independent management audit of the EDP function cannot be useful; it is frequently helpful in estimating efficiency and identifying major gaps in service.

Still, determining the effectiveness of the company's EDP department is dependent on a good understanding of the business. Senior management obviously has this understanding, and it is important that it develops an awareness of the potential for using computing in the company by working directly with the EDP manager. If senior management studies and monitors his plans, feasibility studies, and project-management systems, it will be able to form an excellent estimate of his effectiveness.

CONCLUSION

To view the EDP manager's activities solely in terms of engineering computer technology is a narrow and grossly inadequate view in the environment of the 1970s. Yet this narrow view is all too typical of senior managements. The result is costly—the computer resource is not used effectively and scarce managerial talent is squandered.

To end this waste, senior management and EDP management must jointly reassess the function and focus on the management dimensions of the computer resource. Above all, it is important to recognize that each computer application is only part of a broad program of organizational change that must be brought about before any benefits can accrue from it to the company.

22

Business Needs a New Breed of EDP Manager*

RICHARD L. NOLAN

Top management has never been totally comfortable with the EDP manager. And it is fair to say that the EDP manager has not always completely understood the rationale for top management's actions in regard to EDP.

There are many subtle indications that the relationship between these two groups is less than satisfactory. These indications, to name but a few, include: arbitrarily set budget levels, poorly attended and unproductive steering committee meetings, and jargon-ridden justifications for new computer-based systems instead of explanations presented in language understandable to all at the senior management level.

Not so subtle is the continuing high attrition rate among those who hold top EDP spots. I have estimated that annual EDP management turnover in 1972 was from 40% to 50%.[1] In a more recent 12 month period, 25% to 35% of the EDP managers in more than 450 companies were replaced, according to a survey conducted by a major vendor of computer hardware and software in 1975. These rates compared to 10% to 15% turnover rates among other senior managers.

Four years ago I attributed the high turnover rate among EDP managers to rapid growth of electronic data processing throughout the 1960s. This growth led to radical changes in leadership styles, ranging

[1]Richard L. Nolan, "*Plight of the EDP Manager,*" HBR May-June 1973, p. 143.

from technocrats to entrepreneurs to turnaround managers.[2] Under those circumstances, and given the fact that few individuals are able to change drastically their management styles, it was not surprising that many organizations had to go through so many managers.

But for most medium and large organizations, those circumstances no longer apply. Most have come to accept the function as a more mature, integral, and important part of their business. It is my impression, however, that even within these companies the relationship between top and EDP managers continues to be an uneasy one. For example, the CEO of a major U.S. company that is a sophisticated user of computer technology told me the following:

> "In the last seven years, I have hired and fired three EDP managers. Two years ago, I centralized and grafted our DP activities onto the corporate structure. This is not working out. I don't see an end in sight to the turmoil involved in providing for the needed EDP leadership."

At about the same time, the most recent EDP manager of the company said:

> "As a professional DP manager, I have accepted an average tenure of three years in my job, with some jobs lasting as long as seven years. I'm not complaining because my salary increases have averaged more than 20% per year, and I find the challenge of the technology and its management an unbelievable turn on."

I believe that comments such as these, high turnover rates, and unstable patterns in working relationships all point to a general problem: *"fitting" an appropriate EDP management style with the needs of top management.*

To determine better what "fit" exists at present and to discern how it might be improved, I first interviewed a group of EDP managers. All were associated with medium to large companies that had been using computers for more than 12 years. In general, the managers were technically and managerially competent; as far as I could tell, all of them had established an accepted position of leadership over their company's EDP activities. I asked them how they approached five key tasks:

- organization

- planning and management control

- project selection

---

[2]These leadership styles roughly correspond to management of EDP stages I, II, and III, see Cyrus Gibson and Richard L. Nolan, *"Managing the Four Stages of EDP Growth,"* HBR January-February 1974, p. 76.

- leadership

- future opportunities

Two general styles emerged from the interviews. In order to clarify the nature of these two styles, I next conducted more in-depth interviews with two of the managers who seemed to best typify the two styles. One I call the "architect" management style, and the second I call the "insider" management style.

The architect generally likes to draw a sharp line between technical data processing responsibilities and nontechnical user responsibilities. He manifests the delineation through a highly defined organizational structure and sophisticated control systems. By contrast, the insider purposely keeps the delineation between technical and user responsibilities "fuzzy." The insider attempts to infiltrate user areas with technical personnel, and his control systems are less developed than those of the architect. The accompanying exhibit on page 353 highlights the style contrasts of the two managers for each of the five tasks we discussed in our interviews.

Finally, I obtained independent comments from a group of "experts" (Herbert Halbrecht, President of Halbrecht Associates, Inc; George B. Rockwell, Former Vice Chairman of the Boad, State Street of Boston Financial Corporation; Jules Silbert, Senior Vice President Lane Bryant, Inc and Chief Executive Officer Special Size Division; and Eric A. Weiss, Director of Planning, Sun Oil Services Corporation) on the appropriateness of these two styles to the needs of modern organizations.

What follows are excerpts from my interviews and the experts' comments regarding each task. I shall then draw some conclusions concerning the task of management that the EDP function has now come to require.

ORGANIZATIONAL STRUCTURE PREFERRED

In our conversations together, the architect and the insider both agreed that the way in which an organization structures its EDP activities depends on its particular characteristics.

Although their corporate managements had centralized EDP activities for budgetary control reasons, each manager had tailored the centralized structure to his own liking and questioned the effectiveness of the other's tailored organization.

Pricing Mechanism for Supply and Demand

The architect had set up profit centers for operations, time-sharing services, programming, and systems design. His rationale for doing so was as follows:

"We established an information systems division and a market price mechanism for information services to better allocate the $30 million that the company spends on information processing resources.

"In order to optimally allocate information resources, you need two things. You first need a market-oriented pricing mechanism for the technology, particularly where there are economies of scale. Second, you need a formal sharpening of the procurement and acquisition process. In other words, you have to differentiate between the demand and the supply function.

"The demand function is diffused throughout the entire organization, and we have decentralized systems analysts so that users can effectively trade off capital equipment, more clerks, more manual systems, outside consultants, outside time-sharing services, software packages, and whatever else might help them achieve their objectives with our information services. The demand is manifested through the price, and we supply to meet the demand.

"Before, our systems people were largely responsible for both demand and supply. The whole ethic of the computer profession was driving us to more and more hardware and to a technical orientation to problems.

"The reorganization perforated this bond between supply and demand. Now we have technical systems people worrying about problems, and users worrying about the solutions to the problems."

Profit Centers Confusing

The insider had a much less delineated structure than the architect's. He had placed both programmers and systems analysts into the users' departments and allocated virtually all EDP costs to those departments. He explained how his structure worked:

"Profit-center organization for my management services division, or for any information systems division, is a serious mistake. We don't make any profit. We only incur costs: there is only so much profit to go around, and all we would do is confuse senior managers in their attempt to measure our performance.

"I have had less than two hours with my CEO in the last year and only a little more time with the executive vice president that I report to. I am senior management, and the CEO leaves management of management services to me. My superiors hold me responsible for a budget that doesn't grow faster than sales and for a head count.

"Every year for the last five years, I have been able to charge my total $10 million budget to users, except for a 'residue' of $250,000 to $400,000, which goes directly into corporate overhead. My central systems analysts and programmers are priced at $18 an hour, which is more than competitive.

"Although it is hard to get an accurate measure, I believe that my services cost less than those available from outside vendors. Users, however, are prohibited from going outside."

Comment on Organization

All four commentators concur with the interviewees that it is important to understand a particular company and its management in assessing EDP management style. They all comment as well on the importance of clearly articulating and understanding the objective of the data processing department. Problems don't seem to arise in understanding the concepts but in implementing them. Especially troublesome is establishing performance evaluation guidelines and process for the organization's EDP manager.

Measurement of Effectiveness.   For example, Halbrecht states that in his work with EDP managers, "the most disquieting thing to EDP managers is recognition that there is no universal way for them or their bosses to measure their effectiveness. Remember that almost every information systems manager has substantial analytical background and naturally wants some kind of a quantitative or semi-quantitative measure of his effectiveness. At the same time, most of them recognize that effectiveness at their level is really more important than the efficiency of the EDP budget, per se."

Silbert comments:

> "The objective of any EDP organization, as I see it, is to develop and implement systems that will help the company improve its profitability, its growth posture, and various other factors which any individual company sees as important to its corporate 'health.'
>
> "The architect's organization seems to concentrate more on improving the process of allocating expenses than on addressing itself to fulfilling this prime object. On the other hand, I like the idea of decentralizing the systems analysts; it provides the significant advantage of 'living with' the user and achieving a familiarity with user problems and needs.
>
> "The insider's cost-center organization in principle recognizes that its sole purpose is to design and run systems which will meet the company's needs (as opposed to running a profitable 'service bureau' which would appear to be the architect's purpose). It's the new system that should produce the profit, not the process of designing the system."

The insider's view of profit-center organizations strikes Weiss as naive:

> "[The insider] makes the remark, 'All we would do is confuse senior management.' Concern that senior managers will become confused and that they need to be protected from that terrible state is characteristic of technicians in management positions. If senior managers are not accustomed to the profit-center situation in other parts of the organization, they probably will be confused. If they are accustomed to it, it will be difficult to confuse them.
>
> "The insider goes on to remark that he had 'less than two hours with my CEO in the last year and only a little more time with the executive vice president that I report to.' Here we identify a more serious problem: the parent organization itself is allowing the insider to function without guidance or concern. In this case, he is senior management, as he says, but by default. The parent organization apparently considers the function to

be of such little significance as to require no attention. The insider remarks that he is held responsible for a budget and head count but makes no remark abut being held responsible for benefits or anything relating to corporate profit. This is an organizational flaw that lies outside the EDP department."

The insider's limited interaction with his CEO disturbs Halbrecht even more than it does Weiss: "How any individual, regardless of his title, who acknowledges that he doesn't get more than two hours with his president, can say 'I am senior management,' escapes me. An even more basic question is whether top management really considers EDP important. The small amount of time given to EDP managers in most companies makes the CEO's assertion that EDP is truly important to him suspect."

Question of Centralization. A more fundamental issue of organization is the balance between EDP centralization and decentralization. Although the balance is not clear, advances in technology (for example, minicomputers[3]) and other factors have reduced the potency of earlier economies-of-scale arguments for centralization and increased the importance of such considerations as involving users in system design activities.

Rockwell remarks:

"In terms of organization, I tend more to the architect's side. Data processing should have an identifiable structure, should be centralized, and should have a mechanism by which users are billed for the service they receive. A good pricing mechanism [also helps users in turn] to price their services appropriately to customers of the organization. A less delineated organization with programmer analysts spread across the organization prevents top management from deciding where to place resources (for instance deciding whether to allocate to areas with the highest profit return to the company rather than parcelling out to everybody so that each has some share).

"I do not agree with the architect that users can effectively analyze the trade-offs involved for capital equipment, more clerks, more manual systems, or outside time sharing. This must be done in conjunction with the data processing department. I don't believe users have the knowledge. Furthermore, as a general rule of thumb, users should concentrate on selling and product innovation in their area, rather than on the technicalities of the data processing. They should, however, be able to evaluate the service they receive from data processing in support of their product line."

PLANNING AND MANAGEMENT CONTROL

In their planning, both EDP managers by and large emphasized hardware

---

[3]For a discussion on how minicomputer technology is realigning the balance between centralization and decentralization, see Gerald J. Burnett and Richard L. Nolan, "At Last, Major Roles for Minicomputers," HBR May-June 1975, p. 148.

with an eye to implicit budget ceilings. Their management control systems centered on charges to users for services.

The Architect: Arm's-Length Operations

"We have never had a senior management steering committee review my budget and projects because I think that steering committees are a waste of time.

"Instead, I work with my managers on profit targets for their departments. I review these, target a total profit for the information systems division, and then negotiate with my CEO and financial vice president. This process makes the information systems division an arm's-length business operation as much as is possible.

"If users don't like my prices or service, they can go outside. If this happens to any great extent, I am put in a tough capacity position. That is, because I have a high fixed cost resource, I not only must cover costs, but must also remain competitive with outside suppliers. Consequently, I closely monitor market share for all my major resources such as batch computing, time-sharing, and programming. I also have a comprehensive reporting system that allows me to keep track of such variables as productive time on the computers, programming cost and schedules, and profit-target attainment.

"Planning is now decentralized to the user. My technical people try to sell new services, and users buy them if they help solve their business problems. I depend on my managers to tell me what users are thinking about so that I can plan for the information resources that they will require."

The Insider: Industry Comparisons

"Management control is a particularly difficult problem. First, I try to compare my level of expenditures with the industry average. The industry average is about 1% of sales; I am spending about three-fourths of 1%. I know what my counterparts are doing in similar companies, and we seem to have roughly the same types of applications. In the programming and operations area, I have a very good manager of our data center, and he has built an excellent staff around him.

"We discovered four general types of systems in our environment: plant, operational planning, customer orders, and financial. After analyzing how to improve and integrate these four types of systems, we concluded that our efforts along these lines could have a dramatic impact on the company's bottom line. On investigating how to do this, we drew a wide consensus that data-base technology was the key. Accordingly, we have acquired a data-base package, and have recently brought up a customer order system, as the first installment in our grand scheme."

Comments on Planning and Control

Rockwell thinks that "the insider misses the boat on management control. He is worried about his comparisons, which are worth including but should not be the be-all and end-all. Basically, he is saying, 'I have a great bunch of guys, I have an excellent staff, and we have these types of systems, and that's the way we run.' This has nothing to do with planning and management control, especially if you compare the insider's system to the architect's."

Weiss also feels that industry averages are weak measures.

> "What goes into these general industry averages is very loose," he says, "so loose that the difference between 1% and three-fourths of 1% to which the insider refers is not at all meaningful. The insider discusses the types of systems he works on. This identification is apparently all done in his organization with no participation by the user."

Silbert, however, supports the insider's approach in principle. He states:

> "Although appetizing in theory, the architect's decentralized, 'go-outside-if-you-wish' style of systems development carries with it an absence of the team spirit so essential to success in the EDP-user relationship. It also might prove wasteful because of the staff needed to sell new services and computer applications. Would this waste put the company in a noncompetitive position when compared with companies that do not require these internal sales staffs?

Effect of Style on
Management Tasks

Management tasks	EDP management styles	
	Architect	Insider
Organization	Divisionalized profit center	Centralized corporate cost center
Planning and management control	Decentralized to user: the user budgets for EDP; each EDP group has a profit plan.	Centralized to EDP group: the EDP manager budgets for EDP.
Project selection	Decentralized to user through charge out and budget justification.	Centralized to user steering group and EDP staff.
Leadership*	Boss-centered: the boss makes a decision and announces it.	Subordinate-centered: the boss permits subordinates to function within defined limits.
Perception of future opportunities	Word-processing clerical systems — reduce company overhead.	Improve planning and management decision-making processes.

*Boss-centered leadership and subordinate-centered leadership are defined by Robert Tannenbaum and Warren H. Schmidt in *"How to Choose a Leadership Pattern,"* HBR March-April 1958, p. 95. The two approaches to leadership represent the extremes of a continuum defined by two variables: (1) use of authority by the manager, and (2) areas of freedom for subordinates.

"A centralized 'insider' approach, utilizing an active steering committee (in contrast to the horror described by the insider) can help control planning and dollars spent. A comparison of costs with 'outside' quotes can be a useful check on the efficiency of the EDP group. Stringent cost justification for each proposed application and periodic audits by an outside firm are other methods which might be used to direct planning and help assure a better degree of control over costs."

PROJECT SELECTION

Both the architect and the insider viewed project selection as the key in maintaining an effective EDP activity as well as keeping bounds on efficiency.

Their approaches, again, were markedly different. The architect greatly relied on the user to justify budget funds for the applications required. The insider relied on advice from both his own staff and a steering committee.

The Architect: Neutrality and Manageable Bites

"A key aim of our current organization structure has been to remove the historical bias favoring financial systems. The facts show that 70% of most companies' systems are financial systems. As long as an information systems group reports to finance, this bias is perpetuated and motivates other functional areas to create their own information systems capability.

"By creating a neutral information systems division where everyone's dollar is the same, we have eliminated a most troublesome aspect in project selection. We plan for and manage the supply to best serve the demand manifested by users' dollars.

"The big problem with most information services divisions that have failed is that they eliminated one monopoly and created another. When we create an information services 'utility,' you must be sure that it is more than a regulated utility: it must also be a competitive utility, so that the CEO has a warm, woolly feeling of control, knowing that management can turn the thing off anytime it wants.

"Another important aspect of our project selection, which has resulted from bitter experience, is that we only bid small bites, projects from $5,000 to $25,000. I feel that when you really get into the whole question of technology, nobody knows how to manage the project. Nobody. So, basically, we and the user approach projects one step at a time, agreeing on a finite commitment of resources, a schedule, and an identifiable output.

The Insider: More Involvement and Long-Term Systems

Our steering committee is a necessary mechanism, but meetings have been poorly attended and frustrating. However, in recent budget reviews, divisional presidents have been asked some questions about their systems that they couldn't answer. Consequently, I have been better received by them, and the steering committee attendance is getting better. I can also see interest increasing and more involvement in helping us to determine what systems we should be working on.

"Central to project selection is our data-base project. When I acquired a data-base package in 1970, it was promptly cut out when we had a massive staff reduction. I will tell you that I kept it going right through with slack that I manufactured. In early 1974, the customer order inventory came up and is now a production system.

"For other projects, we work with the users to determine what their savings might be and to develop a proposal. I review these proposals on the basis of the company's long-term strategy, and their long-term implications for the user. As a basic principle, I don't believe in building systems that will only last for a year."

Comments on Project Selection

Some of the commentators question the wisdom of the architect's seeming reluctance to bid on large projects, not because they are inherently bad for the corporation, but apparently because he will have a more difficult time estimating. Second, it appears he will do work for anyone who pays, regardless of the project. Some believe that these are both cop-outs on tough managerial problems.

Silbert sees other dangers:

"I cannot see how the decentralized decisions on project selection can take into account overall corporate priorities. There are distinct dangers in everyone's going his own way. Duplication of efforts is one. Another is that you lose the advantage of developing a better system that would, with a bit of extra effort, provide an additional benefit which may not be recognized if each division acts on its own.

"Beyond the desirability of having corporate control of new project selection, however, I believe it is essential that each division be given the greatest possible responsibility for its own project selection. This should then be subject to a corporate level review, the objective being to maximize the benefits of all systems development ativities within the company.

"The insider's arrangement, with a top-management-involved steering committee, could be an effective means for accomplishing this control; the danger with his arrangement is that too much control is placed in one person's hands. Consider the insider's statement: 'I review these proposals on the basis of the long-term strategy of the company. . . .' "

Weiss notes, "The description of the insider's data-base package—which apparently continued for three years before being put into a production system—is indicative of an immature organization. The insider again emphasizes the fact that he is the person who reviews the user's savings and compares it with the long-term strategy of the company and the long-term implications to the user. These would seem to be user department functions."

LEADERSHIP

Virtually all executives would agree that no matter how intangible the attributes of leadership, it is critical in choosing and developing a management team. An important leadership variable is the degree of authority used by a manager and the amount of freedom available to subordinates in reaching key decisions. Of course, neither extreme is absolute, and both have their limitations.[4]

So far, the comments of the EDP managers have given us some idea of their leadership styles; they also have stated their beliefs about leadership.

The Architect: Creativity and Innovation

"Appropriate leadership is analogous to creating a culture. The information systems function is like a biosymbiotic environment. Just having a fertilized egg in a mother's body doesn't give you a baby. Many hormones must come in at the right time. It's a very complex process.

"Managing the information systems division is dependent on creatively applying the management tools and mechanisms that are available, and on innovating new ones where the existing ones are deficient."

The Insider: Trust in Professional Staff

"My organization is a bit ambiguous. We have some systems analysts and programmers embedded into the division. Some division presidents prefer it this way; others don't want the responsibility. I operate out of our corporate headquarters where I have a relatively small staff.

"I have a good manager at our data center and depend upon him and his staff for running the technical side of our function. As a matter of fact, my success is highly dependent on and interwoven with the trust that my staff is doing the job it should be doing.

"I don't have a single professional that has been here for less than five years. This gives me a tremendous advantage, because all of our senior people know how we operate and know it from the business end, and, to some extent, from a technical point of view. Someone who does not have much sympathy with the management side of things, who is only technically proficient, would not rise very high here."

---

[4]See Robert Tannenbaum and Warren H. Schmidt, *"How to Choose a Leadership Pattern,"* HBR March-April 1958, p. 95; rerun as HBR Classic, May-June 1975, p. 162.

Comments on Leadership

Rockwell disagrees with both the architect and the insider and asserts his own ideas on leadership. He states:

> "The important thing is to have a manager who understands the company's products and the direction the corporation is going. He must be flexible so that he can change his support as the direction of the corporation changes. The good manager should not think of data processing as a technical sandbox in which to play, but as a resource which enables the company to earn a greater profit. Leadership lies in the manager's ability to effectively communicate the necessary change of direction to keep his people going technically, and yet to steer their direction so as to support the corporation.
>
> "In other words, he has to build the bridge between corporate needs and the niceties of technical development, to keep everybody on the same wave length and thinking positively, so that everyone is going in the same direction.
>
> "There is no question that there is a difference of thinking among the people who deal heavily in technology and among the managers of that technology. The manager of technology must show his leadershsip with people—get them to carry out their functions from a technical and operating standpoint and, at the same time, swing the data processing organization as the corporation changes."

Halbrecht believes that leadership problems stem from an inability to manage people. "Too many persons who are in executive capacities in planning, management science, and management information systems have the notion that being a top executive means making the 'right' decision. They talk about management decisions as being 'optimal.' These are cop-outs of very, very capable, but primarily analytically- and quantitatively-oriented people, who are not necessarily managers of people, but of things. If one were to delve deeply into their subordinate turnover and into the caliber of people that they have as subordinates, one would learn that these managers are rarely mentioned as inspirational leaders."

Silbert concurs, adding that "an effective leader is essential regardless of what type of organization is developed. Paramount to achieving success, it seems to me, is management involvement. Top management must take an active role in the selection of the EDP manager and must maintain a close working relationship with him. The hopeful result is that the EDP manager himself takes a more active interest in the total company's business and becomes an insider in a really constructive sense."

FUTURE OPPORTUNITIES

An EDP manager's perception of future opportunities is important because this is where competitive advantages as well as expensive mistakes with computer technology have been made. The architect and insider, characteristically, assess future opportunities quite differently.

The Architect: Reduction in Overhead

"I reject the whole idea that management information systems are systems support for management. I consider the major mission of our information systems division in the next decade to be to reduce the unit administrative cost, and, as our margins are squeezed, to really reduce the burgeoning overhead.

"I'm talking about 10,000 clerks, 5,000 secretaries; I'm worrying about 2,000 people just moving inventory around and picking warehouse parts. I'm talking about 200 people doing nothing but shuffling paper for personnel. I absolutely reject justification of future information systems on the basis that our planners will get smarter, or that we will gain great insight on new markets or product profitability."

The Insider: Forecast of Shortages and Market Shifts

"For the last five years, my key managers and I have really been trying to focus on what the corporation will be needing in the way of information systems in the future.

"Several years ago, I had my management science staff begin developing a pretty sophisticated forecasting capability. We are very susceptible to raw material shortages and to market shifts of end-products that our products are used in. But nobody's interested in sales forecasting today, because we can sell what we make. That worries me a great deal, because it ain't going to stay that way.

"We have carefully reviewed our production processes, our market, and our best guesses about viable long-range strategies. Forecasting plays a key role both in linking end-product relationships with our product lines and in raw material planning."

Comments on Future Opportunities

According to Weiss:

> " 'Reducing unit administrative costs,' as described by the architect, is a very limited approach to future opportunities. This is addressing the question of 'are we doing things right?' rather than 'are we doing the right things?' The architect should, from the shrewd use of information, be seeking opportunities to increase the corporate income rather than simply reducing unit administrative costs.

> "The insider, on the other hand, has focused on better information use but has selected—independent of the user, I suspect—forecasting as the area in which he is going to make money. The fact that 'nobody's interested in sales forecasting today, because we can sell what we make' should indicate to him that he chose the wrong horse. I doubt whether he has the user orientation necessary to identify money-making propositions."

Rockwell disagrees:

"I feel that both the insider's and the architect's ideas are to some extent in line with what we really think here at State Street. The area of compensation is one of ever-increasing expense and, therefore, any inroads that computer technology can make to reduce these costs, or at least hold the line, would contribute greatly to our net profit.

"It is also true that we in data processing at State Street have been focusing on the corporation's current and future needs so that the data-processing capability will be there to provide support."

Silbert believes that, to maximize future opportunities, an EDP manager needs to have "the hard-to-find combination of both technical skill and management skill. Establishing the atmosphere (that is, the organization) which would make this person an 'insider,' and making sure that management is actively involved in the EDP function are the extra ingredients required to assure effectiveness."

DIFFERENT BREED OF MANAGEMENT

The EDP function in most companies is maturing. The continued high turnover of EDP managers now results from top management's search for the right information systems manager than from indecision or ignorance about the role of a rapidly growing and constantly changing function.

This fundamental change is evident from the requests that Halbrecht has received for what he calls a "new breed" of EDP manager (see the Appendix) and from the desire for compatibility repeatedly expressed by CEOs. Silbert's comment is typical:

"Just as senior management style differs from company to company, the sale of the EDP manager differs also. It is important that the styles of the EDP manager and his corporate management are compatible and that the organization of systems development and design activities recognize the management state of development as well as the EDP state of development."

While either the architect or the insider style of management may be appropriate for a mature EDP function in a given organization, I believe that there are some conclusions we can draw from our examination of these two approaches:

● Neither a cost-center nor a profit-center structure is necessarily the "right way" to organize the EDP function. Silbert emphasizes that the structure should fit the overall organizational environment of the company. This means that a financial criterion for performance evaluation must be assessed closely within the company. For any meaningful evaluation of the EDP function and manager, top management's involvement is necessary. Halbrecht points out that, in general, top management isn't facing up to this, as indicated by the little time it spends with the EDP manager.

- A defined EDP management control system is needed in order to provide the means for performance benchmarking and tracking. Rockwell believes that working within a profit center structure is a step in the right direction. Weiss is wary about broad-brush approaches, such as superficially comparing a company's EDP expenditures with industry averages. Benchmarking and tracking are more important than absolute measures against alleged standards; there simply aren't any reliable standards yet.

- Project selection cannot be neatly disentangled from overall corporate objectives and priorities; individual users cannot have the final say on projects, nor can the EDP manager possibly make these decisions himself. Silbert points out that some mechanism such as a steering committee is necessary. He expresses this view, fully aware of how hard it is to make a top management steering committee work.

- Effective EDP management leadership balances both technical and administrative skills. Rockwell says it well: "Leadership lies in the manager's ability to effectively communicate the necessary change of direction, to keep his people going technically, and yet to steer their direction so as to support the corporation." Halbrecht identifies a most hazardous pitfall in providing effective EDP leadership: searching for "optimal" decisions, which don't exist in the first place. Instead managers should choose one course of action from available good alternatives and concentrate on making it work.

- EDP's potential is great and ranges from reducing burgeoning overhead to producing higher quality information for more profitable decision making. This spectrum of opportunities provides wide latitude for formulating an EDP strategy.

In conclusion, it is important to recognize that the information systems manager is a different breed of senior management. He adds a technical element into top management deliberations. The plain fact is that modern senior management teams are going to have to become comfortable with the technical element. This will take place in the same way that Rockwell and Silbert have become comfortable integrating the function into their organizations.

APPENDIX

The "New Breed"

More and more top managers are seeking an individual to fill their company's top EDP slot who will be a true participant in their decision-making process. This concept of participation in management is the key to the distinction between the old and the new breed, which Halbrecht defines below.

Job descriptions:
Old breed — $35,000 to $40,000
New breed — $40,000 to $60,000

The "new breed" understands and has shown that he knows how to manage management information systems efficiently, but, more importantly, how to manage them effectively.

He understands that, as an EDP manager, he is not managing technology as much as he is managing change, change of the decision-making process as well as change of the way in which a company is run.

He should be a participant in top management decisions from the outset, responsible for identifying the systems required as well as the costs of implementing these systems and their implications for the entire organization.

He of course must also be at least "snowproof" in relation to EDP technology and must ensure that his staff is abreast of the state of the art of hardware and software.

Accordingly, he must have the perception of a general manager, be ready not only to "sell" EDP, but also to develop and sell the logic and discipline of how one does business in a particular technological environment. He must be able to develop in other top executives an appreciation of the value of the systems function and a perception of the requirements for implementation.

23

Towards a Theory of Data Processing Leadership

RICHARD L. NOLAN
FREDERIC E. FINCH

Cost/performance of computers has improved six orders of magnitude in the past twenty years. This will occur again within the next twenty years. Management in general, and data processing management in particular, must ready itself for this development so as not to be piloting a biplane in the age of space exploration. To accomplish this, data processing management leadership will need to address the problems created by rapid growth.

What are these problems? As most managers know, the major one is the fact that there are different groups operating within an organization, and that the interaction between these groups is less than ideal. Data processing management operates in conjunction with other groups—namely senior management and users—in making decisions concerning the rapid growth of data processing. Each group operates out of its own power base, making management of their interdependencies critical. The organization, comprised of many players, must pull together and behave like a single unit. Naturally, as the data processing function of an organization grows, the three groups are affected in different ways and at different times.

Effective data processing leadership is dependent on each group accepting the leadership role at different stages in the growth of data processing, and sharing a common base of knowledge about how data processing should function in an organization. Accomplishing this is something different. Clearly an organization needs to have a structure or framework to embrace, support, and understand the growth and to allow it to mature properly. Evidence suggests that elements of the structure are below the level of effective perception. A native from the bushes of New Guinea, examining a telephone for the first time, would marvel at the discovery that he could hear someone at the other end. In an organization, the same type of thing can happen, allowing the data processing function to develop improperly. Leadership is needed to direct the growth.

The need for leadership is demonstrated by the fact that high data processing management turnover rates which have plagued many organizations remain unabated. These results demonstrate an ongoing failure in fashioning a structure which encompasses the requirements of effective data processing management leadership.

Year of Study	Data Processing Management Turnover Rates
1972	40 - 50%
1976	25 - 35%
1980	30 - 40%

To be successful at constructing such a structure, the organization develops a system or pattern on which data processing management leadership can be built. The causes of data processing management turnover demonstrate some specific patterns. In 1972, the primary cause was overemphasis on technical achievement and skills and underemphasis on organizational change skills in specific business functional areas; in 1976, a deficiency in communications between data processing and each of the other two groups; and in 1980, a lack of strong leadership in guiding the penetration of information technology into the company.

The primary cause for turnover has changed, but on closer examination there is a constant. The issue of leadership remains at the core throughout as the causes accumulate. There is a need for strong leadership requiring organizational change skills. Organizational change, in turn, requires communication. Leadership is needed to see that these skills are assimilated during the organization's growth.

A Pattern of Skills

As the data processing environment grows and the organization learns, certain data processing skills emerge in a stage and become more important to effective data processing leadership during that stage. The emergence of these skills, and the rise and decline of their importance, forms a pattern. This pattern reflects the evolution of data processing in an organization and is therefore important as a design on which effective data processing management leadership can be built.

The technical and operational skills, developed in the earlier stages of an organization, give way to organizational skills in the latter stages (see *Exhibit I*). The technical and operational skills reflect a view by the organization towards data processing as a tool. Later, as the data processing function develops, the organization may pass through the transition point, utilizing data processing as a resource. Data processing management leadership should recognize the pattern in this progression. The knowledge of these skills through the stages is cumulative, and ought to be at a data processing manager's ready command through his organization if he does not have them personally.

The progress of data processing and the core of our structure, focuses on three groups—data processing management, senior management, and users. In particular, our concern lies with how these three groups view the function of data processing. The building of a complimentary, unified structure which will enable data processing to be led effectively relies on certain provisions.

To promote the interaction between the three groups, communication among them is necessary. To lead data processing effectively, however, we must go beyond this. The interacting nature of data processing with the other groups must be known and accounted for. The three groups should realize their position and accept the roles that they must play. But how are they to know precisely what these roles are? This is the critical element. The three groups must develop and hold a common base of knowledge—a common paradigm—if data processing is to make the progress it could. To develop this common paradigm requires learning, not only by each of the three groups, but by the organization as a whole.

EXHIBIT I

Skill Change Patterns

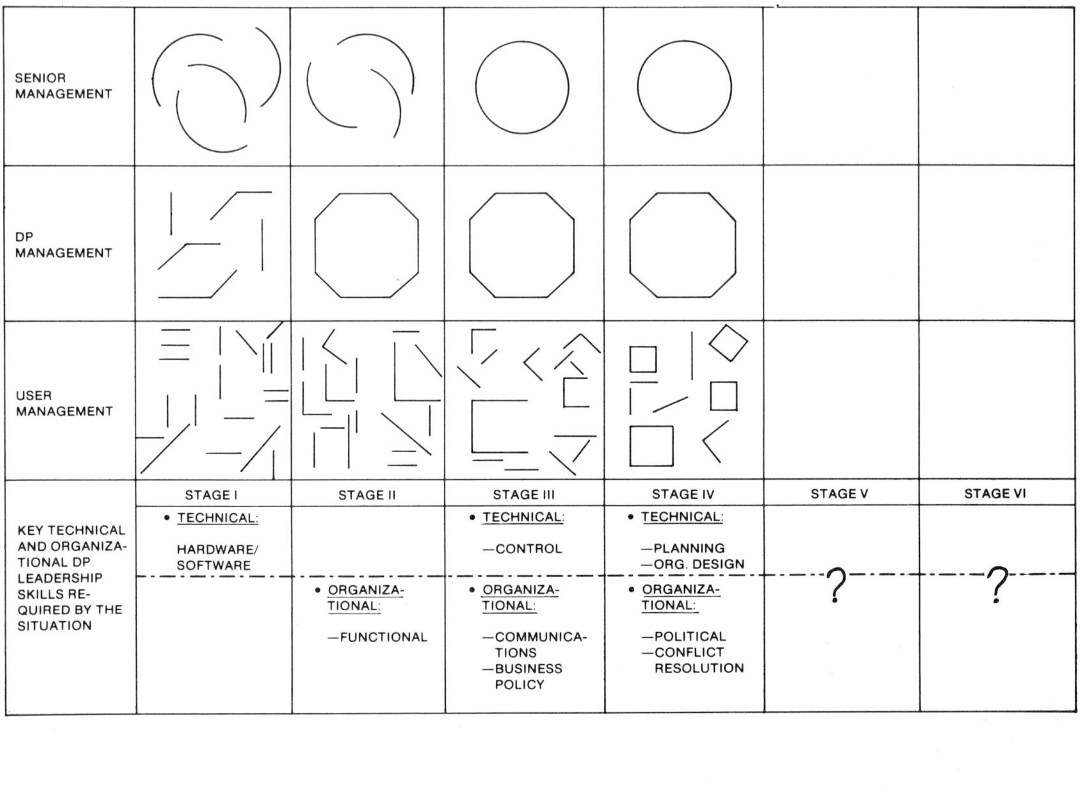
SENIOR MANAGEMENT
DP MANAGEMENT
USER MANAGEMENT
KEY TECHNICAL AND ORGANIZATIONAL DP LEADERSHIP SKILLS REQUIRED BY THE SITUATION
STAGE I
STAGE II
STAGE III
STAGE IV
STAGE V
STAGE VI
• TECHNICAL:
HARDWARE/SOFTWARE
• ORGANIZATIONAL:
—FUNCTIONAL
• TECHNICAL:
—CONTROL
• ORGANIZATIONAL:
—COMMUNICATIONS
—BUSINESS POLICY
• TECHNICAL:
—PLANNING
—ORG. DESIGN
• ORGANIZATIONAL:
—POLITICAL
—CONFLICT RESOLUTION
?
?

The phenomenon of organizational learning can be seen as the product of eclectic learning by senior management, data processing management, and user groups. We recognize the metaphysical problem associated with this extension, and we seek only to point out that the organization gains knowledge as these groups learn.

As the organization grows and learns, with the concurrent rise in the interaction between the groups, the dimension of power evolves as the key element of the structure.

Power and Its Results

A discussion of power requires a definition. Power, as used here, is the capacity of an individual or group to influence or modify the behavior of others in desired ways, and to prevent having one's own (or the group's) behavior changed in ways undesirable to that group or individual. We recognize five kinds of power and the consequences of each.

Legitimate power is the use of authority associated with formal organizational office or position. If the manager is perceived as having the right to influence coworkers and the coworkers have a duty to obey, the result is an effective working relationship.

Reward power is the belief that the manager has valued rewards which will be given in exchange for changes in behavior. If coworkers perceive this, only marginally effective working relationships will result.

Expert power is a way of gaining power by building reputations of expertise in certain areas. If coworkers believe that the manager has proprietary expertise they will be willing to be influenced in those areas. If there is expert power, withdrawal will result as the others feel intimidated by the expert.

Referent power is the power obtained by an individual or group by identifying with a manager or the ideas for which the individual or group stands. Referent power results in alienation if the individual or group over which it is wielded does not identify with a manager of the group.

Coercive power is based on the belief that punishment follows an individual for failure to conform to the power wielder's influence. If coercive power is used, aggression results when an individual or group feels wronged by the punishment or threat of punishment.

As you can see, perception is critical to the capacity of power. The wielder must insure that those over whom he holds power perceive his power as real.

The balance of power directs the growth in areas of an organization. If an individual or group perceives that a particular power base (or bases) is being used legitimately, effective working relationships result. When individuals perceive that inappropriate power is being used (and on some occasions even when perceived legitimately), they will organize together to create a base of countervailing power.

Which group—senior management, data processing management, or users—holds the leadership position in a given stage depends upon the balance of exercised power. This makes interdependencies in an organization a serious concern.

ALIGNING INTERDEPENDENCIES

Dependency, like organizational learning, accumulates through the stages. When building the structure of an organization, the alignment of the interdependencies is critical. The gears of a mechanism may spin fruitlessly alone, or grind when not meshed properly. But when these gears are correctly aligned a harmonious, productive result occurs. The same is true in an organization.

In the first stages, users become dependent on data processing. As data processing growth continues, the organization becomes even more dependent on it. By stage III, senior managers and users feel dependent on and vulnerable to data processing. Data processing in turn is dependent on both senior management—vertically, and users—horizontally. Effective data processing activity must minimize the negative aspects of the growing senior management and user dependencies by developing constructive bases of power. How is this to be accomplished? Data processing must have an understanding with the two other groups.

Hierarchy connotes legitimate power associated with the manager's office, title, budget size, etc. For most managers, workflow interdependencies are lateral (between data processing and users), except for budget. However, legitimate power is of limited effectiveness in the lateral mode. It is vital that data processing develop mechanisms to influence, understand, and work with both senior management and users. An examination of the growth of data processing, as seen in the stages, demonstrates how these mechanisms develop.

Coalitions and the Move Towards Common Knowledge

In stages I and II, data processing operates from a base of expert power. In stage I, dependency relationships have not yet developed since senior management and users see the computer as a mystical, unknown entity. When senior management initially intervenes, data processing may see it as coercive if they perceive that punishment will result if they do not conform. Senior managers need to understand the kind of action with respect to data processing that will lead to long-run goals for the organization as a whole. A senior management steering committee is often created to develop an understanding of current data processing functioning, and to direct the data processing department.

Data processing now perceives power being used appropriately, and the senior management's base of power, if seen as coercive, is transformed to legitimate. The focus on data processing leadership has now moved from the data processing department to senior management, the ultimate users.

Stage III closes when the data processing management team and the senior management coalition share a common understanding of how data processing should be managed.

The role of the user coalitions arises in stage IV. During stage III, the relationship between data processing and users had continued to deteriorate as data processing shift resources from building controls systems to developing controls. In some instances, users even searched for alternatives to the data processing department to satisfy their needs.

To prevent fragmentation, the senior management coalition may have installed policies to limit the use of alternatives. In frustration, the users organized into coalitions, and perhaps tried outside sources. The sequential emergence of the data processing team, the senior management coalition, and the user coalition is indicated in *Exhibit II*.

In stage IV, the coalitions of users learn how to cooperate with data processing in the development and maintenance of needed applications and systems. Users also develop a common system of knowledge, or paradigm, to serve as a catalyst and establish a smooth, cooperative working relationship.

EXHIBIT II

The Sequential Emergence of the DP Team,
the Senior Management Coalition, and the User Coalition

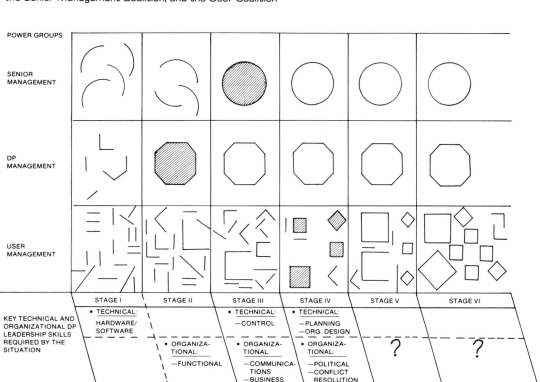

SHADING INDICATES DOMINANT BALANCE OF POWER AND MAJOR LEADERSHIP DIRECTION

ENTRY INTO THE DATA RESOURCE ERA

At this juncture in an organization's growth, the development of paradigms serve as a dynamic factor in moving an organization beyond the transition point of stage III into the data resource era. What exactly do we mean by a paradigm? A paradigm is a representation of reality. An effective paradigm is shared and accepted by members of a group. It increases the ability of decision makers within the group to set goals and develop strategies. It helps identify problems and evaluate information. It permits integration of new information in the existing framework. And the paradigm helps the group take action.

By developing a common paradigm, the data processing function of an organization can be effectively led. An organizational paradigm is a system of knowledge about action/outcome relationships that is held, for example, by members of the senior management.

Congruent paradigms emerge under certain conditions. All three groups—data processing, senior management, and users—must understand the phenomenon of coalition formation and the effective use of power. Further, each group must accept the leadership role at different stages, and accept the shift in the balance of power as the next leader emerges. In addition to these conditions which all three groups jointly observe, the emergence of a congruent paradigm is dependent on the recognition of necessary elements by each individual group.

Data processing needs to maintain open communications with its constituencies before and after coalition forming to build mutual understanding. Data processing must also remember that coalitions are power phenomena. Senior management leadership emerges in stage III. It is critical data processing and senior management establish a common frequency at this time, so as to ensure that management's policies are embodied in the DP/user paradigm in stage IV. Users must understand that it is possible to develop a common understanding with data processing of what data processing can and should accomplish on the user's and the organization's behalf. To do this, users need to develop a shared paradigm in stage IV when user coalitions are in the leadership position vis-à-vis data processing. The emergence of congruent paradigms is summarized in *Exhibit III*.

WHAT SHOULD MANAGEMENT DO?

The rapid growth in the data processing function of an organization, and the concomitant problems which result, necessitates a management structure encompassing a pattern on which successful data processing management leadership can be built. If organizations are at present not quite piloting a biplane in the space age, clearly the data processing management turnover rates indicate that they are at least not keeping up with the rapid progress being made. The problem of leadership exists, and management needs to deal with it. But what should management do?

EXHIBIT III

Congruent Paradigms Result From Linking Paradigms of Power Groups by Exercising Leadership Skills of (1) Communication, (2) Political, and (3) Conflict Resolution

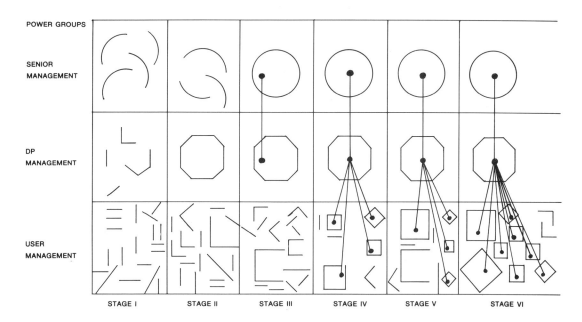

The most important step is to recognize the patterns demonstrated here and act accordingly. Organizations learn how to assimilate and adapt to information technology. To accomodate this knowledge across its structure, an organization must develop stable, consistent, and reliable patterns of behavior so that diverse interdependent groups can take joint action.

These patterns follow a recognized course. Dominant leadership power over data processing passes from the data processing team in stages I and II to the senior management coalition in stage III and to the user coalitions in stage IV (see *Exhibit II*). With management's recognition of this evolution of power shifts, rational power relationships can be institutionalized around a common paradigm of knowledge. When all three groups share this common paradigm, the data processing function in an organization can be effectively led, making entry possible into the advanced stages of the data resource era. This represents a mature data processing function in which the data processing organization is restructured and new management techniques can be installed to accommodate the proliferation of novel technologies. The organization is piloting a modern, adaptable craft which will keep pace with advances in data processing.

24

Steering Committees

WINNIE R. ROGOW
HERBERT W. PERKINS, III

The breakdown of communication between individuals and groups in regard to data processing issues is one of the recurring signs of crisis in an organization as it moves through the stages of data processing growth. The effects are evident in the breakdown of the relationship of data processing management and personnel to users, user area management, and senior management. They may be expressed in terms of specific issues, in open clashes, or as an undercurrent of bad feeling among people in different areas of the organization. In any case, the result is often a contentious situation characterized by accusations and misunderstanding. A successful program for data processing growth must address this problem.

The data processing **steering committee** is an organizational grouping which can serve to diminish conflict and build understanding. Usually it is composed of senior management, data processing management, and representatives of user groups. These different factions work together to solve problems of budgeting, direction-setting, management control, and project management. Through these activities, the three groups develop common priorities and review their needs in the context of shared goals. Technical, functional, and strategic organizational objectives are reconciled and data processing growth is integrated with organizational growth plans.

The introduction of data processing in the organization is comparable to the introduction of any new product or service. There must be an effort to develop a market and, as the nature of this market is clarified, to adjust the product to suit it. However, in the case of data processing there is first a tendency to develop the product autonomously without fully understanding the needs of the user. In addition, there is a tendency on the part of the user to feel that technology can accomplish anything, that the product has unlimited flexibility. Misunderstandings develop easily in this atmosphere and the popularity of data processing will fluctuate widely both within each stage and as the organization moves through the stages.

The steering committee can modulate these fluctuations through a process of mutual education based upon such concrete tasks as funding and planning decisions. In steering committee meetings, representatives of both contentious groups, providers and users, can present their needs to senior management. Senior management can, in turn, coordinate and prioritize those needs according to agreed-upon objectives. Thus, funds can be allocated and plans approved by mutual consent on the part of all three organizational groups.

THE USER-PROVIDER GAP

Before discussing the specific responsibilities of the steering committee, it is helpful to understand the reasons for the tension between data processing—the providers of services—and other divisions or departments in the organization—the users of data processing services. This tension may not yet have surfaced in an organization at the time the steering committee is formed (groups within the organization may either be unconcerned or optimistic about data processing) or it may be severe (users feel data processing is incompetent and falsely representing its potential). Whatever the particular situation, there is a basic difference in orientation between the two groups. Part of the role of the steering committee is to enhance communication and increase understanding of both perspectives.

The users in an organization are market-oriented. They are concerned with support to the goals of the organization through the achievement of objectives set for their particular organizational unit. Their success or failure is often measured at frequent intervals. For this reason, users tend to have short-term sense of their information support needs. They are also, by necessity, people-oriented and see people and not data as the critical resource necessary to achieve their objectives.

Data processing personnel, by contrast, are often technicians. Their careers are more closely linked to the data processing industry than to the corporation employing them. They are concerned with increasing their technical expertise, a goal which is not necessarily dependent upon their ability to service the objectives of a particular organization or user group. An innovative, technical solution to a user problem is more likely to advance a data processing career than a less imposing, steady service approach to user problems. As a result, data processing personnel are task-oriented. Their desire to achieve results to problems in a technically rational manner, not always aligned to long-term business considerations, usually leads them to assume a much longer-term perspective on data processing and information services than the users.

When the steering committee meets to address funding issues, for example, the differences in perspective may be expressed in terms of funding strategy. Users may favor systems and projects which address problems whose immediacy is obvious, or they may suggest grandiose schemes which have hidden development and/or maintenance costs. Data processing may favor a more long-range building of general capabilities or growth in a direction favorable to existing personnel skills and computing capabilities. There may be no way to match the system desired by the users to data processing capabilities within overall funding constraints. However, when all three groups participate in the decision they can weigh priorities and inhibiting factors in order to develop a plan and a budget agreeable to everyone. In addition, as a result of this process understanding and communication about data processing should be improved and growth should be facilitated.

THE STEERING COMMITTEE CHARTER

The steering committee can only be an effective forum for the development of shared, organization-wide data processing plans and budgeting if it is properly sanctioned by senior management as well as data processing and user groups. The purpose of steering committee meetings should be stated in terms of tasks and areas of activity which are clear to all three groups and approved by the organization. If the committee charter is strong, it provides a sound basis for aligning all of its members in a commitment to organizational goals even where this involves moderation or revision of ideas about the role and responsibility of data processing.

For example, if the committee is sanctioned to set up a long-term plan for data processing and then to fix an annual budget for the upcoming year, the discussions prerequisite to decision making will lead naturally to a process of mutual education. In addition to explaining their own needs and constraints, the participating groups will be forced to express themselves in terms of commonly held objectives. Contentions about budgeting which center on clashes between the value of systems to the users (what they feel to be their need for data processing maintenance and the feasibility of the systems in technical terms) can be resolved in terms of the role of the system and its cost on an organization-wide basis.

The maturation and increased sophistication of the members of the steering committee will lead naturally to a broader perspective in all four Growth Process areas. The balancing of growth of technology, users, controls, and applications will occur naturally in the coalition formed by the steering committee members. Coordination will penetrate down through the organization as it matures and, with the delegation of supporting activities by the steering committee to subgroups (a process described later in this chapter), will help to avoid misunderstandings in the future.

STEERING COMMITTEE ACTIVITY

When the steering committee meets, the general charge of education and communication among members is translated into three primary committee functions:

1. direction-setting

2. management control

3. project review and control

In the course of fulfilling these functions, committee members engage in specific activities which are important to organizational planning and operations as well as building communication and understanding of data processing issues. These activities include budgeting, liaison, performance evaluation, and planning revisions.

In brief, the sequence of activities is as follows. The committee addresses a specific problem such as setting a data processing budget. First, the needs of the users are matched to the availability of resources and the feasibility of increased services. A data processing plan is outlined in conjunction with the articulation of a strategy that meets the goals established in the direction-setting process for the organization as a whole. When strategy formulation and planning are complete, the members of the steering committee function as liaisons in their areas of the organization. They promote understanding of data processing strategy and see that measures and standards for control and evaluation of data processing are used. Altogether this process insures that data processing activity is conducted and assessed according to set criteria rather than informal expectations.

To a certain extent, the breadth of perspective and the scope of steering committee activity is stage-dependent. As an organization matures, experience with data processing makes it easier to plan and eventually to delegate some of the reporting and control responsibilities to subgroups. However, before detailing the changes in the steering committees through the stages, it is necessary to identify the basic functions it serves. These include direction-setting functions, management control functions, and project review and planning revision. The direction-setting function is usually largely determined by organizational objectives while management and project control and planning are accomplished through funding, project approval, and project review processes.

Direction-Setting

The steering committee acts in the capacity of a board of directors for data processing. It provides strategic direction to the data processing organization based on an understanding of the company's long-term objectives. Information systems needs are presented in the context of business priorities. This makes it possible to weigh the importance of technically complex or costly efforts against their value as business function support. It provides a basis for decision making which moderates the tendency of users to press for systems inappropriate to the stage of development of data processing staff and/or technology. Conversely, it discourages data processing from pursuing technologies for their own sake without considering business issues.

The range of responsibilities which are a part of the direction-setting function of the steering committee are extensive. Direction setting should provide a rationale for the assessment and selection of data processing strategies. It should function as an underlying framework for funding and management control procedures. More specifically, the direction-setting process should involve a sequence of committee activities comparable to and compatible with corporate planning and budgeting. In addition to general direction-setting activities, the steering committee should be responsible for the following activities:

1. The establishment of procedures to facilitate sharing of responsibility by data processing and other groups in the organization involved in the development and delivery of systems support.

2. The definition of the relative responsibilities of user and systems groups.

3. Annual review and revision of a long-range plan.

4. Funding and budgeting-setting.

5. The resolution of disputes over data processing support.

The result of policy setting should be a corporate strategy which integrates data processing plans with the business plan of the organization. As the organization evolves through the stages, the focus of steering committee strategy shifts and, as discussed below, activities related to the implementation of the direction-setting programs are ordinarily delegated to lower levels within the organization.

Management Controls

The direction-setting activities of the steering committee are expressed in general policy and reviewed annually in the course of long-range planning and project approval. In addition, the steering committee participates in a quarterly review process which is aimed at insuring that data processing activity is monitored and evaluated on a regular basis. In this sense the steering committee is responsible for management control procedures for data processing. It is not concerned with technical data processing control procedures, but is responsible for general monitoring and review of data processing performance. The steering committee must have access to accurate information which can be measured and analyzed periodically, and it must have the authority to act on problems as they develop, before situations become critical.

The means by which the management control process is carried out depends upon accurate reporting and analysis. The details of carrying out plans and many of the supporting activities in the planning and allocation of funds are the responsibility of other groups. However, there must be a good reporting system which channels information to the steering committee for periodic review. On the basis of these reviews, the steering committee should be authorized and willing to alter plans when necessary. This process can be broken into three more specific steering committee management control functions:

1. Variance analysis of performance reporting systems for the purpose of making recommendations for action.

2. Review and approval or deferment of urgent project requests.

3. Revision of project schedules and resource allocation.

While these may seem like common management activities which are the responsibility of managers in each user and/or data processing area, in many organizations there is little or no direct communication between groups and few information sources which provide information. Data processing is often in the position of performing according to its assumptions about its role in the business, while users assume that data processing shares their needs and priorities. When problems arise and disputes occur, there is no way to settle issues through facts gathered in the course of regular operations. It is at this point, in the context of crisis, that the absence of shared assumptions and accurate information about data processing appears as a problem.

The role of the steering committee is to avert such a crisis or, in the face of one, to rely upon a responsible information base to settle the dispute. In other words, the steering committee must manage the relationship of data processing with the organization. Often this need goes unnoticed until it is too late to avert a crisis and communication has completely broken down. If management controls are included among the areas of concern in the formulation and definition of the steering committee, such a crisis can be avoided.

During the later stages, when the steering committee strategies have been incorporated in user and data processing activities, it will be possible to delegate aspects of the steering committee function to user/data processing personnel groups. This includes primarily areas which are project oriented or defined by time or activity such as project definition, project planning, project monitoring, and project review.

In the steering committee these activities are discussed in the context of exception reports and variance analysis. The committee must maintain a high level of awareness regarding project status and will be willing to respond quickly to changes in project feasibility. As knowledge of the project areas increases, project requirements may change. Failure to respond to change can be costly in terms of both the direct cost of expenses and the indirect cost of frustration among users. There are several management control activities which can be utilized by the steering committee to improve project supervision:

1. Provision of guidelines for establishing priorities for new systems development.

2. Review and setting of priorities for major development projects.

3. Review and approval of major projects both at the start and at specified points in the development life cycle.

Initially, the project control function of the steering committee is indirect, involving guidelines and strategy. However, as the organization matures the steering committee matures, expanding in size and scope. It becomes possible to incorporate the mutual efforts of users and data processing personnel in many project phases. This is possible because the steering committee, like the Growth Processes (technology and data processing personnel, management controls, the applications portfolio, and the users) must be synchronized with the growth through the stages of data processing in the organization.

STAGES OF MATURITY: THE EVOLUTION OF THE STEERING COMMITTEE

The changing role of the steering committee can be compared to the stages of data processing growth. Overall, there is a movement from an inactive or nonexistent role through an advisory role to the roles of participant and finally to full responsibility for carrying out the function.

The steering committee is introduced into the organization as an advisory group supporting top management. The group, referred to as the executive steering committee, is composed of senior management, ranking department heads in the major functional areas (e.g., accounting, manufacturing, etc.), and the director of the data processing organization. Its purpose is to address the very broadest strategic issues. These include direction-setting, management control systems, long-range systems planning, and annual budgets.

The executive steering committee can be introduced in a stage II environment or as late as mid-stage III. It is not appropriate for the smaller, ad hoc and concentrated scale of activity in a stage I environment. When the executive steering committee is introduced in stage II, it serves as an advisory group which encourages expansion and establishes the mechanisms necessary to monitor the course of growth. It should not try to constrain the broad and experimental quality of stage II activities. Nonetheless, it can begin to put some monitoring mechanisms in place in anticipation of stage III. In a stage II environment, the executive steering committee is primarily a policy-setting body. Its scope of concern is small and generalized.

In stage III, on the other hand, the executive steering committee is often introduced to avert a potential crisis situation. It functions as a power coalition, a group composed of representatives of contending groups who address areas of potential conflict by setting formal policies and management controls. They moderate differences and set procedures to govern the consolidation process indicative of stage III development. For example, the suspicion on the part of users or senior management that data processing is growing too fast and is out of control can be addressed by the steering committee. This may result in formulation of governing regulations and standards by senior management, users, and data processing.

Whatever the reason for forming an executive steering committee in stage III, the responsibilities are the same. In addition to the broad, policy-setting function of the stage II committee, the stage III committee must also review management control processes and insure that they are consistent with general policies (consolidation, for example, rather than experimentation of stage II) and support the long-range plan. In this context, the executive steering committee assumes a more authoritative role and supplies a forum for airing and resolving disputes, deciding on priorities, and handling general organizational politics as related to data processing.

It is important to insure that the responsibilities of an executive steering committee do not lead to a devaluation of the prestige of the committee and alienate high-level committee members. The objective is to build mutual support among senior managers in the organization and data processing management. Quarterly meetings which address significant issues should not be allowed to become bogged down in specifics. The members should not be taxed with detailed preparation. Instead they should be thoroughly but concisely briefed so that meetings result in decisions on key issues.

The executive steering committee is the first such committee in an organization. It is there to establish a pattern for future problem solving. As the need and/or desire for the discussion of more specific issues by a steering committee arises, it becomes necessary to augment the membership and the role of the group. This cannot be accomplished by the executive steering committee alone. It is time to introduce another level of steering committee activity.

The Tactical Steering Committee - Operating Committee

Upon completion of a plan, responsibility for implementing that plan can be assumed by an operating committee or tactical steering committee. Usually the need for such a group develops during the review of the first annual plan and the subsequent revision of the next year's plan. In this review it becomes apparent that the steering committee as a concept has become more familiar and better accepted. More demands are placed upon the group, necessitating additional support to its members.

In order to preserve the high-level role of the executive steering committee, a lower level tactical steering committee can be formed. While the executive steering committee continues to meet quarterly and to act as a senior advisor, the tactical steering committee meets monthly and acts in a participatory capacity. At this stage the organization is usually involved in consolidation and needs a group of data processing and user personnel who can address problems and monitor planning on a regular basis.

While it may seen inadvisable to remove any day-to-day activity from the control of experienced data processing professionals at this point, the Stages Model demonstrates that user commitment and user involvement enhance the maturity of the user. For this reason, user involvement and experience are critical to successful data processing growth. In the tactical steering committee, data processing management and senior user groups work together. This increases and deepens user understanding of data processing. Reciprocally, it also increases business awareness among data processing management and participating personnel.

The tactical steering committee is effective because it is able to handle more routine issues than the executive steering committee and to disseminate understanding of problems and responses to users and data processing personnel on a more regular basis. This builds an increased sense of shared purpose which is filtered down from the executive steering committee, through the tactical steering committee, to the rest of the organization. Growing knowledge diffuses tensions and maximizes results, two effects which can be critical to the success of the consolidation stage.

Functional Area Steering Committee

The role of the steering committee as a participant in the generation and carrying out of policy, plans, and management control is established by the executive steering committee with the follow-up support of the operating committee. As the organization grows and matures, it becomes possible to build upon that foundation and to push the educational role of the steering committee down through the organization to middle-level management as user coalitions form in stage IV. This is not a matter of didactic education. It involves experiential learning in which the communication forum of the steering committee involves more and more people in data processing function where their talents can be exploited to carry out the broader guidelines and plans set by the executive steering committee.

The functional steering committee is introduced in this role as the organization matures. Its members are largely determined by division or some other organizational unit. They specialize in planning and evaluation functions in a localized context. They carry the communication process begun in the higher level steering committee to their respective divisions or areas. They set policy, formulate plans and controls, and address problems for their functional area. They are also a communication channel for the higher level groups, reporting functional area information up to either the tactical steering committee, or directly to the executive steering committee. These groups are especially important in the latter stages when such new technologies and strategies as data base and distributed approaches change the manner in which data processing services are provided to functional groups.

The Project Steering Committee

The project steering committees are introduced in the latter stages as participating groups which can assume responsibility for carrying out the strategies and plans of the higher level steering committees. They set time schedules and budgets, review projects, and act as a steering committee to insure steady progress, adherence to standards, and regular evaluation. Again, mirroring the role of the higher level executive steering committee, the project steering committee provides a forum for grievances and, where a project does fail, acts to insure that failure is properly explained in order to avoid unwarranted, blanket accusations against data processing.

The project steering committee is composed of managers from data processing and the user departments involved in the project. In a major project, day-to-day input from the user is submitted to the committee. This insures close monitoring and control of project activity and provides a mechanism to increase user involvement without undermining data processing control. This communication and participation in the project by both users and data processing helps promote the alignment of data processing efforts and business needs.

It may be tempting to begin steering committee activity with a project steering committee regardless of the stage of growth of the organization. Project steering committees are localized and their members are more likely to have the time to participate on a regular basis. However, it is important to understand that the basic purpose of all steering committees is to align business functions and data processing activities by building a common strategy for the growth, expansion, and increase in sophistication of services. This in itself is a sophisticated concept. Users in the earlier stages of data processing cannot be expected to fully understand either the general concept or the particular manner in which data processing functions. There is a similar lack of understanding of users on the part of data processing (which in the earlier stages is also quite appropriately concerned with internal, technical issues).

IMPLEMENTATION AND INSTALLATION OF STEERING COMMITTEES

The timing of the installation of each level of data processing steering committee is important. Education is a significant element in the function of the steering committee, and before education can begin there must be some readiness to learn. For this reason, senior management must be committed to the idea of a data processing steering committee. Even when the data processing manager decides that such a group would be helpful or an outside consultant recommends the formation of the committee, it should be presented to the organization with senior management sponsorship and chartered by them.

The charter for each steering committee should delineate the scope of control and the specific responsibilities of the group. It should be approved by the manager, management group, or committee to which the steering committee reports, and should be communicated by them to member groups in the organization. Reporting mechanisms and implementation strategies should be developed, and compliance to chartered responsibilities should be reviewed during and after the installation phase.

The success of the data processing steering committee will be determined, to a large extent, by management sponsorship and the clarity of the charter. However, supporting details are also important. Meetings should be scheduled and staff support provided. The objective should be to make senior management as productive a contributor as possible without overburdening them with homework. The same will be true for department heads and data processing personnel in the latter stages and lower level steering committee.

SUMMARY

The purpose of the data processing steering committee is to create an in-house expert on both business strategy and data processing services which can evaluate issues of supply and demand in the area of data processing. Direction-setting procedures provide fundamental guidelines for alignment of data processing support and corporate objectives. The budgeting and planning activities of the committee provide a forum for reconciliation of misunderstandings on the basis of concrete organizational planning issues.

Through the budgeting and direction-setting process, the steering committee functions as a communication and learning forum in which the mutual education of business and data processing groups makes it possible to claim mastery of both areas by one organizational body. This accomplishment is essential to data processing growth. If business goals and data processing services are not coordinated, data processing remains ancillary and technical. The real power of the computer comes from the sophistication of its use, not its technology.

It is difficult for individuals to accept this idea. In most organizations there is a tendency to separate technicians from users. The data processing steering committee is a mechanism which can be used to correct this situation. It bridges the gap between the technology and its use by acting on issues of strategy and translating strategy into policies, review procedures, standards, and controls which link data processing to business functions. The data processing steering committee sets an important precedent for the direction of data processing growth in the organization and provides a strategic umbrella for related management issues.

Viewpoints-A Case

The early history of an executive steering committee at a regional United States bank is typical.

Use of data processing had been spreading throughout the organization, and much of it seemed to be effective. Still, the anxiety levels of those employees vitally concerned with the function's good performance was increasing. Managerial intuition indicated that something was not quite right. This sense of trouble was expressing itself at three levels.

The bank's leaders were asking broad questions about data processing:

- Is the activity getting anywhere?

- Are we overbudgeting it? or underbudgeting it?

- Should we be spending differently?

- Should we be watching it more closely?

Senior users-managers were raising parallel, but more specific, questions:

- Can data processing be of more help?

- Have we tried to automate things in the wrong order?

In addition to these, the data processing executive was worrying on his own:

- Why do my best analysts always leave?

- Do I need a systems development methodology?

- What, really, is holding the programming back?

From the top down, in other words, management was getting uneasy about its own performance at managing data processing.

If all these managers had had a data processing strategy they believed in, and if the organization had been pursuing it, anxieties like these would not have arisen. They obviously need to build such a strategy. But to build a strategy that made sense to all of them, they first had to have a workplace to build it. Considering that the groups regarded data processing management from three different levels and directions and speaking different languages as they came, the problem of defining this workspace was not simple.

Criteria

The group's broad goal was to nourish a mirror-image relationship between (a) all the bank's data processing applications and (b) the regular business functions these applications were intended to support. First the group had to have a broad right of inquiry and action to approve or disallow or revise data processing directions, services, and service lines, and to set priorities for data processing activities and development.

Second, all the managers had to have confidence that the strategies they would choose were the right ones—they had to have a strong sense of agreement among themselves. Therefore the next criterion was "common language." The only jargon permitted would be jargon that all the managers in the group could quickly master.

Third, the forum membership had to carry enough clout to bring about real change. Characteristically, the problem would be to bring together two parties in the organization that often maintained careful distance from each other because of misunderstanding and open distrust—users and data processing people.

Committee

These criteria make up the start of an executive steering committee charter, and an ESC is precisely what the bank installed. The process began when the bank asked a consulting firm to join with selected bank personnel to look into its data processing affairs.

Just as an investment analyst analyzes a client's financial structure and performance, the firm first investigated the bank's data processing expenditures for the past ten years. Comparing the bank's expense patterns against guidelines, the firm discovered several problems.

Although the bank's data processing expense profiles of several years ago matched the guidelines fairly closely, recent patterns appeared to be drifting. To be sure, many new applications had been added to the portfolio, but a look at the technical and functional quality of the bank's Applications Portfoio indicated the following situation:

As the bank's data processing activity passed into stage III (control), the pressure for more efficiency had induced both increased development and tighter control over data processing spending. The level of normal systems maintenance and enhancement necessary to preserve Application Portfolio quality had been allowed to drop. Efficiency pressures had gone too far and resulted in heavy damage to many existing systems and technical resources. This was the situation which had given rise to management's uneasiness.

The picture was reviewed in several sessions with the executive steering committee which moved first to develop an appropriate data processing funding evaluation/strategy. It developed a data processing funding direction to be used for the next several years.

Continuing

Called into existence by necessity, the executive steering committee continued to oversee the bank's data processing efforts. Its scope now is wider. Its agendas now incorporate a higher level of technical detail than would have been appropriate when it first began to operate; the comprehension level of its members vis-à-vis data processing has increased. The committee is also in a position to decide when a level of detail is high enough to warrant its delegating an issue to another group. The committee reviews its own work regularly, as well as the changes its decisions bring about.

The executive steering committee is bringing the task of overseeing data processing under control. The key to this committee's subsequent success was the process by which its members agreed on the current status of data processing in the bank and the data processing issues they were obliged to deal with to ensure the effectiveness of data processing efforts. They gained this agreement through analysis. They communicated their consensus in business language and business structure to the key members of the bank. Once agreement was achieved in this group, change was easier to implement. Without agreement, an executive steering committee will never function effectively.

Furthermore, without effective oversight, data processing will suffer benign neglect at best. More likely, and worse, ill-informed and half-hearted efforts to manage the effort from the top will result in deterioration of data processing. As this case shows, management can rise to the oversight task if it provides itself with an effective instrument through which to investigate and act. Then, planning for the future of data processing is done on a sound basis.

25

Corporate Planning for Information Resources

THOMAS M. SCURRAH

The last decade heralded great advances in corporate planning as organizations began installing new or improving old planning processes. Much attention and resource is still devoted to corporate planning. Yet planning for information resources is still in its infancy, often operating independently of corporate planning processes. Many cite the need for information resource planning but very few actually plan.

There are several reasons why planning for information processing either is not done or is not done effectively. The first is the view of senior management toward data processing. One view often held by management prior to installing a computer is that data processing is an unlimited resource, and planning in terms of selecting and prioritizing systems is therefore unnecessary. The data processing organization is simply required to convert management wishes to reality. The other view, emerging after some experience with computers, is that data processing is a resource-consuming activity. Having painfully learned that data processing organizations could not meet all their needs management's solution is to control the resource. "Control" usually means firing the data processing manager, restricting investment in data processing, and effectively isolating the data processing organization from the rest of the company. Planning is rarely offered as a solution.

This second reason helps to explain why senior management rarely considers planning as a means of effectively utilizing the data processing resource. Simply stated, there was no established planning methodology—no analytical tools for making sound management decisions about information resources, and no process through which opportunities could be identified and decisions implemented.

This chapter proposes a methodology—analytical tools and procedures—for planning for corporate information resources. However, before developing the methodology, the need for planning must be justified.

The Need for Data Processing Planning-Coping with the Environment. To a large extent, strategic planning is a vehicle through which organizations cope with three aspects of their environments: uncertainty, complexity, and change. *Uncertainty* relates to the unknown, i.e., what the competitor is doing, what the economy will be like. *Complexity* relates to understanding how forces operate in the environment, and *change* relates to environmental dynamics in acknowledgements that the situation today may not be at all like the situation tomorrow. As *Exhibit I* demonstrates, data processing organizations face uncertainty, complexity, and change through the interaction of these variables:

1. Technology. Such as office automation, CAD/CAM, telecommunications.

2. Business Needs. The need for computer support for product-related functions in such areas as manufacturing, marketing, finance, accounting. This support is often aimed at improving product quality.

3. Organizational Needs. The need for computer support within and between organizational units (subsidiaries, divisions, and departments), chiefly through reporting systems.

The dynamics causing uncertainty, complexity and change which impact the data processing organization can be explained as follows. Technology is such that computers are becoming less expensive and more powerful as hardware costs are declining in real terms each year. Likewise, new technologies, as mentioned before, are rapidly being introduced. Less expensive, more powerful computers with greater applicability for a variety of business needs create user demand for more data processing. Research and design engineers may want computer-aided design systems (CAD/CAM). Indeed there are increasing numbers of business applications which appear in support of new, emerging technologies. Likewise, low hardware costs and improved communications software, for example, appear able to meet the information processing and reporting needs of diverse, multinational organizations. New technology and lower hardware costs spur user demand for more data processing resources. This demand, in turn, puts pressure on the data processing organization to bring in these new technologies. Data processing organizations, are therefore forced to cope with technological changes, the complexities and uncertainties of meeting user demands, and assimilating new technologies.

The Need for Data Processing Planning—Resource Application

Organizations have a limited amount of financial resources from operating income and from capital markets. The goal of strategic planning is to

EXHIBIT I

Data Processing
Variables

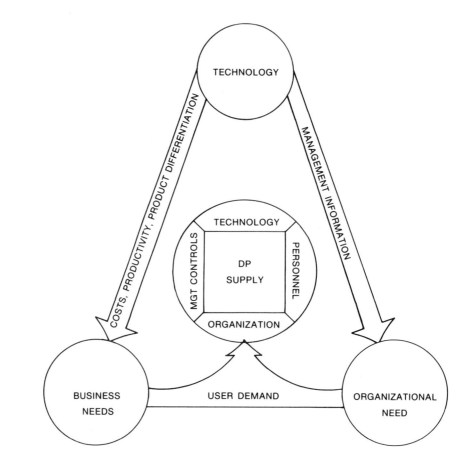

allocate these limited resources to projects which yield greatest value and
meet corporate objectives. Data processing is a scarce resource which also
must be allocated to projects which will yield greatest value. Clearly, user
demand for data processing resources far exceeds the available supply of
the resource, despite proliferation of new technologies and reduction in
hardware costs. This available supply consists not only of technology and
hardware, but also of software to support business functions, and the
number and experience of data processing personnel. Given supply limitations, project selection must take place. Therefore, data processing
projects which support business and organizational functions must be
prioritized through a planning process, using such criteria as risk and
return on investment.

The Need for Integrating Data Processing and Corporate Planning

The motivations for data processing planning are similar to those for corporate planning. Although analytical tools and processes will differ in many ways between data processing and corporate planning, there are good reasons for integrating both types of planning. First of all, data processing applications development projects often span several months or even several years. Therefore, if a business decision is made largely on the basis of analytical data processing support without first consulting the data processing organization regarding systems development implementation time, the decision may end up being an unfavorable one. Secondly, corporate strategic decisions should be communicated to the data processing organization as soon as possible.

There have been cases, for example, where senior management decided to close a factory while, unaware of the decision, data processing management continued to develop systems for it. Finally, data processing can be a competitive tool in terms of lowering costs, increasing productivity, competitively differentiating products, or improving product quality. This is especially true in such service industries as banking, and is becoming increasingly true in manufacturing industries with the advent of new technologies. It is important, therefore, that data processing personnel be involved in the corporate planning activities of project identification and selection.

PLANNING THE INFORMATION RESOURCE: A METHODOLOGY

Having stated why planning the information resource is often not done and why it should be, let us now propose a methodology for planning, following a clarification of planning objectives. Planning is the process of managing change. The planning process has three objectives:

1. Understand the forces which affect an organization.

2. Given this understanding, set direction for the organization.

3. Develop tasks and allocate resources to ensure that the organization moves in the appropriate direction over time.

There are two dimensions to planning: the first is the **time** or **process dimension**, considering who in an organization should be involved, when they should be involved and what they should be involved in. The second dimension is the **analytical** or **substance dimension**.

Several planning models have been developed which deal with the first dimension, a notable one being the Lorange-Vancil corporate planning model.[1] This model is based on three cycles with varying levels of

---

[1]Lorange and R. F. Vancil, *Strategic Planning Systems* (Englewood Cliffs, NJ: Prentice-Hall, Inc., 1977).

involvement from different parts of a corporation with each cycle. The first cycle sets goals and objectives for the organization, the second develops specific programs for obtaining the objectives, and the last involves setting budgets and monitoring controls for those programs.

As *Exhibit II* shows, the analytical dimension involves specific tools used during each cycle. In the objective-setting cycle, for example, which may require an environmental scan of forces affecting the firm, a business portfolio analysis is frequently used. Following an overall environmental assessment, programs which attempt to combat threat and maximize opportunities are developed with business and functional managers. Here questionnaires and meetings become effective tools for program development.

Finally resources are allocated and budgets are drawn up. Variance analysis then becomes a means of controlling costs and measuring the performance of each program. In organizations where planning has been an ongoing process, the objectives-setting cycle consists in part of a review of previous program performance. In organizations about to initiate a planning process, an audit is generally performed which assesses for the first time the position of the corporation within its environment.

There have been a large number of corporate planning models proposed, most characteristically beginning with an objectives-setting phase and concluding with the development of budgets. For that reason, the

EXHIBIT II

The Lorange-Vancil
Corporate Planning Model

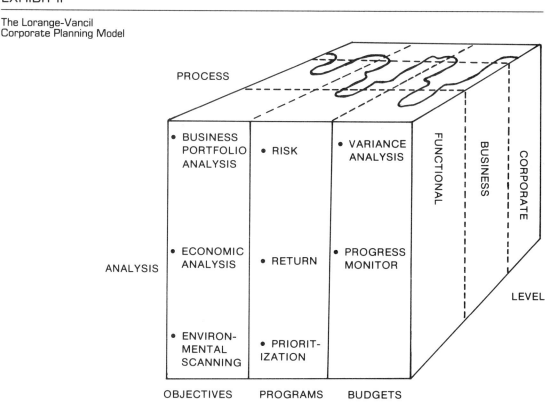

Lorange-Vancil model is a reasonable framework for developing a planning methodology for corporate information resources. However, what needs to be determined is where and how in the corporate planning cycle the data processing organization should be involved. There also needs to be a link between the analytical tools used in corporate planning and those used in data processing planning—i.e., how information systems should be used in order to most effectively support business functions.

We will begin by developing appropriate analytical tools, particularly those used in the audit phase. Using the concept of the product life cycle, we will develop a link between portfolio analysis, a tool used to evaluate businesses in diversified firms, and the Applications Portfolio of information systems, used in evaluating data processing support. Following discussion of these tools, we will present a corporate data processing planning process describing appropriate linkages between the data processing organization and the corporation.

ANALYZING INFORMATION SYSTEMS NEEDS THROUGH THE LIFE OF A PRODUCT

We begin by examining the business and information requirements of a product throughout the four stages of its life as shown in Exhibit III. Information and business requirements for multiple products will be discussed later. We include the initial stage "product consideration" simply because there are information needs prior to initiation of a product.

The key message in Exhibit III is that financial, business, and information characteristics will vary in each stage of a product's life. In general, business conditions will be highly unstable when a product is being introduced and virtually unknown when it is being considered for introduction. During product initiation, market leadership will not yet have been established, distribution channels will still be developing, and new customers are still being identified. As the market becomes saturated or mature, market leadership will have been established and distribution channels solidified. In the initiation and growth stages, the product will require extensive amounts of investment but it will be expected to generate cash as it matures and declines.

Information needs will vary over the life of a product also. As a product is being considered, vast amounts of information on competitors, market conditions, and government regulations will be desired. Likewise, the process of gathering data will be ad hoc in that the informaton sought will answer specific questions relating to the initiation of the new product, rather than, for example, routinely monitoring sales of a currently manufactured product.

Although a firm's financial and information systems policies will differ throughout the life of a product, whether a firm can profitably manufacture a product will depend on its ability to compete with other manufacturers. A widely-held key to a company's success marketing a product is its competitive position measured by its relative market share.

EXHIBIT III

The Business and Information Requirements
throughout the Stages

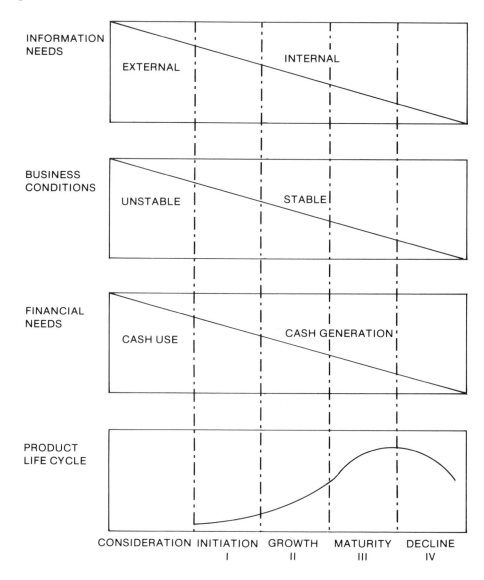

Many studies have shown that the higher relative market share in a
product, the better a firm's competitive position and, therefore, the more it
is able to continue profitable manufacture of that product. As mentioned
earlier, the product portfolio matrix shown in *Exhibit IV* is a useful tool
for helping make product divestment, investment, and acquisition decisions.

The vertical axis represents market attractiveness, measured by
market growth; the horizontal axis represents competitive position,

EXHIBIT IV

The Product
Portfolio Matrix

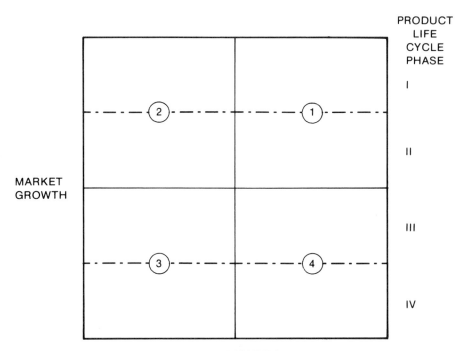

measured by relative market share. The upper-most quadrants, representing high growth rates, indicate initiation and growth phases of a product's life cycle. The lower quadrants, showing small growth rates, indicate maturity and decline phases of a product's life cycle. Products falling within quadrant one require substantial amounts of investment given high market growth rates and unstable business and competitive environments. Those within quadrant two still require substantial investment; however, given its strong competitive position, the product sales should provide nearly all investment funds required.

Given market leadership at this point, there is often the temptation to hold a price umbrella on these products with the effect of generating vast short-term profits. However, the other effect of this policy is to invite into competition those who view the market as highly profitable. Thus this policy endangers the firm's dominant share position. As the product matures and moves into quadrant three it becomes a net cash generator, often providing funds for products within the first quadrant. Little incremental investment is required. Products in the fourth quadrant are unattractive given low market growth and poor competitive position. Consequently they are candidates for divestment.

Exhibit III indicates that there are different information needs at each stage of a product's life. From the product life cycle we note different growth rates at each stage which, when combined with an assessment of competitive position, give rise to a product portfolio matrix. Both the information and financial needs of a product at different stages of its life and competitive position have important implications for the type of information systems required for support and the manner in which they are prioritized.

Yet business and organizational functions which are ultimately supported by information systems must somehow be represented in a way to evaluate those needs. An adaptation of R. N. Anthony's classification of management control systems is a useful tool in this regard.[2] We identify three levels of functions, as *Exhibit V* shows:

1. operational support

2. management control

3. strategic planning

Within each level we identify key areas of the business (marketing and finance, for example) along with specific functions performed in each area. Using the functional portfolio tool we can begin to map existing data processing support to functions and evaluate the quality of that support.

But the functional portfolio goes beyond that as a link to the product portfolio matrix and, therefore, to business strategy. Using the functional portfolio, we can make generalizations regarding the attributes of systems supporting the three levels. Operational systems will support *process*, the impact of which will be gains in productivity, lowered costs, and better product services. Management control systems will *inform*—let management know when and what actions to take. They too will have some impact on costs, more from a control sense. Strategic systems will *evaluate*, helping management make long-term large investment decisions. Although the nature of information will be more from outside the organization as one moves up the triangle, it is important to note that internal information flows from the bottom up. This strongly suggests that, overall, operational systems should be developed prior to management control systems, and management control sytems prior to strategic systems.

There are also two other reasons operational systems should be developed first. The first is that they are likely to require less modification as the business environment stabilizes. The other, and perhaps most important reason is that operational systems which are designed to minimize cost and increase productivity are likely to affect the firm's competitive position. The lack of operational systems may inhibit the ability of the firm to expand. Secondly, competitors with systems in place may have a cost advantage enabling them to lower prices in order to gain market share.

---

[2]R. N. Anthony, *Planning and Control Systems: A Framework for Analysis* (Boston: Harvard University Press, 1965).

EXHIBIT V

Functional
Portfolio

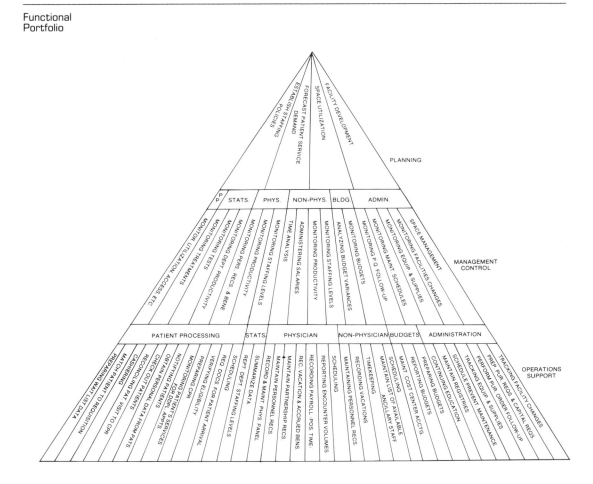

As *Exhibit VI* demonstrates, each phase in the life of a product will require different information needs and, given competitive pressures, induce the firm toward systems which reduce cost, increase productivity, or competitively differentiate the product. The problem is that there are divergent systems needs—information needed is strategic when a product is being introduced. Yet operating systems need to be installed if the product is to remain competitive, as *Exhibit VII* shows. When a product is being considered, the information management requires relates to markets, competitors, and other environmental factors including the economy and government regulations. The scope of the information is vast and often needed on an impromptu basis.

While management desires on-line systems which would provide immediate answers to their inquiries, these systems are impractical, would be very expensive to develop, and are very likely to fail. Likewise, when a decision has been made to manufacture a product and in the first two stages of the product's life cycle, instability in the business environ-

EXHIBIT VI

Information Needs at each Phase of
a Product Life Cycle

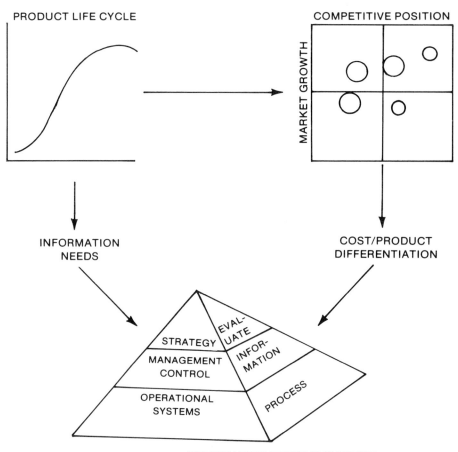

INFORMATION SYSTEMS SUPPORT

ment—regarding competitors, distribution networks, manufacturing
needs, etc.—may prompt the need for environmental information and a
desire to control the environment when in fact it is difficult to control.

Developing computerized information systems to meet these information needs will seem more achievable now than in the consideration phase;
however, they are likely to be very costly and involve several modifications as the business environment stabilizes. It is far more effective to
obtain strategic and control information through communications—written or oral—with sales and manufacturing employees, for example, rather
than through formal computerized systems.

It is suggested that, in the beginning stages of a product's life when
market growth is high, operational systems be developed first, followed
by development of management control systems as the product begins to
mature. Strategic and some control information should be obtained

EXHIBIT VII

Strategic
Information Needs

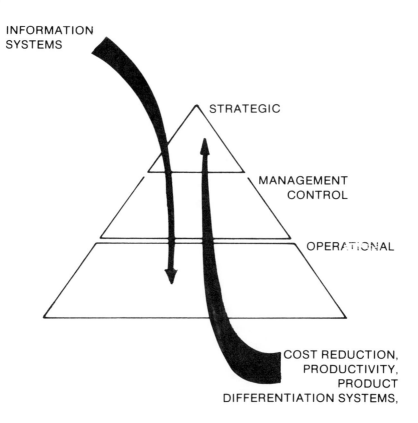

INFORMATION
SYSTEMS

STRATEGIC

MANAGEMENT
CONTROL

OPERATIONAL

COST REDUCTION,
PRODUCTIVITY,
PRODUCT
DIFFERENTIATION SYSTEMS,

outside of the computerized information system. As the product requires investment in the beginning stages of its life, the development of applications to support the product should likewise be considered investments. At this point it is dangerous to directly reflect the cost of applications development in the price of the product. The danger is in potentially losing share because of an effective price umbrella, albeit for cost rather than profit reasons. Similarly, it is dangerous to develop any computer chargeout scheme which discourages management from investing in support applications since the potential for cost reductions and productivity increases through computerized applications make them strategically invaluable tools.

Once the product matures, most of the information needs supporting the product can be met through computerized applications. Operational systems and most management control systems are now in place. As the overall business environment has stabilized with declining market growth and hopefully a dominant competitive position for the firm, there is less need for vast amounts of external information. Generally this information is constant and can be reported on a routine basis. Computerized applications development should consist principally of management control systems—e.g., financial control systems, short-term sales forecasting systems, and some development planned for strategic information systems. This means that, given current sales, profitability, and customer structure, new product introductions should be identified once a product declines. In general, a mature product should be a cash generator, where most costs are noninvestment in nature. Cash should be used to invest in new products. Likewise, applications development should now go towards new products.

MULTIPLE PRODUCT PORTFOLIOS

Although we have presented a methodology for systems development for any one product, organizations with large scale computer systems are likely to have an amalgam of several products. This complicates our methodology. However, the underlying principles should hold for a portfolio of many products. Overall systems development should parallel the particular product portfolio, shown in its simplest form in *Exhibit VIII*. In all four cases, operational systems should precede development of management control systems, and management control systems should precede development of strategic systems. We can compare the computerized Applications Portfolio to the Product Portfolio to see if the Applications Portfolio is properly balanced. The Product Portfolio of a company is more likely to be mixed, however. Given our understanding of different systems requirements at each stage of the product life cycle, we can determine roughly overall what precentage of systems costs should be devoted to development and maintenance and at what level of the Applications Portfolio they should occur—operational, management control, or strategic. Using this as a benchmark against which actual expenditures can be compared, we can assess whether or not data processing expenditures are being allocated reasonably.

THE PROCESS OF PLANNING CORPORATE INFORMATION SYSTEM RESOURCES

Having presented a methodology which links corporate strategy analysis to information systems analysis, particularly useful in the objectives setting cycle, we will now discuss the links between corporate data processing planning and the remaining two cycles. Our methodology is particularly useful when doing the first audit of the corporate business portfolio and supporting data processing Applications Portfolifo to set initial objectives. We might add that an audit should be done prior to initiation of a corporate/ data processing planning process. However, as *Exhibit IX* shows, the audit of the data processing function should also include examining three other growth areas identified by R. L. Nolan in his early studies of data processing organizations—data processing planning

EXHIBIT VIII

Overall Systems Development
Parallels the Product Portfolio

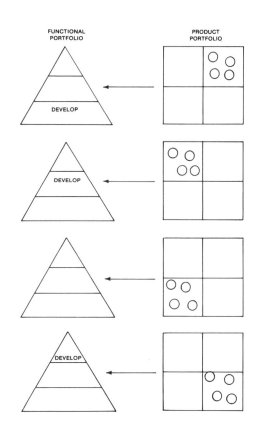

and control areas, data processing resources, and user awareness. It is crucial that these areas be considered in the remaining planning cycles, particularly in program development, since these areas are necessary to the support of the Applications Portfolio.

The Lorange-Vancil planning model broadly describes the remaining two cycles as program development and budgeting. We shall extend these cycles somewhat. Out of the analysis or objectives-setting phase will come identification of opportunities and threats (strengths and weaknesses) facing the organization. Program development will include:

- Identification of projects
- Evaluating of these projects in terms of risk and return, including the risk of developing computerized information systems
- The selection of specific projects

The budgeting cycle will involve not only allocation of financial resources, but also the development of detailed operational plans with specific

EXHIBIT IX

The Data Processing
Audit

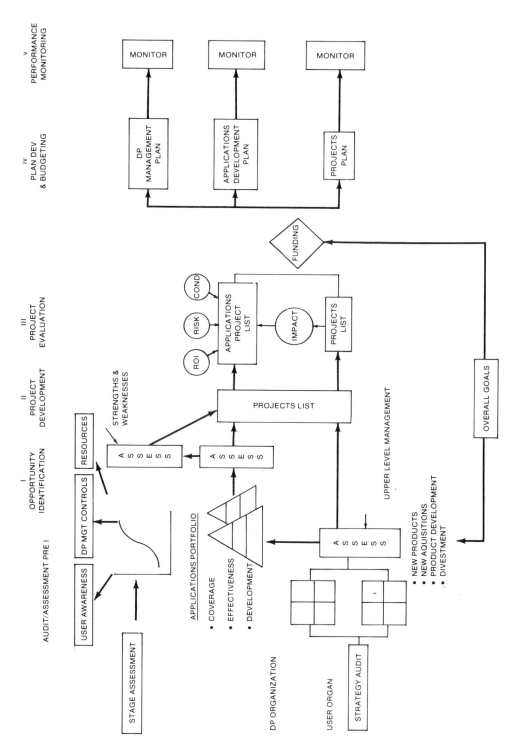

objectives and time frames. A last but crucial phase in the planning process is the development of methods and systems for monitoring and assessing the effectiveness of these programs on an ongoing basis at the beginning of the planning cycle. We begin by discussing opportunity identification.

Identification of Opportunities

As previously discussed, when an audit of the organization and an assessment of the data processing function is performed for the first time, new product needs and development, acquisition, and divestment candidates are identified. For the data processing organization, such management areas as user awareness, controls, technology, and personnel are evaluated. The computerized Applications Portfolio is assessed on the basis of adequacy and effectiveness of coverage. However, when an ongoing planning process has been installed in an organization, usually preceded by an audit as shown on the planning diagram, two processes occur leading to the identification of opportunities within an organization. The first is an objective-setting process, the first of three cycles identified in Lorange-Vancil corporate planning model. In this cycle, the Chief Executive Officer and upper management draft a formal statement of the organization's purpose and objectives. Following this statement, they will set overall direction and broad principles for strategic planning. These principles might suggest seeking more internal than external projects, improving resource management, or developing new technologies. The broad guidelines for the corporation are then passed on to business managers who state their own goals and resource requirements for their businesses. These statements are referred to the CEO and upper management where they are reviewed and modified from the perspective of the entire organization.

The second process, which transpires with the first, is one of review. This is likely to involve some form of corporate audit and data processing Stage Assessment, and will certainly include a review of completed and ongoing projects from the previous planning year at varying levels of the organization. The purpose of the objective-setting and review processes are to determine whether or not previously identified opportunities have been taken advantage of and previous weaknesses have been remedied. This is done by measuring the effectiveness of existing programs. These processes also intend to identify new opportunities and areas of weaknesses so that appropriate programs can be developed.

Program/Project Development

Let us view the organization as an entity composed of business units (product, market, or groups of similar products and markets) and functional units (marketing, finance, manufacturing, accounting, distribution, data processing) supporting the business. Projects either support one or more business functions or the organization as a whole in its outside environment (markets, government), or are developed to integrate certain functional areas. Projects for the data processing organization are related either to the Applications Portfolio or to the management of the data processing organization.

Although each unit will develop a list of projects relating solely to itself, it is crucial to recognize that there is a high degree of interdependence among units and projects, particularly where they involve data processing resources. Business units will need functional support which will often translate into business systems for the Applications Portfolio. Although this phase of planning is designed to identify but not evaluate projects, it is useful to involve data processing managers in discussion of the projects which may or may not utilize the data processing resource. In this way, data processing managers may impose on users realistic views of capabilities and implementation of time frames regarding data processing support systems. Better yet, the data processing manager might identify new systems possibilities or uses of old ones to support viable projects which might otherwise have been scrapped.

In this phase, the data processing organization develops an overall strategy statement and a list of information systems proposals (ISPs). The aim is to create a number of small projects, each taking up to ten man-years' effort and eighteen months lead time to implement. These can then be compared to each other and a priority listing produced in the next planning phase.

Plan, Development, and Budgeting

Developing a plan for the data processing resource involves three steps:

1. Identification of funding levels of information systems proposals (ISPs)

2. Selection of data processing application and management projects

3. Development of detailed implementation schedules and budgets for each project

ISPs are grouped on the basis of the amount of investment required. For example, the first six ISPs might require five percent growth in data processing development costs, and the first fifteen might require ten percent growth in data processing development costs over the previous year's investment. Following grouping on required levels of investment, IPSs are sequenced on the basis of implementation schedules, technology, risk abatement (size, structure, and technological requirements for a project), resource constraints, economics, and user involvement. For example, a computerized order scheduling system may have priority over development of a computerized order entry system. However, it may be more feasible to develop an order entry system first. Resource availability, and needs including technology and personnel in support of the applications ISPs, must be considered and the beginnings of a data processing management plan developed.

Once funding levels and sequencing of ISPs have been accomplished, project funding levels and selection are determined by upper, business, and functional management. Three key questions are answered:

- What business and functional programs should be selected?

- Which of these should have computerized applications developed for support then?

- What subsequent funding is needed for the management of the data processing resource?

Following project selection, detailed implementation schedules and budgets should be developed for each project. This translates into two plans for the data processing organization:

1. The applications plan consisting of a sequenced list of application projects with developments and implementation time frames by quarter for five years.

2. A management plan consisting of personnel hiring and development schedules and time frames for introducing new equipment and technologies.

Performance Monitoring

Often neglected, monitoring and ultimate adjustment of plans must complete the planning cycle as the foundation for comprehensive review of the organization. Formal reporting systems which produce recurring reports addressing the basic elements of the plan must be developed. They will occur principally at two levels. At the strategic level they might involve periodic assessments of Applications Portfolio coverage, particularly at the beginning of the planning cycle. At the operating level they may indicate the need for periodic revision of such plans such schedule adjustments.

It is important to understand that the performance monitoring process functions as the final link in the direction-setting cycle. It is not merely a record of events but the basis for a rationale for future action. If reporting and review mechanisms are in place, the organization will remain responsive to changes in its growth process as data processing matures.

SUMMARY AND CONCLUSIONS

Business needs and organizational demands on the data processing organization make data processing a scarce resource. Technological uncertainty further complicates the data processing environment. Data processing is therefore a resource which must be managed—a resource most effectively managed through a planning process. But planning for information resources cannot be done in a vacuum. Planning must be made an integral part of the corporate planning process.

This chapter has suggested not only a way in which data processing resources can be planned, but also where data processing planning should be linked to corporate planning. Some analytical tools have also been proposed which have been effective in data processing planning. These tools and key process links are summarized below.

Planning Tools

1. The Applications Portfolio. A way of integrating and evaluating corporate and data processing needs.

2. Information Systems Proposals (ISPs). A list of information system products and a methodology for prioritizing them on the basis of business need, implementation risk, condition of existing system resources, and return on investment.

Key Process Links

1. Project Development. Business and functional managers should consult data processing managers in the development of their own project lists to initially assess feasibility of system support. In this way the data processing manager as an educational resource is perhaps adding more realism to the system expectations of users and identifying opportunities where systems can be of greatest value to user departments.

2. Project Evaluation. Data processing managers must be informed of business needs in prioritizing applications project development. At the same time they must be allowed to include data processing risk and condition of system factors in prioritizing applications projects. They must plan their own organizations resource needs according to these factors. Corporations should not expect data processing organizations to support all other projects, and they should recognize various levels of risk—just as there is risk in product development—and effectiveness inherent in any applications project.

INDEX

†